LIFE OF GEORGE BENT

WRITTEN FROM HIS LETTERS

Life of George Bent

WRITTEN FROM HIS LETTERS

BY GEORGE E. HYDE

EDITED BY SAVOIE LOTTINVILLE

UNIVERSITY OF OKLAHOMA PRESS : NORMAN

Books by George E. Hyde
Published by the University of Oklahoma Presss

Red Cloud's Folk: A History of the Oglala Sioux Indians (1937, 1957)
A Sioux Chronicle (1956)
*Indians of the High Plains: From the Prehistoric Period
to the Coming of Europeans* (1959)
Spotted Tail's Folk: A History of the Brulé Sioux Indians (1961)
Indians of the Woodlands: From Prehistoric Times to 1725 (1962)
Life of George Bent Written from His Letters (1967)

Library of Congress Catalog Card Number: 67-15574

Copyright 1968 by the University of Oklahoma Press, Publishing Division of the University. Composed and printed at Norman, Oklahoma, U.S.A., by the University of Oklahoma Press. First edition.

THIS BOOK WAS WRITTEN fifty years ago from the letters of George Bent to George E. Hyde. The coming of the first World War made it impossible to find a publisher, and the manuscript was put away in a box and forgotten. It turned up in the attic two years ago. Its quality was obvious. The Bent material was well worth publishing, but the manuscript needed work to put it in shape. It was then found that a better manuscript had been acquired by the Denver Public Library, through whose friendly co-operation this copy was made available and has been used in the making of the present version, down to the point where my older and longer working copy extended the chronology.

George Bent was the half-blood son of Colonel William Bent, who, with his brother Charles, owned and operated Bent's Fort on the Upper Arkansas River in southeastern Colorado. Bent's mother was Owl Woman, the daughter of White Thunder, who was keeper of the Medicine Arrows and, in effect, was the high priest of the Southern Cheyennes and in some ways more important than any of the chiefs. He was killed in the battle with the Kiowas at Wolf Creek, in what is now northwestern Oklahoma, in 1838.

The Bent brothers began to trade with the Indians in Dakota in the early 1820's. They then decided to shift their operations to the Upper Arkansas, this river then being the boundary between the United States and Mexico. In 1828 or 1829, the Bent brothers built Bent's Fort on the north side of the Arkansas, near the present town of La

Junta, Bent County, Colorado.[1] The place was a big one, built in the Mexican style with adobe bricks. It had all of the Indian trade from north and south of the Arkansas, and also a big trade with the Mexicans at Taos and Santa Fe. The fort employed from eighty to one hundred men, many Americans but more Mexicans. It was here in the old fort that George Bent and his younger brother, Charles, were born and brought up.

By 1849, the Indian trade and the trade with American beaver trappers was much less profitable. Charles Bent, the elder, was dead, and his brother William blew up the old fort. He built another (smaller one) which was called Bent's New Fort. He sent his two sons, George and Charles, to school in Missouri; and then the gold rush to Colorado filled the country with a rough American population, mainly men, and William Bent sold his fort to the War Department, which renamed it Fort Lyon. Bent established a ranch near the post and lived there. He was for a time agent for the tribes on the Upper Arkansas.

The Civil War now broke out, and George Bent and many of the boys at his academy in Missouri enlisted in the Confederate Army. I do not remember what Charlie Bent did. By the time he had gone through the savage Battle of Pea Ridge, George Bent had had enough of the white man's methods of making war. General Sterling Price's army was breaking up, the men leaving.

George Bent returned to western Missouri, joined a wagon train headed west, and went to his father's ranch near Fort Lyon. His brother Charlie also went there. The white men of Colorado were mainly violent partisans of the Union cause; they termed the Bent boys renegades and threatened to kill them on sight. I believe that William Bent advised the boys to join a camp of their mother's people, the Southern Cheyennes, for safety, and this they did. This

---

[1] Charles and William Bent were closely associated with Ceran St. Vrain, who, as a member of the firm of Bent, St. Vrain and Company, must also be credited with the creation of Bent's Fort, as will appear in succeeding chapters. The dates for the construction of the fort are given in footnote 7, Chapter 3, *infra.*—S.L.

was in 1863, and soon after the Bent brothers joined the Cheyennes a violent Indian war was started in the Plains. The Bents found themselves cut off from the world of white civilization. They became separated, George going north with the main hostile camps, Charlie remaining in the Kansas plains with another camp.

It is for this period of war, from 1863 to 1868, that George Bent's information is unique. He was the only man among the hostiles who could and did set down in writing an account of what he witnessed. He described the war customs of the Plains Indians, as he saw them on this last big occasion when the ancient customs were being kept up. He saw the warriors preparing for battle by "renewing" the magic power of their battle charms and having their war bonnets and war shirts refurbished. He was present at the great war parades in the hostile camps, and went with the big war parties, witnessing how the Indian soldier societies herded the warriors together in a dense column and whipped any men who tried to slip away and make premature attacks of their own which would alert their white enemies and thwart the plans of the Indian leaders.

Bent's account of these war operations is particularly important, as he was the only eye-witness to report on them. Out of touch with white civilization, he did not even know the months in which events occurred; but the years he remembered, and by using the Indian reckoning by moons, he had a good idea as to dates. I have found the true dates in official records and inserted them; I have also inserted the names of military commanders who operated against the Indians, as Bent usually did not know who the commanding officer was or the identity of the troops.

Over the years, I have been asked from time to time by some scholar what I thought of George Bent's reliability as an informant, and I have always said at once that I placed him very highly. The late George Bird Grinnell also had a high opinion of Bent, and usually employed him as an interpreter when he paid his frequent visits to the Cheyennes and Arapahos in Oklahoma seeking material. Bent would get together a number of old Indians and interpret what they said, and Grinnell's secretary would make a shorthand version of Bent's interpretation.[2] Grinnell had scores of these interviews carefully type-written, and also interviews from the Northern Cheyennes, Blackfeet, and Pawnees. He used part of the Bent material in his book, *The Fighting Cheyennes*.

George Bent differed from all the other mixed bloods I ever knew in that he liked to write letters. The other mixed bloods would fail to reply to your inquiry or would write a half-page in faint pencil a year after receiving your letter, and then they gave up. Bent would answer you fully, giving what information he had, and he would then look up some old Cheyenne men and women and write down what they had to tell him. He gave their names, ages, and often their tribal affiliations. It was all obviously reliable material, allowing for the fact that no two human beings ever saw the same events eye to eye.

During the fifty years that have elapsed since George Bent's death, I have picked up much additional information concerning the Indians in the north in early times. It seems to me to be apparent that the old people who talked to Bent around the date 1910 were correct in stating their belief that the Cheyennes were closely related to the Crees. It seems to me that the Cheyennes, Blackfeet, Arapahos, and Atsinas were all part of the mass of Algonquian people who, around the date 1600, were wandering in the cold lands between the north shore of Lake Superior and the James Bay of Hudson Bay. These people had canoes. In winter they could not support themselves in large camps but had to separate into family groups, each family living far from all neighbors in the forest. They were snowed in all winter, living mainly on rabbits and probably hunting on snowshoes.

I think it probable that the Blackfeet and Cheyennes may have been a single group that drifted southward into northern Minnesota sometime near the date 1600. The native names for these two tribes

---

[2] Hyde, in response to my inquiry, tells me he was not the secretary in the case, though he was for some time Grinnell's research assistant. That Grinnell, after a growing reluctance on the part of George Bent to interpret for him or supply information, became dependent upon Hyde, whose relations with Bent were excellent, seems probable.—S.L.

seem to be the same, allowing for a difference in spelling, the Cheyennes calling themselves *Dzis-dsis-tas*, the Blackfeet calling themselves *Sik-sika*.[3] I think that the Arapahos and Atsinas formed a
somewhat different group and came down into Minnesota about the
time the Cheyennes and Blackfeet did.

In the Headwaters Lakes country, near the head of the Mississippi,
these Algonquian Indians from the north encountered Siouan Indians,
who were mound builders and had, perhaps, a higher culture than
the Algonquians. The map of the mound groups in northern Minnesota seems to show a clear-cut division between the two Indian stocks,
the mound groups extending up to the upper Mississippi indicating
the Siouan area, the lands farther north, with only a few circular
burial mounds, being those occupied by the Algonquians. We have
only a dim vision of these early times in Minnesota. The Arapahos
remembered that the Blackfeet were there; the Chippewas stated
that the Siouans were Hidatsas, or Hidatsas and Crows, and that they
were driven to the Missouri by enemies. The names, Upper and
Lower Red Lake, Red Lake River, and Red River of the North, were
originally Algonquian, and these names do not mean red but mean
blood. This hints at early wars or massacres, when the natives armed
only with flint weapons were attacked by enemies armed by the French
with steel knives and some guns.

The Blackfeet, if they were there, must have left early. They seem
to have been in Manitoba Province, Canada, about the date 1690. The
Hidatsas, Crows, Cheyennes, Arapahos, and Atsinas perhaps were
forced to remove westward, to and beyond Red River. The Cheyennes who talked to George Bent had forgotten all this. They remembered the kind of life they led in Minnesota, near the lakes and
marshes, but they had no memory of wars earlier than the Assiniboin
and Sioux attacks on them, probably after 1700. Strangely, they did
not recall the savage raids made on their people by the Chippewas

---

[3] Frederick Webb Hodge, *Handbook of American Indians North of Mexico*,
25–51, gives the Cheyenne self-designation as *Dzi'tsüstäs*, after Petter. Note also
slight variation on this same phrase in the opening lines of Chapter 1 which
follows.—S.L.

after 1700, and they all told Bent that they obtained their first horses out near the Black Hills, after 1775. We know from Chippewa tradition that the Cheyennes in the village on Sheyenne Fork of Red River were mounted in 1750, and I think that archaeology has confirmed this by finding horse bones in the ruins of this village.

The Cheyenne tradition of the removal west to the Missouri seems better than the Arapaho tradition, the Arapahos making their tribe, the Cheyennes, and the Atsinas all migrate in one group towards the Missouri. Our other evidence is that these Indians, and the Hidatsas and Crows, moved to the Missouri in small groups at different periods, and this confirms the Cheyenne stories.

It seems pretty obvious that these migrations westward date after 1700, with the exception of the Blackfeet, who were seemingly in Manitoba by 1690. Joseph La France and the [Pierre Gaultier de Varrenes, Sieur de la] Verendrye journals both mention the tribe called Beaux Hommes as being on Red River of the North as late as about the year 1740; the Beaux Hommes or part of that group were still on Red River of the North, between the Assiniboins in Manitoba and the Sioux on Minnesota River. These Beaux Hommes were either Crows or Hidatsas and Crows, and the Bougainville report of 1757 places them on or west of the Missouri, near the Mandans.[4]

The Bougainville material gives the Algonquian name for the People of the Bow, and this name means Bowstring, not Bow. They were met in the plains west of the Missouri by Verendrye's sons in 1742, and the name suggests that they may have been the Cheyenne camp in which the famous Bowstring warriors were prominent. Here we have another dim clue to the early history of the Cheyennes; for in northern Minnesota, north of the upper Mississippi, there is a Bowstring River, and this may indicate the early location of Cheyenne groups. It would fit in with the Cheyenne traditions of the early period when they lived in Minnesota among lakes and marshes.

Returning up the Missouri from the Arikara villages to those of

[4] For Beaux Hommes, see Louis Antoine de Bougainville, *Adventure in the Wilderness: The American Journals of Louis Antoine de Bougainville*, translated and edited by Edward P. Hamilton, 117, 120, 148.—S.L.

the Mandans in the early months of 1743, Verendrye's sons passed a camp of Indians they thought were Sioux; but they gave the name of the group as People of the Painted or Striped Arrows, and here we may have a reference to the second Cheyenne group, the one that had the medicine arrows. Moreover, they seem to have been met in the neighborhood where the Cheyennes later had two earth-lodge villages, just below the later Fort Yates on the west bank of the Missouri, and this suggests that the medicine-arrow camp was part of the earth-lodge Cheyenne group.

I do not know what became of the large number of letters that George Bent wrote to Mr. Butler of Washington, D.C. It is to be hoped that they will turn up and be placed in a library, as Bent's letters to me have been safely housed in the William Robertson Coe Collection in the Yale University Library. The Yale collection has been microfilmed and the letters are being used by scholars.

I hope that in time George Bent will be recognized as one of the leading men in the field of Indian history and ethnology. He deserves such a standing.

GEORGE E. HYDE

Omaha, Nebraska
June, 1966

IN MID-SPRING, 1966, George E. Hyde of Omaha, then living in a rest home with his sister, Mabel Hyde Reed, dredged up from his memories of eighty-four years a fact well known to many historians who had undertaken research on the Cheyenne Indians and events on the Great Plains in the nineteenth century. There was a manuscript, he told me, recounting fifty years of Cheyenne Indian life, related by George Bent, the son of William Bent of Bent's Old Fort and Owl Woman, a Cheyenne, a substantial part of which he had sold to the Denver Public Library in 1930. Perhaps that clear copy of eight of the fifteen chapters he had originally constructed, plus those remaining in his working notes in Omaha, might be publishable.

Thirty-six years had elapsed since Mr. Hyde had closed out of his thinking the frustrations he had experienced in trying to get the manuscript published in the early Depression years. Unable to place it with a publisher, he had offered it through a book and manuscript dealer to the Denver Public Library. Records of the Library establish the sum paid as three hundred dollars, but Mr. Hyde recalls that he actually received two hundred. The sum is less important than the economic condition it depicts. And the existence of the manuscript in Denver, unpublished for more than a third of a century, is more significant in terms of first-hand historical value than in terms of the many syntheses which have emerged on the era, the peoples, and the events on the Southern Great Plains known at first hand by George Bent.

The generous co-operation of the Denver Public Library made it possible for me to secure a copy of the portion of the manuscript which Mr. Hyde had deposited there. Mr. John T. Eastlick, the librarian, and Mrs. Alys Freeze, his associate at the Library, kindly put their holdings of George Bent letters at my disposal. Almost simultaneously with these materials, Mr. Hyde's own working copy of the entire manuscript reached me. It has thus been possible to collate the two versions. It is clear that the Library manuscript is the one originally intended by Mr. Hyde to see the light of day, hopefully through the medium of print. But fortune favored history when he was able to locate the whole account, including the portion which carries forward from the point where the Library copy leaves off, bringing events down to 1875, practically the close of warfare between the Indians and the whites on the Southern Plains. The working copy had rested in the Hyde attic in Omaha up until the time it was sent to me, a matter of weeks before the residence was sold.

The account here published is in the first person, the narrator being George Bent. As Mr. Hyde's introduction explains, it was put together from letter exchanges between the principal and himself, beginning in 1905 and carrying down almost to the time of Bent's death in 1918. There are marginal notes in both copies of the manuscript by both Bent and Hyde, indicating that the narrator himself had an opportunity to give at least a measure of finality to the story of these stirring years of his life. It is not possible at this date to ascertain the authorship of each marginal note, but the footnotes are Mr. Hyde's except where I have added my own with proper identification.

The task of scholarly editorship on these papers might extend for months, even years. But it became clear almost at the outset that the close consultation so desirable could not be achieved. In my association with Mr. Hyde over a period of nearly thirty years, our sole means of communication has consisted of letters and, when we have been together in Omaha, scribbled notes from me and oral responses from him, owing to his total lack of hearing from about his twentieth year. Today, his added handicap of limited vision further complicates the problem. That Mr. Hyde's historical and anthropological achievements have been phenomenal becomes all the more clear from these facts. The soundest course, therefore, as I suggested to Mr. Hyde, was to move ahead as rapidly as possible to the publication of what George Bent saw and heard and did, leaving to future researchers the relation of his narrative of events to official records and to a chronology which today is more meaningful if taken from the calendar than from the moons of Cheyenne time-keeping. This plan has had his entire agreement.

Wherever and whenever possible, I have asked Mr. Hyde for such information as he could supply for footnotes ("My eyesight will not permit me to search out things in books and documents," he wrote recently). Such notes are fully identified.

It is important to say that my determination from the beginning has been (as I wrote Mr. Hyde) to treat the two manuscripts with "reverence," shying away from an all too common tendency among editors to change contexts in the interest of meaning, or simply to make better what was already good. They are, after all, documents, and the Hyde working copy will be delivered, in accordance with his wish, to the Denver Public Library with the publication of this book. My own editorial copy, typed especially for the purpose, will be deposited in the Division of Manuscripts of the University of Oklahoma Library.

The authenticity of any account of this kind, in the absence of supporting documents and the acquiescence of the principal narrator, can always remain in doubt. But in addition to the Denver Public Library holdings of Bent letters, the Coe Collection in the Yale University Library, containing the bulk of the Bent responses to Mr. Hyde's letters, several in the Colorado Historical Society, and a small number in the Southwest Museum, Los Angeles, leave little room for question about what Bent said or the joint intent of himself and Hyde, within the limits of human fallibility. Bent was not only highly literate but wrote in a fair round hand; moreover, he, not Mr. Hyde, appears as the author of "Forty Years with the Cheyennes," a series of six articles which appeared from October, 1905, to March, 1906, in *The Frontier: A Magazine of the West* (Colorado Springs, Vol.

4, Nos. 4 to 9). Mr. Hyde was listed as the editor. That Bent was setting down the stuff of history could scarcely have escaped him this early in the game. What came in the next thirteen years before his death was a much more massive, detailed account of the life at Bent's Fort, the vicissitudes of the Cheyennes, and the part Bent himself played in the life of both.

The stature of a historian is often measured by the extent to which his fellow craftsmen reveal their dependence upon him. Few serious researchers working on the Great Plains and the era in which the Bents lived have been able to escape Bent's letter-reminiscences and the narrative held in the Denver Public Library. For many events there are no other eye-witness accounts or no other dependable sources. It is probable, therefore, that the longer history upon which Bent and Hyde began after their tentative effort more than half a century ago will serve even larger purposes in the future.

Bent's character—or rather characters—have often been misunderstood. He was both white and Indian, but after he was wounded at the Sand Creek Massacre in 1864, when he was in the Cheyenne camp with his mother's people, he became increasingly Indian and often hostile in his actions, outlooks, and interpretations. His clear identification of himself with "my people," the Cheyennes, from that point becomes abundantly clear in his narrative. It also accounts for certain of Bent's glosses upon the actions of his people thereafter, and certain attributions of other tribes, notably the burning of the bodies of Patrick Hennessy and three of his wagoneers by Osages on July 3, 1874, after the men had been killed by Cheyennes. It takes no profound understanding of Indian character to get at these tendencies (some of which have an amusing quality of tongue in cheek), which have been exhibited often by far more sophisticated interpreters of human history than Bent.

The need for giving at least that minimum of annotation which appears in the book has been far more time-consuming than I had earlier expected. But is it hoped that that minimum will be more serviceable to the purposes of the two men who sought to give a unique record of happenings in a heroic age.

To George E. Hyde, who has honored me by entrusting me with the responsibility I have described, my sincere thanks. It is not every chronicler of the past who says, "Bosh, make any change you think necessary in the interest of a good book!" And my thanks to him also for asking me to join him in the editing of the George Bent letters, a large task which is already under way.

SAVOIE LOTTINVILLE

Norman, Oklahoma
April 20, 1967

CONTENTS

William Bent with Little Raven and His Children—Charles Bent,
Ceran St. Vrain, and Christopher "Kit" Carson—Yellow
Wolf—Lieutenant J. W. Abert's Sketch of Bent's Fort— Key to
Lieutenant J. W. Abert's Sketch of Bent's Fort—Lieutenant
J. W. Abert's Perspective of Bent's Fort, 1845—
George Bent and Magpie, His Wife—Edmond Gurrier
Following page 102

Wolf Robe—Black Kettle and Other Chiefs in Denver, 1864—
Old Fort Lyon—White Antelope, Man on a Cloud,
and Little Chief—Cheyenne Camp—Fort Phil Kearny—Fort
Larned and Fort Dodge—Fort Laramie
Following page 198

Fort Benton—Camp Supply—Bull Train Crossing the Smoky Hill
River, 1867—Medicine Lodge Peace Commission—
Battle of the Washita—Little Bear, Hairless Bear, and Island—
Cheyenne Prisoners at Fort Marion—Quanah
Following page 294

LIFE OF GEORGE BENT

WRITTEN FROM HIS LETTERS

CHAPTER ONE

MY PEOPLE, THE CHEYENNES

A short introductory paragraph would not be amiss here setting forth the fact that in the early chapter or chapters Bent will set forth the reliable accounts of early history of tribe, accounts seldom told only among themselves. GB.[1]

OUR PEOPLE call themselves *T'sis tsis tas*, meaning "people alike" or simply "our people," but by the whites we have always been termed "Cheyennes," from a Sioux word, *Shai ena*, which means "people speaking a strange tongue." The Sioux gave us this name over two hundred years ago, and many other tribes, and the whites, have adopted the name from the Sioux.

Indian tribes are grouped by enthnologists in linguistic families or stocks, each stock composed of a number of tribes speaking dialects of the same language. Some of those stocks are very small, including only three or four tribes, while the Kiowas form a stock all by themselves, as no tribe has ever been found speaking a language in any way related to the Kiowa tongue. The Cheyennes belong to the great group of tribes speaking the Algonquian language, in which stock are included the Algonkins, Cheyennes, Arapahos, Crees, Chippewas or Ojibwas, Blackfeet, Atsinas, Missisaugis, Micmacs, Ottawas, Penobscots, Sacs and Foxes, Potawatomis, Piankashaws, Michigameas, Peorias, Narragansets, Powhatans, Mohegans, Delawares, Shawnees, and a great many other tribes, occupying in early times a vast territory

---

[1] Longhand note, signed GB, but too round to be in George Bent's hand.—S.L.

extending from the Rocky Mountains to Newfoundland and from the Churchill River of Hudson Bay to Pamlico Sound.[2]

Our old people say that the Cheyennes were formerly a part of the Cree tribe and that we separated from the Crees long ago and wandered off toward the south and west. The oldest people now living say that the earliest home of the Cheyennes was on the shore of great lakes in the far north. This was very long ago, probably as early as the year 1600. In those times the Cheyennes were very poor, famine dwelt almost constantly in the camps, and the men were so badly armed that they did not go to war and were even afraid of the larger animals, which they had great difficulty in killing with their rude stone-pointed weapons. When the old people tell stories of those far-off times they often begin by saying, "Before the Cheyennes had bows and arrows." The people were fish-eaters in those early times and dwelt on the shores of the lakes the year round. They made seines of willow shoots and used them in the shallow water near shore. These seines were very long, and each one was drawn toward shore by a number of men, while the women and children lined up at the two open ends of the seine and beat the water with clubs and sticks, to frighten the fish back into the seine. In this way they made good hauls and caught some very large fish. The people were so famished that they even boiled the fish bones and pounded them up, extracting a pure white oil, which they ate.

From these lakes in the great cold land of the north, the Cheyennes migrated in canoes and at last came to a land of great marshes filled with tall grass and reeds.[3] On the edge of the marshland the tribe halted and went into camp, while the chiefs selected a number of young men and sent them into the marshes to explore. The grass and reeds in the marshes were so tall and dense that the young men were afraid that they would lose their way, so before entering the marsh they cut a large number of long poles and placed them in the canoes, and as they advanced into the marsh they stuck a long pole up

---

[2] Marginal note, possibly in Bent's hand: "Would this be more proper as an editor's note?"—S.L.

[3] Evidently the great marshes of southern Ontario and northern Minnesota.—G.H.

in the shallow water every little way, to mark their trail. After some days the scouts returned and reported that they had found on the other side of the marshlands a large lake with some fine open prairie along its shore. The tribe then broke camp, loaded the canoes, and by following the line of poles crossed the marshes safely and came out on the large lake the scouts had spoken of.

Here the Cheyennes set up their camp and lived for many years, fishing in the lake and hunting on the prairie.[4] The people lived more comfortably here than they had in the far north. They built good wigwams by fixing long poles in the ground, bending the poles over and tying them together at the top; the frame of poles was then covered with dry grass, which was coated with mud to stop up the holes, and then the final covering, made of sheets of bark or mats woven from reeds, was put on. These were the houses used in winter. When the people went away on hunts they had little lodges made of poles covered with sheets of bark, reed mats or skins. These old-time lodges were very small and light and could easily be packed on a dog's back. While they lived in this village on the lake the Cheyennes had enough to eat except during the hungry time of late winter and early spring. There was abundance of fish in the lake, and wild fowl swarmed in season. In spring the people gathered birds' eggs, and in early summer they caught fledgling ducks and other waterfowl.[5] Out in the prairies, far from the lake, was a hill which was called "the hill of the skunks" because skunks were very plentiful there. Each autumn the whole tribe moved out across the prairies to this hill and held a grand skunk-hunt. All the oldest people who are now living remember the stories about these annual skunk-hunts, two hundred and fifty years ago. They say the northern skunks were very large and

[4] The location of this Cheyenne village on the lake cannot be fixed. It was evidently to the south of Lake of the Woods, in northwestern Minnesota. There are hundreds of lakes in that region.—G.H.

[5] As late as 1850 the Ojibwas and other canoe tribes of the north made a practice of hunting fledgling ducks on the lakes. Men in light birch canoes pursued the flocks of young birds, which, unable to fly, flapped their wings and skimmed over the water, dodging and doubling. Two Indians in a canoe could catch a large number of these birds in a few hours.—G.H.

in fall were fat. With their camp outfits and little lodges packed on dogs, the people went on foot to this hill and there everybody engaged in the hunt. As the hunt went on the skunks that were killed were all placed in one large pile, and when the hunt was over the headmen laid the skunks out in regular rows on the grass and they divided them up, giving each family its fair share of the game. In the prairies around this hill the grass was very tall. There was no wood, nothing but the tall grass, and when the tribe went on these skunk hunts the women gathered the dry grass and bound it into long tight bundles to be used as fuel. By lighting only one end of the bundle, the grass was made to burn slowly and a bundle lasted a long while. In this country there were no buffalo, but deer abounded, and in winter the whole tribe engaged in hunting the deer. Men, women, and children surrounded the deer and drove them into the deep snow, where the men ran up and killed the animals as they floundered about in the drifts.

From this village on the lake the Cheyennes moved farther south and camped on the shore of another large lake. Here they secured corn from some neighboring tribe and began planting fields, and here they abandoned their small wigwams and built a strong permanent village of large earth lodges protected by a surrounding ditch and log stockade.[6] The Cheyennes now for the first time met the Sioux, who lived on the upper Mississippi to the east of the Cheyenne village. The two tribes made peace with each other and for a long time were on friendly terms.

White Frog, a very old Northern Cheyenne, was down here on a visit in 1912. We had several talks, and the old man told me a number of stories of the old days when the Cheyennes lived in the lake country of western Minnesota. One story he told was about a Cheyenne war party that set out from this stockaded village on the lake,

[6] A Sioux tradition asserts that this Cheyenne earth-lodge village was at the head of Minnesota River, near Yellow Medicine River, in southwestern Minnesota. The Cheyennes probably secured corn and learned the art of building earth lodges from the Iowa tribe, who at that time dwelt lower down on the Minnesota River. This Cheyenne earth-lodge village was probably built some time before 1675 and was abandoned before the year 1700.—G.H.

intending to make an attack on some hostile tribe over toward the Missouri. As this party, all on foot, was moving across the prairie the warriors came upon a large buffalo bull that was red in color. The Cheyennes approached the bull and shot him with arrows, and when they went up to examine the animal they found that he had been rolling in some strange kind of red dust or mud, and this had made him bright red all over. Following the trail of the bull back across the prairie the warriors came to a wonderful place where there were rocks and all the rocks bright red. And that was how the Cheyennes first discovered the famous Red Pipestone Quarry.[7]

While living in this village by the lake, the Cheyennes first saw white men. A party of Cheyennes went to the big river and visited a French fort. With these Cheyennes was a party of Red Shields, that is, Cheyenne warriors belonging to the Red Shield or Buffalo Bull Society. These Red Shield men went inside the stockade of the fort and began to dance the Red Shield Dance, but in the middle of the dance the wind blew the gate of the fort shut, and the Red Shield men, thinking that the French had set a trap for them, went out over the stockade pickets in a great hurry. A Frenchman ran and opened the gate, and the Cheyennes being reassured returned inside the stockade and finished their dance. The Cheyennes were camped near the fort, and after the dance the French sent out some presents to the Cheyenne camp. A Frenchman brought the presents in a cart

[7] The Pipestone Quarry is in Pipestone County, the extreme southwest corner of Minnesota, south of Minnesota River. This famous quarry, the "fountain of the pipes," was discovered at different dates by the various tribes. The Iowas discovered the quarry at a very early date, and in the Jesuit Relation [Lenox Papers, New York Public Library] for the year 1676 we are informed that this tribe carries on a large trade in buffalo robes and red stone pipes. The Sioux did not discover the quarry until much later than the Iowas and Cheyennes, probably as late as the year 1725, but in later times the Sioux have always claimed the quarry, and their right to work the quarry to procure stone for pipes was confirmed in the treaty of 1858. The following year a survey was made and a reservation one mile square, embracing the ancient quarry, was set aside. The Sioux still quarry the pipestone, and in recent years the output has been very large, blasting sometimes being employed in getting out the stone. Here on the Pipestone Reserve, the government has established a large industrial school for Indian youth.—G.H.

or wagon, and as he drove to the Cheyenne camp he stood up in the cart, driving his team while standing. The Cheyennes had never seen a wheeled vehicle before and were very much astonished at sight of this Frenchman standing up in the cart and driving his team. An old Cheyenne man stood up and spoke to the warriors. He said, "See this white man doing wonderful things," just as if the Frenchman had been a great conjurer.[8]

After many years in the village by the lake, the Cheyennes moved again, but the old people do not know why or when this movement was made.[9] Abandoning the village on the lake, the tribe moved west of Red River and built a very strong village of earth lodges surrounded by a stockade on a bluff overlooking the valley of Sheyenne Fork, which flows into Red River from the west. This stream is still called by the Sioux, *Shaien wojubi* ("Place where the Cheyennes plant.")[10]

[8] White Frog and the other old people say that this French fort was near "the big river," which is the Cheyenne name for the Mississippi. It is well known that a party of Cheyennes visited La Salle at his post, Fort Crève Coeur (near Peoria) on the Illinois River, in 1680, and it is quite probable that the Cheyenne tradition as given above refers to this visit to La Salle's fort. Perrot built two forts on the upper Mississippi about the year 1685, but there is no evidence that the Cheyennes visited either of these during the short period they were occupied. Fort Beauharnois was built on the Mississippi in the same region about 1727 and was headquarters for the French in the upper country for many years, but the Cheyennes had removed from the village on the lake before Fort Beauharnois was built.—G.H.

[9] The removal from the village on Lake Traverse or Big Stone Lake, at the head of the Minnesota River, occurred just prior to the year 1700. The reasons for the removal are quite obvious: the village by the lake was in a poor position for defense when attacked by enemies armed with guns. Between the years 1680 and 1700, the Ojibwas living to the east and the Crees and Assiniboins living to the north secured guns from the French and from the English traders on Hudson Bay and began making attacks on the tribes of the Minnesota region. The result was that the Cheyennes removed to the west and built this new village in a strong position on a bluff top; about the same time the Iowas removed west to the Missouri and part of the Sioux were driven from the upper Mississippi and forced to retire westward to the head of Minnesota River.—G.H.

[10] Through the courtesy of the North Dakota Historical Society I am enabled to give a description of the site of this old Cheyenne village on Sheyenne Fork. The village stood on the top of a bluff on the south side of Sheyenne River, some seven miles southeast of Lisbon, N.D. (The exact position is in the NW¼ Section 28,

To the west of this new village lay the plains of eastern Dakota; these plains were full of buffalo, and now the Cheyennes began to make regular trips into the plains to hunt buffalo. The home village on the bluff was only occupied at certain seasons. As soon as the corn was planted in May or June the tribe left the village and moved out into the plains to hunt buffalo; in the fall they returned to the village to harvest and store their crops, but as soon as this was accomplished they again returned to the buffalo range for their fall and winter hunt. In those days the Cheyennes had no horses, everyone was on foot, but the tribe had a great number of large dogs, and these animals were employed to pack or drag burdens. When the people were moving about in the buffalo plains these dogs transported the little lodges and lodge-poles, all the camp equipage and baggage. The dogs were used just as horses were in later times. Some of the dogs had little packsaddles or saddlebags and carried loads on their backs; others were fitted up with little travois made of two small poles the ends of which dragged on the ground behind the dog. The load was fastened to the poles on short crosspieces. These dogs of the olden time were not like Indian dogs of today. They were just like wolves, they never barked but howled like wolves, and were half-wild animals. The old people say that every morning just as day was breaking, the dogs of the camp, several hundred of them, would collect in one band and all howl together, waking the whole camp.[11]

Township 134 N., Range 54 W.) In 1908 Mr. Libbey of the North Dakota Historical Society, and Mr. A. B. Stout of the University of Wisconsin examined and mapped the ground on which the village formerly stood. The village was on the highest point of a bluff on the southeast side of the big bend of the river; about half of the ground has been under the plow, the rest is still in grass and the sunken circles in the ground, marking the spots where the earth-houses formerly stood, are still clearly indicated. There are sixty-two of these house rings, averaging above thirty feet in diameter, indicating a population of perhaps one thousand souls. The position of the old "caches" used for the storing of corn are also clearly marked in the grass, and a broad shallow ditch, a part of the old defenses, can be traced, beginning at the steep bluff-edge to the northeast and extending clear around the village and back to the edge of the bluff to the northwest of the village.—G.H.

[11] The travois-dogs of the Plains Indians are mentioned in accounts of the Coronado expedition (1541) and by many of the early Spanish, French, and English explorers. A dog could pack fifty pounds on its back, but with the travois or pole-

Antelope Woman, very old [between eighty and ninety][12] years
old in 1912, recently informed me that when she was small her
mother used to tell her stories about the winter buffalo hunts the
Cheyennes made when all the tribe was on foot. Everyone went on
these hunts, men, women, children, and dogs. A herd of buffalo was
surrounded by the people and driven into the deep drifts; then while
the huge animals were floundering about in the snow, the men ran
up and shot them with arrows. In this way a whole herd could be
killed without one animal escaping. If a buffalo got away the dogs
were set on it, and they quickly drove it back into the deep drifts.
After the kill, the buffalo were skinned and the hides were laid on
the snow, fleshside down; the meat was then cut up and laid on the
hides, which were then folded up over the meat, and the whole
bundle was then corded up with rawhide thongs. Thongs were then
tied to the bundles and the other ends of these long thongs were
fastened to the dogs' necks. The hunters then set out for the camp,
the dogs dragging the bundles of meat over the snow. If a stream was
handy the dogs dragged the loads of meat over the ice, where the
going was much better. As soon as the camp was reached, the dogs
were loosed, and at once the whole pack rushed back across the plain
to the place where the herd had been slaughtered, and there they

---

drag could transport twice that weight. Stephen H. Long, 1820, says the Pawnee
dogs were nearly pure wolf, and John James Audubon, 1843, declares that the Sioux
dogs of the Upper Missouri were so closely akin to wolves that he would have
mistaken them for wolves had he met them in the woods. John Palliser purchased
a travois-dog from an Indian woman on the upper Missouri and says that the
animal was half white wolf, and that after dragging its load all day this dog would
run out on the prairie in the evening and romp and play with the young prairie
wolves. As late as 1833 the Assiniboins of the northern Plains were nearly all on
foot, and to see a village of these foot Indians coming to visit a tribe on the upper
Missouri was a stirring sight. The men marched on foot in long lines, two or three
men deep, with the chiefs in front, marching arm-in-arm. The women and children,
guiding the travois-dogs, were on all sides of the column of warriors, moving like
clouds of skirmishers. Like all foot Indians, the warriors marched with an upright
carriage and a light, quick step, singing war-songs and firing off their guns while
the drums pounded.—G.H.

[12] Bracketed data, George Bent to George E. Hyde, August 2, 1911, left blank
for later insertion in Denver Public Library typescript.—S.L.

feasted on the parts of the game that had been thrown aside while the butchering was going on. I have often heard old people describe how mother dogs who had little puppies in the camp would run to the slaughter ground and gorge themselves with meat and then run back to camp and disgorge part of the meat for their puppies to feed on. Sometimes a mother would make several trips to the slaughtering place, miles from camp, to get enough meat for her litter of young ones.

While the Cheyennes were living in this village on the bluff they were frequently attacked by the Crees and Assiniboins from the north and the Ojibwas from the east. These three tribes had secured guns from the French traders and from the English on Hudson Bay, and the Cheyennes, still armed with bows and stone-tipped arrows, were kept in a constant state of terror by the raiding parties that came against them armed with guns. One time the Cheyennes had gone out into the plains to hunt buffalo, and there was no one left in the village on the bluff except one old woman. This old woman lived in an earth-house near the edge of the bluff. On this side of the village the bluff broke off and descended in a steep precipice to the river below. Down this side of the bluff ran the water paths which were used by the women when they went to the river for water. One evening this old woman was in her lodge preparing a meal. She had some bones in a stone mortar and was pounding them up so she could boil them and get out the grease to mix with her corn. She was sitting on the floor with a crooked pine knot thrust between her robe and the back of her neck, so that she could see to work. The old woman had a big wolf-dog with her. All at once the dog growled. The old woman knew something was wrong. She got up and went out of the lodge, and just as she came out of the door enemies whooped right in her face.

The old woman ran towards the edge of the bluff. This bluff was very steep, and down its face ran the water paths to the river below. As the old woman ran she pulled the blazing torch out from the back of her neck, and when she came to the bluff edge she threw the torch straight out in front of her as hard as she could. Then she ran down

11

one of the water paths a few yards and squatted there. The enemies, seeing the light go straight on ahead of them, ran whooping after it, and all fell over the edge of the bluff. The old woman squatted on the water path and listened. She could hear the enemies groaning at the foot of the bluff. Pretty soon she went back to the lodge. She got ready, took her dog, and set out to find the tribe. The tribe had been gone from the village only one day and the old woman soon found the hunting camp. She told what she had done, and the tribe at once started back for the village. When they arrived they found the enemies, a war party of Assiniboins, lying at the foot of the bluff, some dead and some dying. The ones who were not dead were killed at once, and the Cheyennes gathered up all the guns, iron tomahawks, and knives. This was how the Cheyennes first secured guns. Fearing that some of the Assiniboins had escaped and would bring back a large party to take venegeance, the Cheyennes at once left the village and moved out into the buffalo plains again.

These raids made on our tribe by Indians armed with guns grew so frequent that at last our tribe was compelled to abandon the village on the bluff and move out into the plains toward the Missouri.[13] Thus a new migration was begun. On this journey the Cheyennes were accompanied by the Moiseyu, a tribe whose home was in the lake country of northwestern Minnesota. These Moiseyus were good friends of the Cheyennes, and as they were also being attacked by Indians armed with guns, they determined to go with the Cheyennes to the Missouri. The two tribes hunted buffalo in the plains north of

[13] Alexander Henry, the fur trader, in his journal [*The Manuscript Journals of Alexander Henry and David Thompson . . . 1799–1814*, edited by Elliot Coues] under date of November 9, 1800, gives an account of the Cheyenne removal from this village on the bluff. He says that the Cheyennes were a neutral tribe living between the Ojibwas of northern Minnesota and the prairie bands of Sioux on the head of Minnesota River, to the south. These two tribes were at war. Although the Cheyennes stood neutral, they were suspected by the Ojibwas of favoring the Sioux. About the year 1740 a large party of Ojibwas went against the Sioux, but failed to find them, and on their way home the angry warriors took vengeance on the Cheyennes, destroying their village and nearly exterminating the tribe, the remnant of which fled southward across the Missouri. This account is probably correct except in one detail—the statement as to the number of Cheyennes killed.—G.H.

the Missouri, but after some time the Moiseyus lost heart and moved back to Minnesota. They said that they were hungry for the ducks in the lakes of their old home and that they were afraid to kill any more buffalo for meat, because at night the ghosts of the dead buffalo came into their lodges and stared at them with big eyes. Our old people say that these Moiseyus were Sioux Indians and that for many years they kept moving back and forth, sometimes living with the Cheyennes on the Missouri and then returning again to their old home. Their last visit to the Cheyennes seems to have been made about one hundred years ago (1814); after this visit they moved north again and the Cheyennes lost them; but we still have a clan in our tribe called Moiseyu, which is said to be mixed Cheyenne and Moiseyu.

The Cheyennes and Moiseyus appear to have remained in the plains north of the Missouri for some time before they finally crossed the river. While still living here in these buffalo plains they met a strange tribe, the Suhtais. These people were buffalo hunters who did not plant corn or live in permanent villages, but kept moving about in skin lodges, following the buffalo. When the Cheyennes and Suhtais first met, both tribes lined up and prepared to fight, both sides shouting, but before the battle began the Cheyennes discovered that the Suhtais spoke a dialect of the Cheyenne tongue. The chiefs then met in the middle of the field and made peace. The tribal medicine of the Cheyennes was the bundle containing the four sacred arrows, while the Suhtais had for their medicine the Buffalo Cap, *Issi wun*. The Keeper of the Arrows and the Keeper of the Buffalo Cap became great friends and camped together. One time the Cheyennes, Moiseyus, and Suhtais started south at the end of winter. When they reached the Missouri the river was still covered with ice. The Cheyennes, Moiseyus, and the Keeper of the Buffalo Cap with his band of Suhtais, crossed the river on the ice and camped on the southern bank, while the rest of the Suhtais camped on the northern bank. During the night a strange noise was heard and the criers ran through the camps calling out that something terrible was about to happen. Then there was a sound like thunder and the ice in the river

13

broke up with a great roar. Huge cakes of ice were thrown up on the banks, and the Indians fled. The Suhtais who had camped on the north bank were never seen again. The Cheyennes say that these Suhtais were Cree Indians and that after the ice broke they returned north and rejoined the Crees, but we have never been able to gain any news of the Suhtais. Our old people think that they are still living up in Canada among the Crees but we have never heard anything further about them. The band of Suhtais that was camped on the south bank when the ice went out remained with the Cheyennes and finally joined our tribe as a clan. These people always held to their own customs and spoke their own language. The last of the Suhtais among us died years ago. My father met these people about 1830 while they were still a strong clan, and he used to say that although he spoke Cheyenne well, he had great difficulty in understanding the Suhtai dialect. The funny way the Suhtais said things used to be a standing subject for jokes in the Cheyenne camps.

After being driven from the village on the bluff, the Cheyennes went to the Missouri several times before they finally crossed to live on the south side of the river. This final crossing was made in spring or summer. I recently had a talk with two very old women, Bear Woman and Lightning Woman, and they told me that their grandmothers had a story that when the Cheyennes reached the Missouri this time they were crossed over by the Rees or Mandans in bullboats. These boats were round and bowl-shaped; they were made of rawhide stretched over a framework of willow.[14] These old women told me that when the Cheyennes and Moiseyus crossed the Missouri they

[14] Bullboats: "But the greatest marvel of all the things in the land [of the Assyrians] after the city [of Babylon] itself, to my mind, is this which I am about to tell: Their boats, those I mean which go down the river to Babylon, are round and all of leather: for they make ribs for them of willow which they cut in the land of the Armenians who dwell above the Assyrians, and round these they stretch hides."—Herodotus, *History*, v. 1, p. 96. Straw was placed in the bottom of the boats on which casks of wine were laid. An ass was taken in each boat; two men were the crew. At Babylon the cargo, the willow rods, and straw were sold, while the hide covering was packed on the ass and taken up the river to serve again.

The ancient Irish and Britons used the same kind of boat, which was called a "coracle."—G.H.

were very poor. They had no lodgepoles or skin covers for lodges; all they had was their dogs and a little camp equipment.

After crossing to the south or west bank of the Missouri, the Cheyennes built another earth-lodge village near the famous Standing Rock.[15] There were only two other tribes living on the upper Missouri at that time, the Rees or Arikaras below the Cheyennes near the present Pierre, South Dakota, and the Mandans above the Cheyennes near the present Bismarck, N. D. Both these tribes lived in earth-lodge villages, planting corn and beans and making hunts in the buffalo plains to the westward. The Cheyennes lived near these two tribes for a long time. They lived the same kind of a life that the Mandans and Rees lived, planting their fields and then going off on a buffalo hunt, returning in time to harvest the crop and then going off again on the autumn hunt. Lightning Woman and Twin Woman tell me that their mothers told them stories of how the Cheyennes lived here on the Missouri. These old women say the Cheyennes made seines of willow shoots with which they waded into the river and caught large numbers of fish. The people made wooden dugouts by hollowing out logs with fire. A whole family would work on one of these canoes, keeping the fires burning day and night until the log was burned out and the canoe completed.

At the time when the Cheyennes were living in this village on the Missouri there were no Sioux in that region.[16] The Sioux had not yet

[15] The date of the arrival of the Cheyennes on the south bank of the Missouri cannot be fixed exactly. Alexander Henry says they were driven to the Missouri about the year 1740, and the French explorer La Vérendrye met them on the south bank of the river in the summer of 1743. He does not speak of an earth-lodge village but simply says his party "passed among the squaws and camps, stopping very little." The Cheyenne earth-lodge village was probably built soon after 1743. It stood on the high bank of the river just below Porcupine Creek (above the present Fort Yates). The ruins of this village were still to be seen a few years ago, but the Missouri began eating into the bank and the whole village site has now gone into the river.—G.H.

[16] The first bands of Sioux to move west to the Missouri came between 1750 and 1760 and struck the Missouri about the mouths of the Big Sioux and the James or Dakota rivers. These Sioux made war on the Mandans and Arikaras, but were not strong enough to injure these village Indians seriously. Then in 1780 came the

migrated westward from Minnesota. In those days the Mandans and Rees were the most powerful tribes in all that region. The Mandans had six or more large earth-lodge villages or "forts" surrounded by ditches and picket stockades, and the Rees had as many villages as the Mandans. These two tribes were sometimes at war, and the Cheyennes seem to have aided the Rees. Our oldest people speak of these old troubles with the Mandans, but they do not remember any details. After our tribe moved out toward the Black Hills, we had a quarrel with the Rees about horses and a war followed, but peace was made again and some Cheyennes went back and lived at the Ree villages a long time. Our tribe was not on the river when the great smallpox came. The Cheyennes had already moved to the Black Hills and did not get the disease, but the Mandans and Rees lost terribly. Their old strength was broken; then the Sioux moved to the Missouri and began raiding these two tribes, until at last the Mandans and Rees hardly dared go into the plains to hunt buffalo. The Mandans are now extinct and the Rees are only a handful.

After building the earth-lodge village near Standing Rock, the people made two hunts each year on Cheyenne River and Grand River, at first hunting on the lower courses of these streams, but gradually extending their excursions farther west toward the Black Hills. As time went on Cheyenne River became the favorite hunting ground of the tribe, and our people still call this stream Good River. The two main forks of this stream head close together to the west of the Black Hills; the North Fork flows around the northern side of the hills and the South Fork around the southern side; then reaching the plains to the east of the hills, the two forks join and flow eastward into the Missouri. Thus the Black Hills are practically surrounded by the waters of Cheyenne River. Finding the country near the hills

---

great smallpox epidemic which broke the power of the Mandans and Rees. This epidemic came up the Missouri, attacking the Mandans and Rees with great virulence. A war party of Assiniboins who had made a raid on the Mandans took the disease home to their camp on Red River, where it decimated their tribe. From here it spread north clear to Hudson Bay and west to the Rockies. Fur traders of that period state that this epidemic carried off two-thirds of the Indian population of western Canada.—G.H.

very rich in game of all kinds, the Cheyennes had abandoned their earth-lodge village near Standing Rock and moved into the Black Hills to live. This move was not made all at once, but gradually; and even after they had abandoned the village on the Missouri, part of the Cheyennes continued to plant corn each year in the lower valley of Cheyenne River.

This movement to the Black Hills made a great change in the Cheyennes. They now became a typical plains tribe of buffalo hunters, and securing horses near the hills, they began to wander far afield, waging war on many tribes.[17] Near the Black Hills the Cheyennes met the Arapahos, who are kinsmen of ours, and also the Kiowas and Crows. These tribes all had horses, and from them the Cheyennes secured their first mounts. Many old women still used dogs, and when they went out to gather roots and berries, they took their dogs with them, with little saddlebags fitted on the dogs' backs, in which the berries, fruits, and roots were taken back to camp. These old people did not mix up with the younger Cheyennes but lived alone in little lodges. The rest of the people lived in fine large buffalo-skin lodges. In the old days north of the Missouri the lodges used by the Cheyennes during their hunts were very small and were covered with rawhides. These hides were not sewn together to make a regular lodge cover, but were simply thrown over the lodgepoles and tied down with rawhide cords. In those early times the Cheyennes did not even know how to dress buffalo hides and make them into robes. The old people say the Cheyennes first learned this art from the Sioux. The Sioux women split the buffalo hide in the middle, dressed the two pieces separately and then sewed them together again. When the Cheyennes moved out toward the Black Hills, they learned from the Kiowas and Comanches how to dress

---

[17] "Without it [the horse] he [the Indian] was a half-starved skulker in the timber, creeping up on foot toward the unwary deer or building a brush corral with infinate labor to surround a herd of antelope, and seldom venturing more than a few days' journey from home. With the horse he was transformed into the daring buffalo hunter, able to procure in a single day enough food to supply his family for a year, leaving him free then to sweep the plains with his war parties along a range of a thousand miles."—James Mooney.—G.H.

hides in one piece without splitting them. These two tribes, the Kiowas and Comanches, made the finest robes in the Great Plains in those early days, but the Cheyenne women soon learned to do just as good work. Lightning Woman, born in 1829, tells me that when the Cheyennes moved out to the Black Hills and found game of every kind, they used the skins of the various animals for these purposes: mountain sheep and deer skins for women's dresses and men's leggings; antelope skins for children's clothing and for men's fine shirts and jackets; elk skins and buffalo-cow skins for lodge covers; buffalo-bull hides for shields and other work requiring very thick or tough leather. Young elk skins were as soft as deer skins, and old elk skins as soft as young buffalo skins.

When all the men, women, and children, had hidden themselves behind the lines of brush and the antelope priest was seated on the ground back of the pit with his medicine sticks in his hands, a few good runners were sent out on foot to drive the antelope toward the trap. When the antelope came running toward the pit, the priest kept singing to them and beckoning them forward with his medicine sticks until the whole herd rushed toward him and jumped into the pit. Sometimes there were so many animals that they could not all get into the pit and some of them jumped over the ditch and came right where the priest was sitting; but he kept right on singing and beckoning with his sticks. If any of the antelope ran toward the brush lines to attempt to escape, the Indians hidden behind the brush yelled and drove the animals back. Poles were set in the ground among the piles of brush so the antelope could not knock the piles over. When the trap was full of antelope, the priest gave the signal and the Indians entered and began killing the animals. No shooting of any kind was permitted, as people were running about everywhere and it was very dangerous to use guns or arrows. The antelope were knocked on the head with clubs, and lariats were used to drag some of the animals out of the bottom of the pit. If any antelope broke through the lines and escaped, the priest called to the Indians not to chase these animals but to let them go.

When the antelope were all killed, they were laid out in lines on

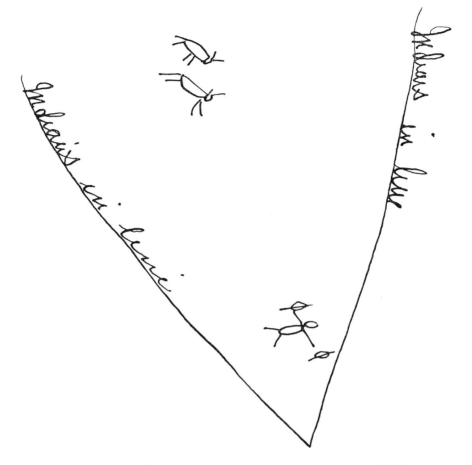

White Face Bull's Antelope Pit with Men Women and Children. My father's men joined in this line.[18]

[18] Drawn by George Bent. He was present at this affair when a boy—it was near Bent's Fort, and one of the last antelope pits made by the Southern Cheyennes. The sketch shows the lines of brush forming a large V with Indians hiding behind the brush "wings" and the antelope priest at the point of the V with his two antelope instruments in his hands. This method of killing antelope is described at length in Grinnell's Cheyenne book.—G.H.

the grass. The priest was given first choice of the game, and he also received all the tongues. White Face Bull made one of these pits near Bent's Fort in 1853 and after the kill gave all the tongues to my father.

The last pits ever made by the Cheyennes, as far as I can learn, were made in 1865–1866 by Black Shin's Suhtai band on Antelope-pit River (the Little Missouri). I recently had a talk with Prairie Chief, son of Gray Beard. Prairie Chief was a boy in 1865 and was with this band when the antelope pits were made. He says one pit was made in the fall of 1865 with Curly Hair an antelope priest, and another pit was made in the spring of 1866, with Black Beard as priest. He told me that the priests always made the pits where other pits had been made in early times, because it was said that the ante-lope priests of the old days had made very strong medicine at these old pits, so that the antelope always came to these places in great numbers. He told me that Black Shin's people found large numbers of clubs lying about near these old pits, and when the new pits were made in 1865–1866, these same clubs were used in killing the game. This kind of antelope trap was used by the Kiowas and other tribes near the Black Hills long before the Cheyennes moved into that country, and old men have told me that when the Cheyennes first moved west of the Missouri they found these old pits at the forks of several streams. When the Kiowas moved south they used a similar trap to catch wild horses, in the Staked Plains. They made these horse pits near water holes, where the wild herds came to drink, and large numbers of horses were caught in these traps.

When the Cheyennes moved into the Black Hills region they found that country occupied by the Arapahos, Kiowas, and Crows. There was also a small tribe, the Prairie Apaches, who lived with the Kiowas, and part of the Comanches were evidently still living near the hills, as our old people say [as noted earlier] that the Chey-enne women learned to dress buffalo robes in one piece from the Kiowa and Comanche women, and that our women also received the mixture used in softening robes from the women of these two tribes.

All these tribes near the hills had horses when the Cheyennes first came, and the Arapahos, Kiowas, and Crows, all have stories that their tribe was the first to give horses to the Cheyennes. The truth probably is that our people secured some horses from each of these tribes. In those early days, 1750–1775, all the Black Hills tribes made annual visits to the villages of the Mandans and Rees on the Missouri, where they traded for goods which the Mandans secured from the English in the north and the Rees from French traders who came up the Missouri. Lightning Woman says the Cheyennes used to trade horses, buffalo robes, dried meat, and other products of their hunts to the Mandans and Rees for guns, ammunition, iron tomahawks, knives, and other goods secured from the whites, and for Mandan corn, dried pumpkins, and tobacco. Porcupine Bear, our oldest man (he recently died and Cedar Grove is now the oldest man among the Cheyennes) told me that the guns the Cheyennes secured from the Mandans were short-barrelled smoothbores of English make ("North West fusils"). They had flintlocks and the Cheyennes made their own flints. They also made gun wads of the inner bark of willows. They had powder horns and small pouches of buckskin in which the bullets and extra flints were kept. The powder was poured into the hand and then put down the barrel of the gun; a small ball of bark was rammed down on top of the powder, and then the bullet was dropped in with another ball of bark rammed down on it.

With the Arapahos the Cheyennes became close friends at their first meeting, and from then until today the Cheyennes and Arapahos are always spoken of together. During one hundred and fifty years we have never had any serious trouble with the Arapahos. With the other tribes of the Black Hills country the Cheyennes were at first on good terms, but quarrels arose and the Cheyennes made attacks on all these tribes. Then the Sioux began to move from the Missouri out toward the hills, bringing more trouble with them.

The Sioux did not come all at once, but slowly, a few small parties at first, then larger bands. Our people say the first Sioux who came to the hills were very poor people who came out all on foot, with dogs, to visit the Cheyennes and to get presents of dried meat and a few horses.[19] Seeing how rich the hills country was in game and how abundantly supplied with horses all the tribes in that region, the Sioux began to come out in stronger bands, to hunt and to steal horses from the hills tribes. The Sioux traditions state that some attacks were made on the Cheyennes, but if this is true the attacks must have been petty ones, for our people have no recollection of ever having been at war with the Sioux. In fact, the Sioux and Cheyennes joined forces and were soon helping each other in raiding the other tribes. The Kiowas were the first to suffer. They were driven into the mountains at the head of the Platte and from there moved south, finally joining the Comanches near Red River in what is now Oklahoma. With the Kiowas went the Prairie Apaches, of course, as this little tribe lived with the Kiowas almost as one people. Having pushed out the Kiowas and Apaches, the Sioux and Cheyennes turned their attention to the Crows. When the Cheyennes first came to the hills, this tribe was living on the Little Missouri and Powder rivers, northwest of the hills. Being constantly attacked, the Crows retired toward the northwest, to Tongue River and the Bighorn country.

In 1819 or 1820, a party of thirty Cheyennes, young men of the Bowstring Society,[20] set out from a Cheyenne camp near the Black Hills to steal horses from the Crows over near Tongue River. Reaching Tongue River, the Bowstring Men soon located a Crow village on that stream, and here the thirty Cheyennes concealed themselves in the valley, to wait until darkness came, when they could slip into the Crow camp and steal horses. While the Bowstrings were lying

[19] The Sioux seem to have made raids and visits among the tribes of the Black Hills as early as 1775, but they did not move to the hills to live, in any force, until just prior to 1800. According to the Sioux winter-counts, Standing Bull, an Oglala Sioux, visited the Black Hills and brought home a small pine tree in 1775–1776. The first attacks made by the Sioux on the tribes near the hills are mentioned in the winter-counts under the dates 1786 to 1798.—G.H.

[20] The Cheyenne warriors all belonged to soldier societies. Each of these societies had its own peculiar dress, dance, and ceremonies. The men of these societies or brotherhoods were called *Nutqui*, "warriors." There were six of these societies: *Hotamitanio*, or Dog Men (Dog Soldiers); *Woksihitanio*, Kit-fox Men; *Himoiyoqis*, Pointed-lance Men; *Mahohivas*, Red Shield Men; *Himatanohis*, Bowstring Men; and *Hotamimsaw*, Crazy Dogs.—G.H.

hidden, they were alarmed by a sudden stir in the camp. They saw the herds driven in and the Crow warriors mounting their war ponies and getting ready for a fight. When they saw this, the Bowstrings knew that they had been seen and that the Crows were preparing to attack them.

The Bowstring Men were all on foot, and they saw that if they were caught in the open valley by the mounted Crows they would be quickly surrounded and ridden down. Already the bands of mounted Crow warriors were searching the valley for them; so leaving their concealment, the Bowstrings ran to a nearby hill and on its top began to pile up stone for a rude breastwork. This hill stands out in the valley of Tongue River all by itself, between the bluffs and the river. It is steep on most sides, but in one place slopes down gently to the valley below, and in this place horses could be ridden right up to the top of the hill. This hill is called by the Cheyennes Crow Standing Butte. The hill is on the south side of Tongue River.

As soon as the Bowstrings came out in the open and ran toward this butte, the Crows saw them and came charging toward them. Now the fight began. The Crows, all mounted, charged up the slope toward the hill top, but the Bowstrings from behind their breastwork drove the mounted warriors back. Thus the fight went on for some time, then the Bowstrings began to run out of ammunition. They hardly had an arrow left. The Crows now gathered in very strong force and a big medicine man on a fine horse put himself at their head. As they came charging up the hill, the medicine man was far in the lead. He reached the top all alone and charged in among the Bowstrings. They pulled him off his horse and cut him into small pieces with their knives; then the great mass of Crow warriors rushed over the brow of the hill and in a minute the thirty Bowstrings were on the ground, all dead.

For some time the Cheyennes had no news of the Bowstrings, but at length another Cheyenne war party which was out hunting for the Crows came to Crow Standing Butte, and there they found the bodies of the thirty Bowstring Men. The wolves had been dragging the bodies about, and they were badly gnawed. When the war party returned to camp and told what they had seen, the relatives of the dead Bowstrings began to mourn, and they would not stop until they had induced one of the soldier societies to take up their cause. It was then announced that the tribe would wait "one winter" and then "move the Arrows against the Crows." This meant that the whole tribe, men, women, and children, would move with the Medicine Arrows into the Crow country to get vengeance for the killing of the thirty Bowstrings.

Accordingly, in the summer of 1820 or 1821,[21] the Cheyennes and a big village of Sioux assembled near the Black Hills and moved west towards Tongue River. Reaching Powder River, the people encamped, the Cheyennes on one side of the stream, the Sioux on the other. Meantime the Crows had learned that the Cheyennes and Sioux were after them, and they sent out ten Crow men to scout. Just at sunset these Crows discovered the two villages on Powder River, and riding cautiously down into the valley they hid themselves near the camps. As soon as it was dark they rode in between the two camps, and here they ran upon a Cheyenne man who was crossing from one camp to the other. They shot this man and scalped him; but, of course, the shots were heard in the two camps, and a large number of Cheyennes and Sioux armed themselves at once and jumping on fast ponies set out to find the Crows. It was very dark by this time and nothing could be seen, but the Crows were quirting their ponies at every jump in their hurry to escape, and by following the sound of the whips the Cheyenne and Sioux warriors succeeded in overtaking two of the Crows, who were poorly mounted, and killed them both. The other scouts got away, and, returning to the Crow village on Tongue River, reported the position of the Cheyenne and Sioux camps on the Powder.

A strange thing now happened. The Crows made up a big war party and set off east to surprise the Cheyennes and Sioux, and at the same time the Cheyennes and Sioux made up a similar party and

[21] The Cheyennes say this expedition against the Crows was in or about the year 1820. The Sioux winter-counts mention the event under the date 1820–1821.—G.H.

set off west to surprise the Crows. In some way these two big war parties passed each other in the night and each went on to attack the other's camp without knowing that their own camp, left unprotected, was in danger. The Cheyennes and Sioux followed the trail of the Crow scouts back toward Tongue River. They kept a force of scouts out ahead, and as these scouts were going along through the darkness they stumbled upon a Crow. This man had remained in the Crow village after the main war party of Crows had left and he was now following along, trying to catch up with the main body. He walked right into the Cheyenne and Sioux scouts, and not wishing to make a noise, they attacked him with their war clubs but bungled the business and only wounded the man.

The man escaped from the scouts and rushed back to Tongue River where he ran into the Crow village, covered with blood, and began to call out that the Cheyennes and Sioux were coming to attack the village. The people would not believe him. He told them to look at him and see what the Cheyennes and Sioux had done to him, but the Crows just laughed at him. "This Crow man had been meddling with another man's wife and now," the people said, "the woman's husband has caught him outside the camp and given him a good clubbing; that is all. He has not seen any Cheyennes or Sioux. If the Cheyennes and Sioux had caught him they would not have left him alive."

At last this Crow man succeeded in convincing a number of people, mostly his own relations and friends, that he was telling the truth and that the village was to be attacked. There were about fifty lodges of these people. They packed all their best things on ponies and, leaving their lodges standing in the village, moved out to the hills, where they sat down to watch and see what would happen. Day came and no attack was made. The sun came up and still the Cheyennes and Sioux had not appeared; and now the people began to say that the Crow man had lied to them, after all, and after waiting some time longer most of them packed their things on the ponies again and moved back to the village in the valley below.

Meantime the big war party of Cheyennes and Sioux had lost

their way in the night and could not locate the Crow camp. It was nearly noon when at last they succeeded in finding the camp, and just as these Crow families were moving back from the hills and were entering the village, the Cheyennes and Sioux charged in among the lodges. It was not much of a fight, for most of the Crow men were away with the Crow war party, and the Cheyennes and Sioux had everything their own way. They rushed into the village, rounded up the pony herds, captured women and children, killed all the men they could find, overturned the lodges, broke the poles, and knocked everything to pieces. In 1865 when I was up there with the hostiles, I visited this place and the ground was still covered with broken lodgepoles, old stone axes, and other stuff. This was the biggest capture the Cheyennes and Sioux ever made. The Cheyennes alone took over one hundred young Crow women, boys, and girls.

The big war party of Crows had also missed its way in the night, and while the Crows were still hunting for the Cheyenne and Sioux camps a runner arrived with news of the attack being made on the Crow village. The Crows rushed back to Tongue River, but arrived too late. Their village was in ruins, a large part of the people had been carried off and the rest were scattered among the hills. It was a terrible blow to the Crows.

On their way home, the Cheyennes and Sioux began to quarrel over the division of the prisoners, and the wrangling grew so fierce that several captives were killed by the angry warriors before the camps were reached. After the war party had reached the Cheyenne and Sioux camps, no more prisoners were killed, as it was a great crime to kill anyone who had been taken into a lodge.

Some years after the capture of this Crow village, the Cheyennes were encamped on Horse Creek on the south side of the North Platte near the present eastern line of Wyoming. One day a young Crow man came out of the hills and rode toward the Cheyenne village. This man had lost many relatives in the capture of the Crow village and he did not care much what happened to him. He was mounted on a very fine pony and rode right down into the edge of the Cheyenne camp. When he was discovered the village was thrown into great excitement. The people rushed out of the lodges, and the men began catching and mounting their war ponies. The Crow rode up and down at the edge of the village singing his death song. Some of the older Cheyennes smelled a trap and called out for everyone to wait until all were mounted and ready to ride. This was good advice, but twelve young men of the Medicine Lodge got mounted ahead of everyone else and refused to wait. They were very eager to win the honor of striking this Crow man before anyone else could do it; so as soon as they were ready they charged at the Crow.

As the twelve young Cheyennes made a rush at the Crow, he turned his pony and began to ride back toward the hills. His pony was very fast, but he held it in and kept just a little ahead of the Cheyennes, drawing them on toward the hills. As they approached the hills they thought they had him; then all at once a big force of mounted Crows charged out of the hills and made for the Cheyennes. The twelve young men of the Medicine Lodge turned their ponies and started back toward the camp, riding hard, but their ponies were already used up, and one by one they were overtaken and killed. Eight fell and the Crows rushed the other four right into the Cheyenne camp, but by this time the main body of Cheyennes was ready and, charging out, they drove the Crows back into the hills and several miles beyond. They chased the Crows clear off the ground, killing several of them.

After this fight some Cheyennes committed a great crime. The relatives of the eight young men of the Medicine Lodge whom the Crows had killed were very angry. When the Cheyennes were going to move away from Horse Creek, the bodies of these eight young men were wrapped up and placed on scaffolds inside of lodges. The families of the dead men had several Crow prisoners who had been adopted into the families and had been living with the Cheyennes ever since the capture of the Crow village several years before. These Crow prisoners were taken by the relatives of the dead Cheyennes and killed and laid on the ground around the lodges in which the eight young Cheyennes had been buried on scaffolds. Then the Cheyennes moved away and left the dead Crows laying around the lodges.

Our old people today say that this was the greatest crime ever committed by Cheyennes, and they say that when the Medicine Arrow
ceremony was next held spots of blood were found on the sacred
arrows—the blood of these murdered Crow captives.

Some time after the Crows had set this trap for the Cheyennes at
Horse Creek, the Crow chief learned that his son was still alive and
was a captive in the Cheyenne camp. He learned of this from the
Arapahos and at once determined to attempt to get the boy back. This
boy was called Big Prisoner by the Cheyennes. He had been with the
Cheyennes several years, and was now grown up and married to a
Cheyenne girl. It was in 1827, as nearly as I can make out, that this
Crow chief started south with a big band of Crows, intending to
recover his son. In the fighting between the Crows and Cheyennes,
the Arapahos had remained neutral, and although living with the
Cheyennes much of the time, they still maintained rather friendly
relations with the Crows. So when the Crows started south the chief
sent a runner to the Arapahos notifying them that his band was
coming to visit them.

The Arapahos, Gros Ventres, and Cheyennes were encamped on
the South Platte, northeast of where Denver now stands and east of
Greeley. These Gros Ventres lived up in Canada, but having had
some trouble with the British traders, they came down to visit their
kinsmen the Arapahos. They stayed several years. When the Crows
arrived they camped about two miles from these other tribes. The
Crows now held a big feast in their camp, and the Arapahos and
Gros Ventres attended, but the Cheyennes stayed away. After the
feast the Crow chief told his guests that he had come to make peace
with the Cheyennes and get back his son. The Arapahos went to the
Cheyennes and repeated what the chief had said. The Cheyennes
spoke to Big Prisoner about it, but the boy refused to return to the
Crows. He had recently married a Cheyenne girl and his adopted
father treated him just like a son and gave him everything he wanted,
so he did not wish to leave the Cheyennes.

These Cheyennes were a small camp, so when the Crow chief
learned that the Cheyennes would not give up his son, he determined

to take the boy by force. He gave another feast for the Arapahos and treated them very well; then, after all had eaten, he requested the Arapahos to hand over the fifty lodges of Cheyennes to him and let the Crows deal with them as they desired. A brave Gros Ventre, who had been made a chief by the Arapahos, replied to the Crow chief. He said the Cheyennes and Arapahos had been living together, eating together, fighting together, and dying together for many years, and that if the Crows wished to attack the Cheyennes they would have to count on fighting the Arapahos and Gros Ventres also. Several Arapahos backed up what this Gros Ventre had said; then the Crow chief made another speech and said that he had done all that he could and now intended to drop the whole business. He said that next day the Crow warriors would come and give a big dance in the camp of their friends, the Arapahos. The Arapahos told him they would feel very much honored, and then the feast broke up, everyone appearing much pleased.

That night a Crow who had some friends in the Arapaho camp slipped over to the camp and told his friends that the Crows were planning a massacre. They intended to come armed and in great force; during the dance they would attack the Cheyennes and Arapahos by surprise, kill them all, and get back the Crow chief's son and all the other Crow prisoners in the Cheyenne camp. Two very big Crow men had been selected to pick up the Crow chief's son and carry him off on a horse between them. The Arapahos at once notified the Cheyennes of this plot; a night council was held in secret, and it was decided that everyone should arm immediately to guard against a possible night attack. That night no one slept in the camps; every man lay on his arms, and both the Cheyennes and Arapahos kept sending out scouts all night. The Crows had learned that their plot had been discovered and they were also under arms with scouts out.

Next day there was no Crow dance. The Crows kept in their own camp, on their guard. Toward noon there was a clash, and at once the Cheyennes, Arapahos, and Gros Ventres mounted and formed a line in front of their camps, while the Crows formed up facing them.

29

The women and children packed up everything and loaded the ponies. Only the lodges were left standing, and places had been selected for the women and children to flee to if a big fight was started. But only a little skirmishing took place. Warriors rode along the lines on fast ponies, firing and yelling, and every little while brave men from each side rode out and fought between the lines, but there was no general engagement, as each side was unwilling to make the first charge. The Gros Ventre chief (Small Man was his name), was very brave in these single combats, and I have heard old Cheyennes say that they saw Dohnsau (Little Mountain), the famous Kiowa chief, fighting among the Crows. He was visiting the Crows at that time. After this skirmishing had gone on for a long time, the Crow women took down the lodges and began moving away. The warriors followed them, retreating slowly and keeping on their guard, and thus the last big meeting between the Cheyennes and Crows came to an end. The Northern Cheyennes, living near the Black Hills, continued to fight the Crows until about 1875, but our part of the tribe (Southern Cheyennes) moved too far south to see much of the Crows after 1826.

CHAPTER TWO

THE MEDICINE ARROWS ARE LOST

J UST AS there are currents in the sea, so also there were regular
currents of Indian migration in the plains. There were no beaten
paths or trails that you could see, but there were well-known routes
which were used by the different tribes. One of these currents of
Indian movement was from the Black Hills of Dakota south across
the heads of the Platte and Arkansas rivers to the Canadian and Red
rivers, and so on clear down into Texas. This route was used long ago
by the Comanches in their migration to the south; later it was used
by the Kiowas, and still later by the Cheyennes and Arapahos. The
Northern Comanches or Quahadi Comanches were living near the
Black Hills in 1700, but about 1750 they were attacked by the
Kiowas, Crows, and other Black Hills tribes and were pressed south
of the Platte. They followed this route of migration clear down to
Red River. Part of the Kiowas, the Southern Kiowas, followed these
Comanches and continued to force them southward, but the rest of
the Kiowas lingered in the Black Hills region until 1800. These
Kiowas were the Northern Kiowas or Cold Men, and they remained
in the Black Hills country until the Sioux moved into that region and
began raiding them.

The last of the Kiowas were forced south of the Platte by the Sioux
about the year 1800, and they retired along the same route the Comanches had followed in earlier times. After they had been pressed
south, part of the Kiowas used to return north to the North Platte
nearly every year to meet the Crows, Arapahos, and sometimes the
Cheyennes. The Kiowas brought horses and Mexican goods to this

31

trading fair on the North Platte, and for these things they received from the Crows, Arapahos, and Cheyennes, guns, ammunition, British goods, eagle feathers, ermine skins, and other articles. Our old people say that the Cheyennes were engaged in this intertribal trade for many years. These Cheyenne traders operated in this way: they secured horses, some by trade from the Kiowas and other tribes, some by stealing from the Pawnees and other hostile tribes. They took part of these animals to the Mandan or Ree villages on the Missouri and exchanged them for guns, ammunition, British goods, corn, dried pumpkins, and tobacco. They also gave the Mandans and Rees dried buffalo meat and robes for corn, pumpkins, and tobacco. They kept part of these articles for their own use and took the rest to the North Platte and exchanged them with the Kiowas and other tribes for more horses. These annual fairs on the North Platte were finally broken up by the Sioux. In 1813[1] the Sioux came to the fair, which was on Horse Creek that year, just west of the Wyoming-Nebraska line, and drove the Kiowas and other traders into the mountains at the head of the Platte. About 1815 the Kiowas ventured up to the Platte again but were a second time attacked by the Sioux and driven into the mountains. After that the Kiowas kept south of the Arkansas, coming north only on rare occasions.

In 1825 the Cheyennes and Arapahos were all still living north of the Platte, near the Black Hills. In that year or the next the Gros Ventres came down from Canada to visit their kinsmen, the Arapahos, and with those Gros Ventres came eighteen or twenty young Blackfeet. These young Blackfeet were all men, they had no women with them. They said their tribe had been fighting with the whites up in Canada, their relatives were all dead, they did not care to stay in Canada any longer, and so had come down to live with the Cheyennes and Arapahos and to steal horses from the Kiowas and Comanches, as they had heard these tribes were very rich in horses.

Left Hand Bull, who was nearly ninety in 1910,[2] told me that he

---

[1] Originally 1803 in Hyde's working copy, corrected in longhand to 1813. But 1803 appears in the Denver Public Library copy.—S.L.

[2] Eighty-four appears in Hyde's working copy, struck over and made to read as

was just a small boy when these Gros Ventres and Blackfeet came south. Soon after they arrived, the Blackfeet made up a war party and set out for the south to steal horses. Left Hand Bull saw them march through the Cheyenne camp, all abreast, in a long line, and singing a song that they knew how to go to war and steal horses better than anybody else. They then went down near Red River and ran off a big herd of Kiowa and Comanche horses. When they got back they boasted again that they were better warriors and horse-stealers than anyone else, and, of course, this made the Cheyennes and Arapahos very jealous, and they decided to send war parties against the Kiowas and Comanches and show what they could do.

This was in 1826. The Blackfeet reported that they had seen great herds of buffalo between the Arkansas and the Platte and that plenty of wild horses were also to be found in that region. Wild horses in large herds had never been reported as far north before, and as soon as they heard this news part of the Cheyennes and Arapahos abandoned the Black Hills country and began to move south of the Platte to live. This new migration was led by the *Hevhaitanio* clan or Hairy Men. This was a large Cheyenne clan and had many famous warriors in its camp. With the Hairy Clan went some Arapahos, and other camps of Cheyennes and Arapahos moved south of the Platte soon after; in this way the Cheyenne and Arapaho tribes each became divided into two tribes: the Southern Cheyennes and Southern Arapahos moved south of the Platte to live, while the Northern Cheyennes and Northern Arapahos remained in the old country north of the Platte. The Gros Ventres and the little party of Blackfoot men moved south with the Southern Cheyennes and Arapahos. The Gros Ventres returned to Canada some years later, but the Blackfeet never went back. Most of them married into the Cheyenne and Arapaho tribes, and their children and grand-children are still living with us down here.[3] I knew five or six of these old Blackfeet.

shown above. The Denver copy shows eighty-four with an interlinear question mark.—S.L.

[3] That is, the Cheyenne and Arapaho country of present Oklahoma. Bent lived with his wife Magpie at Colony in northeastern Washita County.—S.L.

The last of them, Small Eyes, died of old age about the year 1880. He lived with me for a time in my lodge in 1867. These Blackfeet never learned the Cheyenne language. They always talked to us in the sign language, which was used by all the Plains tribes.

As soon as the Hevhaitanio or Hairy Men had moved south of the Platte, they began to raid the Kiowas and Comanches. They also took to running wild horses and soon became very skillful in catching these animals. There were about seventy-five lodges in this band. The name Hevhaitanio is of doubtful meaning. Some of the old people say it means Fur Men, others say Hairy Men, and still others claim that it means Hair-rope Men and that the name was given because this camp was the first among the Cheyennes to use ropes braided from the long hair of the buffalo bull's beard. The old type of rope was braided of rawhide strands, but these hair ropes were much better for use in catching wild horses.

The mustangs, or wild horses, originated in the Texas plains. A few strays, Mexican and Indian horses, formed the first herd, probably about 1650. The herds increased in size with great rapidity and spread northward, first across Red River and the Canadian, then across the Arkansas and on north toward the Platte. When the Cheyennes and Arapahos moved south of the Platte in 1826 to hunt these animals, they found that the largest herds were on the north side of the Arkansas from about the present west line of Kansas up to near Black Squirrel Creek east of Colorado Springs and Pueblo.

These Cheyennes and Arapahos who had moved south camped on the South Platte east of the present town of Greeley, Colorado. The women and children and part of the men remained in these camps along the South Platte while the rest of the men went down near the Arkansas to run mustangs. These hunts were made in this way: the band of hunters set out from camp, taking their best horses with them and also a number of gentle mares. They crossed the Ridge Country, which separates the waters of the Platte from those of the Arkansas, and having arrived near the latter river they formed a camp in some good place near where the scouts had reported large numbers of wild horses were ranging. As soon as camp was made the hunt began.

34

Scouts were kept out ahead the same as in a buffalo hunt, and when they signaled that a herd of mustangs had been sighted, the hunters prepared to surround the herd. The country down there near the Arkansas was rolling and it was not difficult to approach a herd unseen. The hunters moved up-wind to prevent the mustangs winding them, for if the wild herd scented the hunters it would be off instantly. Keeping behind the hills, the hunters advanced cautiously, and after coming as near to the herd as they could get, they began to spread out and make the surround. When everyone was in position the signal was given and a man mounted on a very fast horse rode out toward the mustangs. This man rode slowly, lying flat on his horse's back, until he was quite close; then he sat up and charged into the herd. This scattered the mustangs, which ran in every direction, but everywhere they turned Indians rode out from behind the hills and charged at them. Each hunter picked out the mustang he liked best and ran it down. Running the animals down was not very difficult, as these hunts were usually made in the early spring while the mustangs were still weak from a winter passed in a state of semi-starvation. Besides this, the animals were always full of grass and water and in poor shape for a hard run. Their wind was not good.

Each hunter had a long slender pole with the noose of his lasso fastened to the end of the pole. As he overtook the mustang he was pursuing, he rode up alongside and slipped the noose over the wild horse's head. He then "choked down" the mustang until it was subdued, then threw it, put a rawhide halter on its head, and "tailed it up" to a tame horse. Gentle old mares were usually taken along to be employed in this work. The wild horse's head was tied close up to the mare's tail. This was called "tailing" the mustang. Old mares were best because the wild horses soon became very friendly with them and followed along after the mares without giving much trouble.

Sometimes two or more men worked together in these hunts; one man on a very fast horse doing the running and noosing, while his partners took care of the mustangs he had caught. In this way one man could catch several mustangs in a single run. Eighty years ago

Iron Shirt had a pony named White Antelope, the finest and fastest horse the Cheyennes ever saw. Iron Shirt would take three buffalo-hair lassos and catch three mustangs in a single run.

After the run, the hunters led the old mares back to camp with the captured mustangs tailed up behind them, and when camp was reached the mustangs were hobbled, all four feet, with their heads still tied to the mares's tails. The party remained in their hunting camp until they had taken as many wild horses as they could handle; they then set out for home, leading the mustangs with their heads tied to the tails of the gentle mares. On this trip the wild horses were kept tailed to the mares all the time, and in camp each night they were hobbled, all four feet, to keep them from jumping around and kicking.

When the home camps on the South Platte were reached, each hunter picketed the mustangs he had caught near his lodge with their heads still tied to the mares's tails. The wild horses soon grew used to seeing people moving about. They were left alone for a while, and then their owners began to gentle them. A man would walk up and stand near a mustang; after a while he would rub the animal's nose and ears and then rub his back. The horse soon grew used to this handling. The man next put a buffalo robe on the animal's back and then untied the old mare and led her around the camp with the mustang's head tied to her tail. The next step was to hobble the mustang so that he could not jump around any and then untie his head from the mare's tail. The man then heaped buffalo robes on the animal's back, and as soon as the animal grew used to having the robes on his back the man would mount and sit on the mustang's back while he was still hobbled so that he could not jump around or kick. Next day the man mounted again, untied the mustang and rode him around, leading the old mare alongside to keep the wild animal quiet. After that the Indian could ride the mustang without any trouble. He rode the animal for one month, then turned him loose with the herd to graze and get fat. In this way the mustangs were gentled. They were not broken in the way cowboys broke their horses. The hunters always picked out young animals, not over four years old, because the older horses were much harder to gentle. These captured wild horses made the best mounts for hunting buffalo. The wild herd grazed on the same range right alongside with the buffalo and were not a bit afraid of the buffalo, as most other horses were. Many of the best mustangs were also long-winded and fast, qualities which all good buffalo-runners had to have.

Horses were to the Plains Indians what gold was to the whites, and when the Cheyennes, Arapahos, Gros Ventres and Blackfeet moved south of the Platte their main object was to procure more horses. They caught large numbers of mustangs, but not content with this they at once began sending war parties south of the Arkansas to steal horses from the Kiowas, Comanches, and Prairie Apaches. These tribes, living in the Plains between the Arkansas and Texas, were famous throughout the Plains for the size and quality of their herds. The largest of the wild herds were in their country, and they caught great numbers of these mustangs. Besides this they made annual raids into New Mexico, Old Mexico, and Texas, running off great herds of branded horses and mules. When I was a boy I saw the Kiowas, Comanches, and Apaches camped on the Arkansas near my father's fort, and their pony herds were grazing along the river for fifty miles.

The Comanches, and I think also part of the Kiowas, used to hunt horses for their meat and hides. I have heard many old Indians say that the Comanches preferred horse meat to buffalo meat and used horse hides in the way the other Plains tribes used buffalo hides, in making clothing, lodge covers, etc. The fact that the Kiowas and Comanches were so rich in horses made them the mark for the raiding parties of the other Plains tribes, and they were constantly being plundered by the Cheyennes, Arapahos, Pawnees, Osages, and many other tribes.

It was in 1826 that the Hairy Clan of Cheyennes moved south of

[4] Bent's Fort was located on the north bank of the Arkansas, twelve miles west of the mouth of the Purgatoire River in southeastern Colorado. It is now a National Historic Site, eight miles east of La Junta, Colorado, though not as yet restored (1967).—S.L.

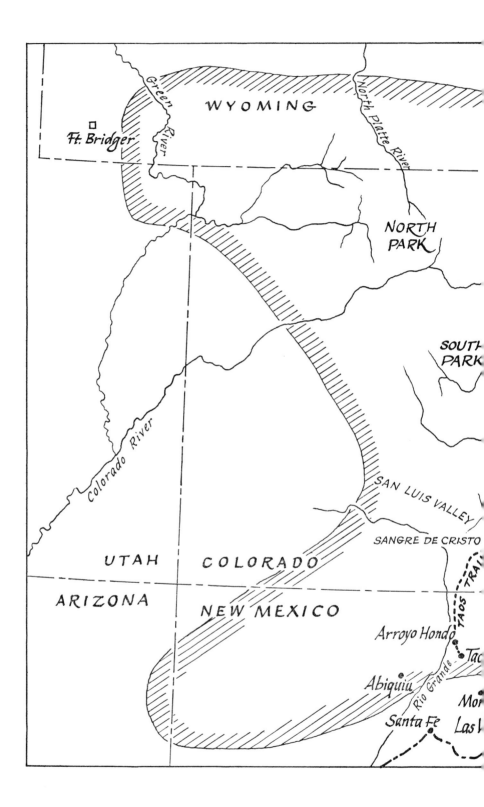

THE WILDERNESS DOMAIN OF BENT, ST. VRAIN & CO.

the Platte, and that same year Yellow Wolf, one of the famous leaders of this band, went down to the Kiowa and Comanche country
with a large war party and ran off a big herd from the North Fork
of Red River. Other parties soon followed Yellow Wolf's example,
and Arapahos, Gros Ventres, and Blackfeet were soon engaged in
this work. The Comanches and Kiowas retaliated by sending war
parties up to the Platte, and the raiding went on year after year.

These horse-stealing expeditions were always on foot and usually
the parties were small ones, as only a few men were required to do
the work and it was very difficult to move large parties through the
enemy's country without their being discovered. Caught on foot in
the open plains by a large body of mounted Comanches and Kiowas,
a war party rarely made its escape; sometimes not a man returned to
tell the story. The war party moved very cautiously, keeping under
cover, traveling in ravines, and never crossing open ground when
they could avoid it. Scouts were always kept out ahead, and whenever
a scout saw anything that looked suspicious, he signaled the warriors,
who at once concealed themselves or lay down on the ground and
waited until the scout signaled them to come on again. These little
parties were not often discovered, but they were in constant danger,
and old men have often told me of the narrow escape they had when
out with these horse-stealing parties. One time a party of Cheyennes,
all afoot, was moving through the Kiowa and Comanche country.
They were crossing an open plain where buffalo were grazing all
about them, when all at once the scout out ahead signaled enemies
in sight. The Cheyennes ran to the head of a small ravine and lay
down in the tall grass. Soon a big body of mounted Kiowas rode up
and charged in among the buffalo. They began killing buffalo all
around the little ravine, but by some chance none of the hunters
came near enough to see the Cheyennes. A Kiowa man shot a buffalo
with an arrow right in front of the ravine, and then he and his wife
dismounted and began to skin the animal and cut up the meat. The
Kiowa cut up the meat while his wife packed it on a horse. All around
other Indians were butchering the buffalo they had killed. Crow
Chief, a great warrior, long dead, told me that there were hundreds

of Kiowa men and women in sight. This Kiowa and his woman who were nearest to where the Cheyennes lay kept looking around toward the little ravine. Crow Chief said they looked around several times and he thought they had seen the Cheyennes, so he said to the warriors, "Be ready. If this man and his woman come any nearer we will all shoot at them at once." Spotted Wolf did not like this. He said to Crow Chief, "That will not do. These people are all around us, cutting up their meat. If we shoot a gun we will all be killed."

After a while the Kiowas began to move off with their ponies loaded with meat. The Kiowa and his wife who were nearest the Cheyennes were among the last to go. The Cheyennes followed this man and his wife until they came in sight of the Kiowa village. They hid themselves until after dark; then they slipped into the Kiowa camp in pairs, cut loose the best horses they could find, and led them silently out of the village. When they had taken as many animals as they could handle, they started for home, driving the stolen herd before them and riding very fast. The Kiowas did not overtake them.

Many old men used to tell me of the war parties they went with to steal Kiowa and Comanche horses in those early days. Yellow Wolf of the Hairy Clan led a party down to the North Fork of Red River, where they ran off a very large herd of Comanche horses. White Antelope and Rock Forehead told me that when Yellow Wolf's party came in with this big herd they went to his lodge and asked him for directions. He told them just where to go and they made up a party and went down there to the North Fork of the Red River. White Antelope and Rock Forehead were the pipe bearers of this party and they had twenty young men with them. When they reached the North Fork they found the Comanches had moved from the place where they had been when Yellow Wolf stole the herd, but after some delay they located the Comanche village farther down the North Fork. They slipped into the camp that night and secured the largest herd of horses ever stolen by a Cheyenne war party. I knew both these men well in 1863 and later. Rock Forehead was the keeper of the Sacred Medicine Arrows after my grandfather was killed in 1838.[5] The whites always called this man Medicine Arrows because he kept the arrows, but his real name was Rock Forehead. He was a famous man.

The Kiowas, Comanches, and Prairie Apaches had so many horses that they let most of them run loose, and these great herds ranged over miles of grass on all sides of the camps. Many of the best animals were herded near the camps and were watched by boys or Mexican captives who acted as herders. These fine horses were driven into camp every evening and tied near their owners' lodges. When the Cheyennes went to steal horses they did not take the common ones running loose on the range but usually ran the danger of going right into the enemy's camp to cut loose the fine animals and lead them out from among the lodges. The men of the Hairy Clan were the most famous horse takers and were also the best at running down wild horses. The leaders of this clan, when the move south of the Platte was made in 1826, were Medicine Snake or Walking Whirlwind, Afraid of Beavers, Yellow Wolf, Little Wolf, and Wolf Chief.

In these horse-stealing raids the Cheyennes did not have everything their own way, for the Comanches, and sometimes the Kiowas, came up to the Platte and stole horses from the Cheyenne camps. Bull Hump of the Comanches came north in 1826 or 1827, hunting for the Cheyennes, and stopped at Bent's Stockade on Fountain River right where the city of Pueblo now stands. Charlie Autobee was working as a beaver trapper for my uncle and my father[6] at that time, and forty-six years ago he told me this story of Bull Hump's war party. My father used to tell the story too. A party of Cheyennes had been out hunting for the Utes and Apaches and were visiting at the stockade when Bull Hump and his party approached. My father used to tell us how he hid these Cheyennes among the trade-goods when the Comanches appeared, as he knew the Comanches would kill them. Bull Hump, however, saw the fresh moccasin tracks of these Cheyennes around the stockade and asked where the Cheyennes were. My

[5] White Thunder was the father of Owl Woman, the Cheyenne wife of William Bent and the mother of George Bent. He was killed by the Kiowas in a battle on Wolf Creek in northern Oklahoma in 1838.—S.L.

father told him the Cheyennes had gone north a little while before to a Cheyenne village on the South Platte. Bull Hump then left the stockade and went up to the Platte. On the South Platte the Comanches found a Cheyenne camp of about one hundred lodges. They thought all the Cheyennes and Arapahos were camped here close together, so they were afraid to make an attack. They waited until after dark, then slipped into the camp and cut loose a large number of horses. With this herd they started south, riding hard, for they feared that a big body of Cheyennes and Arapahos would soon be after them. Many of these horses had been stolen from the Comanches by the Cheyennes, and Bull Hump must have felt tickled at getting them back.

At this time Yellow Wolf of the Hairy Clan was running mustangs down near the Arkansas with a big party of his men. This run was very successful. Yellow Wolf's adopted son, Walking Coyote (he was a Ponca, captured by the Cheyennes when a small boy) ran down thirty mustangs, and the whole party took five hundred head. Yellow Wolf and his band now started home with the wild herd. They made a night march, leading the mares with the mustangs tailed up behind them. They had arrived at a point about thirty miles north of the Arkansas, near Black Lake, when the man who was walking ahead as a scout halted and said that he could smell the smoke of a buffalo chip fire. Yellow Wolf stopped the party and sent his son Walking Coyote and two other young men out to scout. Pretty soon the scouts returned and reported that they had seen a small fire and heard men speaking in a strange language. They had run upon the camp of Bull Hump and his Comanches.

The Cheyenne leaders held a council. Walking Coyote, who was a famous warrior, advised that the main party go on home with the captured mustangs while he with a few young men remained behind to attack the Comanche camp at dawn and run off the herd. This was agreed to, and just at dawn Walking Coyote and his warriors swept down on the Comanche camp and stampeded all their horses except

[6] Charles Bent (b. 1799 at Charleston, W. Va.) and William Bent (b. 1809 at St. Louis, Mo.), partners with Ceran St. Vrain (b. 1802 near St. Louis, Mo.).

43

GEORGE BENT'S ORIGINAL MAP OF THE BLACK LAKE AND
BITTER LAKE AREA

I think Black Lake is shown on the big Colorado Geological Survey Map, at the head of a creek which flows south into the Arkansas—but, of course, the lake is not named Black Lake on this modern map. Bitter Lake was east of Sand Creek and south of Ladder Creek, in western Kansas. Dull Knife and his crowd camped one night at Bitter Lake on their flight north in 1878. The little square mark on the west bank of Purgatoire River is Bent's Ranch, 1864.—G.H.

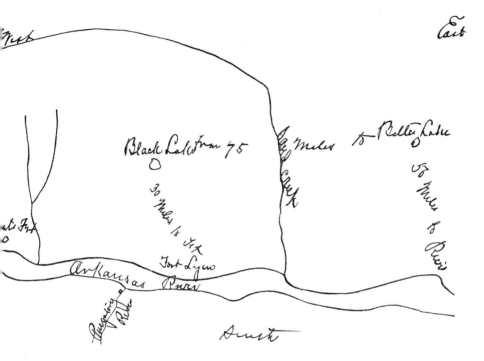

West

East

Black Lake from 75

  miles

to Belter Lake

Creek

55 miles to River

30 miles to Fix

at Fort

Fort Lyon

Arkansas River

Purgatory River

South

a few which had been picketed close to camp. Walking Coyote had only a few men. They turned the herd they had stampeded toward the north and made off as fast as they could go. Walking Coyote and a handful of his men formed up in rear and kept off the Comanches, who were already after them. The Comanches outnumbered the Cheyennes, but they were mostly armed with lance and bow only, while most of the Cheyennes had guns. The running fight had not gone on long when Walking Coyote shot a Comanche and knocked him off his horse. Soon after another Cheyenne named Stone shot another Comanche off his horse, and after that the Comanche drew off and gave up the chase. As the light increased, the Cheyennes were astonished to find that the horses they had captured from the Comanches were Cheyenne horses which they had last seen in the camp on the Platte. Most of these animals had been stolen at least three times, first by the Cheyennes from the Comanches, then by Bull Hump from the Cheyennes, and finally by Walking Coyote from Bull Hump.

This little brush with Bull Hump was at Black Lake west of Sand Creek and about thirty miles north of the Arkansas. This lake or pond was a famous place. It was round and about five hundred yards across. Some old Cheyennes have just been talking about this lake here in the office.[7] They said the water was not good (brackish) but there was a fine spring in a ravine some distance off connected with the lake by a little run of water. Fine buffalo grass grew all about this lake and the vicinity was a famous range for wild horses and antelope. These old men were talking about the water monster who lived in this lake. They say the water in the lake was made by this monster, who guarded the lake. About seventy years ago, they say, some Cheyennes were passing Black Lake and found the water monster lying dead at the edge of the water. They say he was struck by lightning. After that the lake began to dry up. I saw it in 1863–1864 when it was nearly all dried up. East of Sand Creek, about seventy-five miles east of Black Lake and fifty north of the Arkansas, was another

[7] Apparently the Cheyenne and Arapaho Agency at Darlington, present Canadian County, Oklahoma.—S.L.

46

famous little lake called Bitter Lake. These lakes were both famous places for wild horses and antelope. The country around them was flat like a table, with fine grass, but the Indians did not stay around these lakes much to hunt because the water was bad.

While the Cheyennes were raiding the Comanches and Kiowas down near Red River, they were also having trouble with the Pawnees to the east and the Utes in the mountains to the west. With the Pawnees they had been at war from the time they crossed west of the Missouri to live, and when they lived in the Black Hills they secured many of their horses by raids on the Pawnees. The Pawnees had earth-lodge villages on the lower Platte, but they only spent about four months each year in these villages and the rest of the time hunted in the plains, wandering all over the Platte and Republican and their branches and often coming into collision with the Cheyennes, Sioux, and other tribes. Porcupine Bull, who was over seventy-six in 1912, told me this story. About 1822 (before his time) a war party of Cheyennes went to a Pawnee earth-lodge village, probably on the Platte or Loup Fork, to steal horses. The Pawnees had strong log corrals in front of their earth houses, and most of the families kept all of their finest horses and mules in these corrals at night. The Pawnee, unlike most other Plains tribes, liked mules and had large numbers of very fine mules which they stole during their raids into New Mexico.

When the Cheyennes reached this Pawnee village they entered it after dark and found that all the best horses and mules were shut up in the log corrals. This made it very dangerous work getting the animals out. The warriors waited until everything was quiet in the village and then began taking out the animals, bringing them from the corrals one by one and being very careful to make no noise. A young Cheyenne named Bear Feathers went to a big Pawnee earth lodge where he found a number of fine animals in a log corral just in front of the lodge. He was untying the rope that secured the corral gate when a big Pawnee slipped up behind him and threw his arms around him. The Pawnee's wife ran out of the lodge to help her man, but he motioned to her to be quiet. He then signed to Bear

47

Feathers to go into the lodge. Inside Bear Feathers sat down and the Pawnee sat down and looked at him a long time without saying anything. The Pawnee's wife brought water and food and set them before Bear Feathers, and the Pawnee told him in signs to eat and not be afraid. When Bear Feathers had eaten he felt safer. The Pawnee now told him in signs that he was head chief of the village and that he was going to give him a fine mule to ride home on. The Pawnee's wife went out to the corral and saddled a fine white mule. The Pawnee led Bear Feathers to the edge of the village and saw him safely started on his way home.

This was the act of a great chief, but Bear Feathers acted badly. When he reached home he told a crooked story and boasted that he had gone into the Pawnee's corral at great risk and stolen the mule and saddle. Everyone thought him a very brave young man, but some years later my grandfather, White Thunder, the Keeper of the Arrows, went to this same Pawnee village to make peace and had a talk with this Pawnee chief, who told him the whole story of how he had captured a young Cheyenne and had turned him loose after giving him a fine mule and fine silver-mounted Mexican saddle. After that the people did not think so highly of Bear Feathers.

In those early days the Pawnees hunted far up the Platte and on all the head streams of the Republican and Smoky Hill rivers. Their war parties were constantly crossing the plains to New Mexico and southwest to the Comanche and Kiowa country. When we used to camp in the plains of eastern Colorado and western Kansas, old men often showed me places where the Cheyennes had fights with Pawnees. North of Bent's Fort were the Pawnee Hills, where the Cheyennes annihilated a war party of Pawnees, and between the forks of the Platte are Pawnee Creek and Pawnee Hills, where the Cheyennes and Arapahos killed another Pawnee party about 1833. These Pawnee war parties crossed the plains on foot to steal horses, and if they ran into a body of mounted Cheyennes, of course, they had little chance of escape. If they could, they retreated to some nearby hill and fought until they were all killed.

I think it was in 1832 that a small party of Cheyennes went to the

48

lower Platte to make a raid on the Pawnees, but being discovered, the entire party was killed. Some time later another Cheyenne war party was passing the place where this fight had taken place, and they found the bodies of their dead tribesmen in the creek. The Pawnees had cut the bodies in pieces and thrown them into the creek. Wolves had eaten part of the flesh, but there were some marks by which the bodies were easily identified. The killing of this whole party made the Cheyennes very angry, and the relatives of the dead warriors mourned through the camp until they induced a soldier society to undertake a move against the Pawnees. It was announced that the tribe would wait one winter and then move the arrows against the Pawnees. War pipes were sent around to all the different camps, and all the headmen smoked the pipes, thereby promising to join the expedition with all their people.

When the cherries were red the following summer, all the Cheyennes, a large body of Sioux, and some Arapahos came together into one big camp and started to move against the Pawnees. They moved down the north bank of the Platte, taking their women and children, camps, and herds along with them. My grandfather, as has been noted, was Keeper of the Arrows at that time and he and his wife led the move. Scouts were sent ahead to locate the Pawnees, and four of these scouts were discovered by the Pawnees and were all killed. When the main body came to the place where the scouts had been killed, they saw the four bodies, and this made the Cheyennes more angry than ever. Everyone pushed on, eager to find the Pawnees. At last scouts reported the Pawnee hunting camp was on the head of the South Loup, north of the Platte. At this place the Cheyenne, Sioux, and Arapaho lodges were set up and the women put all the property on high scaffolds inside the lodges, so the wolves could not reach anything; the camps were then abandoned and everyone moved forward. They pushed on all day and all night. Toward morning they came near the camp of the Pawnees and the Cheyenne and Sioux warriors formed their lines of battle. The women and children formed up in a great circle in rear of the warriors, where they could watch the fight.

49

These fights in which the entire Cheyenne tribe took part with the women, children, and old men formed up in a circle in the rear to watch the battle, were very formal affairs and full of ceremonies. In fact they were modeled on the old-time battles in which everyone fought on foot and the medicine men used magic to strike the enemy helpless and make their own warriors invulnerable. In these formal engagements the Cheyennes were drawn up in two divisions; in front of the first wing the Medicine Arrows were carried, and in front of the other the sacred Buffalo Cap. These two great medicines protected all who were behind them from wounds and death and rendered the enemy in front helpless. In such a fight a medicine man was always selected to carry the Medicine Arrows tied to the end of a lance. The Arrow Keeper did not carry the arrows into battle himself, and in this Pawnee fight my grandfather turned over the arrows to a medicine man named Bull, who took them into the fight.

After day came, a large body of mounted Pawnees were discovered, coming out to hunt buffalo, as they did not know that the Cheyennes and Sioux in great force were in their immediate vicinity. This big hunting party came right toward the battle lines of the Cheyennes and Sioux. Both sides were thrown into some confusion, and the Cheyenne and Sioux warriors, greatly excited by the sudden appearance of the hated Pawnees, surged forward to meet them. Bull, who was to carry the sacred arrows into the fight was not yet ready. My grandfather called to the warriors to wait, but they paid no attention. He then handed the Medicine Arrows to Bull who hastily tied them to the end of his lance and rode after the warriors. When he came up the Cheyennes and Sioux were in line facing the Pawnees and out between the two lines of battle a Pawnee was sitting on the ground all alone. Some say this man had been wounded, others that he had been sick a long time and was discouraged and wished to die, so he went out and sat down between the lines where he would be killed in the first charge. When Bull saw this Pawnee sitting on the ground he charged him, intending to strike him and count coup on him. As he rushed by the man, Bull leaned over to one side and struck at him with his lance, but the Pawnee avoided the blow and grasped the lance with both hands. To avoid being pulled off his horse, Bull had to let go of the lance, and thus the lance with the great medicine of the Cheyennes tied to its point was lost.

When Bull realized what had happened to him, he turned his horse and rode slowly back toward the Cheyenne lines, mourning in a loud voice. The Pawnee man looked at the Medicine Arrows tied to the end of the lance and saw that he had captured something of great value. He called out to the Pawnee warriors, "Come here. This is something wonderful," and the Pawnee line rushed forward. At the same time the Cheyennes saw that the Pawnee had the Medicine Arrows, and they made a fierce charge to recover their great medicine, but the Pawnees reached the man first and seized the lance. The Cheyennes killed the man who had taken the arrows from Bull, but they could not recover the arrows from the Pawnee warriors.

When they saw that they could not recapture the arrows, the Cheyennes lost all heart and gave up the fight at once. They knew that after this terrible disaster no matter how bravely they fought they could hope for no success. They rode back across the field mourning as they slowly retreated, and thus the great expedition to punish the Pawnees came to nothing. As the great village retired up the Platte, the camps were full of mourning, women and children wailing, and even the men crying. This was the greatest disaster the Cheyennes ever suffered. Some of the old people say that this was in 1830, but most of them say it was in 1833, the year the stars fell.[8] The great meteoric shower came in November and all the Indians thought the world was coming to an end. The dogs collected in bands and howled like wolves, the women and children wailed, and the warriors mounted their war horses and rode about, singing their death songs.

After the loss of the Medicine Arrows a council was held and it was decided that a new set of four arrows should be made. These new arrows were made with great ceremony and care was taken to make them as nearly like the old arrows as possible; but White

---

[8] The Leonid Shower of November 14, 1833. Others proceeding from Leo Major occurred in 1799 and 1866.—S.L.

Thunder, the Keeper of the Arrows, was not satisfied, and he determined to attempt to recover the old arrows by making peace with the Pawnees. About 1835 he went to the Pawnee villages on Loup Fork to make peace. He had his wife, one other woman, and two men with him. They walked right into the hostile Pawnee village and went to the chief's lodge. My grandfather spoke to the Pawnee chiefs in signs and told them that he wished to make peace and get back the sacred arrows. This lodge belonged to the chief who had captured the arrows, and he had them hanging up at the back of the lodge, in the place of honor. After White Thunder had spoken, the Pawnee chief took down the four arrows and said that he would permit the Cheyennes to choose one to take home with them. My grandfather picked out one of the Buffalo Arrows. Of these four Medicine Arrows two were Man Arrows, which gave success in war, and two were Buffalo Arrows, which insured abundance of buffalo to feed the tribe.

After White Thunder had selected the one arrow, the Pawnees made up a large party and accompanied the Cheyennes home. The Pawnees were all on foot. White Thunder conducted them to a big Cheyenne and Arapaho camp at the Big Timbers, below Bent's Fort.[9] This was in 1835 and Colonel Henry Dodge with his dragoons, who was then making a tour among the tribes of the Plains, was camped at the Big Timbers when this big party of Pawnees came with my grandfather to conclude peace with the Cheyennes.[10] The

[9] The Big Timbers, consisting of a fairly dense growth of cottonwoods, a mile deep and extending for several miles along both banks of the Arkansas in Bent County, Colorado. Janet Lecompte to Savoie Lottinville, January 6, 1967, suggests that "the extent and apparently the location of the timbers changed." Zebulon Montgomery Pike, 1806, "found trees thick on both sides of the river nearly to the present state line." Jacob Fowler, 1821, found them near present Lamar, forty miles west of where Pike first noted timber. J. W. Abert, 1847, had the Big Timbers starting twenty-seven miles east of Bent's Fort. J. E. B. Stuart, 1860, had them extending from Bent's Fort 22.40 miles down the river.—S.L.

[10] "Journal of a March of a Detachment of Dragoons, under the Command of Colonel Dodge, During the Summer of 1835," *American State Papers*, Military Affairs, VI, 138–40. Dodge arrived at Bent's Fort on August 6. The meeting at the Cross Timbers occurred two days later. See also Donald J. Berthrong, *The Southern Cheyennes*, 76–80.—S.L.

Pawnees had many guns, and they gave these guns to the Cheyennes as peace presents, for which they received a present of over one hundred horses, besides many other things. The Cheyennes pitched their lodges in a great circle and the Pawnees danced inside. One Pawnee headman wore a fine buckskin shirt trimmed with otter skins and an otter-skin cap. As he danced he kept throwing his tomahawk into the air and catching it. This man the Cheyennes were very much pleased with. They called him Otter Cap, and he married a Cheyenne girl and remained with the Cheyennes, but after some time returned to his own people, as the peace did not last long. His son, Big Baby, is still living with us and is over eighty now (1914).

The Pawnees were suspicious and did not believe that the peace would last long, so they only gave the one arrow, promised to White Thunder, to the Cheyennes. About two years later the Brulé Sioux captured a Pawnee village on the upper Platte, and in this camp they found another of the Medicine Arrows, which they returned to our tribe with great ceremony. As four new arrows had been made when the old ones were captured by the Pawnees, there were now six, and it became necessary to get rid of two of the new arrows, but these could not be destroyed, as they were very sacred. The two arrows were therefore wrapped up with a number of presents, and the bundle was left on Medicine-pipe Mountain in the Black Hills, where, long ago, Sweet Root Standing was given the original Medicine Arrows by the Listeners-under-the-Ground. Old Cheyennes say the Pawnees have been dying off ever since they captured the Medicine Arrows and that they have had no luck from that day to this. The Pawnees still had two of the arrows, one Buffalo Arrow and one Man Arrow.[11]

Fighting with the Pawnees soon began again. The peace only lasted a short time. About 1839 or 1840 Medicine Snake or Walking Whirlwind, a famous man of the Hevhaitanio clan, set out with a

[11] Karl N. Llewellyn and E. Adamson Hoebel, *The Cheyenne Way*, contains much information on the Medicine Arrows. Grinnell, *The Fighting Cheyennes*, 25, 45, appears to be indebted to Bent, among other informants, concerning these talismans.—S.L.

large party of Cheyennes to steal horses from the Pawnees. They reached the head of the South Fork of Republican River and camped. They had no idea that any Pawnees were in that vicinity, so they set out down the river next morning, although there was a dense fog in the valley and they could not see ten feet ahead. They walked right into a big hunting camp of Pawnees and just then the fog lifted and they were seen. Medicine Snake and his men, all on foot, ran toward a small creek near the Pawnee camp, hoping to find a good place to fight; but the Pawnees were already after them, men mounted and men on foot, women, children, old people, and dogs, all running and all howling at the Cheyennes. Just as Medicine Snake and his men reached a little hollow, the mounted Pawnees headed them off, and here in the hollow they were surrounded by a great swarm of Pawnees, men shooting and yelling, women and children screaming insults. In a little time the Cheyennes were all dead.

When Medicine Snake and his warriors failed to return, their families became very anxious about them, and at last some people presented pipes to the spirit doctors and begged them to call up the spirits and ask what had become of this war party. The spirits gave different answers; some said Medicine Snake and his warriors were all right and would soon show up again; others said they were all dead. Some time after this, a war party of Sioux were going along the South Fork of Republican River and came to the place where this Pawnee camp had stood. Here they saw an old dead cottonwood, and on the white trunk of this tree the Pawnees had drawn a picture of the killing of Medicine Snake and his party. Great heaps of ashes were around the tree, where the Pawnees had built fires to dance the scalp dance, and there was a pole leaning up against a log pointing down-stream. Going in that direction, the Sioux found the bones of Medicine Snake and all his party. The Sioux told this to the Cheyennes and a party of Cheyennes went to the place and, wrapping up the bones in fine blankets, brought them home. The South Fork of Republican River has been called Medicine Snake's Creek by the Cheyenne, because it was near the head of this stream that the bones of Medicine Snake and his party were found.

In 1835 a large village of Kiowas ventured north with a fine lot of horses, intending to go up to the Tongue and Big Horn rivers to trade the horses to the Crows for elk teeth and ermine skins.[12] The Cheyennes of Yellow Wolf's Hevhaitanio clan and Black Shin's band of Suhtais were camped on Artichoke Creek east of where Denver now stands. They were hunting buffalo. Early in the morning they broke camp and started on the hunt. The women and children with the old men were marching in an irregular column with the travois and pack horses and the loose animals, while the warriors rode in front and on the flanks of the column. Scouts were far out ahead, looking for buffalo. The light was not yet very strong, when presently the scouts saw before them, far off across the plain, a large number of moving dots. They gathered in a group on a hill and watched the dots, thinking at first that these were buffalo; but as the light increased they saw that many of the moving objects were white and had dark objects on their backs. Then they knew that these were horses and people.

The scouts were now greatly excited and began to signal. The Cheyennes in the rear with the main column saw a scout ride away from the group on the hill and then ride back to it. This meant "enemies in sight." As soon as the warriors saw this signal they rushed to the column, jumped off the common horses they were riding and, taking their war horses and arms, came on, riding very fast. The Kiowas were moving across an open plain when they saw the Cheyennes making towards them. The women, children and old men at once bunched together and made for a timbered creek off to one side, taking all the loose horses with them. In the meantime the warriors formed up in the rear and began fighting off the Cheyennes.

The Kiowas retreated slowly toward this creek, where their women and children were already engaged in digging pits in the sand and making breastworks to fight behind. The Kiowa warriors would retire a short distance, then turn and face the Cheyennes, checking their advance. One Kiowa man on a fine white horse was very brave. Again

[12] Grinnell, *The Fighting Cheyennes*, 43, gives a date of "about 1833," which Berthrong, *The Southern Cheyennes*, 81, accepts.—S.L.

and again he took his lance and charged right through the Cheyenne lines. In one of these charges he struck a Cheyenne named Man Above with his lance such a hard blow that he knocked Man Above right off his horse. As they were nearing the creek, this brave Kiowa came back again and charged right in among the Cheyennes; but this time they shot him with arrows, and he turned and rode slowly back toward the Kiowa lines, but dropped his lance and fell from his horse before he could reach his friends. The rest of the Kiowa warriors lost heart as soon as they saw this brave man fall, and they at once retreated into the timber. Along the creek among the timber, the Kiowa women had tied the best horses, and in the edge of the timber they had dug pits and made a kind of breastworks. The Kiowas now hid behind these breastworks and fought off the Cheyennes. Our men made several charges, attempting to drive the Kiowas out of their defenses, but the position was a very strong one, and all the Cheyenne efforts to reach their enemies failed. The Cheyennes then turned their attention to the Kiowa herd and succeeded in cutting out a large number of animals, but all of the best horses had been tied to trees close to the pits and breastworks, and these the Cheyennes could not reach. After the Cheyennes had run off all the horses they could get at, they gave up the fight and withdrew.

This fight was on what the Cheyennes call Scout Creek, now called Kiowa Creek on the maps. It is just east of Denver.[13] When the Kiowa women and children stampeded for the timber, one Kiowa squaw fell off her horse. She had a small girl on her back, and both she and her daughter were captured by Black Shin of the Suhtais. Snake Woman, who is eighty-three, told me the other day that she was a small girl at the time of this fight, and after the fight she saw this Kiowa woman and her daughter sitting in front of Black Shin's lodge. The woman had been wounded by a lance in the breast. When the

[13] Location of Scout Creek. Bent could never locate it surely on a map, but he told me once that his father had a trading house at or near Denver, sometime about 1850, and that he and the other children used to play around and saw the pits dug by the Kiowas during this fight. There must be a record as to where this Bent trading house stood, and Scout Creek would be very near it.—G.H.

Cheyennes looked at this woman's little girl, they saw that the child was white. She had probably been carried off by the Kiowas during a raid in Texas. She was not Mexican but true white. Some years later, when the Kiowas made peace, they bought back the Kiowa squaw, but they did not care anything about the little white girl, so she remained with our tribe and is still living down here, a very old woman now. The Kiowa on the fine white horse who made so many charges with his lance, wore a sash embroidered with colored porcupine quills across his breast. This is what is known as a "dog-rope" and it was worn only by a few of the most famous warriors among the Plains Indians. This Kiowa was a brave man. The old Cheyennes talk about him when they meet even today.

CHAPTER THREE

BENT'S FORT

SILAS BENT, my grandfather, was born in the Colony of Massachusetts in 1768. He was educated for the bar, and following the purchase of the Louisiana Territory by the United States he removed to St. Louis in 1804,[1] where he soon became a prominent man and judge of the Superior Court. He died at St. Louis in 1827, leaving seven sons. Of these sons, John Bent remained at St. Louis, where, like his father, he became prominent at the bar;[2] Silas Bent was an officer in the old navy and served as a flag-lieutenant under Commodore Matthew C. Perry during the expedition to Japan;[3] Charles, William, Robert, and George became fur traders on the upper Arkansas, in what is now the state of Colorado.

My father, William Bent, was born on the old Bent Farm at St. Louis, May 23, 1809. He and his brother Charles were the first of the Bents to enter the fur trade. Charles was somewhat older than my father.[4] He took service with John Jacob Astor's American Fur

[1] Actually, 1806. See David Lavender, *Bent's Fort*, 20–21, who gives the date of arrival of the Bent family in St Louis as September 17, 1806. Bent was appointed to a judgeship on the Supreme Court of Missouri Territory sometime after 1810 by President Madison.—S.L.

[2] The social and cultural prominence of both the Silas Bents and the John Bents appears in William Clark Kennerly, *Persimmon Hill: A Narrative of Old St. Louis and the Far West*, as told to Elizabeth Russell, 35, 178, 218.—S.L.

[3] Rear Admiral George Henry Preble, U.S.N., *The Opening of Japan: A Diary of Discovery in the Far East, 1853–1856*, edited by Boleslaw Szczesniak, 103, 182.—S.L.

[4] Charles (b. November 11, 1799) was, in fact, nearly ten years older than William Bent.—S.L.

Company in the Sioux country on the upper Missouri in 1816, or about that year, and my father joined him up there a few years later, in 1823 or 1824 I think. At that time my father was only thirteen or fourteen years old, but it was not an uncommon thing for boys of that age to strike out for themselves in those days.[5]

On the upper Missouri, Charles and William Bent soon made friends with young [Ceran] St. Vrain, another St. Louis boy,[6] and about 1824 these three young men formed a partnership, engaged a number of white trappers in the Sioux country, and setting out from the Missouri made their way across country to the upper Arkansas. Here near the mouth of Fountain River they built a stockade, right where the city of Pueblo now stands. This stockade was built before the Cheyennes and Arapahos moved south of the Platte to live, and the Bents and their partner soon met these tribes and made friends of them. The Bent St. Vrain Company was more interested at that time in beaver trapping than in trade with the Indians, but about

[5] William Bent would have been fifteen at the latter date, having been born in St. Louis on May 23, 1809.—S.L.

Lavender, *Bent's Fort*, 17–27, 376–78, traces the Bent family chronology. George Bent's dates for his uncle Charles's Rocky Mountain career are conflicting and inaccurate. Charles was probably not farther west than western Missouri in 1817; he was possibly a clerk (in Missouri) for the Missouri Fur Company in 1818–19, while Manuel Lisa, its head, was still alive; he was at Fort Recovery in present South Dakota in 1823, with the reorganized Missouri Fur Company under Joshua Pilcher, Lisa's successor. But Charles Bent was not then or subsequently of Astor's American Fur Company group.

The earliest William Bent could have been in the Far West was during the winter of 1827–28, when Charles and his partners from Missouri lost their trade goods to the Crows on the Sweetwater as they moved towards South Pass. But the assumption that he was on this expedition is at best conjectural.—S.L.

[6] Ceran de Hault de Lassus de St. Vrain, born 1802 at Spanish Lake near St. Louis, may have met Charles Bent when they were youngsters or at Council Bluffs in 1824, when Charles was returning to St. Louis and St. Vrain was working for Pratte, Cabanné, and Company, fur traders, at the former place. He was in the Santa Fe trade with François Guerin in 1824–25, and in 1826–27 with Ewing Young; in 1827–28 he was largely snow-bound in the valley of the Green River, on a fur-hunting expedition. Both he and the Bents became engrossed in the Santa Fe trade thereafter, but independently. He seems to have become firm friends with Charles Bent in August, 1830, but their actual partnership dates from Santa Fe in December, 1830. Lavender, *Bent's Fort*, 51, 127.—S.L.

two years later, in 1826 or 1827, they moved farther east and built a new stockade on the north bank of the Arkansas and about opposite the mouth of Purgatoire River. Here they came in closer contact with the Indians.

This second stockade was started the same year that Yellow Wolf of the Hevhaitanio clan made his first expedition to the North Fork of Red River, and on their way home Yellow Wolf and his warriors stopped at the stockade and had a talk with the Bents. Yellow Wolf told Charles Bent that the stockade on Fountain River was too near the mountains to be of much use as a trading place; the Indians, he said, could not winter up there because the buffalo did not range that far up the river. The chief advised the Bents to build a post about where this new stockade was, or farther down near the Big Timbers, and he promised that if a trading fort was established here he would induce his clan, the Hevhaitanio, and also the Oivimana clan, to move down to the Arkansas to live near the new fort and trade there. Charles Bent told the chief that he would begin building a large fort in that vicinity as soon as he could get workmen and material on the ground; and that was how Bent's Fort came to be established. I think the Bents and St. Vrain had about made up their minds to build a fort, and what Yellow Wolf said at this meeting decided the matter. Porcupine Bear, who is very old, has just been telling me about this meeting. He says the chiefs who were present were Yellow Wolf, Little Wolf and Wolf Chief, all of the Hevhaitanio clan, and that the party had just stolen a very large herd of Comanche horses on Red River and had these animals with them when they visited the stockade. During this visit Yellow Wolf named Charles Bent "White Hat" and my father "Little White Man," as he was not yet full grown at that time. Yellow Wolf was one of the famous chiefs of the old days, and the whites considered him head chief of the Southern Cheyennes. He was a small man and light on his feet. He lived to be eighty-five and was killed in the Sand Creek Massacre by Chivington's Colorado Volunteers in 1864.[7]

[7] Porcupine Bear of the Cheyennes, who informed George Bird Grinnell in 1912, and George Bent were sometimes wide of the calendar but perhaps deserve less

Bent's Fort was the first permanent settlement in all the central Plains region and William Bent was the first American settler within the borders of the present state of Colorado. He went there in 1824 and lived there until his death in 1869. His partners, Charles Bent

censure for misdating certain events than they have got. It was probably William Bent, with a party of independent trappers, who made the first picket stockade attributed to the Bents, on Fountain Creek at its mouth at present Pueblo, the date being uncertain but after John Gantt's post was built on the upper Arkansas in 1832. The meeting between the Bents and Yellow Wolf is also of uncertain date, but all evidence points to the decisiveness of Yellow Wolf's advice in the final location of Bent's Fort.

Ceran St. Vrain, in a letter to Lieutenant Colonel Eneas Mackay of July 21, 1847, National Archives, says that he and Charles Bent built the fort in 1834. Of critical importance in the chronology was the issuance of a trading license to Charles Bent on December 13, 1834 (*Document No. 97, Abstract of Licenses*, St. Louis Superintendency Records, National Archives), describing not one, but three trading points: "To Charles Bent for two years, with twenty-nine men employed, at Fort William [the original name of Bent's Fort as well as of the picket post at Fountain Creek], on the north side of the Arkansas, about forty miles east of the Rocky Mountains, about twenty miles north of the Spanish Peaks, and about five miles below one of the principal forks of the Arkansas; at Union point, on the north side of the Arkansas, near the foot of the Rocky Mountains, about ten miles below the Black Hills, and at a point near the mouth of Bear river, on the waters of the Grand river, or the Colorado of the West, with the Arapahoes, Cheyennes, Kiowas, Snakes, Sioux, and Arickaras."

If Ceran St. Vrain was right, and it is reasonable to assume that he could remember events of thirteen years before, then Charles Bent's license confirms the existence of Bent's Fort in 1834. Students of cartography, as well as students of grammar, for whom the punctuation in Bent's abstract of license is highly important, will need to be wary of identifying either the picket post at Fountain Creek or Bent's Fort from the distances given in the opening lines: they do not come within many miles of squaring with either.

Finally, the big fort on the Arkansas was complete when Colonel Henry Dodge arrived with his Dragoon expedition on August 6, 1835. Thus, we have no evidence that it was started earlier than 1834 or completed as late as the spring of 1835, no season for the working of adobe.

Janet Lecompte to Savoie Lottinville, January 6, February 5, 1967; Lecompte, "Gantt's Fort and Bent's Pickett Post," *Colorado Magazine*, XLI, No. 2 (Spring, 1964), 111–126; George Bent to George E. Hyde, April 14, 1908, November 29, 1912, Bent Letters, Coe Collection, Yale University Library; Lavender, *Bent's Fort*, 106–108, 130–36, 385n., 388n.; LeRoy R. Hafen, "When Was Bent's Fort Built?" *Colorado Magazine*, XXXI, No. 2 (April, 1954); Berthrong, *The Southern Cheyennes*, 25–26.—S.L.

61

and Ceran St. Vrain did not become, of course, permanent settlers, but in later years moved down into New Mexico to live. The new fort was begun in 1828 or 1829.

The site selected was on the north side of the Arkansas River about fifteen miles above the mouth of Purgatoire River. Charles Bent, had been engaged in the Santa Fe trade, off and on, for a number of years and had lived a good deal at Taos and Santa Fe. He knew the comfort of the Mexican adobe houses, and when the fort was being planned he determined that it should be built of adobe. Adobe buildings were more durable than wooden ones; they were cool in summer and warm in winter, and were almost fireproof. So when the material had been hauled out to the site of the new fort, a large body of Mexican 'dobe masons was brought up from Taos to make and lay the adobe bricks. These Mexicans were housed in a temporary stockade, but hardly had they arrived when smallpox broke out and was soon raging among them.

My father, St. Vrain, and Kit Carson were also attacked by the disease and were all three badly pitted. At that time the Cheyennes were expected down on a trading visit, but as soon as the smallpox made its appearance at the stockade a mounted messenger was sent up to the Platte to warn the Indians off. This prompt action probably saved the tribe from disaster. The Cheyennes never had the smallpox severely, as so many other tribes did, but they took the cholera from emigrants on the Oregon Trail in '49 and suffered terrible loss. After this epidemic of smallpox had run its course, the Mexican stockade with everything it contained was burned; everything was cleaned up thoroughly, and only then were the Indians notified that they might now safely come down to do their trading. This smallpox was in 1829 or 1830, and so many of the Mexicans died that a new force had to be recruited in New Mexico and the work of building the fort was greatly delayed.

Young Carson was with the Bents at the time the fort was begun, but it is uncertain just when or where he entered the service of Bent and St. Vrain. Inman,[8] who is a poor authority, says that Carson

[8] Henry Inman, *The Old Santa Fe Trail* (1897).—S.L.

joined Charles Bent's Santa Fe caravan on the Missouri frontier in 1826 and went with it to New Mexico. However that may be, one thing is certain, and that is that Carson first came into the Indian country in that year, 1826. This is proved by the following notice, which was printed in the *Missouri Intelligencer* of October 12, 1826: "Notice: To whom it may concern: That Christopher Carson, a boy about sixteen years old, small for his age, but thick set, light hair, ran away from the subscriber, living in Franklin, Howard Co., Mo., to whom he had been bound to learn the saddler's trade, on or about the first day of September last. He is supposed to have made his way toward the upper part of the state. All persons are notified not to harbor, support or subsist said boy under penalty of the law. One cent reward will be given to any person who will bring back the said boy. David Workman, Franklin, Oct. 6, 1826." This is the only printed mention of Carson from the time he ran away until he joined Captain Frémont's expedition as a guide, after 1840. Most of the stories about his early life on the plains and in the mountains have been invented by the men who published them. I knew Carson well and many old Cheyennes who are still living knew him also. He came to Bent's Fort in 1826 or 1827 and was employed as a hunter. He supplied all the meat for the fort and continued at this work most of the time until he joined Frémont as a guide.[9]

[Longhand note: The following story, well known to all of the older Cheyennes is absolute proof of Carson's service with the Bents, Geo. B. says:] The timber that was used in building Bent's Fort was mostly cut on a small creek about five miles down the Arkansas. This

[9] M. Morgan Estergreen, *Kit Carson: A Portrait in Courage*, 23–48, has Carson a member of the Bent caravan of 1826, joining it at Independence, Missouri. Both Charles and William Bent were with the caravan, but they left it at the Cimarron. Soon after Carson arrived in Santa Fe in late November, 1826, he left for Taos and spent the winter there. He accompanied the trapper Ewing Young and his party to California in 1829. Carson family tradition says that Carson worked on Bent's Fort in 1830–31, which is here confirmed by George Bent, except that the chronology is off by three to four years. The problem of linking him to construction of the fort is further complicated by the fact that it is known that he was employed by Stephen L. Lee and later by Jim Bridger in 1834 in an entirely different locality from the fort. Harvey L. Carter to Savoie Lottinville, January 16, 1967.—S.L.

stream was called Short-Timber Creek by the Cheyennes. For a while, Carson was in charge of the wagon train and the party of men engaged in hauling timber from this place up to the fort, and in 1830 or 1831 he had a fight with a war party of Crows on Short-Timber Creek. As this story about Carson has never been told before, I will give all the details.

Carson was at this time in command of a small party of Americans who were engaged in cutting timbers for use in building the fort. The only large trees in all that region were at the Big Timbers, thirty-five miles below the fort,[10] but on Short-Timber Creek, five miles below the fort, there was plenty of good-sized cottonwood. Here at the mouth of this creek Carson had established a camp where he and his men lived while they were loading the wagon train with logs. It was winter and grass was scarce, so Carson had brought down to this camp all the horses and mules belonging to the fort, and he had turned the herd loose among the timber where the men were making logs and the ground was covered with cottonwood branches and twigs. Horses and mules were very fond of cottonwood bark, and if they could get plenty of this bark they went through the winter in good shape without grass or grain.

One of my Cheyenne uncles was named Black White Man. My father had a slave at the fort, a very black Negro, and as the Cheyennes had seen few if any Negroes before, they thought this slave was very wonderful. They called him the black whiteman and this Cheyenne uncle of mine adopted the name of this slave. Black White Man was young at that time. He was living in a big Cheyenne camp on the South Platte that winter, and there he fell in love with Otter Woman, the wife of another Cheyenne, and decided to steal her. Of course she was willing to go with him, but this kind of elopement was always called "stealing a woman." My uncle and a friend of his named Little Turtle took Otter Woman and started down toward the Arkansas, intending to stay with the Bent outfit until the husband had had time to cool off a bit.

This little party reached the Arkansas at the mouth of Short-

[10] See footnote 9, Chapter 2.

Timber Creek and there found Carson and his party in camp. They spent the night at the camp. In the morning the Mexican herder went up the creek to see if the herd was all right. Pretty soon he came running back, very much excited, shouting that the animals were all gone. Carson thought the animals had simply strayed off, so he remained in camp with his men and sent Black White Man and Little Turtle, who had horses, to hunt the herd up. Otter Woman remained in the camp. She was standing on a log when she saw Little Turtle coming back, riding fast. He rode up to Carson and began talking to him in the sign language. He was greatly excited and made quick motions. He said the herd had been stolen by hostile Indians. Moccasin tracks were very numerous and the trail could be clearly seen in the snow, leading up the creek. He said the tracks showed that it was a big war party.

Carson saw how serious the matter was. Every hoof belonging to the company had been taken and if the animals were not recovered work on the fort would have to be stopped until more horses and mules could be brought up from New Mexico. He gave his orders at once and the men began to get ready for a fight. When Black White Man presently rode into camp the men were running bullets, but it was nearly noon before everything was ready. Otter Woman was left in the camp alone and the party marched, the two young Cheyennes riding ahead, Carson and his eleven Americans following on foot. The going was slow as there was deep snow in the creek valley, and Carson's men floundered about in the drifts. The Indians kept out in advance, following the trail and watching for signs of the enemy. After a while they picked up two arrows in the snow, and when they saw these they knew that they were Crow arrows. They were surprised that a Crow war party should have come so far south. After a long time they saw sparks coming out of a willow thicket far ahead, and then they rode back and told Carson in signs that the Crows were there in that thicket and had gone into camp for the night. Carson gave his orders at once. His men were to attack the Crows; Black White Man and Little Turtle were to keep out of the fight, watch their chance and, if they saw one, ride in and stampede the stolen herd. Carson knew that the Crows outnumbered his men five or six to one, but he did not hesitate to attack them right out in the open.

The Crows had been very careless, as they knew how many men were in Carson's camp and had not supposed that the whites would dare to follow them. They did not even have a guard set, and Carson had advanced his men very near to the willows when all at once a dog began to howl in the thicket. The Crows at once put out their fire with snow and stood on their guard, but when they saw Carson and his eleven men they were astonished that such a weak party should dare to approach them.

Carson had his men strung out in line, each man a good distance from the next. The little party looked so weak that the Crows believed they could easily kill all the whites, and as Carson's line moved slowly toward the thicket the Crows, sixty of them, rushed out on foot and charged them fiercely. Carson's men were so close and the Crow charge so sudden and swift that in a moment the whites were pushed back and surrounded; then the Americans threw up their long rifles and gave the Crows a volley. Carson told me about this when I saw him just before he died in 1868. He said the Crows seemed to think they could rush his men off their feet, but when his men turned loose with their rifles the Crows had a big surprise. They went back into the bushes on the run, Carson's party right after them with their pistols and tomahawks. The Indians intended to make a stand in the edge of the thicket and hold Carson off until they could round up the stolen herd and make off with it, but when they entered the willows they found the herd gone, and right at their heels Carson and his men came tumbling into the bushes, firing right and left with their rifles and pistols and giving the warriors no time to make a stand. The Crows went right on through the thicket and, bursting out at the other side, made off across the prairie with Carson's party still after them. Carson, however, soon called his men off, as it was more important to make sure of the herd than to chase the Crows.

Just as the Crow warriors had come out of the thicket and charged Carson's line, Black White Man and Little Turtle had slipped in

66

behind the Crows, entered the thicket and stampeded the herd. They drove the animals down the creek at top speed, left them in a safe place and then rode back as fast as they could to join in the fight; but when they reached the thicket again the Crows were gone and Carson and his men were coming back. The whole party now moved down to where the herd had been left, and here a big fire was started and the men bivouacked in the snow. That night Black White Man and Little Turtle went up to the scene of the fight, where they found two dead Crows and took their scalps. One Crow had fallen during the charge on Carson's line and the other among the willows. It is a strange thing that Carson's men, all armed with rifle and pistol and all good shots, should have killed only two Indians in this fight; and queerly enough, not one of the Americans was even wounded, although the Crows, when they charged out of the bushes, shot their arrows right into the faces of the whites. In this kind of a fight on foot, everyone kept jumping from side to side, making sudden springs to disturb the enemy's aim, and this may explain why the shooting on both sides was so poor.

This fight was in 1831, the year before Bent's Fort was finished. Carson remained in the Bents' employ, off and on, for ten years after that, leaving in 1842 or 1843, to join Frémont's exploring expedition. While living at the old fort he married a Cheyenne girl, but they had no children. In later years he married a Mexican girl at Bent's Fort and they went to live at Taos. I do not know whether they had any children or not. Frémont was very fond of Carson and secured his nomination to a second-lieutenancy in the old Mounted Rifle Regiment in 1847, but the Senate refused to confirm the nomination. Carson then became an Indian agent in New Mexico. When the Civil War broke out he entered the service as lieutenant colonel of a New Mexican regiment of cavalry and played a leading part in the battles fought in the southwest. He made a successful expedition against the hostile Navahos but was later nearly defeated by the Kiowas and Comanches at Adobe Fort [Adobe Walls] on the Canadian. In his latter years he returned to the vicinity of Bent's Fort on the Arkansas and died up there in 1868. He was brevetted a brigadier-general "for gallantry in the battle of Valverde and for distinguished service in New Mexico." The Cheyennes call him Little Chief and the old men still talk about him today.

Bent's Old Fort was completed in 1832, and from that time my father lived there and was in command of the post most of the time. About 1835 he married my mother, Owl Woman, daughter of White Thunder, the Keeper of the Arrows, and thus he became a member of the Cheyenne tribe. Part of the Cheyennes and Arapahos moved down from the Platte to live near the Arkansas, and these bands wintered each year at the Big Timbers, thirty-five miles below the fort. They often camped for long periods right around the fort, coming in every day to trade. Other tribes also came to the fort to trade, but as the Cheyennes were at war with the Kiowas, Comanches, and Prairie Apaches, these three tribes could not come to the fort and traders had to be sent to the different camps. In later years two branch forts were established by the Bent and St. Vrain Company: Fort St. Vrain on the Platte, opposite the mouth of St. Vrain's Fork, for the Sioux, Cheyenne, and Arapaho trade, and Adobe Fort on the Canadian for the Kiowa, Comanche, and Apache trade. These two forts, like Bent's Fort, were built of adobe. The St. Vrains usually had charge of Fort St. Vrain while my father was in command of Bent's Fort and Adobe. Bent's Fort was the company's headquarters. Besides these three main posts, the company established temporary stockades and trading houses from time to time at different points in the plains, but these places were usually abandoned after a few seasons. In the '40's the Bent and St. Vrain Company was doing a larger business than any other American company with the exception of Astor's great fur company.

In its best day Bent's Fort employed over a hundred men: traders, hunters, herders, teamsters, and laborers. Most of the laborers were Mexicans who were paid about six dollars a month, usually in goods. My father had several Mexicans whom he had bought from the Kiowas and Comanches. I know of several instances of this kind, and there must have been many others. One peon who was bought by my father from the Kiowas in early days is now living down here at the

Kiowa Agency and was eighty-two in 1906. Another captive my father bought was a German who was carried off by the Kiowas from the German colony in Texas when he was a small boy. He was known as Kiowa Dutch. He did not remain at the fort long, but rejoined the Kiowas and became a regular wild Indian. He spoke nothing but Kiowa, and yet his features were typically German. He died among the Kiowas in 1906, about eighty-five years old at that time.

A strange thing about these captives was that they nearly always returned to the tribe if someone ransomed them from the Indians. They liked the wild life. Among the Kiowas and Comanches nearly every family had one or two Mexican captives. The women captives married into the tribe; the boys and men were employed by the Indians as herders, to guard the horses when out grazing; but after the men had lived with the Indians a number of years they became regular warriors, and the more intelligent and brave ones led war parties of Indians on raids into Mexico and Texas. Some of these peon war leaders had friends among the peons in Mexico, and they learned from these friends where the finest herds of horses and mules were to be found, and the movements of the Mexican troops. By making use of this information the peons often led their war parties into the heart of the Mexican settlements and made big hauls of plunder.

Besides trading with the Indians, my father used to send some of his best traders down to New Mexico—to Santa Fe and Taos—with wagonloads of goods from the fort. They brought back from New Mexico horses, mules, cattle, Mexican blankets, silver dollars, and silver bullion in bars. I remember when a boy seeing the wagons come in with their loads of bright colored blankets. The Indians prized these blankets with their stripes of bright coloring very highly, and a good blanket was traded at the fort for ten buffalo robes. The silver, horses, mules, and cattle, were taken to Missouri and sold. In later years when the emigrant travel on the Oregon Trail up the Platte Valley grew heavy, many of the horses and mules were driven up there and traded to the emigrants. One good mule or horse was traded for two broken-down ones; the broken-down animals were then taken to the fort and kept until they were in good shape again, then they were taken up to the Platte and traded again to the emigrants. I remember several of the traders who were employed at the fort in early days: Fisher, Hatcher, Tim Goodall, and Tom Boggs. These were all good men who could speak Spanish and were experts in the Indian sign language, which was most used in trading with the tribes.

The Bents had cowboys whose business it was to break and ride the wild horses which were brought up from New Mexico. When I was a boy I used to go to the big corral back of the fort and watch these riders at work. One-eyed Juan was the best of them. He did nothing but break and ride the broncos and teach the younger hands how to handle the animals.

Every spring my father sent the wagon train down the Arkansas to Missouri (usually to Westport [now Kansas City],) with all the furs, robes, silver, horses, and mules that had been traded for during the past fall and winter. It was 530 miles to the Missouri River, and in all that great stretch of plains between the fort and the river, there was not a settlement, not a single house, not even a trading post or a government fort.[11] Oxen were usually employed in drawing the big wagons, six yokes to each wagon, and twenty-five to thirty wagons in the train. The loose herd of horses, mules and cattle was driven along in rear of the train by Mexican herders. There were four of these herders; two drove the herd during the day while the night herders slept in the wagons, and at night these two men guarded the herd while the day herders slept. At night the wagons were corraled and the oxen turned loose inside the corral. In the morning the oxen were yoked up inside the corral and then led to their places. The train started very early, even before day, but at ten a halt was made and breakfast cooked. The men then took their siesta. At two or three in the afternoon, after the heat of the day was over, the train pulled out again and did not halt until about dark. The distance made

[11] For locations and distances on the Santa Fe Trail, see Josiah Gregg, *Commerce of the Prairies*, map facing p. 58, table of distances 217n.; Max L. Moorhead, *New Mexico's Royal Road*, 98–102.

each day was not fixed, sometimes a long move was made, and again only a short one. The wagon boss knew all of the best camping places along the five hundred miles of trail, and he regulated the train's movements so as to reach a good camping place with good wood, water, and grass each evening. A hunter was always taken along to provide the outfit with fresh meat, and as the greater part of the march was right through the heart of the buffalo range, meat was usually supplied in abundance. These hunters were usually Delaware Indians or Shawnees, who were very skillful at this kind of work.

The journey to the States was usually made without accident, but occasionally the Indians were troublesome. In 1847 the train was attacked at Pawnee Fork, near the present Dodge City, Kansas, by a big body of Comanches, but the Indians were beaten off and their chief, Red Sleeves, was shot and killed. All the Plains Indians call Pawnee Fork "Red Sleeve's Creek" after this Comanche chief. This little fight was about the worst trouble the Bents ever had with the Indians. As the company was trading with all the tribes and the tribes were often at war with one another, great care had to be taken by the company to avoid trouble. My father always ordered the men to keep out of the Indian quarrels and not to mix in when one tribe was fighting another. As my father had married a Cheyenne girl, he always treated the Cheyennes better than any of the other tribes, and this made it rather difficult to keep on good terms with the Kiowas and Comanches, whom the Cheyennes were constantly attacking; but my father managed to do this and kept on friendly terms with most of the Kiowa and Comanche chiefs, especially with Bull Hump and Baldhead of the Comanches. Bull Hump came up to the fort twice with Comanche war parties, hunting for the Cheyennes. His first trip was about 1826, when he came up and had a fight with the Cheyennes at Black Lake. After the fort was finished, about 1836, Yellow Wolf went down to the North Fork of Red River and stole a large herd from a Comanche camp, and Bull Hump chased him up to the Arkansas with a big party of mounted Comanche warriors. This was the biggest mounted party of Comanches ever seen on the Arkansas, and the Comanches were in a very ugly humor at missing

71

Yellow Wolf, who had already gone on north when Bull Hump reached Bent's Fort. To make matters worse, Yellow Wolf had presented to my father a very fine Comanche horse. If Bull Hump had seen this animal he would probably have attacked the fort, but luckily the horse was inside the fort and as the Comanches were only permitted to enter the trade room they did not see the horse. This horse was used by Carson in running buffalo while he was hunter at the fort, and he told me it was the best buffalo horse the Bents ever owned. The horse was named Yellow Wolf after the Cheyenne chief.

Every year war parties of Cheyennes went south to attack the Kiowas and Comanches. These small parties were mostly engaged in stealing horses, but if they saw their chance they made attacks on small parties of the enemy. The custom was that no Cheyenne parties should go to war until after the ceremony of renewing the Medicine Arrows had been held. This was the great annual medicine ceremony of the Cheyennes, and my grandfather as keeper of the arrows always decided when the ceremony should be held. I think it was in 1837 that the men of the Bowstring Society of soldiers wished to go to war against the Kiowas, and asked my grandfather to hold the ceremony so that they could start out at once. White Thunder told them that the time was not right to hold the ceremony. They argued with him, but he held to his decision, and at last the Bowstrings lost their tempers and made a fierce attack upon him with their quirts, whipping him until he gave in and agreed to hold the ceremony. White Thunder was a very old man at that time and was, next to the Prophet, the most venerated man in the tribe. His person was sacred, but the Bowstrings were all hotheaded young men and carried matters with a high hand.

My grandfather held the ceremony and renewed the arrows, but afterward he told the Bowstring men that they would have no luck. They, however, paid no attention to what he said, but at once made up a party of forty-two men and set out for the Kiowa and Comanche country. From the start they had no luck, and by the time they arrived on the Canadian they had used up most of their ammunition in killing game for meat. They located the camps of the Kiowas, Comanches, and Prairie Apaches on the Washita, between the Canadian and Red River, and slipping up as near to the camps as they dared, they concealed themselves and waited for dark. The place where they were hiding was nearest to the Kiowa camp, and the Bowstrings had two scouts out ahead, lying on the bluffs where they could look down into the valley and watch the Kiowa camp. While these scouts were lying here on the hilltop, a Kiowa man who had been out hunting alone rode up the hill. He came from behind them, his pony's hoofs making no noise in the grass, and the two Bowstrings did not see him until he was within one hundred yards of them. Even then, the Kiowa might not have seen them, but with the recklessness usual among the men of their society, the Bowstrings jumped up and fired on the man.

They missed him, and quirting up his horse he rushed down the steep hillside and into the Kiowa camp below, where he gave the alarm. The two scouts ran back to the place where the rest of the Bowstrings were hiding and told what had happened. All the Cheyennes were on foot and had no hope of getting away; there was not even a ravine to hide in or a strong position in which they might be able to defend themselves. All that they could do was to pile up a few stones and make a little breastwork to lie behind. Meantime the Kiowa warriors were arming and mounting, and now they came racing over the bluffs in small groups, each party eager to be the first to find and attack the Cheyennes. They spread out in long lines, searching every foot of ground as they advanced, and soon a yell announced that the Bowstrings had been found, lying there in the open behind their little heaps of stones. The end came swiftly. The Bowstring men held off the enemy for a time, but they had very little ammunition, and soon their last bullet and last arrow had been used. Then the mounted Kiowas charged in from all sides, and the little band of Bowstring men stood up to meet the lances with nothing but knives in their hands. It was all over in a few brief moments.

For a long time the Cheyennes did not know what had become of the forty-two Bowstrings, but at last a Prairie Apache man who was married to an Arapaho woman visited an Arapaho camp and told the story of the death of the Bowstrings. The Arapahos told the Cheyennes, and at once the Cheyenne camp was full of mourning. The relatives of the dead warriors went about weeping and begging the chiefs and soldier societies to take pity on them. At length the chiefs took the matter up and referred it to the Red Shield Society; the Red Shields, I think, passed it on to the Dog Soldiers, and Porcupine Bear, chief of the Dog Soldiers, announced that he would wait one winter and then move the arrows against the Kiowas.

Porcupine Bear now took the war pipe and started to visit all the camps of the Cheyennes and Arapahos. When he arrived in a camp the principal men of that band assembled in a council lodge and Porcupine Bear explained everything to them and then went around and offered the war pipe to each man in turn. Everyone smoked the pipe and thereby pledged themselves to join in the move against the Kiowas.

At last Porcupine Bear reached the village of the Omissis (the present-day Northern Cheyennes) on the South Platte. While he was in this camp the American Fur Company men from Fort Laramie traded a lot of liquor to the Omissis and the whole camp went to drinking. Porcupine Bear was in a lodge with some of his relatives and friends. Everyone was drunk. Two of Porcupine Bear's cousins, Little Creek and another young man named Around, began fighting. They rolled about on the floor, and Around kept calling to Porcupine Bear to come and help him, for he was getting the worst of it. Porcupine Bear paid no attention. He sat alone in a corner of the lodge, singing to himself in a low voice. He was very drunk and was singing Dog Soldier war songs. Presently Little Creek rolled on top of Around, and drawing his knife raised his arm to strike: but at that moment Porcupine Bear leaped up in sudden rage and springing upon Little Creek he wrenched the knife from his hand and stabbed him two or three times. He then forced the knife into Around's hand and standing over him compelled him to finish Little Creek.

For this deed Porcupine Bear and all his relations were outlawed by the tribe, and the Dog Soldier Society, of which Porcupine Bear was the first chief, was also disgraced. Moving the Medicine Arrows against the enemy was a sacred task, and the Dog Soldiers, who had undertaken this work, were now deprived of the leadership. I under- stand that Yellow Wolf, second chief of the Dog Soldiers, handed this work over to the Bowstrings. The Bowstring men had been practically annihilated in the recent fight with the Kiowas, so Yellow Wolf organized a new Bowstring Society, and this band was entrusted with the task of moving the arrows against the Kiowas.

In the spring of 1838 the Cheyennes and Arapahos assembled on the Arkansas below Bent's Fort and began the move against the enemy. Snow was still on the ground when the different bands began to come in. The Omissis from the north were among the last to arrive. The great village of Cheyennes had pitched their lodges in a circle, and the Arapahos were also there in great force. The Arapahos had taken little part in the war on the Kiowas, Comanches, and Apaches, but they had now accepted the war pipe and were going with the Cheyennes to help punish the Kiowas.

The big village now moved to a place called the Sand Hills on the south side of the Arkansas, and here the Cheyennes pitched their lodges in a great circle, while the Arapahos camped by themselves a short distance off. In the center of the Cheyenne camp circle a large council lodge was set up and the chiefs prepared to hold a feast and council. In the Arapaho camp was a young man whom the Cheyennes called Owner-of-Flat-War-Club because he was armed only with a large flat wooden war club. This young man was not a chief, not even a famous warrior, but just a handsome young dandy. When the Cheyenne chiefs had assembled in the council lodge, this young Arapaho sent a messenger to request the chiefs to come to his lodge and carry him to the council lodge on a blanket. The chiefs were amazed that an unknown young man should make such a demand, but they went to Flat-War-Club's lodge, put him on a fine blanket, and carried him to the council lodge. After the feast, Flat-War-Club made a speech and said to the Cheyenne chiefs that he was going to help the Cheyennes fight the Kiowas, that he was not coming back from this war trail, but was going to leave his body among the ene- mies. He said that he had but a short time to live now, and he wished

75

the Cheyennes would grant him the favor of permitting him to "talk to" the Cheyenne girls and women. "Talking to" the women meant making love to them. Cheyenne custom did not tolerate this; fathers and husbands were very strict, and Cheyenne women and girls were famous among the Plains tribes for their virtue; but as Flat-War-Club was giving his body to the enemy and had only a short time left to live, the chiefs did not like to refuse what he asked; so a crier was sent around the camp to announce what Flat-War-Club was going to do and to order that no husband or father should interfere with the young Arapaho's love-making. During the rest of the march, Flat-War-Club enjoyed himself. Every day he painted himself up, put on fine clothes, mounted a splendid war horse and rode around inside the Cheyenne camp circle, with his flat war club in his hand, singing his death song as he went. After this parade he would dismount and go down to the stream and stand beside the water trail along which the women and girls came through the thickets to get water at the creek. Whenever he saw a pretty girl or married woman he would stop her and "talk to" her. No one interfered with him. Some old women are yet living who were "talked to" by Flat-War-Club, and they tell the story with pride. My step-mother, who was only a young girl at that time, used to tell us how Flat-War-Club talked to her, in the camp on Crooked Creek.

Before the big village left the Sand Hills on the Arkansas to move south to Crooked Creek, the Cheyenne chiefs selected some brave young men and sent them south to locate the camps of the Kiowas, Comanches, and Apaches. The Kiowas were all in camp on Wolf Creek near its mouth. This stream joins Beaver Creek, just east of old Camp Supply in northwestern Oklahoma, and the two creeks, after joining, form the North Fork of Canadian River. The Kiowas intended to hold a great Medicine Lodge ceremony here and were getting ready for the dance. Near them the Prairie Apaches and part of the Comanches were encamped; the rest of the Comanches were on the South Canadian but were on the point of moving north to join the Kiowas. The Kiowas had just made peace with their old enemies, the Osages, and were expecting a big force of Osages, who had promised to come to the Medicine Lodge ceremonies.

The scouts whom the Cheyenne chiefs sent out were all brave young men who were swift runners, for they all went on foot. In the first party sent out were Pushing Ahead, Howling Wolf, and two other young men. These scouts went south as far as the head of Wolf Creek, passing the hostile Kiowa camp without seeing it. On the head of the creek they saw a small mounted war party of Kiowas going north. The Cheyennes lay hidden and watched the Kiowas riding down the creek. After the Kiowas had gone by the scouts turned back north and ran most of the way to the Cheyenne and Arapaho camps, which they found on Crooked Creek, north of the Cimarron. The Cheyennes had their lodges pitched in a great circle with the chiefs' council lodge in the center of the circle. This was the way the Cheyennes camped during this whole expedition. The four scouts were called to the center of the circle and reported to the chiefs what they had seen. A mounted crier was then sent to ride around the camp circle and call out the news the scouts had brought. That night the chiefs sent Gentle Horse and two other young men out, with orders to go to Wolf Creek, find the trail of the Kiowa war party and follow the trail to the Kiowa village. Gentle Horse, when he was an old man, told me that he had a talk with Pushing Ahead and Howling Wolf before he started out, and from what they told him he got the idea that the Kiowa camp was somewhere near the mouth of Wolf Creek; so instead of going to the head of the creek to pick up the trail of the war party, he led his two companions to the mouth of Wolf Creek and began to go up the creek, examining the country with great care.

Gentle Horse and his two friends were lying on a hill. All at once a big herd of buffalo rushed up over another hill in front of them, and behind the buffalo came a swarm of mounted Kiowa hunters. Gentle Horse and his partners crawled quickly down behind their hill and hid on a small creek. The Buffalo ran right toward where they were lying, and one Kiowa hunter on a fine mule almost rode

77

over the three young men. After the Kiowas had killed all the buffalo they wished, they cut up the meat and packed it on ponies. As the hunters moved away, Gentle Horse and his two companions came out from their hiding place and followed the hunters. Presently they came in sight of a large belt of timber along Wolf Creek, and they saw great herds of ponies scattered out all over the prairie. When Gentle Horse saw this, he knew that the Kiowa village was right there in the timber, and he and his men, after watching for a time, turned back north. They ran all night, and at daylight located the Cheyenne and Arapaho camps on the Cimarron.

That day the Cheyenne and Arapaho warriors prepared for battle and the women got everything ready for the march. The lodges with nearly everything they contained were to be left where they were; so the women put up scaffolds made of poles inside the lodges and piled their property on top of these scaffolds, where the wolves could not reach anything. The skin lodge covers were also tied up several feet from the ground all around so that the wolves could not gnaw them. At evening the two tribes assembled and formed in column. Everyone was to go, men, women, and children, and all of the horses and dogs were to go too. Children too small to sit a pony were put in the baskets of the travois and were tied down so that they could not drop out while sleeping. Skins of water were tied to the travois poles. These skins could not be placed on the ground, because they collapsed at once and all the water ran out of them. The warriors marched in regular organized bands: Dog Soldiers, Bowstring Men, Kit Fox Soldiers, Red Shields, etc. The horses, with the old men, women, and children, moved in a great column by themselves, and on each flank and in the rear rode the soldier bands. The line of chiefs led the march and a screen of scouts was kept far out ahead. No one was permitted to drop out of the column or straggle. The soldiers quirted anyone who did not obey orders. Off to outside of the main column, Porcupine Bear and his outlaws marched by themselves. After he had killed Little Creek and been outlawed by the tribe, Porcupine Bear had formed a camp of his own, made up mainly of his relations; and

78

all these people were treated as outcasts and were not permitted to camp or move with the rest of the tribe.

All that night the column moved forward, and I have been told by old people who were present that all through the night the men of the different soldier societies kept singing war songs as they rode. The main column moved southeast while Porcupine Bear and his little band of outlaws marched straight for the south. The intention was to reach the neighborhood of the Kiowa and Apache villages at dawn, but when daylight came it was found that the columns had moved in the wrong direction and had struck the Canadian River far below Wolf Creek. The columns swung around farther toward the west and the march went on, but the sun was high above the horizon before Wolf Creek was reached. Porcupine Bear and his outlaws were the first to strike the enemy. As the outlaws swept forward they suddenly came on a number of Kiowa men and women. The women were digging roots and the men hunting. Porcupine Bear, armed with a long lance, rode at a Kiowa mounted on a fine mule. He struck the Kiowa with the lance with such force that he knocked him clear off the mule; and without a pause he rushed on after the other Kiowas.

It was a great fight that followed, but somehow I cannot gain a very clear general idea of the battle. Wolf Creek near its mouth flows northeast to join Beaver Creek. The Cheyennes advanced from the southeast to cross the creek and attack the Kiowa and Apache village, which was in the timber on the north side of the stream. As they approached the creek, the Cheyennes left their women and children with the old men on the hills, and the Arapaho women and children stopped at this point also. Here they were in a safe place and could see everything that went on in the valley below.

As the Cheyennes and Arapahos advanced toward the creek, they appear to have moved forward in several detachments, striking the stream at different points. As one body of Cheyennes neared the creek opposite the Kiowa village, Sleeping Wolf, a brave young Kiowa man, crossed the creek with a body of warriors and attacked the Cheyennes. Sleeping Wolf was on foot and was wearing a fine yellow buckskin war shirt. He rushed in among the Cheyennes, but the Cheyennes counted three coups on him and drove him and his warriors back across the Creek. As the Cheyennes were starting to ride through the shallow water to cross the creek, Sleeping Wolf mounted a horse and led a large body of mounted Kiowas into the creek. He drove the Cheyennes back and out of the creek. My grandfather, White Thunder, Keeper of the Arrows, was killed here, but the sacred Medicine Arrows were not captured by the Kiowas, as my grandfather had given them to a medicine man who took them into the fight. Four other Cheyennes were killed, and Flat-War-Club also fell. This young Arapaho, who had told the Cheyennes that he would not return from the battle, fought very bravely. Although he was armed only with his war club, he took his stand in the creek and held the Kiowas back, riding in rear of everyone else as the Cheyennes and Arapahos retreated. He picked up a Cheyenne whose horse had been shot under him and took this man on his own horse, but the Kiowas killed both riders before the horse reached the south bank. Meantime other Cheyennes and Arapahos had come up, and now the warriors turned on the Kiowas and drove them back across the creek and into the village. In this charge the Cheyennes counted three more coups on Sleeping Wolf, but they could not kill him. This brave man mounted a fresh horse in the village and soon came out again. He charged right into the midst of the Cheyennes; but this time they shot him and he fell from his horse with a broken thigh. The Cheyennes counted three more coups on him and killed him. The nine Cheyenne warriors who counted coups on this Kiowa named their children after him. His name was Sleeping Wolf, but the Cheyennes called him Yellow Shirt because of the fine yellow buckskin war shirt he wore in the fight. Yellow Wolf is a common name among the Cheyennes and Arapahos even today.

While Sleeping Wolf was standing off the Cheyennes and Arapahos and disputing the ford with them, another large band of Cheyennes struck the creek some distance from the village and crossed without meeting any opposition. As they charged into the timber they came on a number of Kiowa women taking sap from the trees, and there were here a good many young Kiowas who were making love to their sweethearts among the trees. The Cheyennes killed nearly all of these people and then charged on toward the village. Meantime the Comanches, who were camped some distance off, had been warned that the Kiowas were being attacked, and Comanche warriors were now coming in in small bands, riding hard. The Kiowa and Apache women had begun cutting down trees to form a breastwork as soon as the first alarm was given, and the village was now surrounded by a high wall of these felled trees. The Kiowas, Apaches, and Comanches retired inside the breastworks, and when the Cheyennes and Arapahos charged in they were greatly disappointed to find that they could not get at their enemies. Here around the village the fight went on from about noon until nearly dark. It is hard to get many details about this fighting, as nearly all the old people who were present that day are now dead. The battle was fought seventy-six years ago. I understand that when the Cheyennes and Arapahos charged the breastworks, the Kiowa and Apache women were terribly frightened. The women had the ponies all packed and everything ready for flight, but they could not get away. The Cheyennes and Arapahos kept charging up to the breastworks, but they could not get their horses over the fallen trees. Once or twice small parties on foot got through the trees and right in among the Kiowas, Apaches, and Comanches, but they were soon either killed or driven out.

On the hills south of the creek the Cheyenne and Arapaho women, children, and old men, sat all day watching the fight, and to this place the wounded were taken, where the women could care for them. Toward evening the fight slackened and gradually the Cheyennes and Arapahos drew off across the creek and to the hills where the women and children were waiting. The two tribes then started back for their villages on the Cimarron.

In this battle on Wolf Creek, the Kiowas, Comanches and Apaches suffered very heavy loss, the Kiowas in particular having many men and women killed. Toward evening when the Cheyennes and Arapahos were withdrawing, a little party of Apaches and Kiowas met some

Arapahos near the edge of the Kiowa village and begged for peace, but the Arapahos told them that they could not make peace as long as their friends the Cheyennes refused to do so. Little Raven was with this Arapaho party and he told me this incident himself years ago. The day after the fight the Osages came in in strong force to join in the Kiowa medicine lodge, to which they had been invited; but they found the Kiowa camp in mourning for the dead. Porcupine Bear counted twenty coups in this battle. He counted the first coup, but as he was an outlaw the tribe would not permit him to count this coup, and they gave the honor of the first coup to another man who had counted the second one.[12]

[12] Bent's account conforms in major details to George Bird Grinnell's in *The Fighting Cheyennes*, 45–62; James Mooney, *Calendar History of the Kiowa Indians. Seventeenth Annual Report* of the Bureau of American Ethnology, 271–73; Berthrong, *The Southern Cheyennes*, 81–83.

CHAPTER FOUR

WHITE WAR AND INDIAN SKIRMISHES

THERE WERE FOUR CHILDREN, all born at the old fort, from the marriage of my father and mother about 1835. Mary was born January 22, 1838, Robert about 1840. I was born July 7, 1843 (the same summer that Carson was married at the fort to a pretty Mexican girl of Taos), and Julia was born in 1847.[1] Our mother died at Julia's birth, and sometime later our father married her younger sister, Yellow Woman. By this second marriage there was only one child, my half-brother Charles.[2] Julia and I are the only ones now alive. Mary died May 6, 1878. She was married to Judge R. M. Moore at the old stockade on the Purgatoire in 1860. She had six children, four girls and two boys. Robert married into our tribe and died down here in April, 1889. Julia married Edmond Guerrier[3] and is still living down here. Charles died on the Kansas frontier in 1868.

We were a large family at the old fort, and something was always going on. My uncle Charles stayed at the fort off and on a good deal, but his home was at Taos. Sometime after 1840 my uncles Robert and George came to the fort to live. Robert died there in 1847 and George about a year later. I do not think that Robert and George were partners in the company, although George was sometimes left in charge of the fort when my father went to St. Louis to sell his furs

[1] Still living 1928.—G.H. "Aunt Julia." [Handwritten.]
[2] The chronology of the issues of the two marriages of William Bent are rather difficult to follow, as Lavender suggests (*Bent's Fort*, 314)—S.L.
[3] Son of William Guerrier and a Cheyenne woman, noted as a scout.—Berthrong, *The Southern Cheyennes*, 218–20, 225, 258–60, 273–74, 276–79, 293–94, 370, 377. —S.L.

and lay in a new stock of goods. My father made this trip every year, leaving the fort usually in April and going with the wagon train to Westport (now Kansas City). From here he went to St. Louis by boat, returning to the fort with the train in fall. This trip to the Missouri River and back to the fort was over one thousand miles, and my father made the journey every year from about 1832 to 1852. For about ten years after 1852 he made the trip twice each year.

When I was a boy there were a hundred men employed at the fort, and many of the men had families. There were Indian women of a dozen different tribes living at the fort, and a large number of children. Something was always going on, and we children had no lack of amusements. In fall and winter there was always a large camp of Indians just outside the fort—Cheyennes and Arapahos, and sometimes Sioux, Kiowas, Comanches, and Prairie Apaches. The trade room was full of Indian men and women all day long; others came just to visit and talk, and there was often a circle of chiefs sitting with my father or his partners, smoking and talking. Wagons came in from New Mexico loaded with gaudy striped Mexican blankets, silver dollars, silver in bars, and other strange things. We could go out and play with the Indian children, or go to the corral back of the fort and watch One-eyed Juan and his men riding and breaking the wild horses. In summer the wagon train and many of the men were away and the Indians were all off hunting, but there was still plenty of stir about the post. Sometimes a war party going against the Utes, Apaches, or Pawnees stopped at the fort and gave a dance, and there were usually some white visitors staying with us. Even in those days that upper country (now Colorado) was beginning to gain a great reputation for healthfulness, and there were often several invalids at the fort. Frank P. Blair, Jr., of St. Louis, who did so much to save that city for the Union in 1861, stayed at the fort for his health for several years. They often had balls at the fort, and Blair would sit up all night playing the banjo in the "orchestra." Mr. Blair later became a general in Sherman's army, and his father was postmaster-general in Lincoln's cabinet. They were both great friends of the Bents, and Frank Blair, Jr., was guardian of my uncle Robert's son.[4]

In those days the Arkansas River was the boundary between the United States and Mexico. The old fort stood on the north bank of the river, and right across the stream was Mexican soil. In the '40's my father and some other men secured a huge land grant from the Mexican government there on the south side of the river, and they attempted to found a colony there, but the scheme was not a success. The Mexican colonists were very lazy and in deadly fear of the Indians, so the little settlement soon broke up. I do not know how my father lost his interest in this land grant. Many other grants were taken up by old fur traders and mountain men there in southern Colorado and northern New Mexico; our government later recognized most of these grants and the lands finally proved of great value. The Colorado coal fields where the strike is going on this year [1914] is right there among the old land grants, and for all I know these rich coal fields may be part of my father's old grant.

In 1846 came the Mexican War, and General [Stephen Watts] Kearny led the Army of the West across the plains, to invade New Mexico, Arizona, and California. The army crossed the plains in detachments and assembled in a camp below Bent's Fort. From this camp the army marched up to the fort and crossed the Arkansas at Bent's Ford, just in front of the fort. The army was very small— about 1700 men, mostly cavalry, but the Indians had never supposed there were as many men as this in the whole "white tribe," and they watched the passing of the troops in amazement. My father had a huge American flag flying on the flagpole on the tower over the big east gate of the fort, and as the General rode up at the head of the column a salute was fired from a brass howitzer on the walls of the fort, but the gun burst. For many years this old brass gun lay in the main court of the fort. Many of the officers came into the fort and were given mint juleps. (We had a fine ice house on the river bank, and there was plenty of wild mint across the river in Mexican territory, up Purgatoire Canyon.) After fording the river in front of the

[4] Francis Preston Blair, Jr., St. Louis lawyer, congressman, was the brother of Montgomery Blair, Lincoln's postmaster-general. *Concise Dictionary of American Biography.*—S.L.

fort, the army pressed on toward the southwest, making for Santa Fe. The news was that Armejo,[5] the Mexican governor, had assembled a strong force and intended to make a stand among the mountains, where his troops were fortifying themselves in the narrow passes. My father led the march with a "spy guard" made up of old trappers and mountain men, and Frank Blair went with this party. The scouts went ahead to examine the mountain passes, but on August 10 they captured a party of Mexican spies and brought them back to camp. These Mexicans were ragged peons and were mounted on tiny asses. The men sat on the rumps of the little beasts, guiding them with clubs. They had no bridles, but steered the asses by tapping them with their clubs, first on one side, then on the other. When my father's men led these Mexican scouts into camp they were greeted with shouts of laughter. The big American dragoons on their fine big Missouri horses were too disgusted even to swear when they beheld the kind of enemies they had marched six hundred miles across desert plains and mountains to meet, and old Thomas Fitzpatrick, a huge, grim mountain man who hardly ever smiled, burst in roars of laughter every time he looked at the prisoners.[6]

The Americans had expected a hard struggle among the mountains, where the enemy were reported to be holding very strong positions; but there was no fight in the Mexican troops and they abandoned the passes without firing a shot. General Kearny marched into Santa Fe without meeting any resistance, and after detaching a small force to hold New Mexico, he moved on at once with his main body, to invade southern California. Before marching from Santa Fe he had appointed a civil government with my uncle Charles Bent as the first American governor and Frank Blair as attorney-general. The people seemed very friendly and pretended to welcome the change of government, but hardly had Kearny's army moved out of

[5] Manuel Armijo, governor of New Mexico, 1827–29, 1837–44, 1845–46, actually abandoned his state to the invading Americans. Moorhead, *New Mexico's Royal Road*, 110.—S.L.

[6] "Broken Hand," the famous frontiersman. Berthrong, *The Southern Cheyennes*, 106ff.—S.L.

Santa Fe when a plot was formed and plans for an uprising against the Americans began to be secretly discussed. My uncle discovered this conspiracy almost at its start and had the ringleaders arrested; then, thinking that an uprising was now impossible, he left Santa Fe and went to visit his wife and children at Taos.

Taos is a mountain valley north of Santa Fe, and in this valley was the Indian pueblo of Taos and the Mexican town known as San Fernando de Taos. It was in this town of San Fernando that my uncle, Kit Carson, and many other fur traders and old trappers had established homes. A few days before my uncle reached San Fernando some pueblo Indian thieves had been arrested and locked up in the town *calabozo*. The Mexicans now laid a plot for an uprising against the Americans, and being too cowardly to make an attack themselves, they planned to instigate an outbreak among the Indians of the Taos Pueblo. The excuse for this outbreak was the arrest of the pueblo thieves. On January 19, 1847, a mob of Indians entered San Fernando and made a rush toward the *calabozo*. Vigil, the town prefect, met them alone and attempted to disperse them, but they killed him and cut his body to pieces. This was early in the morning. They broke into the *calabozo* next and released the Indian prisoners, then the whole mob of them rushed to my uncle's house, a flat-roofed, one-story adobe building. The doors and windows were heavily barred, so some of the Indians got upon the flat roof and began to cut a hole. My uncle went to a window and spoke to the Indians, reminding them of their old friendship for him, that he had lived among them for years and had helped nearly all of them out of trouble at different times; but they jeered him and fired in at him. His wife brought him his pistols but he would not touch them, as he knew that if he fired a shot the Indians would kill his wife and children. By this time the Indians on the roof had cut a large hole and they now leaped down into the room and shot my uncle down at the feet of his wife and children. They shot his body full of arrows, a chief ran up and fired a pistol in my uncle's face; then they tore off his scalp. The mob now went through the whole town, breaking into houses and killing every American they could find. They also murdered all the Mexi-

87

cans who had taken office under the new American government and everyone who was known to be on friendly terms with the Americans. While these bands of murderers were breaking into houses, one of the Indians stretched my uncle's scalp on a small piece of board, fastening it with brass-headed tacks, and paraded it through the streets.

The news of my uncle's murder was brought to Bent's Fort by Charlie Autobee, and when the Cheyennes heard what the Pueblos had done they offered to send a big war party down there and clean out the whole Taos pueblo. But their help was not needed. The mountain men gathered at Santa Fe in force—Santa Fe traders, fur traders, free trappers and some Indians. They marched to Taos with the regulars, stormed the pueblo, and killed a large number of the guilty Indians. The Mexicans who had instigated the murders of course escaped punishment. A big party of traders and trappers had been assembled at our fort and was just ready to move when a runner came in with the news that Colonel Sterling Price had stormed Taos and killed two hundred Indians.[7]

Charles Bent was killed in January, 1847; Robert Bent died at the fort the same year,[8] and George died at the fort of consumption about a year later.[9] My father was now the only one of the Bent brothers left in the mountains, and he ran the business alone. Ceran St. Vrain was his partner for a few years longer, but seems to have dropped out before 1850.[10] By this time the fur business had fallen off heavily

[7] Charles Bent was killed January 19, 1847, and on February 3 and 4, after his forces, aided by Santa Fe volunteers under Captain Ceran St. Vrain, had defeated the revolting New Mexicans at La Cañada, Sterling Price reached Taos Pueblo, killing an estimated 150 of the rebels.—Warren A. Beck, *New Mexico: A History of Four Centuries*, 134–38. The eye-witness account, first, of the effect of the news of Charles Bent's death on his brother William at Bent's Fort, and, second, the trial of the conspirators, is the now classic *Wah-to-yah and the Taos Trail*, by Lewis H. Garrard (1850).—S.L.

[8] Robert Bent was killed by the Comanches in October, 1841, not in 1847, as George Bent asserts. His death occurred as he left a Bent wagon train on the upper Arkansas to hunt buffalo. Youngest of the Bent brothers, he was 25 at the time. Lavender, *Bent's Fort*, 84, 189.—S.L.

[9] George Bent, brother of William and Charles, and two years older than Robert, died of a wasting illness in October, 1847, aged 33. Lavender, *op. cit.*, 303–304. —S.L.

and all the big companies were cutting down their establishments. The silk hat had been invented and the beaver hat was going rapidly out of use; the price of beaver skins fell so greatly that trapping was no longer profitable. Many trappers left the mountains; others remained to pick up a living by hunting and doing a little farming; some of the old free trappers formed a little settlement above Bent's Fort where they lived by hunting and planting a little corn. They called this settlement El Pueblo, and this was the beginning of the present city of Pueblo, Colorado.

In the '30's the Delawares and Shawnees were settled on a new reservation on the west side of the Missouri River, near the present Fort Leavenworth, Kansas. The men of these two tribes were very bold and adventurous, and they were perhaps the most dreaded Indians in the whole West. Their war and hunting parties penetrated everywhere in the plains and in the mountains, down into Mexico and west to Great Salt Lake. While crossing the plains they never missed an opportunity to attack any small party of plains Indians they might meet, and as they were all armed with good rifles and were fine shots they usually had little difficulty in getting the upper hand of the poorly armed plains warriors. Many fights with these parties of Delawares and Shawnees are on record. About 1825 a party of them returning home from a trapping expedition among the mountains ran into a war party of sixty or seventy mounted Pawnees in the plains of western Kansas. The trappers were outnumbered four or five to one, but they made a breastwork of their packs of beaver skins and without losing a man drove the Pawnees off, killing several of their bravest warriors. In 1844 another trapping party of Delawares ran into some of our people, but did not get off so easily.[11]

[10] The dissolution of the partnership between the surviving William Bent and Ceran St. Vrain may have occurred in 1849. Lavender *op. cit.*, 311–12.—S.L.

[11] The Delawares and Shawnees were both Algonquian peoples, allied historically in a migration in and after 1789 to Missouri and later to Arkansas, by permission of the Spanish government. The Pawnees, on the other hand, were of the Caddoan group. F. W. Hodge, *Handbook of American Indians North of Mexico*, I, 385; II, 213–14, 531.—S.L.

That summer a band of Cheyennes and a band of Brulé Sioux were camping together on a creek near the forks of the Republican, about on the present western boundary of Kansas. One day a Cheyenne man named Plover went out on the prairie with his wife and a boy—his wife's brother. They were digging roots when all at once a party of seventeen Delaware trappers made their appearance. The Delawares were returning home from a trip in the mountains with their pack ponies loaded with furs. The minute they caught sight of the three Cheyennes they set up a yell and leaving their pack ponies set off in pursuit. Plover, his wife, and the boy jumped on their ponies and rode for their lives, but the Delawares kept gaining on them, and when they reached a line of bluffs the Delawares were very close. The fugitives rode over the bluffs and disappeared; the whooping trappers galloped after them, expecting to catch them just beyond, but as the pursuers rushed over the top of the bluffs they were amazed to find themselves right in the edge of the Cheyenne and Sioux camp, which was in a little valley hidden between two lines of bluffs. The Delawares jerked in their horses, whirled around, and made off at top speed. They rounded up their pack ponies and rushed them to a nearby creek. Here they dismounted and put all their horses in the bed of the creek, under cover of the high banks; then the trappers came out on foot and lined up on the open ground.

When Plover, his wife, and the boy had come rushing into camp, closely followed by the Delawares, the Cheyenne and Sioux men had armed at once and begun catching their horses; and now they came streaming over the bluffs in little bands and groups. Soon a big body of mounted warriors was lined up facing the little party of trappers. The Cheyenne chiefs High-Back-Wolf and Standing-on-Hill rode forward, making signs of peace, but the Delawares fired on them and drove them back. Three or four times the chiefs attempted to approach and parley with the trappers, but each time they were fired on. The Cheyennes and Sioux did not wish to fight, but after the chiefs had been shot at several times the warriors began to get mad. They held a council and decided to attack the trappers; but as the Delawares all had fine rifles and the Cheyennes and Sioux had only a few old smooth-bore fusils, the chiefs determined to "empty the enemy's guns" before signaling the charge.

Among the Cheyennes was a man named Medicine Water who owned a Spanish coat of mail. Some years before, a band of Arapahos had been camped down in Mexico and the Mexicans came to trade in the camp. One day a Mexican rode into camp with this old suit of armor and offered to trade it for horses. While he was bargaining with the Indians, a young Arapaho rode into camp with a fine big American mule, which he had found straying, and when the Mexican saw the mule, he rode up to the young man and offered the armor for the mule. The trade was made, and some time later Medicine Water saw the Arapaho with the armor and traded him some good horses for the suit. Medicine Water wore this coat of mail in the big fight with the Kiowas, Comanches, and Apaches on Wolf Creek in 1838, and some years later he gave the suit to his son, Touching Cloud.

When the council decided to fight, Medicine Water told his son to go back to camp and put on the coat of mail, and Touching Cloud went at once. The armor was made of little iron scales about as big as half-dollars. These scales were sewn upon a leather shirt, each line of scales lapped over the one above, so as to leave no openings. There was also an iron cap with a flap coming down to protect the neck.

Touching Cloud put on the mailed shirt and wrapped a scarlet blanket over it, completely hiding the armor. He then mounted and rode back to the place where the Cheyennes and Sioux were sitting on their war ponies all in a line. Touching Cloud put his fine pony into a run and rode out toward one end of the Delaware line; then sweeping around in a broad circle, he rushed along the Delaware line, so close that it seemed impossible to miss him. As he swept past the trappers all fired at him, but the bullets fell harmless off his armor; then, as he cleared the end of the Delaware line, the signal was given, and like a flash the Cheyenne and Sioux warriors charged. They rode right over the Delawares, lancing them and knocking them down with their war clubs. Not a Delaware had time to fire a shot. Most of the Delawares were killed with the ramrods sticking from the muzzles of their rifles, the bullets rammed halfway down the barrels. Not a man escaped, and all of their horses, rich packs of furs, rifles, and equipments were captured.

The small creek on which this fight took place flows into the Republican near its forks and is called Shawnee Creek by the Cheyennes. Our people always called the Delawares Shawnees or Black Shawnees. The old traders and trappers called the stream Delaware Creek, and it is so marked on some old maps. After the fight the Cheyennes moved down to the Arkansas and met Frémont's exploring party near the Big Timbers. The chiefs told Frémont how the Delawares had been killed and requested him to inform the Delaware chiefs that the Cheyennes were not to blame for the affair. Frémont evidently did not do this, for a year or more later a party of Delawares came out to Bent's Fort to ask about this party of trappers, and there learned for the first time that the men had all been killed. Yellow Wolf, and my father also, told the Delaware men that the Cheyennes had not been to blame, as the trappers had fired the first shots and had refused all attempts made to parley with them. The Cheyennes were afraid the Delawares would make war on them because of the killing of the trappers, but this was avoided.

Touching Cloud went to Washington in 1850 and was the first Cheyenne who ever went east. In 1852 he was killed by the Pawnees and part of his armor was captured. A big war party of Cheyennes, Kiowas, and Apaches was out after the Pawnees. One morning Touching Cloud with twenty Cheyennes and one Apache set out ahead of the main body, and the first thing they knew they came on a big body of Pawnees hunting near the Pawnee camp. The Cheyennes made an attack but the Pawnees turned on them, killing Touching Cloud and six other Cheyennes and the one Apache. The big war party then came up and drove the Pawnees to their camp, killing a number of them. When the warriors reached the place where Touching Cloud's party had been killed, they found that boys and women had come out of the Pawnee camp and mutilated the dead. Touching Cloud's body was all cut up and the Pawnees had carried off part of his armor. The rest of the armor was kept by the Cheyennes many years and was finally hidden in a hole in the ground and was never found again.[12] The Mexicans had a number of these old coats of mail and traded several of them to the plains Indians. An "iron warrior" was killed up north away back about 1750; another one was killed about 1790, and a Comanche chief who had one of these coats was killed in a fight with the Texas Rangers at Antelope Hills in 1858. His name was Iron Jacket, and he had gained a great reputation as a warrior. He always wore a yellow buckskin war shirt over the armor, to hide it, and as few knew that he had the armor it was generally believed that he had a "medicine" that made him bullet-proof.

After the Mexican War the fur business had fallen off to such an extent that it was no longer profitable to maintain large trading posts, so when the War Department offered to buy Bent's Fort and turn it into a military post, my father said that he was willing to sell.[13] The government, however, offered him only $12,000, and as he did not think that a fair price, he refused to sell, abandoned the fort and blew it into the air. This was in the fall of 1852.[14] I remember well the day we left the old post. With the big wagons loaded with goods, we moved down the river and camped for the night at the mouth of Short-timber Creek. In the morning the train pulled out down the river before daylight and my father rode back to the fort alone. My stepmother told us children that he was going to blow up the fort. Soon we heard an explosion, and then my father rode back and joined us. The old fort was not completely destroyed. After the Civil War part of it was used as a stage station. Today crumbling bits of the old adobe walls are still to be seen, and a few years ago the ground on which the fort stood was made into a park and a stone monument was

---

[12] This may be the armor discovered in western Nebraska a few years ago and, of course, attributed to Coronado and his men.—G.H.

[13] The opening proposal of sale appears to have been made by Ceran St. Vrain (Letter to Lieutenant-Colonel Eneas Mackay, July 21, 1847, General Land Office Records, National Archives).—S.L.

[14] Actually about August 22, 1849, after a cholera epidemic had brought disaster to the Indians who normally traded with the fort. Berthrong, *The Southern Cheyennes*, 114; Lavender, *Bent's Fort*, 313–16.—S.L.

erected inside the old walls by the Colorado Society of the Daughters of the American Revolution.

We moved down to the Big Timbers, thirty-five miles below the old fort, and here at the lower end of the timbers my father built a temporary stockade and two trading houses at the foot of a high bluff near the river. That winter the buffalo were thick in this vicinity and all the tribes were in winter camp here and came in every day to trade. The Cheyennes were camped right at our stockade, the Arapahos two miles below on the north side of the river; the Kiowas and Prairie Apaches about opposite the stockade on the south bank, and the Comanches farther down on the south bank. When the different soldier societies were having dances, we could hear the drums beating in the camps all night long, and every day the Indians came in to trade their robes. The Cheyenne and Arapaho women packed the robes in on their backs, while the Kiowa and Comanche squaws brought their robes loaded on horses and mules.

This was the last I saw of the Indians for ten years. In the spring of 1853 my father sent us children to Westport, five hundred miles by wagon train. He had a fine big farm at Westport, and there we lived and went to school until the Civil War broke out. As my father was out among the Indians most of the time and could not see us very often, he induced his friend Colonel A. D. Boone to act as our guardian while we were at Westport. Colonel Boone was a son of Daniel Boone.[15] From Kentucky Daniel Boone moved to Missouri while that country was still under Spanish rule. He obtained a grant of land from the King of Spain, became a Spanish subject, and founded a small colony on the Missouri River, up above St. Louis. Col. A. D. Boone went up the Arkansas and joined my father after gold was discovered in the Pike's Peak district. He took up some land on the Arkansas above Bent's Fort and founded the town of Booneville, Colorado.

When my father sent us children to Westport in the spring of 1853, he remained at the Big Timbers and began building Bent's

[15] Albert D. Boone was Daniel Boone's grandson, not son. The arrival of the Bent children in Westport was more likely the fall of 1853.—S.L.

New Fort. This fort was completed that same year. It stood on the north bank of the river, below the Big Timbers and about thirty-eight miles below Bent's Old Fort. The post was a small one and the main building was built entirely of stone.[16] My father kept up this post from 1853 until 1859 and then sold out to the War Department.[17] During these years he traded with all the tribes of the Upper Arkansas, sent parties out to trade in New Mexico and with the emigrants on the Oregon Trail in the Platte Valley, and he also engaged in hauling government supplies across the plains. He used to go down to Westport in the spring with his wagons loaded with the robes and other articles he had traded for during the winter; he would then haul the Indian annuities up the Arkansas, deliver these goods, and then return to Westport to haul his own trade goods out to the fort. He used to say that he made enough money hauling the annuities each year to pay for all the trade goods he bought. Freight rates were very high in those days. In 1858 the War Department had to pay to the wagon freighters $1.50 per hundred pounds for each one hundred miles. From the Missouri River to Bent's Fort, five hundred miles, the rate was therefore $7.50 per hundred pounds. In 1850 it cost $34.24 to feed a cavalry horse for one month at Fort Laramie.[18]

The time was now at hand when trouble between the Indians and the whites was sure to come. Emigration to California and Oregon began about 1842, and even as early as 1845 the Indians were begin-

---

[16] Here George Bent's memory is far more accurate than that of others who tended to exaggerate the size of Bent's New Fort. Major John Sedgwick's report of September 8, 1860, to the quartermaster general interpolated, gives a square with one hundred feet to a side, much closer to George Bent's impressions and probably reliable. (Lavender, *Bent's Fort*, 415). Bent's chronology is also close. Stone quarrying began in the fall and winter of 1852 and construction seems to have been completed in the summer of 1853.—S.L.

[17] Date of a rental lease, not a sale, was September 9, 1860 (General Land Office File, Abandoned Military Reservation Series, Fort Lyon File, National Archives).—S.L.

[18] Freight rates for this period for the trip to Bent's New Fort ran as high as 6¢ per pound (c.f. Henry Pickering Walker, *The Wagonmasters*, 249–50).—S.L.

ning to grow restless under this heavy movement of whites through the heart of their hunting grounds. Then came the discovery of gold in California and the great rush across the plains in '49. By this time grass, wood, and game had been so nearly destroyed on the Oregon Trail up the Platte that large trains of emigrants began to use the Arkansas route; thus the Cheyennes and Arapahos who lived and hunted in the country between the Platte and the Arkansas found themselves caught between two great streams of white emigration. The buffalo began to decrease with alarming rapidity and the tribes foresaw the hungry years to come. Famous groves of cottonwood trees where the Indians had camped in winter for generations disappeared in a single season; the Big Timbers of the Arkansas themselves began to go, and in all the valleys for miles away from the river the grass was eaten down into the ground by the emigrants' hungry herds.

Then, in '49, the emigrants brought the cholera up the Platte Valley, and from the emigrant trains it spread to the Indian camps. "Cramps" the Indians called it, and they died of it by hundreds. On the Platte whole camps could be seen deserted with the tepees full of dead bodies, men, women and children. The Sioux and Cheyennes, who were nearest to the road, were the hardest hit, and from the Sioux the epidemic spread northward clear to the Blackfeet, while from the Cheyennes and Arapahos it struck down into the Kiowa and Comanche country and created havoc among their camps.[19] Our tribe suffered very heavy loss; half of the tribe died, some old people say. A war party of about one hundred Cheyennes had been down the Platte, hunting for the Pawnees, and on their way home they stopped in an emigrant camp and saw white men dying of cholera in the wagons. When the Cheyennes saw these sick white men, they rushed out of the camp and started for home on the run, scattering as they went; but the terrible disease had them already in its grip, and many of the party died before reaching home, one of my Indian uncles and his wife dying among the first. The men in the war party be-

[19] The Osages [to the east] also brought it out on the plains, to the Comanches and Kiowas.—G.H.

longed to different camps and when they joined these camps they brought the cholera with them and it was soon raging in all the villages. The people were soon in a panic. The big camps broke up into little bands and family groups, and each little party fled from the rest. The Hevhaitanio Clan was down on the Arkansas when the disease broke out. This clan started north, but on the way met Gentle Horse's band with the cholera raging among the tents. The Hevhaitanio turned and fled, scattering over the prairie in little parties, but prompt as was their flight some of the band took the disease and died. This clan lost less than any of the others. The Oktoguna Clan was practically wiped out and the Masikota Clan was so reduced that the survivors joined the Dog Soldier camp and became merged into that band. This cholera epidemic of '49 began the destruction of the old Cheyenne clans, and the Chivington Massacre of '64 finished the work.[20]

The War Department had begun to establish military posts in the plains to protect the emigrant roads soon after the Mexican War. On the Platte, to guard the Oregon Trail, Fort Kearny was built on the lower river and Fort Laramie was purchased from the American Fur Company and turned into a military post. On the Arkansas, to protect the Santa Fe Trail, Old Fort Atkinson was built in 1850 on the site of the present Dodge City, Kansas, and, as I have told, an

---

[20] I do not remember clearly Bent's account of his own experiences during the cholera: he said, I think, that his grandmother (White Thunder's widow) and his stepmother, Yellow Woman, took the children that summer out among the Cheyennes, and they went to the Canadian, I think, where the Kiowas and Comanches were to make medicine. During the medicine dance an Osage visitor fell down in the crowd with cholera cramps. The Indians broke camp at once and fled in every direction, the Cheyennes north toward the Arkansas. They fled all night and halted on the Cimarron. Here a brave man whose name I've forgotten—a famous warrior—mounted his war horse with his arms and rode thro the camp shouting "If I could see this thing [the cholera] if I knew where it was, I would go there and kill it!" He was taken with the cramps as he rode, slumped over on his horse, rode slowly back to his lodge, and fell to the ground. The people then broke camp in wild fright and fled north through the big sand hills all that night. I think Bent said his grandmother died this night among the sand hills. His stepmother had the children on a poledrag. She left the Indians on the Arkansas and went up to Bent's Fort.—G.H.

attempt was also made to purchase Bent's Fort for military purposes, but this failed, and Atkinson remained for some years the only government fort on the upper Arkansas.

No sooner were these posts established among the plains tribes than trouble made its appearance and, as one chief justly complained, the soldiers who had been sent to keep peace in the country were the first to make the ground bloody. The garrisons were all very small and young and inexperienced officers were often left in charge of the posts, mere boys who treated the Indians like dogs, and being more eager to see service than to keep the peace, these young officers carried matters with a high hand and overlooked no opportunity to stir up the tribes. The natural result was war, and it came quickly.

The first trouble was at Fort Atkinson in 1853. Lean Bear,[21] a young Cheyenne, was visiting the fort and took hold of an officer's wife's hand, to look at her ring. The lady's husband rushed up and attacked Lean Bear with a big whip. The Cheyenne camp was near the fort. Bear, a famous warrior, mounted his war horse and rode through the camp, haranguing the warriors and urging them to attack the post. He had his face painted black and white and held a big tomahawk in his hand. The warriors were very angry and were already beginning to arm when the chiefs stopped Bear's harangue and prevented the affair from going farther.

The following year, 1854, some Sioux found a lame ox straying near the road below Fort Laramie and killed and ate the animal. A man at the fort then laid claim to the ox and demanded payment. The Sioux chiefs offered to pay, but the officer in command also demanded that the "thieves" be given up for punishment, and this the chiefs said was impossible, so a young Irishman, Lieutenant

[21] Chief who was killed by Lieutenant Ayres' Colorado troops in 1864.—G.H. [Lieutenant George S. Eayre, commanding the Independent Battery of Colorado Volunteer Artillery, encountered the Cheyennes on Smoky Hill River on May 16, 1864, and there at a point about fifty miles northwest of Fort Larned, Kansas, Lean Bear, accompanied by Wolf Chief and a number of others, went out to treat with the commander and his troops. As the Indians approached, the troops according to Wolf Chief, who survived, fired, killing Lean Bear. Grinnell, *The Fighting Cheyennes*, 145–46; Stan Hoig, *The Sand Creek Massacre*, 50–52.—S.L.]

Grattan, was sent to the Sioux camp with a detachment of infantry and a howitzer, to arrest the Indians wanted. Grattan marched into the center of the camp, lined up his little party of soldiers and pointed the howitzer at the lodges. The young men had armed themselves and were determined not to give up the men who had killed the ox. The Sioux chief kept going back and forth, trying to prevent a clash. Anyone but a fool could have seen that no good could result from pushing the matter further, while everyone was armed and excited; but Lieutenant Grattan had said many times that the Indians were all cowards and would run like sheep at the first fire. In the midst of the parley the howitzer was discharged among the Indians and the soldiers suddenly fired a volley. The friendly chief, Whirling Bear, was killed at the first fire. The Indians, before the troops could reload the cannon, poured in a volley of bullets and arrows, killing Grattan and many of his men. The rest of the soldiers fled back along the road toward the fort, but the Sioux mounted, overtook them, and killed them all.[22]

The young men were now out of hand and began making raids along the road. In the following summer Colonel W. S. Harney marched up the Platte with a strong force, surprised a Sioux camp on the Blue Water, killed a number of Sioux, and destroyed the whole village. I think these Sioux belonged to another band which had not been mixed up in the Grattan fight and the raids that followed.[23]

Harney's attack (the Indians called him "the Hornet") quieted the Sioux, but the following year, 1856, the troops drove the Northern Cheyennes out of their own country and declared them "hostile."

[22] Lieutenant J. L. Grattan, serving under Lieutenant Hugh B. Fleming at Fort Laramie, was after the Miniconjou, High Forehead, who had shot the ox with an arrow. In the resulting battle, in which the troops may or may not have fired the first shot, Brave Bear of the Miniconjous went down immediately. With Spotted Tail and the Brulé Sioux, Red Cloud and the Oglalas, and the Miniconjous all joined against the troops, the whites were all killed on the field, except one, who died later. George E. Hyde, *Spotted Tail's Folk: A History of the Brulé Sioux*, 48–54.—S.L.

[23] Actually, these were the same Brulé Sioux who had been involved in the Grattan fight—Little Thunder, Spotted Tail, Red Leaf, and Iron Shell, and their people. It was not a surprise attack by the troops under Harney, a brigadier general at the time. Hyde, *op. cit.*, 57–60. The battle occurred September 3, 1855.—S.L.

The trouble started at Platte Bridge, 125 miles west of Laramie, where the emigrant trains crossed the Platte. There was a small infantry guard at the bridge with a young lieutenant in command. In April the Northern Cheyennes were camped near the bridge, trading, and one day some young men found four horses straying. They took the animals to camp, and, of course, a white man at once laid claim to the whole four. Four young Cheyennes took three of the horses to the bridge and offered to give them up; the fourth animal they said the white man had not described correctly and they did not believe he had ever seen the horse before. The officer demanded the fourth horse be also given up, and when the Cheyennes refused he promptly ordered the soldiers to seize the young men.

Now, in those days, Indians did not understand being arrested. They never took full-grown men prisoners but always killed them in the fight and had it done with; so when the soldiers attempted to arrest any Indians, the Indians, of course, believed that the troops intended to disarm them and then kill them; so whenever such an attempt was made the Indians usually fought for their lives. Now when the lieutenant ordered his men to arrest the four young Cheyennes, the young men attempted to break through the soldiers. Two were captured, one was shot down, and the fourth, Little Wolf, who was a famous runner, got away. When he got to the Cheyenne camp with this news, the people were thrown into a panic and fled at once, abandoning everything, for they believed that the Grattan affair was to be repeated. And they were not far wrong, for no sooner had they left their camp than the troops marched up.

The soldiers plundered the camp, "confiscating" everything they took a fancy to and burning the rest. The Northern Cheyennes fled south and joined the Southern Cheyennes between the Platte and the Arkansas. Here they remained, moving about, hunting buffalo, and going to my father's fort to trade. They made no raids and kept out of the way of the troops, because they knew what the Sioux had suffered in '55, and they were not at all anxious to meet the Hornet and his troopers. The whites, however, had made up their minds that the Cheyennes were hostile, and trouble was sure to come.[24]

In August that year the Cheyennes made up a war party of seventy or eighty men and went up to the Platte to hunt for their old enemies, the Pawnees. This war party was camped beside the road on August 24 when the mail wagon came along. Some of the Cheyennes went out into the road to ask for tobacco, but the mail conductor, who had heard that the Cheyennes were hostile, drew a pistol and fired it into the group of warriors. A Cheyenne promptly replied with an arrow, wounding the white man slightly. The wagon then made off along the road at top speed, the Cheyennes making no attempt to follow, as they wished to avoid trouble.

When the mail outfit reached Fort Kearny and told what had happened, a company of the First Cavalry was at once sent in pursuit of the Cheyennes. The troops followed the Indian trail down the river and along Grand Island. This island, very narrow, but seventy-five miles long, was pretty heavily timbered in those days, and the Cheyennes were moving along the island, to keep out of the way of more trouble. Late the following afternoon the cavalry discovered the Cheyennes in camp on the lower end of the island, and without any talk or explanation a charge was ordered and the Indians were driven from their camp, and the troops drove them several miles down the river, killing six warriors and capturing twenty-two horses, two mules, and a number of lances, shields, saddles, etc. That this party was not hostile is proved by the fact that the same day, before the fight, four of the warriors, who had left the main body, went into Fort Kearny to ask for food. These men, Big Head, Good Bear, and Black-Hairy Dog (Cheyennes) and one Sioux man, were all arrested, but the Cheyennes broke through the guard and got away. Big Head (my uncle) was shot in several places by the troops and he broke through them.

When this war party returned home and reported how they had been attacked and had lost six men killed, the young warriors got completely out of hand. The chiefs could not hold them in any

[24] This fight is not to be mistaken for the much greater engagement involving Sioux, Cheyennes, and Arapahos, attacking Platte Bridge in July, 1865, for which see J. W. Vaughn, *The Battle of Platte Bridge.*—S.L.

longer. Two unprovoked attacks had been made on the Cheyennes by the troops; and now the young men broke loose and began to raid on the Platte Road. Several small war parties left the camps and went up to the Platte. They captured a large wagon train east of Kearny and another farther up the river: and by the end of September they had made so many attacks on small parties of travelers that the road was no longer safe except for large trains of armed men. All these raids were made by the Northern Cheyennes; the Southern Cheyennes kept out of it, and in fall went to Bent's Fort for their annuities, the same as usual.

Even before these raids were made on the Platte Road, the government had determined to attack the Cheyennes. The expedition was, however, delayed, because of the Border Ruffian troubles in Kansas, and the punishment of our tribe had to be put off one year. In the following spring, 1857, Colonel E. V. Sumner, First Cavalry, assembled a large cavalry force at Fort Leavenworth, and in the middle of May set out to seek the "hostile" Cheyennes. The Cheyennes were all camped together hunting buffalo on Solomon's Fork of Kansas River when some young men brought in word that troops were in the vicinity. When this news was received most of the chiefs and middle-aged men were for moving camp and keeping out of the way of the soldiers, but the younger warriors wanted to fight, and two famous medicine men also threw their influence for war. The chiefs in this camp were Black Kettle, White Antelope, old Whirlwind, and Rock Forehead, the Keeper of the Arrows. These were Southern Cheyennes. Also Brave Wolf, Little Grey Hair, Dull Knife, and Spotted Wolf, leaders of the Northern Cheyennes. Grey Beard was the Southern Cheyenne medicine man, and Ice or White Bull was medicine man for the Northern Cheyennes. These two medicine men persuaded the young warriors that they had a medicine which would make the guns of the soldiers useless and that the bullets of the whites would not harm the Indians.

The Cheyennes had very few guns in those days and most of these weapons were cheap, short-range smooth-bores. Our warriors had never had a fight with troops, and now they were to meet more than

William Bent with Little Raven and His Daughter and Sons

Charles Bent, *upper left*; Ceran
St. Vrain, *upper right*; Christopher
"Kit" Carson, *lower left*

Yellow Wolf
From the Painting by Lieutenant J. W. Abert

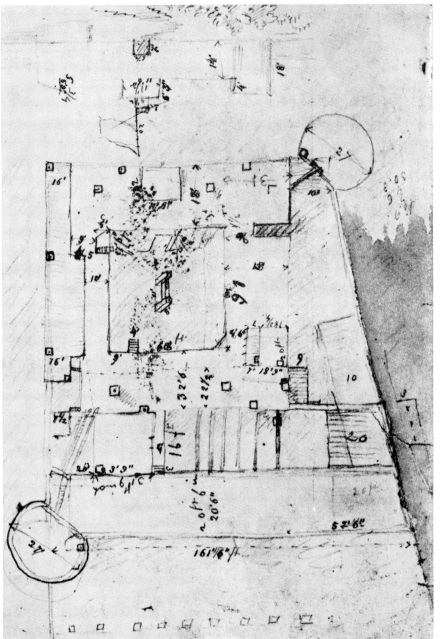

Lieutenant J. W. Abert's Sketch of Bent's Fort. From J. W. Abert, *Western America in 1846–1847*, edited by John Galvin

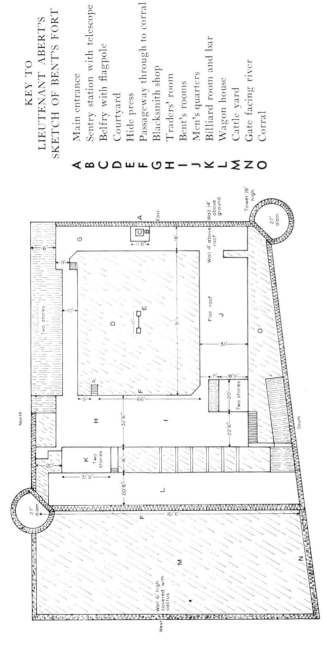

KEY TO
LIEUTENANT ABERT'S
SKETCH OF BENT'S FORT

A Main entrance
B Sentry station with telescope
C Belfry with flagpole
D Courtyard
E Hide press
F Passageway through to corral
G Blacksmith shop
H Traders' room
I Bent's rooms
J Men's quarters
K Billiard room and bar
L Wagon house
M Cattle yard
N Gate facing river
O Corral

Key to Lieutenant J. W. Abert's Sketch of Bent's Fort. From J. W. Abert, *Western America in 1846–1847*, edited by John Galvin

Lieutenant J. W. Abert's Perspective of Bent's Fort, 1845

George Bent and Magpie, His Wife

Edmond Gurrier

their own number of cavalry, all armed with carbines, pistols, and sabres. The belief that the medicine men's power would protect them from bullets put heart into the young men, and when on July 29th news was brought in by the scouts that the troops were approaching the camp, three hundred young warriors mounted and rode up the valley to meet the whites. Colonel Sumner was pushing ahead with his cavalry, the infantry companies toiling along three miles in rear, when suddenly he came upon the Cheyennes drawn up in a long line, reaching from the river to the bluffs and facing the advancing troops "with remarkable boldness," as Colonel Sumner said later in his report. It was the boldness of ignorance, however, and the warriors did not know what they were facing.

As the six companies of cavalry fronted into the line, the flank-companies moving at a gallop, the Cheyenne line began to advance, the warriors singing war songs as they rode slowly toward the troops. They were firm in the belief that the guns of the soldiers would fail to go off; and strangely enough this prophecy of the medicine men came true. Colonel Sumner was an old Dragoon officer and loved the sabre; and now, to the astonishment of all his officers and men, he gave the command, "Draw sabres!" and immediately afterward, "Charge!" and for the first and last time in the annals of Indian warfare a large force of cavalry swept forward to attack a body of mounted Indians with the steel. The Cheyennes faced this unexpected form of attack boldly enough for a short time; then, even before the troopers had come within striking distance, the warriors turned and fled, scattering in every direction.

The troops split into small groups and chased the Indians many miles, but the Cheyennes were mounted on fresh horses and had little trouble in making good their escape. A few officers and men, mounted on fast horses, overtook and attacked individual warriors. Lieutenant J. E. B. Stuart, later the famous Confederate cavalry general, came up with a Cheyenne man and attacked him with the sabre, but was shot in the breast and badly wounded. Colonel Sumner reported his loss as two men killed, Lieutenant Stuart and eight men wounded, and the Indian loss he gave as nine killed, but the old people tell me that only four Cheyennes were killed: Coyote Ear, Black Bear, Yellow Shirt, and Otter Man. Sumner was much blamed by some officers for ordering the sabre charge. They said that the Indians were so close that if the troops had fired a volley before charging they might have killed a third of the warriors.[25]

The Cheyennes abandoned their camp right after the fight and fled south toward the Arkansas. The following day the troops continued their advance down the Solomon, and fourteen miles below the place where the fight had taken place they came on the deserted Indian camp. They found 171 lodges still standing (about the same number had been taken down and removed) and these lodges with all they contained were burned by the troops. Colonel Sumner then set out to follow the Indians, hoping to overtake them and force them to fight again. The trail was followed south to within forty miles of the Arkansas, but at that point it suddenly vanished: the Indians had scattered in every direction, leaving no trail behind.

Moving down Walnut Creek, the troops encamped on the north bank of the Arkansas, not far from the site of old Fort Atkinson, which had now been abandoned for five years. At this camp a rumor was received that my father's fort was in danger of being attacked by the Cheyennes, who intended to seize all of the annuity goods, including a large supply of guns and ammunition. On hearing this report, Colonel Sumner took his best cavalry and marched up the river to Bent's Fort, where he arrived on August 18th. A month before this, Agent [Robert C.] Miller had come up to the fort with the Cheyenne and Arapaho annuities which he wished to store in the fort, as usual, until the Indians came for the goods. My father, however, refused to permit him to store the annuities inside the fort, as he was afraid that if Sumner attacked the Indians they might come to the fort and attack it, to get at the goods. The matter was talked over all one night, and at last my father proposed to move out of the fort and turn the place over to the agent. This was agreed upon,

[25] See also Percival G. Lowe, *Five Years a Dragoon* (ed. by Don Russell), 219–20; Grinnell, *The Fighting Cheyennes*, 117–23; Berthrong, *The Southern Cheyennes*, 138–40.—S.L.

and early in the morning my father moved out with all his family, employees, goods, wagons, and stock. The agent then moved in with the annuities. When Sumner arrived a month later he seized the Cheyenne annuities and handed them over to the friendly Arapahos. He then began to plan a further pursuit of the Cheyennes, but at this moment orders arrived for him to break up the expedition and send Major Sedgwick with most of the troops to Utah, where the Mormons were in open revolt against the United States government. Thus the first military expedition came to an end. The Cheyennes had fled south of the Arkansas, into the Kiowa and Comanche country. They remained there, hunting, until fall, then returned north of the Arkansas, and the Northern Cheyennes went back to their own country, north of the Platte.

A great change now came over the Cheyenne and Arapaho country. In the spring of 1858 a party of thirty Cherokees and twelve white men, all from Georgia, came up to Bent's Fort and from there went through the eastern foothills of the Colorado mountains, hunting for gold. They prospected the whole country from the old fork northward to beyond the Platte, but although they found gold in several places it was never in paying quantities, and in the fall all of the party except seven of the whites returned east. They took with them several little goose quills filled with gold dust; not a man had enough gold to pay his board for a week, and yet when they made their appearance in the frontier towns and showed the little quills filled with dust, the whole frontier was thrown into excitement. In Kansas, Nebraska, Missouri, and Iowa, thousands of men began to prepare to set out for the mountains in the following spring, and several parties set out at once and reached the new gold region before winter set in.

Failing to find gold in any quantity, these new men began to lay out townsites. There on the edge of the mountains, in the heart of the wilderness, they set to work and fell to planning cities. One party laid out El Paso town on the site of the present Colorado Springs, but soon abandoned the place. They moved up to near where Denver now stands and laid out the town of "Montana." St. Charles and Auraria were also laid out at Denver. In the dead of winter a party from Leavenworth, Kansas, arrived and "jumped" the townsite of St. Charles, which had been abandoned. They renamed the place "Denver" in honor of James W. Denver, governor of Kansas Territory.

Here on Cherry Creek in the edge of the bleak mountain wilderness, a bitter fight was fought between the rival owners of the townsites of Denver and Auraria. There was only a handful of men in each camp, but more were arriving all the time, and every few weeks a new storekeeper would come in with his goods loaded on wagons. Every new arrival, and especially the storekeepers, had to be fought over, each town-company offering inducements and squabbling over the relative advantages of their two "cities." When Auraria secured a new merchant there was gloom in Denver, and when Denver succeeded in capturing another grocer there was gnashing of teeth in Auraria. The fight went on for a year and was only ended in the fall of '59 when two big trains loaded with goods made their appearance and were both secured by Denver. Auraria then turned up its toes and died.

The Indians watched these mad proceedings of the whites with astonishment, but they were still further amazed, and alarmed, when the real rush began in the spring of '59. Even before the snow was melted on the plains and the ice had broken up in the streams, parties of eager gold-seekers began to make their appearance. Some left the Missouri in February and reached Bent's Fort and Denver in April. But the great rush came in May. The broad valleys of the Platte and Arkansas were filled with hurrying bands of "Pike's Peakers." Wagon trains, bands on horseback, and ragged parties afoot; they poured into the mountains in a ceaseless stream. Even the Smoky Hill and Republican routes were used by parties which attempted to cross the sandy waste east of Sand Creek, and here, old Cheyenne men have told me, the Indians found many a white man wandering about, temporarily insane from hunger and thirst. The Indians took them to their camps and fed them. They did not understand this rush of white men and thought the whites were crazy. A stage line, the Leavenworth and Pike's Peak Express, was soon opened along the Smoky Hill line and daily coaches were soon running right through the heart of the Cheyenne and Arapaho hunting grounds. During that spring and summer one hundred thousand whites are said to have crossed the plains to Denver and Pike's Peak, as all that region of eastern Colorado was then called.

Meantime the first arrivals in the mountains had found little gold and much hardship. No one was making money except the store-keepers; and now these men who had rushed into the country on the mere rumor that gold had been discovered turned around and started a new rush, this time toward home. "Pike's Peak or Bust" had been their war cry coming out, but on their return journey they altered the slogan to "Kill Byers and Oakes" (two men who had written gold-seekers' guidebooks to the Pike's Peak country, in which they had given rather rosy accounts of the new gold-diggings).[26] Sixty ragged and angry men, returning home on foot by the Platte route, are said to have turned back 50,000 men with their tale of gloom, and all these men went hurrying back down the Platte, calling for the blood of Byers and Oakes. They abandoned everything when they turned back, and the Platte road was strewn with picks and shovels, gold-washing pans, knapsacks, clothing, and provisions. Carts and wagons were left standing everywhere, and even some store-keepers, discouraged by the stories of the returning miners, dumped their stocks of goods by the roadside and turned back with empty wagons. No one knows how many set out to cross the plains that year. A hundred thousand reached the mountains, but most of them returned home in the fall and early winter.

That year my father was appointed agent for the Upper Arkansas tribes, but the great rush of men into the mountains upset everything

[26] W. N. Byers, founder of the *Rocky Mountain News*, Denver, wrote *A Hand Book to the Gold Fields of Nebraska and Kansas*, 1859; D. C. Oakes (1859) had, as pp. 19–27 in Luke Tierney, *History of the Gold Discoveries on the South Platte River*, "Smith and Oakes Guide," which may have been issued earlier as a pamphlet. Henry R. Wagner and Charles L. Camp, *The Plains and the Rockies: A Bibliography* (1937), 218–19, 237–38.—S.L.

and he gave up the agency in the fall. He sold Bent's New Fort to the War Department that year, 1859, and it was garrisoned and renamed Fort Fauntleroy, but the name was soon after changed to Fort Wise in honor of Governor Wise of Virginia. In 1861 Governor Wise joined the Confederates and the name of the post was changed again, this time to Fort Lyon, in honor of General [Nathaniel] Lyon, the first Union general killed in the war. My father moved across to the south bank of the Arkansas and built a new stockade on the west bank of Purgatoire River. Here he lived and traded with the Indians. Most of the old-timers, traders and trappers, disliked and despised the emigrants and gold hunters and would not be mixed up with them. They kept by themselves and did not seem to care anything about gold, and were the only class of men, bar army officers, who were not carried away by the gold fever. They knew every foot of the country, knew the Indians, and were seasoned men; if they had gone to hunting gold they would have had a great advantage over the greenhorns from the States, but they simply did not seem to care about it, and very few of them took to prospecting. There had been stories going around for many years about trappers and Indians who had found gold here in the Colorado foothills, but the fur men were more interested in beaver skins than in nuggets and paid little attention to these old tales.

There appeared to be little gold in Colorado, and it soon began to look as if the miners would all return home and leave the upper country to the Indians, traders, and trappers again. But during '59 several great discoveries were made: Gold Hill, Deadwood Diggings, Jackson's Bar, and, richest of all, the placers along Cherry Creek near Denver. The result of these strikes was a new rush in 1860, greater in volume even than the famous stampede of '59. The plains swarmed with hurrying bands of gold-seekers; the buffalo were frightened off, the last of the timber in the big groves along the streams was cut down, and the Indians did not know where to turn. The newcomers wished to get rid of the Indians and began to talk of putting them on reservations and letting them take their choice between farming and starving. The tribes were discontented at the invasion of their hunting grounds but were overawed by the great inrush of white men. They had never dreamed there were so many men in "the whole white tribe" as they had seen crossing the plains in the last two years. Some of the younger warriors were restless and wished to go to war on the invaders, but the chiefs and older men knew what the result of such an undertaking would be and held the hotheads in check. Then came the Civil War, and the Cheyennes and all their friends were drawn into the great struggle.

CHAPTER FIVE

CONFLICT ON THE UPPER ARKANSAS

WHILE THESE EVENTS were taking place in the Indian country, we children were living at Westport, now Kansas City. Here I went to school from 1853 until 1857, but in the latter year I was sent to St. Louis to attend the academy, and I was still there when Fort Sumter fell and the whole state of Missouri was thrown into intense excitement by the outbreak of the Civil War. The Southern sympathizers attempted to hold St. Louis for the South, but before their plans could be matured, the Union men, led by Captain [Nathaniel] Lyon and my father's friend Frank Blair, seized the city and compelled the secessionists to retire to the western part of the state. When I went home for vacation I found the whole of western Missouri arming for the South. In every little town the young men were flocking in to join the State Guard (a Confederate organization) and it did not take me long to make up my mind to enlist. I was not yet eighteen years old when I signed the roll and became a member of Colonel Green's cavalry regiment.

The Union forces soon invaded western Missouri, but we met them and defeated them at Wilson's Creek. In this first large battle of the war the Union commander, Nathaniel Lyon was killed, and his name was given to my father's fort. The fort had been named Fort Wise, in honor of the Governor of Virginia, but Governor Wise had now joined the Confederacy, and so the post was again renamed, this time Fort Lyon.

The next battle I was in was at Pea Ridge in the Ozark Hills. After that fight we were forced out of Missouri, and I then took part in [General Earl] Van Dorn's campaigns in Arkansas and Mississippi. I was at the siege of Corinth (Mississippi) in 1862, but during the retreat from that place the Union cavalry got in on our rear and succeeded in cutting off and making prisoners of several hundred of our boys. That ended my Civil War experiences. They took us to St. Louis, and there, while being marched through the streets with the other prisoners, I was lucky enough to be recognized by a young fellow who had attended the academy with me. He went straight to my brother Robert, who was in the city purchasing Indian goods, and told him that I was among the Corinth prisoners. Robert went to see some officers of the old regular army, who were old friends of the Bents, and the result was that I was released on parole that same day; but I had to give my word that I would not take any further part in the war and promise to return home with Robert. We left St. Louis a few days later, and late in the fall I found myself on the Upper Arkansas again, after nearly ten years' absence.

I found everything in the Upper Country greatly changed, since I had left in 1853. At that time there had been very few whites in all that region, and practically all of these had been engaged in the Indian trade and fur business. The country did not even have a name in those days. It was spoken of vaguely as "the Upper Country," "the Upper Arkansas," or "the mountains." Now, in 1862, it was Colorado Territory and had an organized government and some thirty thousand whites, mostly men, were within its borders. When we went to Westport in '53, we made the journey by wagon, and along the five hundred miles of trail between Bent's Fort and the Missouri frontier there was not a single house or settlement of any kind. Now there were two stage lines running up the Arkansas, stage stations, and ranches every few miles; Fort Larned (old Camp Alert) had been built near the site of the present Larned, Kansas, and my father's fort had been purchased by the War Department and garrisoned with troops. Denver was a city; Pueblo, Colorado Springs, Booneville, and a score of other towns had been founded, and hundreds of farms and ranches had been started around Denver and in the upper valleys of the Arkansas and the South Platte.

My father was now living in a stockade on the south side of the Arkansas and on the west bank of Purgatoire River, a few miles above his old fort, which was now known as Fort Lyon and was garrisoned by Colorado volunteer cavalry, the regular troops having all been ordered east soon after the outbreak of the war. My father still kept up his trade with the Indians, but the trade was now very small compared with what it had been in the forties and early fifties, when the Bent company had maintained two large posts and several smaller establishments. The business was now almost entirely confined to trade in buffalo robes, but my father also raised stock and was sometimes engaged in wagon freighting for the Indian Department. I stayed at the stockade that winter, but in spring, 1863, joined my mother's tribe, the Cheyennes. My younger half-brother, Charlie, had come up the river a year before me and had been with the tribe for some months before I joined it. From that time until today, fifty-one years, both in war and in peace, I have been with the Cheyennes.[1]

I spent the spring and summer with some of my Cheyenne relatives. We moved about from one place to another, hunting buffalo and visiting other Cheyenne and Arapaho bands. Some of the young men made up war parties and went out against the Pawnees on the lower Platte and the Utes among the mountains. In late summer the band I was with ran into a party of Delaware trappers on Solomon's Fork, in central Kansas, and right there I saw my first Indian fight. The Cheyennes killed two Delawares and captured all the party's horses and packs of beaver and otter fur. One Cheyenne, Big Head, was killed. In June the Cheyennes, Dog Soldiers, and Spotted Tail's band of Sioux met on the Republican River, and the Sioux held their sun dance. The tribes were encamped about a mile from each other in separate villages, and the Sioux invited the Cheyennes and Dog Soldiers to the dance. In this dance the young men who had pledged themselves underwent the sun-dance torture. Slits were cut in their breasts and skewers of wood were then thrust through these slits, under the muscles; long rawhide cords were then tied to the skewers

[1] The time of this portion of Bent's narrative, then, was 1914. His exchange of letters with Hyde had begun ten years earlier.—S.L.

and the other ends of the cords were attached to the center pole in the dance lodge. These young Sioux kept going around the pole, staring straight at the sun, throwing themselves backward, and jerking and pulling at the cords. They kept this up until they had pulled the wooden skewers right through the muscles of their breasts. These dancers always gave away many presents during the ceremony; usually they gave away ponies, but some of them, wishing to make a big show, gave away everything they had, and some gave their sisters away.

At this Sioux dance the Cheyennes and Dog Soldiers received many presents. The Cheyennes now made their medicine lodge and invited the Sioux, and gave them many presents. After that we all moved to Beaver Creek, and there the Dog Soldiers made medicine. These Dog Soldiers were a part of our tribe, but they did not live with the rest of the Cheyennes much. They ran with the Sioux who hunted on the Republican, and the Dog Soldiers and Sioux intermarried and camped and hunted together a great deal.[2]

As soon as the whites had secured a foothold in Colorado, in 1858 and 1859, they began to plan to oust the Indians, and one of the first things they did was to send a delegation to Washington to make the government believe that the Cheyennes and Arapahos wished to settle down on a small reservation and begin farming.[3] The Colorado men put this deal through easily enough and secured an appropriation of $35,000 to be spent in holding councils with the Upper Arkansas tribes and to induce those tribes to give up their lands. So Commissioner [A. B.] Greenwood came out to Bent's Fort to hold a council with the Cheyennes and Arapahos, but the Indians

---

[2] Compare Grinnell, *Fighting Cheyennes*, 17, 151.—S.L.

[3] Superintendent A. M. Robinson of the Indian Bureau had appointed William Bent, George's father, as Indian agent for the Indian tribes living between the Platte and the Arkansas in the summer of 1859, his appointment to which was called the Upper Arkansas Agency being confirmed April 27, 1860. Actually the plan for making the Cheyennes and Arapahos an agricultural, settled people was expressed as early as 1846 by Yellow Wolf to Lieutenant J. W. Abert. William Bent restated it in 1859. Grinnell, *Fighting Cheyennes*, 124 ff.; Berthrong, *Southern Cheyennes*, 148–49.—S.L.

had not been informed of the meeting, and so only a few Arapahos were at the fort. Greenwood then handed over the treaty to Boone, whom he appointed special agent, and then he returned east.[4] In the fall Boone brought part of the Arapahos and a few Cheyennes together at the fort, held a council and induced the chiefs to sign the treaty; but the Cheyennes would never recognize this treaty, as only a small part of the tribe was present during the council, and even the few chiefs who signed the treaty did not know what they were agreeing to. It was the old, old story of the white man with plenty of fine presents and a paper which he wished the Indians to sign. By this treaty the Cheyennes signed away most of their lands and agreed to live with the Arapahos on a small reservation on the Arkansas, below Bent's Fort. The paper set forth that the Indians were very eager to begin farming and someone had stuck in a clause in which the Indians begged the government to sell to their "friends," the whites of Colorado, all the land they desired at fifty cents an acre. This clause was struck out by the senate, but the rest of the treaty passed and became law.[5]

Three months after this treaty was signed the Civil War broke

[4] Albert G. Boone, grandson of Daniel Boone, was chosen by Commissioner Greenwood at the suggestion of William Bent, who apparently had misgivings about the treaty which he had helped to negotiate, to take Bent's place as Indian agent for the Upper Arkansas Agency. Greenwood left Bent's Fort on September 20, 1860, with the expectation that Boone would secure agreement by the absent Cheyenne and Arapaho chiefs to the tentative treaty, the talks about which had begun September 18. Grinnell, *Fighting Cheyennes*, 126; Berthrong, *Southern Cheyennes*, 148–50.—S.L.

[5] George Bent may not have been privy to certain details of the Treaty of Fort Wise, finally signed by part of the Cheyennes and Arapahos on February 18, 1861, but the man who conceived the need for a treaty was his father, who may have seen to it that Robert, his son, was provided 640 acres along the Arkansas from the restricted lands now finally proposed for the Cheyennes and Arapahos. By the treaty, the enormous domain ceded by the two tribes was to be compensated for by the government in the amount of $450,000 payable over fifteen years. In sum, the tribes were agreeing to a very small reservation, and from the small compensating payment were to acquire their own agricultural tools and equipment. Lavender, *Bent's Fort*, 341; Grinnell, *Fighting Cheyennes*, 126; Berthrong, *Southern Cheyennes*, 149–51.—S.L.

out. This prevented for the time any attempt being made to force the Indians to abandon their old hunting grounds and settle down on their new reservation. In the summer of 1861 all of the regular troops were withdrawn from the Plains; only a few caretakers were left at the posts, and the whites in Colorado soon began to feel uneasy. Rumors were started that the Indians were planning to take advantage of the absence of the troops to begin a general uprising. These tales were simply inventions. The Indians were hunting and trading, living their usual lives, and none of the Plains tribes had any intention of attacking the whites.

Another story was that the Confederates were plotting with the Indians and preparing for a combined attack on the frontier settlements and the overland roads. This rumor was about half true, as the Confederates were really planning an attack on the Arkansas River posts. In the summer of 1861, Captain Albert Pike, the author of the version of *Dixie* which was sung in the South during the war, was sent by the Richmond government to attempt to gain over the tribes in Indian Territory. Pike had been an Indian agent when the war broke out, and he was very skillful in dealing with Indians. He had no difficulty in getting four of the Five Civilized Tribes of Indian Territory to sign treaties and come over to the Confederates; and he also induced many of the smaller tribes of the territory to sign such agreements. In the midst of this work, Pike was made a brigadier general and was ordered to begin enlisting the civilized Indians for service in the Confederate Army.

Pike soon had a large force of Indians under arms, and then, in the winter of 1861–1862, he began to work on the wild tribes of the plains. He sent out Indian runners to visit the Kiowas and Comanches, and other runners up to the Arkansas to see the Cheyennes and Arapahos. His message to the Cheyennes was that the "Texans" (which is the name for all Southerners among the Plains Indians) were "very mad" and that as soon as grass was up in the spring a large force of these "Texans" would come up to the Arkansas and clean out the Union forts on that river. When the Cheyennes were given this message the chiefs came to my father and told him all about it; he advised them to have nothing to do with Pike and his "Texans" and the chiefs acted on this advice.

This plan for raiding the Arkansas River posts, and perhaps attacking Denver also, was spoiled by Pike's superiors who sent him an order, early in the spring of 1862, to march with his civilized Indians to the support of the Confederate Army, operating in the Ozark Hills. Pike arrived in time to take part in the Battle of Pea Ridge, and I saw his Indians in action on that field; but the warriors did not understand the white man's method of fighting, all standing up in a row in the open, and they had no liking for the big guns. Many of them deserted during the fight, and Pike was then ordered back to Indian Territory, to command the Confederate forces there (mostly Indians) and to oppose the Union general, J. W. Denver, the man whom Denver was named after.[6]

As soon as he had returned to the territory, Pike took up his old scheme of making a raid on the Upper Arkansas and stirring up the Plains tribes. Some wild Kiowas and Comanches visited him at Fort Cobb, Indian Territory, and he told them that they might raid the Arkansas River road if they wished. He reported to headquarters that this would keep them "amused" until he could find more useful work for them; then he set to work to organize a force with which to attack the forts on the upper river. Early in the summer he ordered Colonel John Jumper (a Seminole Indian)[7] to march his Indians north and attack Fort Larned on the Arkansas. Jumper's Indians, however, did not have much heart for this adventure, and before long most of them deserted and went home. At this time there was but a handful of Union troops at Fort Larned and one company at Fort Lyon, and both posts could have been easily taken if the Confederates had made a push at them. If Pike had had one or two good

---

[6] Battle of Pea Ridge, March 6–8, 1862, fought north of Fort Smith, was a Union victory.—S.L.

[7] The prominent western Seminole, important in the gradual removal of his tribe to Indian Territory after he and many others had preceded them. His service in Indian Territory as a Confederate officer, finally having conferred upon him the rank of lieutenant colonel, was extensive. Edwin C. McReynolds, *The Seminoles,* 277, 284, 292, 299, 312.—S.L.

regiments of white cavalry he might have made a great deal of trouble at this time. He could easily have taken the posts on the Upper Arkansas, then pushed on to the Platte and broken up the Overland Stage Line and the Overland Telegraph. He might have raided Denver and by stirring up the Indians might easily enough have cut off the government from all overland communication with Colorado, New Mexico, Utah, California, and Oregon for many months.

Pike's opportunity was now lost. In May a friendly Kiowa-Apache chief, Poor Bear, who had been approached by some of Pike's Indian emissaries, went in to Fort Larned and laid the whole business before the Union commandant. The result was that the Arkansas posts were heavily garrisoned with Colorado volunteer cavalry, and General Pike's chance to make trouble was gone forever. The only permanent result of his plotting was that the people of Colorado and Kansas were alarmed and soon became firmly convinced that all the Plains tribes were for the South and were planning a general uprising. From this time on the men of Colorado began to speak of the Cheyennes and other Indians as "Red Rebels" and to look upon them as hostile. Then in August, 1862, the Sioux of Minnesota, who had had nearly all of their lands taken away from them by the greedy settlers and several thousand of whom were actually on the verge of starvation, suddenly rose and massacred over two hundred whites, carrying off a large number of women and children into captivity. When the news of this terrible event was received, the whole frontier was thrown into a panic. The governor of Minnesota called on the War Department to send an army and exterminate all of the Sioux tribes; the governors of Dakota, Nebraska, Iowa, and Kansas all sent in appeals for more troops; and everywhere along the frontier the Indians (most of whom were quite friendly) were looked upon with suspicion and dread. Even the army officers became panicky. General Craig, commanding the troops along the Overland Stage Line, sent in a report that one thousand Sioux were on their way to attack the stage line and begin a general war along the frontier. Of course these Sioux never turned up. There was not one hostile Indian within three hundred miles of the stage road. In September, on the rumor that Indians were coming to make an attack, the whole Nebraska frontier stampeded and fled wildly toward the Missouri River, abandoning everything in their rush for safety. All this time there were only two or three hundred hostile Minnesota Sioux in the field, away up near the Canadian border, and even this small band was too hard pressed by the troops to think of making any raids. In October nearly all of them surrendered to Sibley. The frontier population, however, had become thoroughly frightened, and from this time on the people looked on all Indians with hatred and suspicion.[8]

In the summer of 1863 the Cheyenne treaty of 1860–61 bobbed up again and made more trouble. The Cheyennes still refused to recognize the treaty, as it had been signed by only a few men and without the consent of the tribe; these men had deeded away most of the tribe's lands and had consented to the cooping up of the people on a small reservation; they had not even understood what they were signing, and had been induced to put their cross-marks on the paper by bribery, by the liberal distribution of presents. The Cheyennes therefore said that the treaty was worthless; the whites, on the other hand, claimed that the paper was a "solemn obligation" and that if the Indians did not hold to the agreement it was a pretty good sign that the tribe was hostile and was plotting an uprising.

Governor Evans of Colorado, late in the summer of 1863, made up his mind to attempt once more to induce the chiefs to recognize the treaty. He sent out Little Gerry to hunt up the Cheyennes and inform them that the governor was coming out to meet them in council. Gerry was married to a Sioux woman and kept a small trading house and ranch on the South Platte, northeast of Denver. The Dog Soldier band of Cheyennes and the Brulé Sioux (Spotted Tail's tribe) traded with Gerry and liked him very much. Well, he came out and found the Cheyennes and Sioux camped on Beaver Creek, and there he told the chiefs that "a big chief from Denver" (Governor Evans)

---

[8] There was more to the Minnesota alarm over the Sioux than Bent had knowledge of. The substantial nature of conflict and its accompanying bloodshed is recounted in Robert Huhn Jones, *The Civil War in the Northwest*, 37ff.—S.L.

was coming out to meet the Indians in council. My uncle, Long Chin, was a leader among the Dog Soldiers and was present during this talk with Gerry.[9] He told me after the council that the chiefs informed Gerry that it would be impossible to meet Evans, as the Indians were already breaking up into small bands and scattering over the country for the fall buffalo hunt, to get in a supply of meat, skins for new lodge covers, and to get better grass to fatten the ponies. The Indians had come together here on the Beaver to make medicine, but they could never remain together in large villages for very long, because of the immense pony herds. The grass soon became eaten into the ground for miles on every side of the village, and the Indians then had to break up into small bands and move away to get fresh pasture. That was what the chiefs explained to Gerry, but he went back to Denver and told Governor Evans that the Cheyennes did not wish to meet him and were evidently hostile. He said they did not care about peace any longer.

Meantime the Sioux in the Black Hills region had begun to grow really hostile. The Minnesota Sioux who had massacred the whites in 1862 had now surrendered, but the Minnesota whites were very vindictive and they compelled the government to keep a strong body of troops in the field. These troops attacked the western Sioux, who had taken no part in the massacres. In this year, 1863, General Sully[10] crossed west of the Missouri, attacked the Sioux on the Little Missouri, and drove them down into the Black Hills. This attack stirred up all the western Sioux, and during the winter of 1863–64 they sent a war pipe down to the Cheyennes and other tribes who lived south of the Platte. If the Cheyennes had smoked this pipe it would have been a pledge that they intended to join the Sioux in the war against the whites; but the chiefs refused to smoke. The Arapahos also refused to have anything to do with the Sioux pipe bearers. Here the matter would have ended, but a miserable white man who had been loafing around the Arapaho camp, living on the Indians and

[9] "I think Gerry married one of my uncle Long Chin's Sioux neices, as Long Chin was always talking about Gerry."—Geo Bent adds this in a letter.—G.H.
[10] Brigadier General Alfred Sully.—S.L.

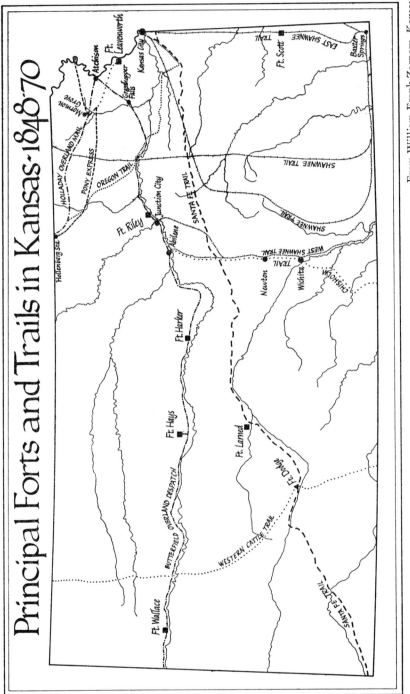

Principal Forts and Trails in Kansas·1848·70

From William Frank Zornow, *Kansas*

FORTS AND TRAILS IN KANSAS, 1848–70

keeping an Arapaho "wife," now went to Denver and told Governor Evans that he had seen the Arapahos holding secret councils and smoking the war pipe, and that all the tribes were preparing for war and intended to attack the whites as soon as grass was up in the spring. I was in the Cheyenne camps at this time and know that this white man's story was a lie from beginning to end, but Governor Evans believed him and he was made a lieutenant in one of the Colorado volunteer regiments in reward for his valuable services.

I was in the camp of the Hill Band of Cheyennes on Smoky Hill River that winter.[11] Everything was quiet, and the First Colorado Cavalry which was guarding the Upper Platte and Upper Arkansas roads had no work to do. The Cheyennes and Arapahos during the winter made up some small war parties and these went into the mountains west of Denver, hunting for the Utes. The war parties passed right through the Colorado settlements and made no trouble at any place. There was not even any talk among the young men of making raids on the whites. In March, 1864, Agent Colley[12] met part of the Cheyennes and Arapahos on the Arkansas,[13] and here the chiefs told him how the Sioux up north had sent down a war pipe, but that the Cheyennes and Arapahos had refused to smoke. The agent sent a report to Governor Evans that the Indians were all friendly and everything was quiet, but Evans had made up his mind that the tribes intended to start a war and he would not believe the agent. General Curtis,[14] commanding the department, now sent an order for the Colorado troops to march east and take part in the campaign against the Confederates. Immediately after this order to go east was received, the Colorado cavalry made an unprovoked attack on our tribe and drove the Cheyennes into war.

[11] Chief Sand Hill's band.—G.H.

[12] S. G. Colley was appointed agent for the Upper Arkansas on August 26, 1861, in succession to Albert Boone, but notice of his appointment did not reach Colorado until mid-November.—Berthrong, *Southern Cheyennes*, 156n.—S.L.

[13] Actually at Fort Larned, Kansas, on the right side of the Pawnee River, eight miles above its junction with the Arkansas. Robert W. Frazer, *Forts of the West*, 55; Berthrong, *Southern Cheyennes*, 175.—S.L.

[14] Major General Samuel R. Curtis, the victor of Pea Ridge, b. 1805, d. 1866.—S.L.

The first attack was made on a party of young Cheyennes who were going north to fight the Crows. In the summer of 1863 the Crows had killed Brave Wolf, a noted Northern Cheyenne, and during the winter the Northern Cheyennes had sent runners down to visit our camps and invite the Southern Cheyennes to join them in an attack on the Crows, to be made in the following spring. A number of young Dog Soldiers made up their minds to join this expedition, and early in April, 1864, they set out for the north. In the party were Mad Wolf, Wolf-Coming-Out, Bull-Telling-Tales, Bear Man, Little Chief, and ten other young men. The Dog Soldiers were in camp on Beaver Creek and Little Gerry (who had told Governor Evans that the Cheyennes were hostile) had been trading in the camp for robes all winter and was still there when this party of young men left the camp in April. The party had almost reached the South Platte when they found four mules straying. They took these animals with them and went on until they were near the river, then went into camp for the night. Pretty soon a white man named Ripley rode into camp and demanded the mules, claiming that they belonged to him.[15] Bull-Telling-Tales and another young man, who had found the mules, told Ripley that they had had a good deal of trouble catching and taking care of the mules and that they wished him to give them a small present for what they had done.

Ripley rode up the river to Camp Sanborn and told the officer there that some hostile Indians had run off his stock and the stock belonging to his neighbors. Next morning, April 12, the party of young Dog Soldiers crossed the South Platte just below a place known as Frémont's Orchard. They were riding slowly toward the hills north of the river when all at once a detachment of the First Colorado Cavalry, guided by Ripley, made its appearance and charged at them. No attempt was made by the officer in command to hold a parley or make any explanations: he simply led his men out and charged the Indians. Little Chief,[16] who was present, tells the story in this way:

[15] W. D. Ripley, a rancher on Bijou Creek.—S.L.

[16] Still alive 1912.—G.H. [The official white accounts of what occurred differ

"We saw fifteen or twenty soldiers riding toward us at a gallop with pistols in their hands. We all jumped on our ponies, which we were leading, and turned to face the soldiers with our bows and pistols ready. Bull-Telling-Tales and Wolf-Coming-Out still stood on the ground in front of the rest of us, holding their ponies with one hand and their weapons in their other hand. Without any talk the soldiers rode up to us and began shooting. The officer, who was in front of his men, rode straight at Bull-Telling-Tales with a pistol in his hand. Bull-Telling-Tales dropped his pony's bridle and jumped at this officer with his bow and arrows in his hands. The next time I looked in that direction the officer was lying on the ground. Bull-Telling-Tales had shot him right through the heart with an arrow. As soon as this officer fell the soldiers all stampeded. We did not chase them as we were not at war with the whites and did not wish to kill any more of them, after they had stopped trying to kill us. As the soldiers charged up Bear Man stood right in their way, and before he could move they shot him two times in the body. Mad Wolf was shot in the hip, Wolf-Coming-Out in the leg, but we did not have anyone killed. Right after the fight we had a talk and decided to go home. When we reached the village we told the chiefs what had happened to us. Next day the Dog Soldiers broke camp and moved south to the Smoky Hill, to keep out of the way of the whites."

I was in the Hill Band camp on the Smoky Hill when the Dog Soldiers arrived, and I had talks with several of the young men who had been in this Frémont's Orchard fight. Mad Wolf, who was wounded, told me that the soldiers had "acted very foolishly," charging right up and beginning to shoot without even attempting to hold a talk. I also saw the jacket, field glasses, and watch of the officer whom Bull-Telling-Tales had shot dead with an arrow.[17]

sharply from the Indian testimony. See Berthrong, *Southern Cheyennes*, 179–80; Grinnell, *Fighting Cheyennes*, 141–42.—S.L.]

[17] The official report does not mention any officer killed in this affair. But George Bent stuck to this story and gave me the account of Indians who were present in the fight to show that he was not mistaken. Since his death I had seen in Eugene Ware's book, *The Indian War of 1864*, that soon after this fight word was brought to his

Irwin and Jackman, government freighters, were wintering a herd of 175 head of oxen in Bijou Basin and on Sand Creek, about seventy-five miles southeast of Denver. There were no settlements in that region, in fact the oxen were being herded right in the edge of the Cheyenne hunting grounds, and two camps of Cheyennes were wintering not very far east of where the herders had these oxen out at grass. One day in April some Cheyennes from one of these camps were out hunting and found a number of oxen straying about among the sand hills. As they did not know to whom the animals belonged they drove them to camp, intending to keep them until someone should lay claim to them. A day or two later the herders went in to Camp Weld near Denver and reported that Indians had run off the entire herd of oxen. I never believed this story and do not believe it now. The Indians had no use for the oxen; there were plenty of buffalo on that range that winter, and the Indians never would eat "tame meat" when they could get buffalo. Besides, I have talked to many men who were in these two Cheyenne camps; all denied that the oxen were stolen, and I know they told the truth. It was not an uncommon thing for herders, who had been careless and let their herds stray off or get stampeded, to tell the boss that Indians had run off the animals, and I believe that this was what happened to Irwin's and Jackman's herd. But at Denver, as soon as the herders had given their version of the story, the troops were ordered out, to recover the stock and punish the Indians. Lieutenant George S. Eayre commanded the expedition, and he was given only one section of artillery and a single company of cavalry. The force was so small that if the Cheyennes had been really hostile and on the watch they could easily have annihilated the whole party.

Eayre's orders were to hunt up the Indians, demand the oxen, and if the Indians refused to give the animals up, attack the camp. Of

post on the Platte that Indians had had a fight with Colorado troops, and had killed a sergeant; that they had taken this sergeant's jacket and other articles to Sioux camps and exhibited them. Ware's account seems to me undoubtedly a reference to the Frémont Orchard affair, and it bears out Bent's statement, though it was a sergeant, not an officer, who was killed.—G.H.

124

course he did not carry out these orders to hold a parley first. He simply marched his outfit toward the Indian hunting grounds and attacked every camp he ran across. This was the way the Colorado troops acted in all the early fights. They seemed to be afraid that the Indians would submit to any demands they might make, so they made no demands but just marched up and opened fire.

The first Cheyenne camp that Eayre ran into was that of Crow Chief's band, seventy lodges. These people were quietly hunting on the head of the Republican Fork, east of Denver, and had no suspicion that troops were out after them. One morning a man named Antelope Skin got up very early, to go out hunting alone. He ate breakfast, mounted his horse, and rode out of camp about dawn. He went up on a hill near camp, to look for buffalo, and the first thing he saw was Lieutenant Eayre's company of cavalry coming down the creek toward the Indian camp at a gallop. This was the way Eayre carried out his order to demand the oxen from the Cheyennes and punish them if they refused to give the animals up!

Antelope Skin put his pony into a run and rushed back toward camp, hallooing "Jump on ponies! Soldiers are coming!" The Cheyennes usually let their ponies graze at large during the night, but just about daylight each morning the herds were driven in near camp. Luckily for Crow Chief's people the boys had just driven in the herds when Antelope Skin came rushing back toward the camp, shouting his warning. Hardly anyone was up yet, but at the first halloo, men, women, and children came pouring out of the lodges. They jumped on the bare backs of the ponies, sometimes two or three on one mount, and fled out of one end of the camp just as the cavalry charged into the other end. The soldiers were so close behind Antelope Skin that he had to leap off his pony as it was going at a dead run and hide among the bushes. As the cavalry rode by he shot several arrows at them.

The Cheyennes had no time to save anything, and one old woman who was so feeble that she could not ride had to be left in the camp. Her family had been carrying her around from camp to camp for several years in a travois or pole-drag. She was never heard of again, and as Lieutenant Eayre does not mention her in his report, I suppose she hid among the bushes and starved to death. Her family went back after the soldiers were gone and hunted everywhere for her, but they could not find any trace of her.

Eayre stayed in this camp three days. He found none of the "stolen" oxen, but plenty of plunder, as the Indians had not had time to take anything away with them. The troops took everything that they fancied, and at the end of three days set the camp on fire and marched out to hunt up more "hostiles." They had luck and soon struck the trail of Chief Coon's band of Cheyennes, leading toward Beaver Creek, a tributary of the Republican. As I am writing this Chief Coon's daughter is sitting in the next room with my daughter Mary. She says that she was just a small girl in 1864, but remembers this affair very clearly. Coon's people (his real name was Racoon) were on the move, but had stopped and pitched camp. Fortunately for them some young men had remained behind, and while these young warriors were following along after the rest of the camp they discovered Eayre's troops sneaking along the trail to attack the camp. The young men rode to camp at once and gave the alarm; the soldiers were still some distance off, and so the people had more time than Crow Chief's outfit had had. They packed up nearly everything, but did not have time to take the lodges down; so they hurried away leaving the empty lodges standing. When Eayre came up and charged the camp he did not find any Cheyennes to kill, and nothing worth stealing; so he ordered the camp burned and marched back to Denver. During this trip his men picked up some of the strayed oxen and took them back to prove that the Cheyennes had stolen the herd.

As I said before, I was in the camp of the Hill Band on Smoky Hill River when the Dog Soldiers came in with the story of how their young men had been attacked by the troops at Frémont's Orchard on the South Platte. Just a few days later Crow Chief's band came in and joined us, with the news that their camp had been attacked and plundered by Eayre's outfit, and soon afterward Chief Coon and his band came in with similar news. The Dog Soldier chiefs, Tall Bull, Bull Bear, and White Horse, wished to send some young

126

men out to scout and see if the soldiers were headed our way; so High-Back-Bear, Spotted Wolf, Elk River, and myself offered to go. We had not gone very far when we met Antelope Skin, the man who had given the alarm as the soldiers charged up to Crow Chief's camp; and he told us that the troops had gone back west toward Denver, so we returned to camp together.

I never could understand why the soldiers made these attacks on the Cheyennes in April, 1864. There was no reason for it. One of Colonel Chivington's political enemies once hinted that there was politics back of the whole business, and that is the only possible explanation I can see. Chivington and the clique of officers he had gathered about him were all in politics. These Colorado volunteers had just been ordered to go to Kansas, to fight the Confederates, and the attacks on the Cheyennes began immediately after this order was received. The attacks were evidently planned at headquarters, for the troops went after our people at about the same time at widely separated points. If Colonel Chivington did not wish to obey the order to go east, the easiest way out of his difficulty was to attack the Indians and stir them up. The troops would then be needed in Colorado, and the officers would have a splendid chance to make reputations as Indian fighters. On the frontier this was the shortest road to the people's hearts: give the Indians a whipping and the voters would give you any office you asked of them. The Colorado population was mostly made up of men, men of the old frontier stock who hated Indians by instinct and training. The Colorado troops included the roughest of these frontiersmen, and from Chivington down the officers thought no more of shooting an Indian than of killing a wolf. I do not think that they would have hesitated a moment at hustling the Cheyennes into a war, to win popularity and gain the hearts of the voters. Like most frontiersmen, they had a poor idea of the Indians as fighters and believed that they could knock the Cheyennes and Sioux about pretty much as they pleased. They did not dream what a hornets' nest they were stirring up.

From the first it was clear that the troops had no desire to preserve the peace, and that their only object was to push the tribes into

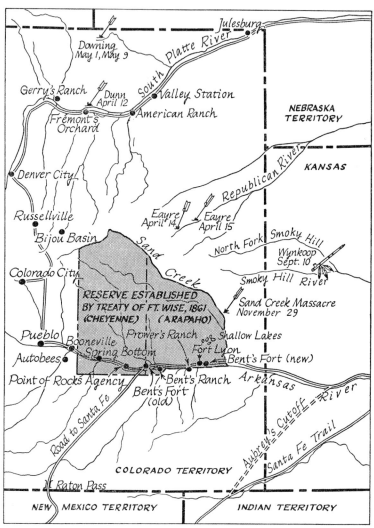

From Stan Hoig, *The Sand Creek Massacre*

BEGINNING OF THE CHEYENNE WAR OF 1864

hostility. At the very time when the soldiers were opening their attacks on our tribe, three Dog Soldiers visited Little Gerry's ranch on the South Platte and told Gerry all the news of the camps. Gerry sent word to Major Downing[18] that the Cheyennes were all quietly hunting, that there was no talk of war and that the tribe was still in the winter camps, each small band camped in its own wintering grounds. Downing sent back word for Gerry to send the three Dog Soldiers away from his ranch at once and to tell them that his troops would attack any Indians they met, whether they pretended to be friendly or not. There was a camp of friendly Sioux on the South Platte at the mouth of Beaver Creek and another camp of them farther down the river, near Valley Station. These Sioux, like our people, thought that everything was all right; then all at once they learned that small bands of soldiers were riding up and down the river, attacking every Indian they met, and the Sioux broke camp and got out of the way in a hurry.

"The Indians have a big scare," Major Downing reported, in evident delight, to Colonel Chivington; but a few days later the major was in deep gloom. Chivington had probably issued orders to take no prisoners, and Downing was himself warmly in favor of exterminating the "Red Rebels," but now the troops had taken an Indian captive and the major had to write in haste to explain why this Indian was not dead. "If I obeyed my own impulse I should kill him," he wrote headquarters, and then went on to explain that, unfortunately, the man had to be kept as a guide. The Indian was a half-Cheyenne (that is, half Cheyenne and half Sioux) and was very unwilling to guide the soldiers to the camps of his own people; so the major had him tied up and "toasted his shins over a small blaze" until he changed his mind. (These quotations are in Major Downing's own words and are taken from the official record).[19]

Setting out with this now willing guide, Downing went up to Cedar Canyon, about sixty miles north of the South Platte, and here

[18] Major Jacob Downing.—S.L.
[19] Grinnell, *Fighting Cheyennes*, 143, refers to Downing's recollections published many years later in the Denver *News*.—S.L.

a little camp of five lodges of Cheyennes was found in the canyon of Cedar Creek. These people did not know that there had been any trouble between the Indians and the troops, and most of the men were out hunting when the troops appeared. The soldiers came on the little camp by surprise and the major "ordered the men to commence killing them," as he cheerfully remarks in his account of the business. The troops were between the Cheyennes and the pony herd, and the Cheyennes, seeing no chance for flight, took refuge among the rocks. Here the few warriors who were present stood off the troops while the women and children sought safety. Lame Shawnee, a brave man, shot a trooper with an arrow and knocked him off his horse. He then ran out in the open, killed the soldier with his war club, and taking the man's carbine reached the rocks again without being hit. The fight went on for some time, and at last, seeing that the Indians could not be reached without losing many of his men, Downing drew off, taking the captured pony herd with him. These animals he divided "among the boys," as he says himself. This practice was forbidden by law but was always winked at by the Colorado volunteer officers, who were more interested in maintaining their popularity among the men than in carrying out the War Department's regulations. The dividing up of the ponies and other property captured from the Indians "among the boys" was one of the things that made Indian fighting very popular with the Colorado troops. The War Department sometimes attempted to compel the officers to account for the ponies and other property captured but could never secure any satisfactory reply.[20]

Lieutenant Eayre returned to Denver after his first raid on the Cheyennes, but only to secure fresh teams and more wagons. He seized a number of wagons on the streets, loaded them with supplies, and set out again, intending to hunt the Cheyennes from camp to

[20] The number of lodges in this camp, placed at five by George Bent, was asserted by Downing in 1865 Congressional hearings to have been fifteen large and several smaller ones. Bent casts doubt on Downing's report of killing twenty-five Cheyennes and wounding more than thirty. Stan Hoig, *The Sand Creek Massacre*, 45–46; Grinnell, *Fighting Cheyennes*, 143–44; Berthrong, *Southern Cheyennes*, 183–84. —S.L.

camp and force them to fight. By this time we had a camp collected on the Smoky Hill River: Dog Soldiers, Hill Band, Crow Chief's Band and Chief Coon's outfit, and farther east, on the Solomon, was a big village of Brulé Sioux. Eayre missed both these camps and passed between them without being seen by the Indians, which was fortunate for him, for by this time the Cheyennes were very angry and the Dog Soldiers, in particular, were eager for a fight. Having passed these camps without seeing them, Eayre turned southeast, intending to scout as far as the Arkansas in his hunt for the Indians. Large bodies of Cheyennes and Arapahos had been in camp all winter on Ash Creek, near Fort Larned, but in the middle of May they began to grow uneasy. They had been going in to the fort to trade and visit all winter, and were quite friendly, but in May they received news, by runner, of the attacks that had recently been made on the Cheyennes on the South Platte and the head of the Republican. This made the Cheyennes near Larned very anxious, and on May 15 they broke camp and started north to join the rest of the tribe.

They made one day's march and went into camp. Next morning at dawn the hunters went out, but before long some of them returned to camp and went straight to the crier's lodge. The crier now came out and went through the camp, calling out that the hunters had seen soldiers with cannon approaching the camp. He then went toward the chiefs' lodges, haranguing the chiefs and telling them to mount and go out to greet the soldiers and find out what they wanted. Black Kettle and Lean Bear were the head chiefs in this camp; both of them had been to Washington about a year before, and they were both great friends of the whites. Lean Bear got mounted first, and escorted by a large number of Indians he set out to meet the soldiers. The party rode up on a hill near camp and saw Eayre's troops advancing, the cavalry in front "in four bunches" or companies, the guns in the center, guarded by more cavalry, and the wagons in the rear. The outfit was strung out over a great deal of ground. Wolf Chief was present and recently told me the story:

"As soon as they saw us, the soldiers ran together and made a line. Lean Bear, a big friend of the whites, told us warriors to stay where we were, so as not to frighten the soldiers, while he rode forward to shake hands with the officer and show his papers. He wore on his breast a medal President Lincoln had given him. When the chief was within only twenty or thirty yards of the line, the officer called out in a very loud voice and the soldiers all opened fire on Lean Bear and the rest of us. Lean Bear fell off his horse right in front of the troops and Star, another Cheyenne, also fell off his horse. The soldiers then rode forward and shot Lean Bear and Star again as they lay helpless on the ground. I was off with a party of young men to one side. There was a company of soldiers in front of us, but they were all shooting at Lean Bear and the other Cheyennes who were near him. They paid no attention to us until we began firing on them with bows and guns. They were so close that we shot several of them with arrows. Two of them fell backward off their horses. By this time there was a great deal of confusion. More Cheyennes kept coming up in small parties, and the soldiers were bunching up and seemed badly frightened. They were shooting at us with the cannon. The grapeshot struck the ground around us, but the aim was bad. Black Kettle, the other friendly chief, rode up soon after the fight began. He kept riding up and down among the warriors, calling out, 'Stop the fighting! Do not make war!' But it was a long time before the warriors would listen to him. We were very mad. At last he stopped the fight. The soldiers ran off. We captured fifteen cavalry horses, with saddles, bridles, and saddle bags on them. Several soldiers were killed: Lean Bear, Star, and one more Cheyenne were killed, and many were wounded."[21]

If Black Kettle had not stopped the fight, not one of Eayre's men would have escaped. Eayre had only about one hundred men, and there were five or six hundred Cheyenne warriors on the ground. As it was, Black Kettle could not control all of the warriors, and a

---

[21] This celebrated fight occurred May 16, 1864. The subsequent white testimony agrees generally with Bent's and Wolf Chief's accounts, that Eayre and his men started the fighting, operating under orders from Chivington to "kill all Indians he came across." Grinnell, *Fighting Cheyennes*, 145–46; Berthrong, *Southern Cheyennes*, 185–87.—S.L.

large body of angry Cheyennes pursued the retreating troops for many miles. Eayre finally got his command to Fort Larned, where the men arrived nearly exhausted and still pretty badly frightened. The Cheyennes were so stirred up over the killing of Lean Bear that the chiefs could not control the young warriors. They made up a war party and raided the stage road all the way from Fort Larned to near Fort Riley, killing several white men and plundering all the stations. At Walnut Creek Station there was a white man who had a Cheyenne wife. When the warriors got there they took the Cheyenne girl away from her husband and warned him to get out in a hurry. They told him that the soldiers had just murdered their chief and that they were going to clean out the road and kill every white man they could find.

We broke up our big camp on the Smoky Hill about May 15 and started south. A couple of days later runners came in with news of the killing of Lean Bear, and a short time afterward the Cheyennes who had had this fight with Eayre's troops moved in and joined our camp. In spite of the attacks that had been made on them by the soldiers, most of the Cheyennes were still opposed to going to war. The Dog Soldiers were for war. The rest of the tribe decided to move south and get out of the way. We moved camp south to Ash Creek, near Fort Larned, and then crossed south of the Arkansas and went to Salt Plain on Bluff Creek, where the Kiowas, Comanches, Prairie Apaches, and Arapahoes were encamped. Our tribe camped near the Apaches and Comanches; the Kiowas and Arapahos were some distance from us, near Fort Larned. My father was down there attempting to prevent war. I met him in the Arapaho camp and had a talk with him, and then he took the chiefs of all the tribes and went in to Fort Larned to have a talk with the commandant, but without any result. This officer was drunk pretty often and permitted his soldiers to get drunk; they all treated the Indians badly when they visited the fort, and the chiefs who came in with my father to have a friendly talk were insulted by the commandant and went away angry. Dr. Elliot Coues, the famous scientist, came up the Arkansas at this time (the end of May, 1864) and he writes in his journal:

133

"At 2 P.M. we brought up at Fort Larned—mean place, built of adobe and logs, with a drunken officer in command; everybody half drunk already; and all were whole-drunk by bed-time."[22] This was the class of volunteer officers who had been assigned the duty of holding the frontier posts and keeping the Indians quiet.

When my father took the chiefs to the fort, Lieutenant Eayre was still there with his men, afraid to venture out with his little command after the fright the Cheyennes had given him when they ran his whole outfit into the fort after the killing of Lean Bear. Someone, possibly Eayre, now advised the drunken commandant to be more careful about permitting the Indians to visit the fort, so the sentries were ordered to keep the Indians at a safe distance. Of course the Indians were not told of this new rule, and as they had been visiting the post whenever they pleased during the winter and spring, they had no idea that it was now dangerous for them to come.

A few days after this new regulation had been put into force, Setangya (Sitting Bear)[23] a famous Kiowa chief came in on a visit accompanied by his cousin and a few other Kiowas. As they drew near the fort a sentry shouted something at them, but they did not understand English and continued to come on. The soldier then threw up his gun and pointed it at Setangya, but the Kiowa chief, who was very quick, drew his bow before the soldier could fire and sent two arrows at the man, shooting him through the body. In a moment the post was in an uproar, the soldiers running and shouting and the Kiowa women and children getting out of the way without losing any time. The Kiowas were camped very close to the fort and had been there all winter. When the sentry was shot, the women and children ran for safety, the soldiers rushed to get their arms,

[22] Author of *Birds of the Colorado Valley* (1878), among other eminent ornithological works; editor of Alexander Henry, *The Manuscript Journals of Alexander Henry and David Thompson . . . 1799–1814* (1897); and *The Expeditions of Zebulon Montgomery Pike* (1895), among others.—S.L.

[23] Variously spelled: by W. S. Nye (*Carbine and Lance*) and his Kiowa informant, the late George Hunt, as Set-ankeah; by Frederick Webb Hodge (*Handbook of American Indians North of Mexico*) as Setangya; and commonly by white contemporaries as Satank.—S.L.

and a party of young Kiowas, taking advantage of the confusion, made a dash for the post herd and ran it off. They secured every hoof belonging to the fort and 240 of Eayre's horses and mules. The Kiowas then made off, leaving their lodges standing near the fort.[24]

The Kiowa leaders did not wish to go to war and were willing to compel the young men to return the herd; so the next day Nawat (Left Hand), an Arapaho chief who was always very friendly with the whites, rode up to the fort with some other Arapahos to have a talk and arrange for the return of the stolen herd. Nawat carried a white flag as he rode forward, but the commandant was now convinced that all the tribes were hostile, so he ordered the soldiers to fire on the Arapahos, and Nawat and his friends had a very narrow escape from being shot. When the Arapaho warriors learned that their chief had been fired on, they went up the river and made a raid at Point-of-Rocks, below Fort Lyon, running off a large herd there. When the ranchmen farther up the river heard of this, they abandoned their places and fled up the river, some of them going clear into the mountains. But the Arapahos made only this one raid and then returned to camp.

I now went up to visit my father at his stockade at the mouth of Purgatoire River, and the Kiowas, Comanches, Apaches, Cheyennes, and Arapahos settled down in their camps south of the Arkansas, to make medicine and hold dances. This was the condition of affairs at the end of May. The Cheyennes had been attacked several times by the troops without any provocation given, and the Kiowas and Arapahos had become embroiled with the commandant at Fort Larned; the Indians had made some counterattacks while they were angry, but they had now quieted down and, with the exception of the Dog Soldiers, were in favor of keeping the peace. The situation, however, was very serious, for the volunteer officers had no intention of giving up their policy of harassing the tribes. A regular-army officer

[24] Satanta, or Set-t'aiñ-te (White Bear) sent word back to Fort Larned a few days later, saying that he hoped the quartermaster would provide better horses in the future, as the last lot he had received were inferior in quality. Nye, *Carbine and Lance*, 35.—S.L.

who was making an inspection on the Plains at this time reported to General Curtis that if the Indians were not treated better a general war in the plains would be the result. "I think that if great caution is not exercised on our part there will be a bloody war. It should be our policy to try to conciliate them, guard our mails and trains well to prevent theft, and stop these scouting parties that are roaming over the country, who do not know one tribe from another, and who will kill anything in the shape of an Indian. It will require but a few more murders on the part of our troops to unite all these warlike tribes." This was Major McKenney's view of the situation, and Major Wallen,[25] another regular officer who happened to be crossing the plains at that time, held the same opinions and telegraphed to army headquarters at Washington that if the volunteers were not stopped at once the government would be saddled with an expensive Indian war. But no prompt action was taken and in a few weeks more the Indian war was in full swing all along the Platte and Arkansas.

[25] Major T. I. McKenny, inspector general of the Department of Kansas; Major Henry D. Wallen, commanding officer at Fort Sumner.—S.L.

CHAPTER SIX

DISASTER AT SAND CREEK

As I said at the end of the last chapter, I met my father in the Arapaho camp near Fort Larned in May and went home with him to the stockade at the mouth of Purgatoire River. Here I remained for some weeks, and during this time Black Kettle with a large Cheyenne village was camped with the Kiowas and Comanches on Medicine Lodge Creek, at the Salt Plain, and here all the Indians held sun dances and made medicine. These people were quiet and did not make any raids, but between the Arkansas and Platte were some large camps of Cheyennes and Sioux, and during May small parties from these camps made several raids on the Platte. Part of the Sioux (Spotted Tail's Brulés and the Ogalala bands under Bad Wound and Whistler) did not wish to get mixed up in the war, so in May they moved up near Camp Cottonwood, a large fort with log buildings and stables on the site of Fort McPherson, and here the Sioux had a council with [Brigadier] General [Robert Byington] Mitchell who commanded the troops in Nebraska. Mitchell seems to have suspected the Sioux were not friendly; at any rate he ordered them to keep out of the Platte Valley, but Spotted Tail replied that the valley belonged to his people and that they would come there to trade and to cross north and south of the river whenever they liked. Old Spot, as the soldiers called the chief, and the General both lost their tempers, but after a while the General cooled down and told the Sioux to come back for another talk in fifty days.

This second visit of the Sioux to Cottonwood in June nearly brought on a fight. Mitchell brought with him to the conference a

137

company of eighty Pawnees who had recently been recruited and armed and uniformed as cavalry. These Pawnees were bitter enemies of the Sioux, the two tribes having been at war constantly since they first met, about the year 1750. At this time, 1863–64, a number of ministers and other good men in the East had formed the Peace Party, the members of which kept after President Lincoln all the time, urging him to make peace with all the Indian tribes and to put a stop to intertribal wars. The result of this was that General Mitchell was ordered to attempt to make peace between the Sioux and Pawnees during this council at Cottonwood in June; but when the Indians were brought together the Sioux at once prepared for a fight and began riding up and down very fast and yelling. The Pawnees in their cavalry uniforms also began to get ready, and before long the two bodies of Indians were making for each other, yelling taunts and making insulting gestures. General Mitchell came up with a brass cannon and a body of the Seventh Iowa Cavalry just in time to get in between the two tribes and prevent their attacking each other. He then made a speech and opened the peace talk; but it was of no use. The Sioux and Pawnees sat and glared at each other and no one said a word for a long time; then a Sioux got up and said that he did not mind making peace with the Pawnees, who were a poor lot any way you looked at them, and always easily whipped by the Sioux, and then he gave a long catalogue of the number of Pawnees who had been killed by his ancestors. After this Sioux sat down, the Sioux and Pawnees sat and glared at each other for ten minutes. Then a big Pawnee stood up and replied to the Sioux speaker, saying he did not mind making peace with the Sioux, who were a very poor lot, etc., etc., and before long the Indians were yelling taunts at each other again, and in order to avoid a fight the General had to break up the council and send the Sioux away in a hurry. Thus ended the new Peace Party's first attempt to interfere in Indian affairs.

These Sioux, after leaving Camp Cottonwood, crossed north of the Platte, as the chiefs wished to keep out of the way of the hostiles who were south of the river. Later on some young men from these friendly Sioux camps began raiding, and the chiefs "soldiered" them, cutting up their lodges and shooting their horses and dogs, but as much as the chiefs wished to keep all their people at peace they could not prevent some of their young men from joining in the raids. Dur-the early summer the Northern Cheyennes and Red Cloud's Ogalalas were hunting on Powder River north of the Platte, and they also kept peace.

In May there were only a few raids on the Platte, and these were made by the Dog Soldier Cheyennes and some Sioux who were their friends. Toward the end of June or early in July Black Kettle's village left the Kiowas and Comanches on Medicine Lodge Creek and started north. These Cheyennes did not make any raids on the Arkansas road but crossed the Arkansas River quietly and started north toward the Smoky Hill. Soon after they crossed the Arkansas some runners from a Sioux camp met this Cheyenne village with news that raiding had begun on the Platte. The Cheyennes at once made up several war parties and these started north and made raids on the South Platte. The war was now started in earnest.

I do not intend to give a detailed account of the raids that were made during July and August. They were terrible affairs, but after all, the Indians were wild people in those days; they had been at-tacked again and again by the troops without any cause, and they were retaliating in the only way they knew how. The big raids were mostly on the Platte. The Arkansas River road was not of much importance, as there was little travel there, the stage line was unim-portant and there were very few stations and ranches. In the Platte Valley, on the other hand, was the great Overland Stage Line with stations every ten or twelve miles and daily coaches carrying the mail passing both ways, east and west. This was also the great emigrant and wagon-freighting route, and you could often see wagon trains extending unbroken for miles along the valley, the huge freight wagons with their white canvas tops looking from the distance like fleets of ships at sea. Into the great valley the war parties of Chey-ennes and Sioux broke, attacking and burning the ranches and stage stations, chasing the coaches, running off stock, and forcing the freighters to corral their trains and fight.

Early in the summer I left my father's stockade and started north to rejoin the Indians. I found them on the Solomon Fork in central Kansas—Cheyennes, Dog Soldiers, Sioux and Arapahos, all camped close together. It was one of the largest villages I ever saw and the camps were full of plunder. War parties were setting out every day, and other parties coming in loaded with plunder and driving captured herds of horses and mules. As I rode past each village I saw war dances going on in each one, and every lodge was full of plunder taken from captured freight wagons and emigrant trains. I saw fine silks heaped up on the ground in the lodges, and cloaks, groceries of all kinds, ladies' fine bonnets, canned goods, bolts of fine cloth, sides of bacon, bags of coffee and sugar, boxes of crackers, boots and shoes— everything you could think of, all piled up together. Old Indian men were going around wearing ladies' bonnets and veils, and most of the young warriors were wearing fine silk shirts of bright colors and stripes which the women had made out of captured bolts of silk. I had a half-dozen of these silk shirts made for me and wore them for some time.[1]

One day in this big village there were only about fifty of us men, all the others being out with war parties or out hunting. That day we heard firing in the distance, and as we ran out of the lodges we saw Hawk, a Cheyenne man still living, coming off a hill, running his horse as fast as it could go and signaling with his hands that soldiers were running some Indian hunters toward camp. When we saw this, we all ran for the pony herd. At such times it was the custom for a man to mount the first horse he came to, no matter who it belonged to. The owner could not prevent this, but the rule was that if a man riding a borrowed pony captured anything in a fight the captured articles became the property of the owner of the horse which the warrior was riding.

About fifty of us ran for the herd. We took only bridles and saddle blankets and our arms. I put my blanket and bridle on the first good

---

[1] Hyde, *Spotted Tail's Folk*, 89ff., gives a synthesis of these events, but written long after the present book was constructed from the Bent letters. Hyde, *Red Cloud's Folk*, 108ff., is also pertinent.—S.L.

horse I came to and the others did the same, then we mounted and charged up the hill and over it, and there we saw a number of Sioux hunters running in every direction, with cavalrymen scattered out in little bunches chasing the Sioux. A large body of hunters had also heard the firing and as we charged over the hill these hunters swarmed up along the divide. The troops saw us coming and the hunters riding up from every direction; then the officer called his men together and started back the way he had come, riding very fast. We went after them in a large body. Two soldiers fell behind, their horses giving out. They pounded the animals with their guns to make them go faster, but the Indians caught them and killed them both. The rest of the soldiers were well mounted and got away, but we chased them many miles. This body of troops was commanded by Captain Mussey.[2] He came from Ft. Kearny on the Platte to scout toward the Republican. On that river he came upon a party of twenty Sioux who were out hunting and chased them, overtaking one Sioux man and killing him; then coming close to the village and seeing the Indians collecting in force, the Captain turned and rode away as fast as he could. He says in his own report that the Indians chased him twenty miles.

Meantime the raiding along the Platte Road went on, and on August 15 they blocked the road completely, breaking up the stage line and forcing the freighters to corral their wagons and remain where they were, waiting for "better weather." For six weeks the Indians held the road, raiding the ranches and stage stations and attacking the corraled wagon trains. Traffic was completely suspended, and letters for all western points had to be sent by sea to Panama, across the Isthmus, thence by sea to San Francisco, and there by coach to Salt Lake City, Denver, and other points which could not be reached from the east. As the wagon trains hauling food supplies were unable to move, food soon grew scarce in the mountains. In Denver flour went up from $9 to $16 per 100 pounds, and then jumped to $25; all other food rose to equally high prices, and swarms

[2] In Grinnell, *Fighting Cheyennes*, 156, identified simply by rank and surname. —S.L.

141

of "grasshoppers" (red-legged locusts) attacked and devoured the crops around Denver, and the people of Colorado were soon facing a famine.

On the Platte, General Mitchell was operating with a strong force of cavalry, but he could not reach the Indians, who were raiding in small parties and were careful to keep out of reach of the troops. As soon as the troops were out of sight the Indians rode down from the bluffs where they had been watching and again began raiding the stage stations and attacking wagon trains. Mitchell marched down toward the Republican, hoping to locate our village and attack it, but he found no Indians on the Republican and so returned to the Platte, where he strung the troops out along the road and did his best to guard it. Not until September was the road reopened for travel, the first east-bound coach leaving Latham, north of Denver, on Sept. 4.

Late in August, while the young men were still busy raiding on the Platte, the chiefs called a council. Most of the older men in our camp were in favor of peace, although the young men were still raiding, and at this council it was decided to write to the authorities, ask for peace, and offer to give up the white prisoners who had been captured during the raids. My brother-in-law, Edmond Guerrier, and I were present at this council, and at the chiefs' dictation we wrote two letters, one to the officer commanding at Fort Lyon and the other to Mr. Colley, agent for the Cheyennes and Arapahos. These letters were both alike and were signed "Black Kettle and other chiefs." One Eye took my letter, which was addressed to the agent, and Eagle Head took Guerrier's copy, which was addressed to the commandant, and they both went to Fort Lyon. There they were arrested by Major Edward W. Wynkoop, the commandant, who put them in the guardhouse and treated them very harshly.

The Major, wishing to recover the white captives mentioned in the letters, left the fort [Sept. 15?] with a body of cavalry and came out to our camp. When the troops appeared, part of the Dog Soldiers and Sioux, who were still for war, got ready for a fight and rode out to meet the troops with bows strung and arrows in their hands, but Black Kettle and some of the chiefs interfered, and requesting Major

Wynkoop to move his troops off to a little distance, they prevented a fight. Black Kettle and the other friendly chiefs had purchased the white captives from their owners, and they now gave these captives up and went in with Major Wynkoop to Fort Lyon. They wanted to surrender to him, so the major took Black Kettle, White Antelope, Bull Bear, One Eye, and Left Hand with him to Denver and there they had a talk with Governor [John] Evans of Colorado. Evans told the chiefs that they were in the hands of the military and that he could not make peace with them. He advised them to make peace with the military, but Colonel Chivington of the First Colorado Cavalry would not tell the chiefs whether they could have peace or not. They then returned with Wynkoop to Fort Lyon and he told them to bring their people in near the fort and they would be treated as prisoners.

While the chiefs were at Denver we broke camp and started to move down Hackberry Creek, a tributary of Walnut Creek, toward the Arkansas. At that time General Blunt[3] had a strong body of cavalry on the Arkansas, and just as we started for that river he started north toward the Smoky Hill, to scout the country in search of Indians. The people in our village belonged to the bands of Black Kettle, White Antelope and War Bonnet, Cheyennes; Little Raven, Spotted Wolf, and Storm, Arapahos. On the evening of September 23 we went into camp near the head of Ash Creek, which runs into Pawnee Fork.[4] We had heard from the Sioux that a big party of Pawnees were going to hunt buffalo on the Republican, and that evening six of our young men, including Wolf Robe and White Leaf, made up a war party to go and attack the Pawnees.

These six young men left our village and went off alone. About ten miles from the village they went into camp for the night. Just at dawn in the morning one of the party got up and went to see if the horses were picketted on good grass, and the first thing he saw was a body of soldiers coming up. These men were General Blunt's advance

---

3 Major General James G. Blunt, commanding the Military District of the Upper Arkansas. Berthrong, *The Southern Cheyennes*, 198.—S.L.

4 Hyde's longhand note inserted in text reads, "The fight was on the 24th."—S.L.

guard under the command of Major [Scott J.] Anthony. As these troops came charging up, the young Indian who had seen them gave the alarm and the other five Indians jumped for their arms and then ran toward their horses. The pony belonging to White Leaf, the leader of the war party, broke loose, leaving him afoot; the other five young men threw themselves upon their horses and started toward the big Indian village, White Leaf running after them.

In advance of the soldiers were a number of Delaware scouts, dressed as cavalrymen, but it was easy to tell them from the soldiers by their dark faces and long hair. Soldiers and Delawares were firing rapidly at the six Indians as they retreated as fast as they could toward our big village.

In our camp the firing soon gave warning that a fight was taking place, and the warriors, arming themselves quickly, caught their horses and rode out of camp. These went riding across the prairie in two's and three's and small parties, and before long they came in sight of the six young Indians and the soldiers and Delawares strung out behind them in pursuit. White Leaf, on foot, was being chased by two cavalrymen and was fighting them off bravely as he ran. Three young men named Spotted Horse, Big Bear, and Little Bear, charged on these two cavalrymen and killed them both.

By this time the Cheyenne and Arapaho warriors, coming up in small bands, had gathered in force, and they now got around Anthony and his men, surrounded them and began circling about them, firing as they rode. When Major Anthony saw the Indians coming he had taken the advice of his Delawares and retreated away from Ash Creek to a small hill. This was what saved his party. The Indians charged and circled all around this hill, firing on the soldiers. White Horse, an Arapaho, charged right in among the troops. We saw him shot and fall from his horse and the Delawares ride forward and kill him and take his scalp.

Early this morning, before the fight with Anthony started, about fifty Cheyennes and a few Arapahos left our village with Chief Standing-in-Water, Cheyenne, and rode on ahead toward Fort Larned. These people met General Blunt's column coming up Pawnee Fork and the chief rode forward and shook hands with General Blunt; then the Indians turned around and rode alongside of the soldiers back up the creek. As the Indians and soldiers marched up the creek, talking together quite friendly, they suddenly came in sight of Major Anthony's men on the hill with the Indians all about him, circling and charging. When they saw this, the Indians with Blunt knew there would be trouble, so they made a break for the creek and got behind the high bank. General Blunt halted his men and did not seem to know what to do. They did not fire on the Indians as they made for the creek, but just sat in their saddles watching the fight away off on the hill.

Blunt halted only a minute or two, then he advanced at a rapid rate toward the hill where we had Anthony corralled. We saw him coming and knew that he had too many soldiers for us to fight, so we drew off as he advanced. He followed us for some distance, then gave it up and went into camp. Next day he followed our trail nearly as far north as the Smoky Hill, but his horses were played out, so he had to give up the pursuit.

This was how we failed to go down near Fort Larned and go into winter camp near that post. If Anthony and Blunt had let the Indians alone there would have been no trouble, as the people wanted peace. In this fight we lost only one man, White Horse, Arapaho, killed and scalped by Anthony's scouts. These Delaware scouts found a poor Mexican buffalo hunter on the prairie and took him to camp and the guard shot him. They seem to have thought this Mexican was me; at any rate it was reported by the troops that they had killed me during the fight.[5] I did not even know that there had been a fight until the little war party I was with rejoined the main camp on the Smoky Hill. We had left camp the night before Blunt made

[5] Wolf Robe in his statement says the Blunt fight was after the chiefs got back from Denver. The official reports say the council with the chiefs in Denver was on September 26 and Blunt's fight was on September 25, so Black Kettle and the other chiefs could not have been with the Cheyennes when Blunt came up. Wolf Robe says the chiefs were given a lot of rations and annuities and these goods were brought to camp just before the Indians started down Pawnee Fork.—G.H.

his appearance and had gone north toward the Republican, hunting for Pawnees; but we had failed to find any of that tribe.

When the Cheyennes and Arapahos fled north to get away from Blunt, they hardly knew which way to turn next; but they had not been on the Smoky Hill long before Black Kettle and the other chiefs rode into camp, having just returned from Denver, where they had talked briefly with Governor Evans, who put the negotiations in the hands of Colonel Chivington, as has been said. The chiefs remained puzzled by what Chivington had said and could not make out clearly what his intentions were. The truth probably was that he had already laid his plans for the attack on our camp, which he carried out with such terrible effect a few weeks later; so in his talk he said nothing to alarm the chiefs or to disturb their belief that peace was soon to be concluded. He was careful, however, to make no promises. The chiefs now thought that the question of peace had been put in the hands of the higher authorities and that they would receive a good answer in a few weeks.[6] Major Wynkoop had reassured the chiefs, telling them that it was all right and that they might bring their bands in near the fort and camp there until an answer to their peace proposals was received. So now we broke up our camp on the Smoky Hill and moved down to Sand Creek, about forty miles northeast of Fort Lyon. From this new camp the Indians went in and visited Major Wynkoop, and the people at the fort seemed so friendly that after a short time the Arapahos left us and moved right down to the fort, where they went into camp and received regular rations.

A rumor now reached General Blunt's headquarters that Major Wynkoop had been holding unauthorized peace talks with the Indians and issuing rations to the "hostiles," so he was immediately removed from command and Major Anthony was sent up the river to take charge at Fort Lyon. When Anthony arrived he found the Arapahos camped at the fort and the Cheyennes from Sand Creek visiting the post almost daily. All the Indians had the idea firmly

[6] The peace talks spoken of by George Bent as taking place in Denver were actually held at Fort Weld near Denver on September 28, 1864. Berthrong, *Southern Cheyennes*, 210.—S.L.

fixed in their minds that they were here under protection and that peace was soon to be concluded. Anthony soon found his new command a difficult one. He did not like Indians and was only too eager to treat them as hostiles and order them to leave the vicinity of the fort; but when he arrived he found the Indians exchanging friendly visits with the garrison and behaving so well that he could find no excuse for sending them away. His first act, therefore, was to disobey his orders, permit the Indians to remain, and continue to issue rations to the Arapahos; but he soon grew uneasy as to what headquarters might think of his action, and, calling the Arapaho leaders to the fort, he gruffly ordered them to move their camp down the Arkansas and supply themselves with food by hunting. The Arapahos were alarmed at the major's new manner and lost no time in breaking up their camp near the fort. On their way down the river they sent a runner up to our camp on Sand Creek with word that "the little red-eyed chief" (Major Anthony, who was suffering from inflammation of the eyes) did not seem very friendly, and that the Cheyennes had better look out. The Arapahos were very anxious for peace, but they felt instinctively that something was wrong, and after their hunt they did not return to Fort Lyon. Part of them came up and joined us on Sand Creek, but most of them moved far south of the Arkansas and camped there all winter, out of the way of the troops.

Shortly after the Arapahos moved away from the fort, fifty or sixty Cheyennes from our camp went in with Black Kettle and the other chiefs to have a talk with the new commandant. Anthony met them in my father's old stone fort, which was now a part of Fort Lyon, and when the chiefs asked him about peace, he told them that he had no authority to deal with them but that they might remain in this camp on Sand Creek until he heard from his superiors. What he told them convinced the Cheyenne more than ever that peace was sure to be made, sooner or later. In a report made after our camp had been attacked and nearly wiped out, Major Anthony says that in this talk with the Cheyenne chiefs he attempted to lull any suspicions they might have as to his intentions, and to induce them to remain encamped on Sand Creek until he could secure reinforcements which would enable him to attack their camp. In order to deceive the Cheyennes still further as to his intentions, the Major permitted John Smith to leave the fort and come to our camp to trade. He also gave his soldiers leave to visit our camp and remain with us for several days at a time. One of the soldiers was in our camp the day the attack was made, and he was almost killed by the troops as he ran from the camp toward the advancing lines of cavalry.

And now, out of a blue sky, the great blow was struck. Colonel Chivington had been planning this attack for weeks. He and his troops were soon to be mustered out of service. The colonel and most of his officers were in politics, and their idea seems to have been to win the hearts of the voters by striking one terrible blow at the "Red Rebels" before they were mustered out of service. The plan was kept carefully secret. Most of Chivington's own officers, and the general commanding the department, were kept in the dark, and pains were taken to prevent news of the movement reaching Fort Lyon. Chivington did not trust Major Anthony and the troops at this post. He suspected them of favoring the Cheyennes and was afraid that they might warn the Indians of the coming attack. All travel down the Arkansas was stopped, so that no word of the movement might reach Fort Lyon, and when the blow fell Major Anthony was taken as completely by surprise as the Indians themselves.

Chivington began gathering his troops about November 20.[7] Most of his force was made up of the Third Colorado Cavalry (one hundred-days-men) who were not real soldiers at all. This regiment had been hastily recruited from among the worst class of frontier whites—toughs, gamblers, and "bad-men" from Denver and the mining camps, rough miners, "bull-whackers," and so on. The men were not disciplined at all, their officers had been selected by the vote of the men and had no real control over the men. The men were not even

---

[7]Actually, the plans for the attack on the Cheyennes must have taken shape early in November, 1864. But Chivington took command of the Third Colorado Cavalry and three companies of the Colorado First, after Colonel George L. Shoup had concentrated the troops at Camp Fillmore on the Arkansas River, on November 23. Hoig, Sand Creek Massacre, 136; Berthrong, Southern Cheyennes, 216.—S.L.

in uniform, and they were alike only in one thing: they were all eager to kill Indians. This force marched from Bijou Basin and reached Booneville, a little settlement on the Arkansas above Fort Lyon, on November 24. At this point Colonel Chivington stopped all travel down the river, to prevent word of his march reaching Fort Lyon. He even stopped the mail. From Booneville the troops marched down the river to my father's stockade at the mouth of Purgatoire River. The column surprised the place and a line of guards was thrown around the stockade at once, to prevent anyone leaving to warn the Indians. Chivington forced my elder brother Robert to act as guide, threatening to have him shot if he refused to serve.[8]

On the morning of November 28, to the surprise of everyone in the post, Chivington suddenly appeared before Fort Lyon and at once surrounded the place with a line of sentries who had orders to permit no one to pass out. Colonel Chivington then went into the fort and told Major Anthony that he intended to attack Black Kettle's camp on Sand Creek. The major made strong objections, not because the camp was a friendly one but because he did not think Chivington's force was strong enough to follow up the first attack. He said that an attack on our camp would simply stir up the Indians again, and that there was not a large enough force of troops in Colorado to deal with a new outbreak of raiding. Chivington, however, was grimly determined to carry out his plan, and after a long angry argument, Major Anthony was compelled to give in and consent to join the expedition with part of his garrison force. That evening the troops, nearly one thousand strong, all volunteers and all mounted, left Fort Lyon and guided by my brother Robert marched all night, reaching the vicinity of our camp about dawn next day.[9]

In our camp on Sand Creek there were about one hundred lodges of Cheyennes and ten lodges of Arapahos, under Chief Left Hand.

[8] Jim Beckwourth, the mountain man, was also taken as a guide, but old Jim gave up shortly to the intense cold prevailing at that season.—S.L.

[9] Whatever was said between Anthony and Chivington, it remains that Anthony added 125 men from the garrison to the Chivington force and wrote on November 28, 1864, that "I believe the Indians will be properly punished." Berthrong, *Southern Cheyennes*, 216.—S.L.

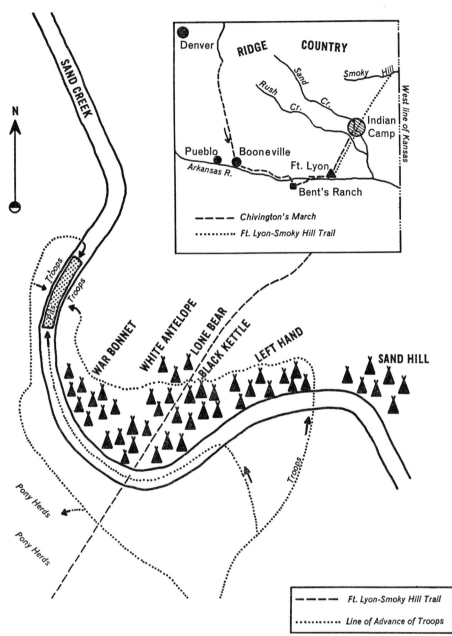

From George Bird Grinnell, *The Fighting Cheyennes*

THE CHEYENNE CAMP AT SAND CREEK

These people were the most friendly ones in the two tribes and had camped here on Sand Creek with the understanding that they were under the protection of the garrison at Fort Lyon and that they were to remain quiet in this camp until word could be received from headquarters in Kansas as to whether peace was to be concluded or not. Sand Creek heads in the ridge country to the southeast of Denver and flows in a great half-circle toward the east and then toward the south, entering the Arkansas River some miles below Fort Lyon and near the west line of Kansas. This stream was usually dry, except after heavy rains, but in a few places there was running water in the creek all the year round. Our camp was near one of these places where there was running water, about forty miles northeast of Fort Lyon. A lodge trail ran from near Fort Lyon in a northeasterly direction to the head of the Smoky Hill, and we were encamped where this trail crossed Sand Creek. This place was well known to all the Cheyennes and Arapahos and they had used it as a camping ground for many years. There were several chiefs in our camp, and instead of being all camped together in one large village, each band was camped by itself with its lodges grouped together and separated by a little open space from the camps of the other bands. The accompanying map will show the positions of the camps, the creek, trail, etc. This map was carefully made with the aid of several old Cheyennes who were in the camps at the time of the massacre. [Bent's map has evidently been lost, for it does not appear in either the Denver Public Library manuscript or Hyde's original working copy. Grinnell's related map in *The Fighting Cheyennes*, here reproduced, may owe something to Bent's sketch.—S.L.]

At dawn on the morning of November 29 I was still in bed when I heard shouts and the noise of people running about the camp. I jumped up and ran out of my lodge. From down the creek a large body of troops was advancing at a rapid trot, some to the east of the camps, and others on the opposite side of the creek, to the west. More soldiers could be seen making for the Indian pony herds to the south of the camps; in the camps themselves all was confusion and noise—men, women, and children rushing out of the lodges partly dressed;

women and children screaming at sight of the troops; men running back into the lodges for their arms, other men, already armed, or with lassos and bridles in their hands, running for the herds to attempt to get some of the ponies before the troops could reach the animals and drive them off. I looked toward the chief's lodge and saw that Black Kettle had a large American flag tied to the end of a long lodgepole and was standing in front of his lodge, holding the pole, with the flag fluttering in the grey light of the winter dawn. I heard him call to the people not to be afraid, that the soldiers would not hurt them; then the troops opened fire from two sides of the camps.

The Indians all began running, but they did not seem to know what to do or where to turn. The women and children were screaming and wailing, the men running to the lodges for their arms and shouting advice and directions to one another. I ran to my lodge and got my weapons, then rushed out and joined a passing group of middle-aged Cheyenne men. They ran toward the west, away from the creek, making for the sand hills. There we made a stand, but troops came up on the west side of the creek and opened a hot fire on us; so after a short time we broke and ran back toward the creek, jumping into the dry bed of the stream, above the camps. Hardly had we reached this shelter under the high bank of the creek when a company of cavalry rode up on the opposite bank and opened fire on us. We ran up the creek with the cavalry following us, one company on each bank, keeping right after us and firing all the time. Many of the people had preceded us up the creek, and the dry bed of the stream was now a terrible sight: men, women, and children lying thickly scattered on the sand, some dead and the rest too badly wounded to move. We ran about two miles up the creek, I think, and then came to a place where the banks were very high and steep. Here a large body of Indians had stopped under the shelter of the banks, and the older men and the women had dug holes or pits under the banks, in which the people were now hiding. Just as our party reached this point I was struck in the hip by a bullet and knocked down; but I managed to tumble into one of the holes and lay there among the warriors, women, and children. Here the troops kept us besieged until darkness came on. They had us surrounded and were firing in on us from both banks and from the bed of the creek above and below us; but we were pretty well sheltered in our holes and although the fire was very heavy few of us were hit.

When the fight opened, my friend Little Bear was in the thick of it. He tells the story in this way: "I got up before daylight to go out to where my brother-in-law Tomahawk had left our pony herd the evening before. He told me where he had left the ponies and said he did not think they would stray far from that place. As soon as I was dressed I went out of the lodge and crossed the creek; but as I was going up on the hill I saw Kingfisher running back toward the camp. He shouted to me that white men were driving off the herds. I looked toward the Fort Lyon Trail and saw a long line of little black objects to the south, moving toward the camp across the bare brown plain. There was some snow on the ground, but only in the hollows. I ran back to the camp as fast as I could, but soldiers had already come up on the other side of the creek and were firing in among the lodges. As I came into camp the people were running up the creek. As I passed Black Kettle's lodge I saw that he had a flag tied to the end of the pole and was standing there holding the pole. I ran to our lodge to get my bow, quiver, shield, and war bonnet. My father, Bear Tongue, had just recently given me these things. I was very young then and had just become a warrior.

"By this time the soldiers were shooting into the camp from two sides, and as I put on my war bonnet and took up my shield and weapons, the bullets were hitting the lodge cover with heavy thumps like big hailstones. When I went out again I ran behind the lodges, so that the troops could not get good shots at me. I jumped over the bank into the creek bed and found Big Head, Crow Neck, Cut-Lip-Bear, and Smoke standing there under the high bank. I joined these young men. The people were all running up the creek; the soldiers sat on their horses, lined up on both banks and firing into the camps, but they soon saw that the lodges were now nearly empty, so they began to advance up the creek, firing on the fleeing people. Our party was at the west end of the camps, not one hundred yards from the lodges. At this point the creek made a bend, coming from the north and turning toward the southeast just at the upper end of the village. As the soldiers began to advance, we ran across to the west side of the creek to get under another high bank over there, but just as we reached this bank another body of cavalry came up and opened fire on us. We hardly knew what way to turn, but Big Head and the rest soon decided to go on. They ran on toward the west, but passing over a hill they ran into another body of troops just beyond and were surrounded and all killed.

"After leaving the others, I started to run up the creek bed in the direction taken by most of the fleeing people, but I had not gone far when a party of about twenty cavalrymen got into the dry bed of the stream behind me. They chased me up the creek for about two miles, very close behind me and firing on me all the time. Nearly all the feathers were shot out of my war bonnet, and some balls passed through my shield; but I was not touched. I passed many women and children, dead and dying, lying in the creek bed. The soldiers had not scalped them yet, as they were busy chasing those that were yet alive. After the fight I came back down the creek and saw these dead bodies all cut up, and even the wounded scalped and slashed. I saw one old woman wandering about; her whole scalp had been taken off and the blood was running down into her eyes so that she could not see where to go.

"I ran up the creek about two miles and came to the place where a large party of the people had taken refuge in holes dug in the sand up against the sides of the high banks. I stayed here until the soldiers withdrew. They were on both banks, firing down on us, but not many of us were killed. All who failed to reach these pits in the sand were shot down."

When the soldiers first appeared, Black Kettle and White Antelope, who had both been to Washington in 1863 and were firm friends of the whites, would not believe that an attack was about to be made on the camps. These two chiefs stood in front of their lodges and called to their people not to be afraid and not to run away; but while they were still trying to quiet the frightened women and children, the soldiers opened fire on the camps. Black Kettle still stood in front of his lodge, holding the lodgepole with the big American flag tied to its top. White Antelope, when he saw the soldiers shooting into the lodges, made up his mind not to live any longer. He had been telling the Cheyennes for months that the whites were good people and that peace was going to be made; he had induced many people to come to this camp, telling them that the camp was under the protection of Fort Lyon and that no harm could come to them; and now he saw the soldiers shooting the people, and he did not wish to live any longer. He stood in front of his lodge with his arms folded across his breast, singing the death-song:

> "Nothing lives long,
> "Only the earth and the mountains."

while everyone was fleeing from the camp. At length the soldiers shot him and he fell dead in front of his lodge. Black Kettle stood in his camp until nearly everyone had gone, then took his wife and started up the creek after the rest of the people. Soldiers kept firing at them, and after a while Black Kettle's wife fell. He turned and looked at her, but she seemed to be dead; so he left her and ran on up the creek until he came to the place where the people were hiding in the pits. After the soldiers had withdrawn about dark, the chief went back down the creek to find the body of his wife, but he found her still alive, although wounded in many places. He took her on his back and carried her up the creek to where the rest of us were waiting. Her story was that after she had fallen and her husband had left her, soldiers rode up and shot her several times as she lay helpless on the sand. At the peace council in 1865 her story was told to the peace commissioners and they counted her wounds, nine in all, I believe.

Most of us who were hiding in the pits had been wounded before we could reach this shelter; and there we lay all that bitter cold day from early in the morning until almost dark, with the soldiers all around us, keeping up a heavy fire most of the time. If they had been real soldiers they would have come in and finished it; but they were nothing but a mob, and anxious as they were to kill they did not dare to come in close. They finally withdrew, about 5 o'clock, and went back to spend the night in the Indian camp. As they retired down the creek they killed all the wounded they could find and scalped and mutilated the dead bodies which lay strewn all along the two miles of dry creek bed. Even this butchers' work did not satisfy them, and when they reached the Indian camp they shot Jack Smith and wished to shoot my younger brother Charlie. These two young men (they were half Cheyenne and half white) had remained in the camp when the Indians fled and had later surrendered to some soldiers they knew. Old John Smith was trading in our camp and remained with his son when the Indians fled. When the whites came back to camp after dark, an officer came and told old John that some of the Denver roughs (one-hundred-day-volunteers) were talking of shooting his son Jack. Smith induced some officers of the Fort Lyon garrison who were his friends to go to Colonel Chivington and ask him to save Jack, but Chivington in the morning had given orders to take no prisoners, so when these officers came in and asked him to prevent the shooting of young Smith, he told them roughly that he had given his orders and had nothing further to say. Old John was sitting in his lodge, waiting for the return of the officers, when shots rang out close by. Then men came into the lodge and told him that his son was dead. The Denver men then wished to shoot my brother also, but Charlie had fallen into the hands of some New Mexican scouts belonging to the Fort Lyon garrison; men who knew all of us Bent boys and who had known our father for years; so when the Denver crowd wished to take Charlie out and shoot him as they had just shot young Jack Smith, the New Mexican men ordered them off and threatened to shoot any of them who attempted to touch Charlie.

After the troops withdrew to the Indian camp, we lay in our pits for some time, suspecting that the whites might come back; but they did not return, and at last we crawled out of the holes, stiff and sore, with the blood frozen on our wounded and half-naked bodies. Slowly and painfully we retreated up the creek, men, women, and children dragging themselves along, the women and children wailing and crying, but not too loudly, for they feared the return of the whites. After a long time we met Indians with horses. These men had gone out before dawn to see that the herds had not strayed, and reaching the herds just before the troops came up, they succeeded in getting away with some of the animals before the soldiers surrounded the rest of the herds. On seeing the soldiers coming, these Indians had thrown themselves upon the first ponies they could catch and had then rounded up as many more as they could and driven them up the creek. They went away up the creek and waited until the firing stopped after dark, then came cautiously back to see what they could learn, and this was how they happened to find us. They helped the wounded upon the ponies. One of my cousins was with them and gave me a pony to ride, but my hip was so stiff and sore that I could not mount and had to be lifted on the animal's back. After meeting these young men with the horses, our party went on up the creek a few miles farther, moving very slowly, and then, as the wounded and the women and children could go no farther, we all bivouacked on the open plain for the night.

That was the worst night I ever went through. There we were on that bleak, frozen plain, without any shelter whatever and not a stick of wood to build a fire with. Most of us were wounded and half naked; even those who had had time to dress when the attack came, had lost their buffalo robes and blankets during the fight. The men and women who were not wounded worked all through the night, trying to keep the children and the wounded from freezing to death. They gathered grass by the handful, feeding little fires around which the wounded and the children lay; they stripped off their own blankets and clothes to keep us warm, and some of the wounded who could not be provided with other covering were buried under piles of grass which their friends gathered, a handful at a time, and heaped up over them. That night will never be forgotten as long as any of us who went through it are alive. It was bitter cold, the wind had a full sweep over the ground on which we lay, and in spite of everything that was done, no one could keep warm. All through the night the Indians kept hallooing to attract the attention of those who had escaped from the village to the open plain and were wandering about in the dark, lost and freezing. Many who had lost wives, husbands, children, or friends, went back down the creek and crept over the battleground among the naked and mutilated bodies of the dead. Few were found alive, for the soldiers had done their work thoroughly; but now and then during that endless night some man or woman would stagger in among us, carrying some wounded person on their back.

At last we could stand the cold no longer, and although it was still pitch-dark and long before dawn, we left that place and started east, toward the headwaters of the Smoky Hill, where we knew Indians were encamped. It was fifty miles to the nearest of these camps, and we could go but slowly, most of the people, and even many of the wounded, being still on foot. Then we had to dread the pursuit which would probably begin as soon as the coming of day made it possible for the troops to follow our trail, and we knew that if the troops overtook us on the open plain, barely a handful of us could hope to escape. But luckily for us a few of the men who had escaped on their horses at the beginning of the attack had made straight for the nearest camps on the Smoky Hill, and riding all day they had reached these camps about dark with the news that our camp had been surprised by a thousand white men.[10] Large numbers of men had at once set out from these camps on the Smoky Hill, bringing led ponies with them loaded with blankets, buffalo robes, and food; and soon after day broke these people began to join us in little groups and parties. Before long we were all mounted, clothed, and fed, and then we moved at a better pace and with revived hope; but it was late in the day when we reached the first camp on the Smoky. As we rode into that camp there was a terrible scene. Everyone was crying, even the warriors and the women and children screaming and wailing. Nearly everyone present had lost some relations or friends, and many of them in their

[10] The strength of Chivington's command was between 675 and 700 men. U.S. Congress, Senate, "Sand Creek Massacre," *Report of the Secretary of War, Sen. Exec. Doc. 26*, 39 Cong., 2 sess., 1867, p. 47.—S.L.

grief were gashing themselves with their knives until the blood flowed in streams.

This Sand Creek Massacre was the worst blow ever struck at any tribe in the whole plains region, and this blow fell upon friendly Indians. The hostiles were camped on the Smoky Hill and Republican, far away from the troops, and our camp would never have been where it was if the chiefs and people had not been assured that peace would probably be made soon and that in the meantime they need fear no attack. From a third to a half of these friendly Indians were butchered in the attack, and of those who escaped very few were without wounds.[11] The women and children were by far the heaviest sufferers. As I have said, the camp was divided up into several groups of lodges, each band camped with its own chief. The people in each camp all belonged to the same clan. Of these clans, Black Kettle's (the Wutapiu Clan) was the heaviest loser. Very few men of this clan escaped. Chief Sand Hill's band (the Heviqsnipahis Clan) had few killed; this band was camped farther down the creek than any of the others and most of the people escaped before the soldiers could reach their camp. Yellow Wolf's band (Hevhaitaniu Clan) lost half its people in killed, including the old chief, Yellow Wolf, who was then eighty-five years old, and his brother Big Man. War Bonnet's band (Oivimana Clan) lost half its people. The Ridge Men, Chief White Antelope (Hisiometanio or Ridge Men Clan) lost very heavily also. Chief One Eye was killed together with many of his band, and the Suhtai Clan lost a few people, but not very many. The Masikota Clan and the Dog Soldiers, together with some other small Cheyenne bands, were not present. Left Hand was also with us, with

[11] On the day of the massacre, Chivington reported to Major General S. R. Curtis that his command had killed "chiefs Black Kettle, White Antelope, and Little Robe, and between four and five hundred other Indians," with losses of "nine killed and thirty-eight wounded." Chivington to Curtis, November 29, 1864. *O. R.* I, Vol. 41, Pt. 1, 948, as cited in Berthrong, *Southern Cheyennes.* Edmond Guerrier, who was with the Cheyennes, gave a figure of 148, and George Bent much later placed the killed at 137. Black Kettle, mistakenly identified among the bodies of nine chiefs killed, survived, as George Bent here indicates. John Smith was the one who supplied Chivington data on the chiefs. Grinnell, *Fighting Cheyennes*, 173. —S.L.

MAP I. AFTER SAND CREEK

George E. Hyde's Sketch Map, Lacking Bent Notes or Changes

This is an old work map that I sent to Bent a couple of times but he was too inert to mark it—just wrote a letter and left the map for me to mark. Bent sometimes marked maps very nicely and occasionally branched out and made quite good maps all on his own; at other times he didn't even mark the maps sent to him. This map marked with trail in red [here printed in black] shows the movements after Sand Creek. I had suspected for a long time that there must have been a camp north of Cherry Creek at the time of the Julesburg raid, because the distance from Cherry Creek to the South Platte was too great. Bent now told me of the new camp near White Butte and that fits the case. Besides, it is well known that the Cheyennes usually camped near White Butte when moving through this district. I have no map that shows this region properly. From Indian information, there should be here White Butte, a very conspicuous landmark; Summit Springs near or at the Butte, and a creek, White Butte Creek, flowing eastward.—G.H.

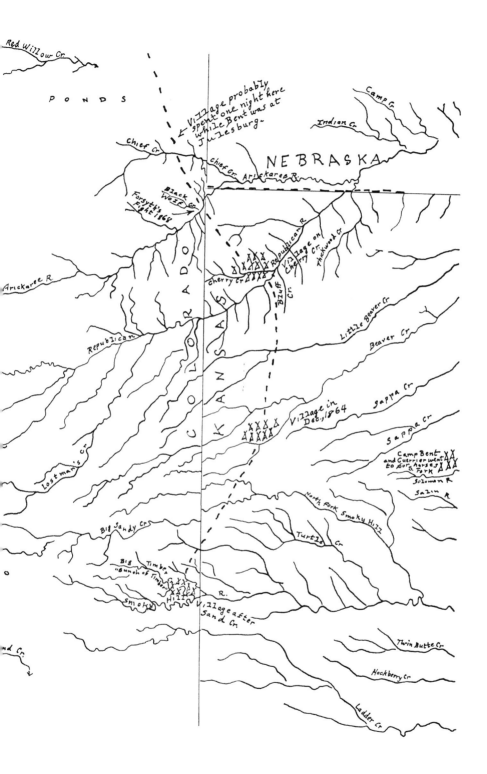

ten lodges of Arapahos—say fifty or sixty people; and of these only four or five escaped with their lives.

Besides killing all these people, the troops captured our village with everything it contained, and the pony herds, between six and seven hundred animals. Having "cleaned out" the Cheyennes so successfully, Colonel Chivington wished to move at once on the Arapahos and massacre them, but his troops were engaged in plundering the captured lodges and squabbling over the division of the pony herds, and they could not be induced to move. Of the one thousand men present, the few who belonged to the First Colorado Cavalry were disciplined troops who had seen real service; the rest—the one-hundred-days-men—remained in the Cheyenne camp two or three days, then marched down to the Arkansas to butcher the Arapahos; but the Arapahos had long since smelled danger and were now safely encamped near the Kiowas and Comanches, far south of the river.

Disappointed in his hope of winning another "victory," Colonel Chivington now turned back up the Arkansas. Major Anthony with the detachment of First Colorado Cavalry went to Fort Lyon, while Chivington and Shoup (colonel of the one-hundred-days-rabble) went on up to Denver. At Denver the men were received as heroes and the town went wild over the great "victory" over Black Kettle's "hostiles." One evening at a Denver theater a band of these heroes stepped upon the stage during an intermission and exhibited fully a hundred Cheyenne scalps, mostly those of women and children, while the audience cheered and the orchestra rendered patriotic airs. A few of the men had still more ghastly souvenirs: tobacco bags made of pieces of skin cut from the bodies of dead Cheyenne women. The wagons of the command had come back to Denver loaded down with fine buckskin clothing, buffalo robes, blankets, etc., taken from the plundered camp, and most of the men had received at least one of the captured ponies. The War Department later made a determined attempt to recover these animals, but only about one hundred broken-down ponies were turned in. The rest, five or six hundred head, had "disappeared."

Chivington's superiors were at first deceived as to the character of the Sand Creek affair. They believed that the troops had surprised a hostile camp and had won a notable victory over the Indians; but the details of the massacre could not long be kept from leaking out, and before long the whole terrible story was known: the fact that the Indians had been camped on Sand Creek under a promise of protection and that they were eagerly waiting for word that peace had been granted them when they were attacked; the story of the wholesale butchery of women and children, and the scalping and mutilating of the dead. When these details became known, an order was issued to try Colonel Chivington by court-martial, but in the meantime he had been mustered out of service and was now safely beyond the reach of any military court. Colonel Shoup and his one-hundred-days-men always stood up stoutly for Chivington; even those who admitted that the Indians "might have been friendly" and that hundreds of women and children had been scalped and mutilated would not admit that Chivington and his troops had done anything wrong. As for Colonel Shoup, he was long a favorite on the frontier; he later became U.S. Senator.

CHAPTER SEVEN

THE GREAT RAIDS

THE CHEYENNE CAMP we went to after the Sand Creek fight was on the head of the Smoky Hill at a place called Bunch Timbers.[1] For a while the Indians were pretty mad at Black Kettle, as they thought he was to blame for getting them to camp on Sand Creek and telling them peace was going to be made, but they soon saw that the chief was not to blame as he had really believed his camp was under the protection of Fort Lyon and that peace would soon be concluded.

We remained in this camp some days, then moved across to the Solomon,[2] where the Sioux were encamped, and here my brother-in-law Edmond Guerrier and I secured horses from friends and we then set out, taking a young Cheyenne with us, for the Arkansas River. Before we left this camp I asked Grey Beard, a Cheyenne chief, where the camp would be moved to next, and he told me to Cherry Creek, a branch of the Republican.[3]

[1] George Bent's writing, "Bunch of Timbers."—G.H.

The location of this camp appears on George Hyde's accompanying sketch map. It was approximately twenty miles west of Fort Wallace, on the South Fork of the Smoky Hill River, just east of the present Colorado-Kansas line. This map, "Great Raids, January-February, 1865," is in conflict with Map 1, which places this site inside the Colorado line.—S.L.

[2] This site is shown on Map 1 sketched by George Hyde. The sketch places it much too far south of its location on the Solomon River in northwestern Kansas. —S.L.

[3] The Cheyennes had shortly before sent war pipes to all of the Brulé Sioux and Arapaho camps on the Solomon. The Northern Cheyennes had come south, hoping to visit their kinsmen of the Southern Cheyennes, and they too smoked the war pipes. Hyde, *Spotted Tail's Folk*, 93.—S.L.

We went slowly, as I was wounded in the hip and could not ride very well, but at length we arrived near Fort Lyon and there we went up on a hill and from there we saw the fort and my father's ranch on the south side of the river; also some soldiers' tents below the ranch, and the sight of these tents discouraged Guerrier. He said he was going right down there and give himself up; that he was tired of the whole business and did not care much what the soldiers did to him. We talked this over a while, and then Guerrier rode down and gave himself up. He was not treated badly, but Major Anthony tried to get information from him about the position of our camps and our plans. Ed. told him about some of the camps but did not give him any information that was of value, and he did not say anything about my being near the fort.

I went to my father's ranch with the young Indian who had come along with us, and we stayed at the ranch about five days, resting up until my wound was better. It was sometime in December when we set out for the camp, and we took with us my step-mother and two women who had been captured at Sand Creek and turned over by the soldiers to my father. We travelled four days and then found the camp on Cherry Creek, a small stream that flows into the South Fork of the Republican in the present Cheyenne County, Kansas. This place is in the extreme northwestern corner of Kansas, right on the Colorado line and not ten miles south of the Nebraska line.[4] Here the Cheyennes were all encamped, and with them were Spotted Tail's and Pawnee Killer's Sioux bands and a camp of eighty lodges of Northern Arapahos. These Arapahos lived up north and they had come down in the fall to visit their kinsmen, the Southern Arapahos. They crossed south of the Platte and joined Pawnee Killer and Spotted Tail on the Republican, and here they learned that the Southern Arapahos were south of the Arkansas with the Kiowas and Comanches. So the Northern Arapahos stayed with the Sioux, intending to return north in the spring of 1865.

---

[4] See George Hyde's Map 1. He however places this site "on Cherry Creek, a branch of the Arikaree Fork of the Republican River" in his *Spotted Tail's Folk* (93).—S.L.

MAP 2. BENT TRACES THE MOVEMENT NORTHWARD

Work map, sent to Bent twice. The first time he returned unmarked; the second time with camps and trails in pencil. He marked: 1. Camp after Sand Creek, on the head of Smoky Hill. 2. Camp on Cherry Creek, tributary of South Fork of the Republican. He connects these camps with a trail in pencil and continues this trail on northwest to the camp I had marked in ink on the north bank South Platte just west of Moore's Creek. Bent told me in a letter there was another camp near White Butte somewhere north of Cherry Creek and south of the Platte, and that they found the village at this camp when they returned from the Julesburg raid. They left this camp near White Butte and moved up to the South Platte. He told me he could not mark the White Butte camp because *this map is not right*. He thinks the White Butte camp was due south of old Julesburg. Is it possible that the three buttes shown are the White Butte?—George E. Hyde.

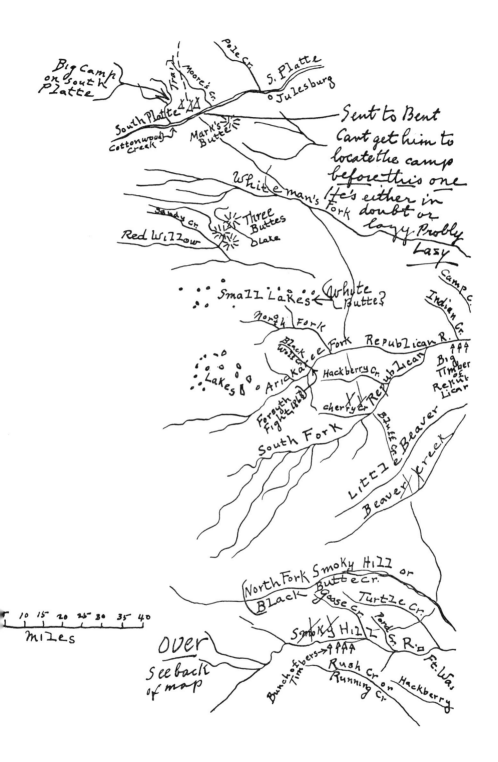

After Sand Creek, in the camp on the head of the Smoky Hill, while the Indians were all mourning for the dead, they made up their minds to send around a war pipe and attack the whites at once. This was an uncommon thing, to begin a war in the dead of winter, but the Cheyennes were very mad and would not wait. The pipe was first taken to the Sioux on Solomon Fork, and it was with this party of the Cheyenne that Guerrier and I went to the Sioux camp. The Sioux smoked the war pipe first, then the Northern Arapahos smoked, and after that the Indians—Cheyennes, including the Dog Soldiers, Spotted Tail's Sioux, Pawnee Killer's Sioux, and the Northern Arapahos—all moved over and camped on Cherry Creek, and here I found them when I got back from my father's ranch.

About New Year's Day, January 1, 1865, all the chiefs assembled in council and decided to attack Julesburg, on the South Platte, in the northeast corner of Colorado, two hundred miles from Denver. The criers rode through the camps announcing the chiefs' decision, and all the warriors began to get ready. We set out about one thousand strong,[5] and a number of women came with us with extra ponies, to bring back the plunder we would take from the Julesburg store. We marched in regular order, the soldier societies seeing to it that no one slipped off to go on ahead and do something that might warn the soldiers and put them on their guard. The chiefs led the column and the Sioux chiefs were ahead of all the others because the Sioux had smoked the war pipe first and must be given first place. This was the custom, that when a war pipe was sent around, to ask aid in making war, the tribe that smoked first, thus promising their aid, was the tribe that was given the lead in all moves. The chiefs who smoked the pipe first had to be treated with respect, and so they were given the lead in all movements.

Old Julesburg, also called Upper Ford or Upper California Crossing, was on the south side of the South Platte one mile east of the

---

[5] The assembled lodges of Spotted Tail's Brulés, Pawnee Killer's Oglala's, and the Southern Cheyennes and Northern Arapahos probably numbered between eight hundred and nine hundred lodges, hence George Bent's estimate of one thousand warriors is not excessive. Hyde. *Red Cloud's Folk*, 109.—S.L.

mouth of Lodgepole Creek, and two hundred miles east of Denver. In the '50's a large part of the emigration to California and Oregon forded the Platte at this place, and there was here a ranch and store. When the Overland Stage began running up the Platte a stage station was established at Julesburg and here the coaches forded the South Platte and struck northwest toward the North Platte, up the North Platte to Fort Laramie, and so on west; but in 1863 the road up the North Platte was abandoned by the stage company because of danger from Indians, and in January, 1865, the coaches leaving Julesburg ran on up the South Platte to Junction House, thence to Denver, crossing the Platte at Denver on a bridge, and running thence on west.

Julesburg stood some distance from the river bank, out in the level sandy valley, which at this point was several miles broad, closed in on the north and south by low sand hills and bluffs. The river here is about two thousand feet wide, dotted with small islands covered with bushes and other vegetation. The banks are low and there is very little water in the river, often less than a foot, and in the highest stages of the river about three to four feet. In '65 there was not a stick of timber in the Platte Valley at this point, and all wood had to be hauled sixty to seventy miles, from Cottonwood Canyon on the lower river.

In 1865 Julesburg was an important place on the stage line; here the company had a large station house or "home station," with an eating house, a big stable, blacksmith and repair shop, granary and storehouses, and a big corral enclosed by a high wall built of sod. Besides the stage company's property, there was a large store selling all kinds of goods to travelers and emigrant trains, and the Overland Telegraph Company also had an office at this point. Altogether, Julesburg Stage Station was quite a large place for the Plains in those days, and there were at the place forty or fifty men—station hands, stock tenders, drivers, telegraph operators, etc. The buildings here were partly built of cottonwood logs and partly of sod.

Since the beginning of the Indians' troubles in the summer of 1864 a small post had been established just above Julesburg Station, opposite the mouth of Lodgepole Creek. This little post was called Camp Rankin, but later a large post was built here and renamed Fort Sedgwick. The first post was a small affair of logs and sod buildings surrounded by a sod wall and stockade. At the time of our raid the place was garrisoned by one company of the Seventh Iowa Cavalry.

On the night of January 6–7, the Indians pitched camp among the sand hills south of Julesburg and every precaution was taken to prevent any warning of our presence reaching the whites at Julesburg. Indian soldiers guarded the camp all night to prevent any young men from slipping away to make an independent attack which would give the troops warning that Indians were in the neighborhood. Long before daylight, everyone was astir and preparations were being made for the events of the day—the women cooking, the men putting on their war dresses, examining their arms, and painting themselves. My brother Charlie and I both dressed ourselves as warriors, as we intended to take part in the fight. The Indian soldiers guarded the camp to prevent anyone going off alone. This was always necessary, as you could not depend on the young men, who were so eager to secure plunder that they would slip off alone and spoil the chiefs' plans by making an attack before the time appointed.

Our main body, a thousand strong, was among the sand-hill bluffs that edge the Platte Valley, about three or four miles south of the river. To the north of us lay the flat, bare valley, and up near the river bank the little buildings of Julesburg, with the stockade of Camp Rankin some distance farther up the Platte. The chiefs had their plans all made. They knew if the little company of soldiers at Camp Rankin saw all our party they would not come outside their stockade, and Indians did not like to attack troops behind breastworks, as there was little to be gained in that kind of fighting. The chiefs therefore planned to draw the soldiers out in the open.

As I have said, the valley was flat and bare with no cover, not even a bush except on the little islands in the river; but there was a small ravine or gully running from the sand hills where we were hiding out across the flats to the river. This gully started in the hills about south of Camp Rankin and ran northeast, passing east of the stage station. Big Crow, chief of the Crooked Lance Society, was the man who had been selected to draw the soldiers out. He picked ten men, including Starving Elk and Old Crow, who are still living and I saw both of them only a few days ago and they told me the story over again. Big Crow took his men down this little ravine and got quite close to the station and Camp Rankin without showing his men. Just at daylight, these ten Indians saw some soldiers walking about outside the stockade at Camp Rankin, so Big Crow and his men rode up out of the gully and charged on these men, shooting and yelling. We who were behind the hills, and some of our men who had been put out to watch heard the shooting, and then a bugle blew, and a few minutes later about sixty soldiers led by an officer rode out of the stockade and charged Big Crow's party.

As soon as this was seen, the criers rode about camp calling to the warriors to mount and get ready. Big Crow and his men retreated back toward the hills, drawing the soldiers after them. They came nearer and nearer and it began to look like they would ride right into the trap; but, as usual, the Indians would not wait for the right moment, and some young men suddenly broke away from the main force and charged out of the hills toward the soldiers. The rest of the thousand followed them, as there was no longer any use in hiding. The soldiers saw us swarming out of the hills and halted at once, then began to retreat. Big Crow and his party at once turned and charged the soldiers, being joined by a large body of Indians coming up from the rear. They struck the soldiers about three hundred yards from the stockade. In this first charge Starving Elk killed the bugler, and several other soldiers fell. Some of the cavalrymen jumped off their horses to fight on foot, but were at once surrounded; the rest of the troops, with their officer, galloped away toward the stockade, the Indians attacking them on all sides but not in strong enough force to cut them off and surround them. Some of these soldiers were killed, and all those who had dismounted also fell. Lieutenant [E. F.] Ware, who belonged to the Camp Rankin garrison but was not present during the fight, says that fourteen men were killed, one sergeant, three corporals, and ten privates. He gives all the names. I thought that more than this number fell, and a few weeks later, when the Indians attacked Julesburg again, I counted eighteen fresh graves near the stockade, but all these men may not have been killed in that fight.[6]

As the Indians charged out from among the hills, the west-bound coach came up the road. The driver saw the Indians charging the troops and whipped up his horses. The Indians saw the coach, and a large body of them at once turned off from following the soldiers and charged toward the stage station. The coach came up to the station at a dead run and stopped. The driver threw down his line and jumped off the box. The one passenger, an army paymaster, jumped out of the coach and the station hands and storekeeper ran out of the station. These men all started for the post as hard as they could run, and they got inside the stockade just as the Indians drove the officer and the survivors of his party into the stockade.

The Indians circled around the stockade, yelling and shooting; but they soon turned off and charged down on the stage station, which they began to plunder. The women came out of the hills with the extra ponies, and these were soon packed with all sorts of goods. At the station breakfast had just been put on the table and was still hot. I sat down with several Indians and ate a good meal. It was the first meal I had eaten at a table for a long time. One old warrior took a great fancy to the big sugar bowl and tied it to his belt. I saw him afterward riding off with the big bowl dangling from his belt behind him.

The shelves in the store were packed with all sorts of goods, groceries and canned goods. The Indians took whatever they wanted, but they did not touch the canned goods, as they did not know what they were. The big warehouse belonging to the stage company was also plundered. From it the Indians secured all the flour, bacon, corn, and sugar their ponies could carry. On the north side of the river was a herd of cattle. A party of warriors crossed the river and drove the

[6] The officer who was decoyed with his troops was Captain Nicholas J. O'Brien. Berthrong, *Southern Cheyennes*, 226.—S.L.

herd over on the ice. The soldiers saw them and opened on them with a howitzer or two, but the shells did no damage. The troops then turned their fire on the groups of Indians about the station and other buildings, but they fired over our heads, evidently not wishing to damage the buildings, and after giving us a few shots they ceased firing. Some of the warriors found a big tin box and knocked the lock off. It was full of pieces of green paper. The Indians handled the paper but did not know what it was. One man took a big bundle of paper, chopped it into three or four pieces with his tomahawk, and then threw it up in the air, laughing as the wind blew the fragments across the valley. I came up and secured good deal of the money, but the Indians had already nearly emptied the paymaster's box. They threw the bills away, as they did not know what they were. The soldiers later had a fine paper hunt and picked up money all over the prairie.

Nearly all day the Indians kept up the plunder, taking load after load of goods and provisions into the hills. The soldiers did not interfere and could not even come out to pick up the dead bodies of their comrades. At the station I found an express package addressed to some officer in Colorado, and in the package was a new major's uniform. I took this and later wore it during the fighting on Powder River when we fought General [P. E.] Connor's troops.

We withdrew late that day, January 7, and started south with the plunder. The ponies were so heavily loaded that it took us three days to reach the village on Cherry Creek. I believe that a few days later part of the Sioux went back to Julesburg and carried off another big lot of plunder, but as I was not present I am not sure about this. It was the Sioux who first made the plan to attack Julesburg, as they knew there was a fine store there and a big warehouse full of supplies. When we withdrew some of the Indians wanted to fire the buildings, but the chiefs stopped them, saying that we might wish to come back some other time to get more provisions.

There are no good official reports of this affair at Julesburg, January 7, 1865. Captain O'Brien who commanded the troops at Camp

Rankin must have made a long report, but it is lost and the only report of his that I have seen is a brief telegram dated the next day, Jan. 8:

"Julesburg, Jan. 8, 1865.
Had a desperate fight (Indians went south) and will report in a few minutes.

N. J. O'Brien.
Captain, Etc."

On January 10 General Curtis, commanding the department, reports by wire that Captain O'Brien "repulsed" the Indians and "drove them south," and that fifteen soldiers and thirty-five Indians were killed. This makes me smile. The Indians drove O'Brien and his men pell-mell into their stockade and they did not show their noses outside again that day, while we were plundering the stage company's property and the store and taking our time about it. None of the reports from the army mention this plundering of the station; they pretend the Indians were driven off without doing any damage; but the stage company mentioned it all right and made a terrible fuss, telling the government it would abandon the whole line if its property was not protected. Also the man who owned the store put in a big bill for damages, $50,000, I believe, and his widow was paid, years afterward, by the government. Even Lieutenant Ware who was stationed at Camp Rankin and was O'Brien's second in command, does not give a fair account of this raid. He does not say a word about our plundering the station and remaining on the ground until nearly evening. He says in his book "The number of Indians killed and vouched for was fifty-six," while in reality we did not lose one man, and he tries to make out that we retreated right after the fight, carrying off our dead. Of the plundering of the station he does not say a word.[7] The newspapers are better in their accounts than these reports of the army officers. The *Nebraskian* of January 19 reports there were fifteen soldiers and four citizens killed. That makes nineteen men, and as I said before, I counted eighteen fresh graves the

[7] Captain Eugene F. Ware, *The Indian War of 1864*, 448–50.—S.L.

second time I visited Julesburg. This newspaper says that some citizens were at the post and joined the soldiers.

On the way home, our pack ponies were so heavily loaded with plunder that we could not move very fast, and it took us three days to reach the big camp, which was still on Cherry Creek, the branch of the Republican. There was great rejoicing in the village when we came in with the plunder from Julesburg. Ever since Sand Creek the Cheyennes had been mourning for the dead, but now that the first blow had been struck in revenge, everyone began to feel better, and that night the young men and young women held scalp dances in all the camps, for all the soldiers who had been killed at Julesburg had been scalped by the warriors, and the young people kept up the dances and drumming until after daylight.

That night, while the dances were going on, the chiefs of the Cheyennes, Sioux, and Northern Arapahos held a council and decided to move north to the Black Hills and Powder River country and join the Northern Cheyennes, Northern Arapahos, and Sioux up there, and to ask these tribes to join in a war against the whites. After the council, runners were sent up north to notify the tribes there that we were coming, and the criers announced the plans in all the camps.

For a few days there was great feasting and dancing in all our camps; the people had never had so much "white man's food" before, and they had tame beef, which most of the Indians had never tasted, and also bacon and all kinds of smoked and canned meats, flour, corn meal, shelled corn, sugar, molasses, and all kinds of groceries. Most of the people did not know how to prepare any of these strange new foods, but they soon began to learn, and the tomahawks were put to the new use of opening tin cans.

We stayed in this camp on Cherry Creek a few days after getting back from Julesburg, and some war parties went out during that time, striking the Platte above and below Julesburg; then, about January 15, I think, we broke camp and moved north to a stream the Indians called White Butte Creek because there was a bald white butte near the stream. This was a small stream, dry most of the year, and I cannot locate it on the modern maps of Colorado. It was about halfway between the South Fork of the Republican and the South Fork of the Platte, in the middle of the dry plains of northeastern Colorado.

Meantime our plundering of Julesburg had stirred up the soldiers, and the wires along the Platte were kept hot with telegrams and orders. The Overland Stage officials were in a panic and were frantically demanding protection for their line. [Brigadier] General Mitchell, commanding on the Platte, believed that the best way to protect the road was to attack the Indians in their own country, south of the Platte, and he at once began collecting troops and wagons for an expedition. Ten days after we had struck Julesburg, he set out with 650 cavalry, four 12-pound howitzers, two three-inch Parrott guns, and 100 wagons hauling supplies and camp equipment. He struck south from near Camp Cottonwood on the Platte, struck Medicine Creek, and marched from there to Red Willow, where he found some old Indian camping places; he then examined Blackwood Creek, Whiteman's Fork, Stinking-Water and Ten-Mile Creek, finally going into camp at the Big Timbers on the Republican and sending out from there scouting parties to examine the country to the south and west. These parties found some of our old camps, but we had already moved up to White Butte Creek and somehow the soldiers missed our trail. If they had found us, there would have been a big fight, for the Indians were all very mad.

Thinking we had gone east, down the Republican, the general broke up his camp at the Big Timbers and marched down the Republican, scouting the creek on both sides. The weather was bitter cold, and the horses and men suffered almost beyond endurance, many of the men being so badly frosted that they had to be mustered out of service as soon as the command returned to the Platte. Marching down as far as the mouth of Medicine Creek, on January 25, Mitchell gave up the search and turned north, up the Medicine. He reached the Platte again January 26. The general was terribly disappointed at the failure of the expedition, but the next day, January 27, he thought of a new plan. There was a wind from the northwest that day. "Just the day I want," said Mitchell. "I will give them ten thousand square miles of prairie fire." And he at once set to work, wiring to all officers at the different stations along the Platte to send out detachments and fire the grass south of the river, and, according to the reports, that evening the grass was fired from Denver to Kearny, three hundred miles along the Platte. Lieutenant Ware, describing this business, tells how the fire was started and rolled off to the south, and that three days later it reached the Arkansas River and some of the fire went on clear down into the Texas Panhandle. Although I was south of the Platte at the time and right in the way of such a fire, I did not see a sign of it, and never saw an Indian who knew anything about such a fire. Meantime, while the General was amusing his troops with the ten thousand-square-miles of prairie fire, we were on our way to clean out the stage line, and this time we did the work thoroughly.

Ever since Sand Creek, Black Kettle had been for peace. Even that terrible affair could not make him join the war against the whites, and he even succeeded in keeping a large part of the Cheyennes from taking part in the raids. He came with us to White Butte Creek, but the day before we left that camp to strike the Platte Road, he left us with eighty lodges of Southern Cheyennes who did not wish to join in the war. I went around among the lodges and shook hands with Black Kettle and all my friends. These lodges under Black Kettle moved south of the Arkansas and joined the Southern Arapahos, Kiowas, and Comanches, and in the spring they made peace and signed a new treaty.

I think it was January 26 or 27 when we broke camp on White Butte Creek and started north. The main village with the women and children struck about due north so as to reach the South Platte some miles west of Julesburg, but a large part of the warriors formed themselves into war parties with the purpose of striking the Platte Road simultaneously both east and west of Julesburg. I went with the Cheyennes who intended to strike high up the South Platte, about midway between Julesburg and Denver; the Sioux struck east of Julesburg, and the Northern Arapahos in between the Sioux and Cheyennes.

I went with a war party of about one hundred Cheyennes and we struck the South Platte near Valley Stage Station, fifty miles west of Julesburg. There was a company of soldiers stationed at this point, but they did not trouble us much. On the morning of January 28, we struck the road at Moore's American Ranch a few miles east of Valley, and here we ran off a herd of over five hundred head of fat cattle, and we also burned a big stack of one hundred tons of government hay, valued at $50 a ton. We moved off down the river, taking our time, herding the cattle ahead of us, and the soldiers did not do a thing. That night we camped on the north side of the river about twenty-five miles or so below Valley, and at daylight next morning we discovered the soldiers near us and had a little fight with them. Some of the cattle were not much good and we turned these loose, driving the fat animals into the bluffs north of the river, and the cavalrymen rounded up the lean cattle we had dropped and drove them across the river. The officer reported by wire that night that he had attacked us, recaptured four hundred cattle, and killed twenty warriors. Some of our men followed the soldiers up the river, skirmishing all the way, and wounded two cavalrymen. We did not have any men hurt in this little brush, which did not amount to anything anyhow.

The same day, January 28, on which we ran off the herd and burned the hay, war parties struck the Platte all along the line, from Alkali, east of Julesburg, to Valley, fifty miles west of Julesburg. The main village, with the women and children, struck the Platte at Harlow's Ranch, about twenty-five miles west of Julesburg, and the warriors with the village attacked and burned Harlow's and a couple of other stations and ranches. Harlow's Ranch, which the Indians struck first, had a wooden building and emigrant's store, built of planks, and built onto the back of this frame building was a log house used as living rooms, and behind the log house was the corral. There were three men and a woman at this place when the Indians attacked, and the men put up a good defense. About seven hundred Cheyennes, Sioux, and Arapahos charged up to this ranch. The people were in the store at the front, but ran into the log building at the rear as soon as they saw the warriors, and the men began firing through loopholes between the logs. The Indians drew around to the front of the store, where the whites could not reach them with their fire, and soon the men and the woman ran out of the log building into the corral, and there the Indians charged in, killed the men at once, and Cut Belly, a Sioux, captured the woman live.

At this ranch the Indians found whisky, and while they were drinking an Arapaho was accidentally shot in the head by a drunken Cheyenne. That same day, January 28, the Indians attacked and burned, besides Harlow's Ranch, Antelope Stage Station, Buffalo Springs Ranch, Spring Hill Stage Station, attacked two other ranches without burning them, and ran off large herds from Alkali east of Julesburg and Morre's Ranch near Valley station, 50 miles west of Julesburg. That evening the big village was put up on the north bank of the South Platte, just opposite Harlow's Ranch.

The party I was with got into the village the day after it reached the Platte, and we killed the fattest of the cattle at once. I never saw so much plunder in an Indian village as there was in this one; besides all the ranches and stage stations that had been plundered (and nearly every one of these places had a good store of goods to sell to emigrants and travelers), two large wagon trains had been captured west of Julesburg. Three Sioux had been killed in an attack on one of these trains, and these are about the only Indians I can remember being killed in these raids and small fights with the troops. The camp was well supplied with fresh beef and had a big herd of cattle besides; then there were whole wagonloads of bacon, hams, big bags of flour, sugar, rice, cornmeal, shelled corn, tins and hogsheads of molasses, groceries of all sorts, canned meats and fruit, clothing, dress goods, silks and hardware—everything you could think of. Most of these things the Indians had never seen before, and they were all the time bringing things to me and asking me what they were and what they were for. I remember an old Indian who brought me a big box and wanted to know what was in it. It was full of candied citron and I told him what it was for. Another thing that puzzled the Indians was the canned oysters.

From the day we struck the South Platte, January 28, until February 2, the Indians raided up and down the road, burning every ranch and stage station between Julesburg and Valley, capturing wagon trains loaded with goods, and running off all the cattle. Besides this, the Sioux made some raids east of Julesburg and the Cheyennes west of Valley nearly to Junction House; the raiders swept the road clean and even destroyed the telegraph line that ran from Julesburg up the South Platte to Denver. We camped there right on the road and held the line, and the soldiers could not do a thing.

In Colorado the people were nearly frantic. At that time very little food was raised in the territory and the people depended largely for food and supplies on what was brought up the Platte in the big freight wagons. The wagons were usually drawn by slow plodding oxen and it took weeks for a "bull train" to move from the Missouri River to Denver. That summer, 1864, the Indians had stopped the ox trains from moving, and when the road was at last opened again, late in the fall, it was too late in the season for bull outfits to reach Denver. For this reason fast freight trains hauled by mules and horses were put on the road to rush supplies to Colorado, and just as the trains got a good start, we struck the road again in January, capturing all the trains west of Julesburg and forcing those lower down the river to corral and "wait for better weather."

The result was a panic in Colorado. There was only enough food to last a few weeks, and prices jumped to famine rates, and even then there was little on the market. Besides this, the stage line was broken up and no coaches were running; every station for a distance of nearly one hundred miles had been burned and the stock run off; the Overland Telegraph had been destroyed and the government was cut off from all communication with Colorado, Utah, Nevada, and the Pacific Coast. All of this trouble was the result of Col. Chivington's "great victory" at Sand Creek.

During these raids a war party of young Cheyennes ran across nine of Chivington's men who had taken part in the Sand Creek affair and had recently been discharged, as their term of service had expired, and they were now on their way east to the States. These men were all killed by the Cheyennes, and after the fight the Indians found in the valises two Indian scalps which were at once recognized as those of White Leaf and Little Wolf or Little Coyote (the son of Two Thighs). The scalps were easily identified, as one of them had hair unusually light in color, while the other scalp still had attached to it a peculiar little shell which Little Coyote had always worn on his scalplock. Little Bear and Touching Cloud, both still living, were with this war party, and they say when the Cheyennes recognized these scalps they were so enraged that they cut the bodies of the dead men all to pieces. They also found in these men's valises several other trophies from Sand Creek which the men were taking east to the States.

I did not see a tenth of the things that happened along the South Platte during those stirring days, but I saw many strange things. At night the whole valley was lighted up with the flames of burning ranches and stage stations, but these places were soon all destroyed and darkness fell on the valley. Our big village strung along the north bank of the river for some distance, the Cheyennes, Sioux, and Northern Arapahos camped separately, but all the camps near together. In every camp the fires were burning all night, and until daylight feasting and dancing and drumming went on. I remember that, when I was out with raiding parties at night, we used to halt and look for the campfires to tell which way the village lay, and when we could not see the fires we would listen for the drums. On a still night you could hear them for miles and miles along the valley.

On the morning of February 2, the village was broken up and the Indians moved north between the two forks of the Platte. The Sioux knew this country north of the South Platte best, and so their chiefs led the march and picked out the camping places. The way the village moved was this. A body of warriors went ahead as advance guard, as we knew that soldiers were stationed on the North Platte and we might run into them; another body of warriors remained behind as rear guard to warn the people if soldiers came up from that direction; the chiefs and some of the Indian soldiers led the march and behind them came the village, all spread out across the prairie, making a trail a mile wide. The lodgepoles were tied to the sides of ponies in bunches and the lodge covers and camp equipment fastened on the poles behind the ponies. Besides this, many ponies were loaded with plunder of all sorts, small children rode on ponies or in pole-drags, and the women and boys drove the extra ponies and the herd of captured cattle. When the chiefs and old men at the head of the village reached a good place to camp they would halt and call out "Camp here!" and the women would at once set to work putting up the lodges. If the camp was to be for only one night the chiefs would call out "Camp here one sleep!" and then the women would only unpack a few of the things, just what they would need during the night. Writers of books are constantly speaking of "Indian trails" and give you the impression that there were regular beaten paths constantly used by the Indians. This is all wrong; there were no well-marked trails in the plains. The Indians knew the whole country like a book and took any route they pleased. They traveled by landmarks from one stream to the next. As the Indians did not travel in "Indian file," as the whites seem to suppose, they did not leave a deep-marked trail, and after the village had gone on the trail would soon disappear and leave no mark in the grass.

When the village left the South Platte and started north a big war party, Sioux, Cheyennes, and Arapahos, left the village and started down the river to finish up Julesburg. I went with this war party, and again the Indians tried the old trick of luring the soldiers out of their stockade by hiding the warriors among the hills and sending out a small party to tempt the soldiers out; but the troops this time were on their guard and would not stir outside their defences, so after waiting among the sand hills for some time, our whole body charged out and raced across the flats to the stockade. Here we saw the fresh graves of the soldiers who had been killed in our first attack on Julesburg, and I counted eighteen graves in all.

The Indians circled around the stockade, yelling and shooting and taunting the soldiers, to get them to come out and fight; but it was no use (the garrison was very weak and Captain O'Brien was away), so after a while we withdrew east to the stage station. Here the warriors, about six hundred strong, broke into the store and stage company warehouse, and completely plundered both. The stage company had a big supply of shelled corn in bags in their warehouse, and the Indians took this corn on the pack ponies and carried it north of the river, later sanding the ice of the Platte so the ponies could cross without slipping. In the hope of drawing the soldiers out, as soon as they had plundered the buildings, the Indians set fire to them, one by one, burning the stage station, telegraph office, store, warehouse, stables, etc., each separately. But no one came out. The great column of smoke floated up in the air, and it could be seen for twenty miles along the valley.

After plundering and burning Julesburg, the Indians, who were over a thousand strong,[8] broke up into three parties; the largest part camped on the north bank of the river with all the plunder that night, holding scalp dances around the fires, in plain sight of the soldiers at Camp Rankin. Next morning, February 3, these Indians with the plunder moved up Lodgepole Creek to rejoin the main village. Meantime a big party of Cheyennes and Arapahos had left Julesburg on the afternoon of the second, just after burning the buildings, and this party made a raid up the river, while at the same time a big Sioux party made a raid down the river. West of Julesburg the Cheyennes and Arapahos attacked a ranch, and near this ranch they captured a wagon train loaded with bottled liquor for Denver.

The main village, which left camp on the north side of the South Platte February 2, moved north, making a trail a mile wide, and on February 3 crossed Lodgepole Creek at a point twenty-five or thirty miles northwest of Julesburg and two miles east of Pole Creek Crossing where the road crossed Lodgepole Creek. This road was the old Overland Stage road from Julesburg to Fort Laramie, but the stage company had abandoned this road in 1863 because of danger from Indians and had adopted a new route up the South Platte to near

[8] Berthrong, *Southern Cheyennes*, 228, accepts Bent's second figure of "a thousand strong," rather than his first, *supra*, of six hundred. Hyde's figure in *Spotted Tail's Folk*, 96, is "fifteen hundred strong." Grinnell, *Fighting Cheyennes*, 192–94, wisely does not estimate.—S.L.

Map 3. Great Raids, from Julesburg to Mud Springs

Mud Springs Ranch was on the site of the modern town of Simla, Nebraska.—G.H. [Hyde's sketch map shows the movement of the Cheyenne camps northwestward from early January to the first week in February, a difficult tracing because George Bent and even the whites of the period attached different names for places and physical features than those later in use, as Hyde's notes to the map make clear.—S.L.]

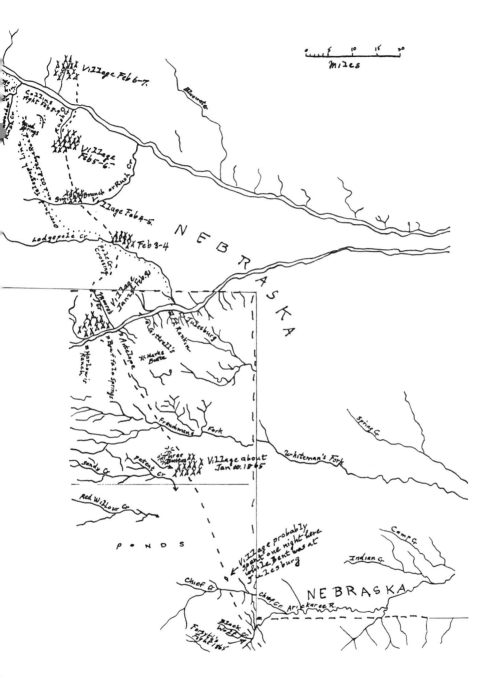

Denver and thence west of Salt Lake. The old "Laramie" road up
the North Platte was thus thrown out of use and all stations abandoned, and only a few trains used that route; but the Overland Telegraph was strung along that road, up Pole Creek to the North
Platte, and thence to Laramie and on west (the wire up the South
Platte being only a branch line to Denver), and in early fall 1864
two small garrisons were placed at Mud Springs and Camp Mitchell
on the Laramie road to protect the Overland Telegraph.

Between the forks of the Platte the country was unoccupied; there
were no ranches and no troops except a few at Mud Springs and
Camp Mitchell, and not even any Indians lived in that country. The
main stream between the two Platte rivers was Lodgepole Creek,
which emptied into the South Platte one mile west of Julesburg. The
stream never has much water in it and at times is dry, it has no tribu-
taries of any importance, just dry arroyos and small creeks, dry most
of the year; the valley was wide and level, covered with short grass
and without a stick of timber. As the Indians who had burned Julesburg retired up this valley, they destroyed the Overland Telegraph
line for many miles. The method the Indians used in destroying the
each group gathered around a telegraph pole and either began chop-
ping it down with axes and tomahawks (the poles were mostly small
cedar ones, not at all thick), or else, if any fuel was handy, they built
a small fire around the pole and sat down and waited until the fire
burnt through and the pole fell. They then cut off the wire and
either carried it away or tangled it all up and left it on the ground.
Sometimes the poles were dragged into camp and used in making the
campfires and for the fires around which the Indians held scalp dances
every night. During these raids the Indians destroyed the line from
east of Julesburg to Valley Station, fifty or sixty miles, besides breaking the line in places west of Valley, and on the Pole Creek line they
destroyed fifteen or twenty miles of telegraph. As the poles were
nearly burnt or carried off, and new poles had to be hauled from
Cottonwood canyon and other points on the lower Platte, 100 to 150
miles, it took the soldiers a long time to reopen the line.

Our war-parties rejoined the main village about twenty-five or thirty miles up Lodgepole Creek near where the old stage road crossed the stream.[9] From here the road struck northwest for the North Platte, along what was known as Jules' Stretch or Thirty-mile Ridge, a high, dry divide or tableland with no water until Mud Springs Ranch was reached.

On the night of February 3–4 our village was on Lodgepole Creek, about twenty miles north of the place where we had been in camp on the north bank of the South Platte during the great raids. We stayed here one night, and on the morning of the fourth broke camp and moved north across the high, dry divide toward the North Platte. That night the camp was pitched on a small stream, near what the Sioux called Muddy Spring, at which place Mud Springs Ranch was located.

Mud Spring was "a little run of clear water in a black miry hollow." It was down in the bottom of a little valley and was a camping place of the Sioux in early days. In the early 60's, when the Overland Stage line ran from Julesburg to Laramie, there was a stage station at Mud Springs, and later a telegraph office was established there. In 1863 the stage company abandoned that line, but the telegraph company still kept an office there, and the ranch continued to be a place of importance, as here was the only water on the road between Pole Creek and the Pumpkin Seed, near the North Platte, and the wagon trains that passed along the road always halted at Mud Springs. In February, 1865, when we came on this place, there were at the ranch nine soldiers of the Eleventh Ohio Cavalry, and five citizens, including the ranchman, telegraph operator, and some herders in the employ of the telegraph company, which had a herd of cattle, horses, and mules wintering near the ranch.[10]

On the morning of February 4 our advance party, led by the Sioux, came upon Mud Springs and after reconnoitering the place

[9] " 'Seven hundred lodges crossed six miles below Pole Creek Crossing.' Official Report."—George E. Hyde's longhand note.—S.L.

[10] Ellsworth's command consisted of thirty-six men, who, with the nine or ten whites already at the Springs, provided a meagre force in walled combat with what clearly must have been hundreds of Indians. C.f. Berthrong, *Southern Cheyennes*, 229.—S.L.

187

ran off the herd which was grazing on a small creek about five miles from Mud Springs. The operator at once wired to Camp Mitchell, 55 miles west of Mud Springs, and to Fort Laramie, 105 miles west, for help, and troops from both these posts were immediately started for Mud Springs, marching night and day. Lieutenant [William] Ellsworth, Eleventh Ohio Cavalry (who established Camp Ellsworth in 1864, where Ellsworth City, Kansas, now stands) set out from Camp Mitchell, 55 miles from Mud Springs, and after marching hard all night, pulled into Mud Spring Ranch about daybreak on the morning of the fifth. Of course, the Indians did not know anything about these movements of troops at the time, as they did not even know that Mud Springs had a wire connection with the posts farther west.

Early on the morning of the fifth we broke camp on the small stream south of Mud Springs, the village moving off northeast while over a thousand warriors started due north, to attack Mud Springs. As we approached the ranch we heard firing and knew that the party of warriors who had left camp during the night, to run off stock at the ranch, was engaged with the soldiers. As we came over the hills and down into the Mud Springs Valley we saw these warriors fighting the soldiers, but the soldiers had shut the horses and mules up inside a strong corral, where the Indians could not get at them.

The soldiers were all inside the buildings (which were very strong) and were firing out through loopholes. It was a hard place to attack successfully. From the spring a little stream ran out between high banks, passing close to the ranch, and seeing this, a large body of warriors crept up under the shelter of the banks and succeeded in getting quite close to the buildings. From this point they opened fire on the troops, who returned the fire from their loopholes. It was not very interesting, as neither side cared to come into the open, and no one could tell what effect was being made by the shooting, as you could not tell whether anyone had been hit or not.

The shooting match kept on in this way from early in the morning until about noon; then all at once the soldiers opened the corral and turned loose the horses and mules. This incident is not mentioned in the official reports, but that is what the soldiers did. The frightened animals scattered and ran in every direction, and the Indians, eager to capture the animals, started after them in a swarm, riding their war ponies at top speed. It was the custom that the first warrior to touch any animal or other sort of property became the owner of the plunder, and the warriors were always very eager to be the first to touch or "count coup." Little bunches of warriors now rushed after these horses and mules, trying to touch the animals with anything they had in their hands—bows, lances, or gunbarrels. Few of the Indians carried regular coupsticks. As soon as one animal had been touched, the warriors would turn off and chase another one.

I believe the soldiers were running out of ammunition and turned loose the stock to induce the Indians to leave. If this was their object, they succeeded, for the Indians were as tired of wasting their ammunition and arrows in that sort of a fight as the troops were, and as soon as the horses and mules had all been captured, we left the ranch and set out for the village. No Indians were killed in this brush at the Spring. These animals were all branded "U.S." and the horses were probably those of Lieutenant Ellsworth's command.

We found the village at the new camping place at some springs on a small creek, about ten miles east of Mud Springs. Just before daylight next morning (February 6) Lieutenant Colonel [William O.] Collins, Eleventh Ohio Cavalry, pulled in to Mud Springs with reinforcements from Fort Laramie.[11] He had been on the road, marching night and day, since the telegram had come to Laramie from Mud Springs on the afternoon of February 4 notifying him that our warriors had appeared on Pole Creek and near Mud Springs. That morning early, a large body of warriors set out to make another attack on Mud Springs, where they arrived about daylight and kept up the fight until long after noon. The soldiers were now in stronger force, but the fight was much the same as that of the preceding day, and many of the Indians soon tired of the business and left

[11] Collins was commandant at Fort Laramie at the time.—S.L.

the ground. This day, as on the day before, none of our men were killed.[12]

That day, February 6, the village broke up in the morning and moving down the creek on which we had been encamped, reached the North Platte, about five miles from the place where the village had stood the night before. Sanding the ice so the herds could cross without slipping and injuring themselves, we crossed the river and struck north into the bluffs, which at this point are about five miles north of the river, level flats filling in the space between the river and the bluffs. Among the bluffs the camp was set up along a little creek, the name of which I have forgotten, if I ever knew it.

We thought that we had now seen the last of the soldiers, as the country north of the North Platte was an unknown region to the whites, and the troops never went into that country. The criers now went through the camps, announcing that the chiefs had decided to stay here four days, to rest the ponies and let them grow strong, as the country north of us was nothing but desolate sand hills and we would have to make a long hard march to reach the next camping place far to the north, where we could find water.

I was up all that night, dancing with a party of young men and women. It was full moonlight and not very cold, and scalp dances were going on around the fires in all parts of the big village, the drums beating and the echoes coming back from the high bluffs among which we were encamped. Toward daylight the dancers began to tire, and by the time the sun was well up the camp had quieted down and most of the dancers had gone to bed.

I think it was about two in the afternoon that some of us in the camp noticed a Sioux warrior up on the bluff south of the village, signaling "Enemies across the river." He rode his horse up and down on the bluff, riding slow and making motions with his arms, and then stopping and holding his buffalo robe up to one side of his head. The signal for "Game in sight," was riding up and down in this way; if the game was far away the man who was signaling rode

[12] The relief force under Collins amounted to 120 men, of whom seven were wounded during the morning's encounter.—S.L.

slow, if the game was near, he rode fast, and that meant that the hunters would have to get ready in a hurry and ride fast if they expected to secure the game. The same signal was used for enemies in sight, except the signaler made motions with his arms as he rode up and down, and if the enemies were far away, he held up his robe, and if they were near, he turned and rode toward camp as fast as he could, and everybody knew what to expect when they saw him coming. I have seen these signals made from a distance of four or five miles.

When we saw this Sioux riding his horse back and forth on the bluff and signaling with his buffalo robe, we knew soldiers were across the river, and all the warriors made a rush for the pony herds, as each man was anxious to get mounted first, in order to reach the troops before the others and have a good chance to capture some of the soldiers' horses and mules. In a few moments a thousand or more warriors had mounted, and off they went in little bands, swarming over the bluffs and down into the Platte Valley. When I had mounted I rode to the bluffs, from whose summits I had a fine view of the great valley, several miles wide and perfectly flat, with the frozen Platte winding through it. The flats to the north of the river were covered with Indian trails, and over to the southwest loomed up Courthouse Rock, Jail Rock and the Chimney.[13] Along the road on the south side of the river I could see a train of white-topped wagons crawling slowly along, guarded by cavalry, and toward this train the warriors were hurrying, looking like a swarm of little black ants crawling across the ice of the Platte.

I left the bluffs and rode down into the valley, and as I reached the river I saw that the soldiers had corralled their wagons on the south bank, at the mouth of the little creek on whose upper waters our village had stood the day before. The wagons were corralled on a bit of level ground, but all around the wagons were little knolls and sand ridges, and the soldiers hastily dug rifle pits among these hillocks and ridges and formed a circle of defense all about the wagons. The

[13] It is difficult to reconcile Bent's earlier statement about the absence of Indian trails with this and subsequent statements indicating well-defined routes.—S.L.

warriors in strong force, as soon as they had assembled on the south bank of the river, charged at full speed across the knolls and ridges, yelling and shooting as they came; then, as the soldiers opened fire, the Indians turned and began to circle round and round, whooping and shooting, but they soon saw that there was no chance of getting at the horses and mules inside the corral. As I crossed the river they drew off and adopted the same tactics as the soldiers, hiding among the hillocks and ridges and crawling forward, firing at a soldier whenever they caught a glimpse of one.

One party of warriors went down to the river and, getting under the cover of the high bank, crawled along the ice until they reached the rear of the soldiers' position. From here they opened fire and warmed the troops very successfully. After a while their fire became so galling that Colonel Collins (for this was Collins and his outfit who had left Mud Springs that morning and was following our trail to see what had become of us) now ordered one of his officers to clear this body of warriors out. I saw the cavalrymen lead their horses out of the corral, mount, and form line, but as they charged down toward the river bank, the warriors saw them coming and, mounting quickly, got out of the way. Yellow Nose, the man who captured Custer's flag at the Battle of the Little Big Horn in 1876,[14] was with this party behind the river bank. Yellow Nose (he is still living, an old blind man now) is a little man, that is, not very tall, and at that time, 1865, was only a boy. When he saw the soldiers coming he started to get on his horse, but he was too small to mount quickly and the pony gave him a good deal of trouble.

While he was still struggling with the animal, the soldiers charged up and one of them shot Yellow Nose in the breast. The boy then made one last effort and managed somehow to get on the pony's back; then he rode as fast as he could after the rest of his party, who were making for a sand hill some distance off to one side. The cavalry were right at Yellow Nose's heels and very close to the rest of the party, and it looked as if all our men were lost. Then all at once a

[14] Cf. Edgar I. Stewart, *Custer's Luck*, 472n.; Grinnell, *Fighting Cheyennes*, 201n.

large body of warriors charged out from behind this sand hill and rushed at the troops. The soldiers turned at once and rode toward the corral at a hard gallop, but they had been very near to the sand hill when they turned back and the warriors were close after them. One by one the rear-most soldiers were overtaken and killed, and I think only about half of the company reached the corral in safety.

One trooper, mounted on a very fast roan, dashed right through the band of charging warriors and got away westward along the Laramie Road. A few Indians on fast ponies went after this man, and after chasing him a long way (his horse was a fine animal and very fast) they caught and killed him. They found on him a paper and after the fight brought it to me. It was a note from Colonel Collins to the officer commanding at Fort Laramie or at Camp Mitchell, I have forgotten which, and it said that he had been forced to corral and was fighting three thousand Indians and needed aid at once. Sergeant MacDonald, who died at Taloga, Oklahoma, about 1900, was with Collins in this fight, and he once told me that during the engagement the Colonel gave copies of this dispatch to two men and ordered them to go through the Indian line. I suppose the other soldier got through with his copy of the dispatch.

After this charge of the cavalry and the counter-charge of our warriors, the fight went on until nearly evening without any incident of note. Both sides stuck close to their rifle pits and did not expose themselves much. Toward nightfall the Indians began to withdraw across the river in small parties, and by dark the last of them had started back for the village. The following morning several hundred warriors recrossed the river, still hoping to get Colonel Collins' animals, but after exchanging shots with the soldiers for some hours and seeing that the troops had no intention of breaking their corral and moving out, the warriors gave up hope of a chance to stampede the stock and retired across the river again. The Indians lost no men killed in this engagement and had only two men wounded—Yellow Nose and a Sioux. This was our last fight with the troops until the following spring.[15]

[15] No two commanders ever see a battle in the same light. Bent indicates many

193

Very early in the morning after this fight with the troops at the corral, the women took down the lodges and packed the ponies, and we started north through the Sand Hills of western Nebraska, a very bad country with no wood and no water. That day we made forty miles and camped on a small stream called Snake Creek by the Sioux (it still bears the same name and can be found on any large map of Cheyenne County, Nebraska). Here there was no wood and fires had to be made of buffalo chips. In the morning we again made a very early start and this day was another march of forty miles through the Sand Hills. Our camp this night was on a small stream which has no timber or bluffs or anything else to mark its course. You could not see that a stream was there until you came right upon it; and for this reason the Indians called it Surprise River. I think this is the stream known to the Sioux as Miniloosa and on modern maps put down as Running Water or Niobrara. Our next camp was on a small sand creek; here again we struck good country, with plenty of timber, as we were now getting up close to the Black Hills of Dakota. We stayed in this camp four days, resting the tired ponies and hunting. There were plenty of elk and antelope, but buffalo were far away. Our next move was to what the Sioux called Bear Lodge River. I think this is Cheyenne River, North Fork, of the maps. It was a fine stream, flowing through the Black Hills, on which the Indians loved to make their winter camps. Here we waited for the runners who had gone on ahead of us to find the Cheyenne and Sioux camps near Powder River. When these runners came in, and reported the location of the camps, we moved on to Red Paint River, where the Indians used to dig red clay in the banks to make red paint. Spotted Tail's Sioux bands left us on Bear Lodge River and moved off eastward; and at the same camp, the Northern Arapahos left us and went to join their tribe over west of Powder River. From Red Paint River we moved to Antelope-pit River—the Little Missouri. Here Gray Beard and his band of fifty lodges decided to remain and dig

whites were killed, but Collins reported two, with sixteen wounded and ten disabled from frostbite. He put the Indian losses at from one hundred to one hundred and fifty; Bent at two wounded, as indicated above.—S.L.

pits to capture antelope in. The rest of us moved on toward Powder River. This country was all new to us, and I cannot locate these streams on the map.[16]

Before we started on this move toward the north the chiefs sent runners from our camp on Republican River, to notify the tribes up north that we were coming, and to ask them to send back runners to meet us and let us know where the northern tribes were encamped. When our big village reached the Cheyenne River, near the Black Hills, in February, runners came in with news that the Northern Cheyennes and Red Cloud's Sioux were in winter camps on the Powder River at a place where there was plenty of timber and good grass. Criers went through the camp announcing the news to all the people, and that night several of the soldier societies held feasts and there was dancing and drumming until daylight.

These runners were Southern Cheyennes and Sioux of Spotted Tail's tribe. They were the same men who had been sent north from our camp on the Republican; but when they came into camp now they brought several Northern Cheyennes with them. These northern kinsmen of ours were dressed very differently from us and looked strange to our eyes. Our southern Indians all wore cloth blankets, cloth leggings, and other things made by the whites, but these northern Indians all wore buffalo robes and buckskin leggings; they had their braided hair wrapped in strips of buckskin painted red, and they had crow feathers on their heads with the ends of the feathers cut off in a peculiar manner. They looked much wilder than

---

[16] Bent's Snake Creek is Snake Creek, in southern Box Butte County, Nebraska, and his distance of forty miles from Platte to Snake Creek is correct. Surprise River must be the Niobrara, which in this locality is about twenty miles north of Snake Creek. Beyond the Niobrara Bent's Indians would come into a well-watered country in the southern edge of the Black Hills. His account clearly shows that they passed around the east side of the hills. His Bear Lodge River was probably either the North Cheyenne or the small tributary of that river still called Bear Butte Creek. West of this creek is another, Red Water Creek, which may be Bent's Red Paint River; beyond the Red Water is the Little Missouri, which is very well known as the old Antelope-pit River of the Indians. The Bear Lodge itself lies south of the big bend of the North Cheyenne, and the Indians must have crossed Cheyenne River here, to the south of Bear Lodge.—G.H.

any of the southern Indians, and kept up all the old customs, not having come much in contact with the whites.

These runners also brought news that the Northern Arapahos were encamped near the Cheyennes and Sioux on Powder River, and the next day the eighty lodges of Northern Arapahos who had come north with us sent out runners to find the camp of their tribesmen on the Powder. Crow Lance was the leader of these runners, and the day they set out he came to our lodge to get some gun caps.

We now broke camp on Cheyenne River and moved north along the eastern side of the Black Hills.[17] We camped on Bear Lodge Creek on the northeast side of the hills for a few days. Here Spotted Tail and his Sioux left us and moved off to the east, and the Northern Arapahos also left us, moving off to the northwest, their runners having returned with news that their tribe was in camp on Red Paint Creek. Our village, now mostly made up of Southern Cheyennes, moved west toward Powder River, sending runners ahead to notify the Northern Cheyennes of our coming. Leaving Bear Lodge Creek, we moved over and camped on Red Paint Creek, a stream near the northwest corner of the Black Hills. Here there were bluffs from which the Indians procured red paint in early days. Our next camp was on a stream the Indians called Noted River, and the next on Antelope-pit River (the Little Missouri) where the Indians pitted antelope in primitive times.

From this camp we moved to the Powder and found the Northern Cheyennes and Red Cloud's outfit camped in a fine location with plenty of timber, good grass, and large herds of buffalo near. The two tribes were camped some distance apart, and we put up our lodges about half a mile from the Northern Cheyennes. Then the visiting began, and all our people were invited to feasts day after day in the other camps. We had long talks, and the northern Indians asked us all kinds of questions about our march to the north and all

---

[17] "Where is authority for this? Other accounts put this camp on Bear Lodge River and do not mention this camp on Cheyenne River; in fact, he thought Bear Lodge was probably Cheyenne River. *Ask him.*"—George E. Hyde's longhand marginal note.—S.L.

the fights we had had with the troops. They told us that they had been in camp at this place for some time, and that in two days they would move down the Powder to get on fresh grass.

We Southern Cheyennes were very much surprised at the appearance of the Northern Cheyennes. The two divisions of the tribe had been separated from each other about forty years (the first bands of our people moved south about 1826), and now in 1865 we found these northern kinsmen of ours very different from us. They were growing more like the Sioux in habits and appearance every year. They did not dress like us at all, and their language was changing. They used many words that were strange to us. This change in language is still going on, and today when Southern Cheyennes go up to Montana to visit they often find it very difficult to understand what the Northern Cheyennes are talking about.

Two days after we arrived, camp was broken up and we all moved down the Powder (which flows north and empties into the Yellowstone). The Sioux led the march, and when we reached a good place with plenty of grass and timber, they were the first to camp. The Northern Cheyennes camped next, and we southerners last. The lodges were set up in irregular groups and the whole village extended along the river for a mile or more. Old men tell me that this camp of ours on the Powder had very much the appearance of the one Custer attacked on the Little Bighorn in 1876, but that this later camp was larger than ours. There was plenty of timber at this new camp, and the Indians made a number of crude log corrals, in which they kept their best horses at night. Several families would club together and build one of these corrals close to the lodges, and each evening all of the valuable horses were driven into the corral for safekeeping. The poorer and wilder animals were permitted to run loose on the range during the night.

Two nights after we reached this place a small war party of Crows slipped into the village after dark, intending to steal horses; but they found all of the best animals shut up securely in the corrals, so close to the lodges that it was extremely dangerous to attempt to lead them out; so the Crows contented themselves with rounding up a number of the loose animals on the range. One Crow mounted a wild horse, an unbroken animal, which bucked around until it succeeded in dumping the warrior off on the grass. When he fell, the Crow dropped his bow and quiver, and as he could not find the weapons quickly in the dark, he hurried off after the rest of his party and left the bow and quiver. About day, some of our herders went out to see if the herds were safe, and the first thing they saw was the Crow's bow and quiver. They gave the alarm at once, and in a few minutes several small parties of warriors were armed and mounted on fast ponies. We had no difficulty in following the trail, for trails up north are much clearer than they are down here. Other parties were ahead of the one I was with. They rode fast toward Tongue River and we rode hard, trying to overtake them. Near Tongue River we heard shooting far to the front; and then we rode harder than ever. When we came up we found that the leading party of our warriors had overtaken four of the Crows and killed them all. The fight had not lasted long, as the Crows had nothing but bows and a few poor arrows. The trail showed that there were nine Crows in the party, but we saw no trace of the other five. I suppose that finding they could not ride fast enough on the unbroken animals they had stolen, they turned the horses loose and hid themselves.

The scalps of the four Crow men were split in halves, making eight scalps, and when we got back to camp one of the biggest scalp dances I have ever seen was started. These northern Indians were great scalp dancers, both men and women, and the way they kept up the dancing, drumming, and singing beat anything I have ever seen. These northern Indians danced a great deal more than we Southern Cheyennes and Arapahos did, and the Southern Plains tribes (Comanches, Kiowas, and Prairie-Apaches) danced less than we did. These three southern tribes were no better fighters than dancers. You will read in old books what splendid fighters the Comanches, Kiowas, and Prairie-Apaches were, but that is all nonsense. These tribes made great raids into Mexico, slaughtering the poor peons and running off great herds of horses and mules, but they would not stand up and

Wolf Robe

Black Kettle and Other Chiefs in Denver, 1864
Black Kettle center, holding pipe

Old Fort Lyon

White Antelope, Man on a Cloud, and Little Chief

Cheyenne Camp

Fort Phil Kearny

Fort Larned, *top*; Fort Dodge, *lower*

Fort Laramie as Seen by Alfred Jacob Miller

fight like the tribes farther north. They were great raiders and full of tricks, but not much account in a real fight.

For three long weeks the scalps of those unfortunate Crow men were danced through all the camps, almost without a pause, and the beating of the drums made such a racket that the buffalo herds left our vicinity. The Indians used to say that buffalo were terribly afraid of the sound of the drums, though, queerly enough, they did not mind singing at all. Scouts were now sent out to locate the vanished herds, and they soon reported plenty of buffalo on the Little Powder, southeast of our camps. We made two moves and camped on that stream, right among the herds. Criers went through the village and announced that no one must touch a drum but that singing was permitted: so the Crow scalps were given no rest. A soldier society known as the Crazy Dogs had issued this order about the drums. They were a Northern Cheyenne society and had been selected by the chiefs to police the camps. This was the custom in all big villages; the chiefs selected a society to act as police and keep order in the camps, and after this society had served for some time it was relieved and another society went on duty.

There was some good hunting at this new camp on the Little Powder, as the buffalo were all about us. When the scouts reported that a large herd was near, the criers went through the camps calling on everyone to get ready for the hunt. This was the Sioux call:

> Your saddles bind,
> The buffalo,
> Half a day,
> We will hunt.

This call was sung by the criers. When the hunters left the village the soldiers went ahead and the hunters straggled along in the rear. Reaching the vicinity of the herd, the soldiers halted behind a hill and gave everyone time to come up. Then the run began. If there were two herds the hunters split up into two bodies and one band of soldiers accompanied each party, to keep order. Arrows were always used by the hunters, to avoid quarrels, for each man had his marks on his arrows and he could tell by the arrows which animals belonged to him. If guns had been used there would have been constant squabbling.

Spring was now at hand, the new grass was coming up, and we moved camp often, to secure good grazing for the horses, most of which were mere skin and bones. This was in April. Up there the grass was not very abundant until the middle of May, and early in the spring the Indians had to keep moving camp every few days to get grass for the herds. In May we crossed over west to Tongue River. Grass was plenty by this time: the ponies were fattening up, and the young men were beginning to talk of making raids. Here on the Tongue the Sioux (Red Cloud's [Oglala] outfit) camped by themselves, and all the Cheyennes camped together, pitching the lodges in a great circle—the old-time tribal circle which had not been set up since the Northern Cheyennes came down to join us in our attack on the Kiowas and Comanches in 1838. Each clan of the tribe had its lodges grouped together in its own part of the circle: the position in the circle assigned to that clan in ancient days. There was an opening in the circle, and in the open space inside the circle the two sacred lodges were set up, one for *Issi wun* (the sacred Buffalo Cap), and the other for the *Mahuts* (sacred Medicine Arrows). Most of us younger Southern Cheyennes had never seen the Buffalo Cap, which was kept by the Northern Cheyennes, and most of the younger Northern Cheyennes had never seen the Medicine Arrows, which belonged to our half of the tribe. The opening in the camp circle was toward the northwest, as we were moving in that direction, down Tongue River. The opening in the circle was always in the direction in which the tribe was moving. Red Cloud and his Sioux camped in our rear, about half a mile up the river. They did not use a circle but pitched their lodges in groups strung out along the river bank.

Here on the Tongue that spring the Indians lived just as they had in the old days, before the whites came. There were all kinds of ancient customs, ceremonies, and dances. The soldier societies of our tribe were the Bone Scrapers or Crooked Lances, Crazy Dogs, Dog

Soldiers, Red Shields, Kit Foxes, Bowstring Men, and Chief's Band. All these societies held ceremonies and feasts and dances at night. I belonged to the Crooked Lances, of which society Young-Man-Afraid-of-His-Horses, a Sioux, was also a member.[18] Our men all had lances with one end curved like a shepherd's crook. We had a piece of elk horn shaped to represent a lizard. This lizard was laid on a heap of wild sage in the center of the dance lodge and a man with a stick scraped the lizard, making a rasping noise in time with the drumming while all of the warriors with their crooked lances danced around and around in a circle. The Sioux societies also held dances, and the chiefs held war councils at night. After these councils the chiefs would come into the dance lodges to announce the decisions of the council. At last one night they announced that the ponies were now nearly fat enough to be used, and that raiding parties could soon set out for the Platte. They told the warriors to note everything they saw on the Platte and pick out the best place to make a grand raid, which they were planning to organize in June.[19]

All this time we kept moving camp, advancing slowly down the Tongue until we reached the eastern base of the Bighorn Mountains. Here we had clear, cold mountain water and plenty of fine grass. The buffalo now started to move south and we followed them in that direction, camping again on Powder River. Here the first war parties were made up and I joined a band of about one hundred Northern and Southern Cheyenne men who intended to raid on the North Platte Road. At the same time a big Sioux party was made up, and both parties left camp the same day, the Sioux striking due south, our party southwest. As we moved up the Powder, we could see the Sioux

[18] One of the most famous of Oglala Sioux warriors, of the same name as his father, Old-Man-Afraid-of-His-Horses, to be understood as meaning "They Fear Even His Horses." See Grinnell, *Fighting Cheyennes*, 220n.—S.L.

[19] At this stage there were perhaps one thousand lodges in the great camp, as it moved, held councils, and had skirmishes with the whites. Although Bent does not identify all the bands present, we know there were, in addition to the Cheyennes under Dull Knife, White Bull, and Roman Nose, the Arapahos, Red Cloud's Oglala Sioux, Little Thunder's Brulé Sioux, and Sioux bands of the Miniconjous and Sans Arcs. J .W. Vaughn, *The Battle of Platte Bridge*, 40.—S.L.

MAP 4. CAMPS AND FIGHTS ON THE POWDER RIVER

This map is entirely of my making except that Bent has marked a village and some trails. The information on the map as to villages and trails I obtained mainly from Bent, set it down and then sent the map to him for comment and additions.

Bent's entry is on the Little Powder north of Pumpkin Butte and reads "Camp here when Connor came to Powder River." He has drawn a blue pencil line from this camp south to point where the fight with the wagon train occurred. Then a black pencil mark (showing the Indian trail) to the camp on Powder after Platte Bridge and another trail north along Little Powder, going to the camp of the day of Roman Nose's fight. As I remember this, Bent said these Indians left the camp after Platte Bridge (the camp at mouth of Lodgepole Creek and went from there to the camp he marks on Little Powder; here they got word of the wagon outfit and went south and fought this outfit. After returning to camp, they took the trail he shows up Little Powder and went to the camp where Cole ran into them the day of Roman Nose's fight. Soon after the Roman Nose fight the Southern Cheyennes returned home by the trail marked in red [here reproduced in black]. They cleaned out the new Smoky Hill Stage Line and then went on south of the Arkansas.

This map shows, from Bent information, the camp before they went to Platte Bridge, their trail; the camp after the big Platte Bridge fight and, in red ink, the trail from this last camp to the one they were in when Cole struck them. Or, rather, when they struck him. It is to be understood that the Indians were not all together on one camp at any time. Only a part of them were in the camp on Little Powder and took part in the scrap with the wagon outfit, then went up Little Powder and rejoined the big village before Cole arrived.— George E. Hyde.

men riding over the bluffs on our left. The Northern Cheyennes in our party knew the country, so they led the way, and that night they picked out a fine camping place. The next morning we went on up the Powder (toward the south), finding lots of fat buffalo bulls and plenty of deer and antelope. Bulls and bucks are pretty good meat when fat, but always coarser than cows and does. The Northern Cheyennes also killed and ate three bears, but we southerners did not like bear.

Our party struck the North Platte about thirty miles below old Platte Bridge. At this point the old Overland Stage Road came up the south bank of the river from Fort Laramie, crossed the Platte at the bridge, and went on up the north bank into the mountains. The stage company had taken its stock off this road a year or two before and was now running its coaches along a new road from near Denver straight west to Salt Lake. On the North Platte there were the abandoned stage stations, with here and there a small garrison of cavalry. Nothing else, and there was very little travel on this road. On the south side of the river near where we struck it was the old Deer Creek stage station, at the mouth of Deer Creek, and we found this place garrisoned by cavalry, who had built a strong stockade here.

The Platte was in flood and there was no ford; but we swam across with our war ponies and took the troops by surprise, running off all their horses. There was only one company here, I believe, and the soldiers were afraid to come out. The Indians kept up a fire on the stockade all that day, but the soldiers did not show themselves, and little harm was done to either party. The official report of Colonel Plumb, who commanded the troops, says that the attack was made May 20 by two hundred warriors and that the Indians lost seven killed and had several men wounded. We had about one hundred men and we suffered no loss at all. He says that the Indians were led by a white man, "supposed to be Bill Comstock, formerly of Fort Laramie" I suppose that I was the man he meant, but I was dressed and painted just like the warriors.[20]

[20] Lieutenant Colonel Preston B. Plumb, commandant at Camp Dodge, was in

After this little affair, the Indians swam back to the north side of the river, taking the captured cavalry horses with them. Colonel Plumb states that he led his men out and drove the Indians across the river, but could not follow them because the stream was in flood. This is all fiction; the troops did not come out of the stockade at all. The official reports are full of such statements about driving the war parties across the Platte, and the officers always say that they did not follow because it was impossible to cross the river. We never had any trouble in crossing, even when the river was at its worst, and I do not see why the soldiers could not cross. If Indian women encumbered with their children could swim across, why not a cavalryman? The truth is that they never tried it.

We moved up the river a short distance and camped for the night. Next morning we moved up to Platte Bridge and exchanged shots across the river with the troops who were holding this point in some force. We camped here and the soldiers made no attempt to cross and attack us. In the morning young Wolf Chief and I went up on the bluffs and examined the bridge and stockade with our field glasses. The Indians had captured several pairs of glasses during the raids on the South Platte the winter before, and these proved a great help to our scouts. We saw tents all around the stockade, which stood on the south bank, at the southern end of the bridge; and it looked as if there were quite a number of soldiers stationed at this point. We thought this would be a good place to make the big raid the chiefs were planning for June.[21]

We returned to camp, and soon after scouts rode in with word that a large wagon train was coming up the road on the south side of the river, so we broke camp and moved down the Platte. We left all our loose stock with the three women and two boys who had accompanied us, telling them that if we were chased by a large body of troops we would retreat in another direction and give them a chance to get away

command at this engagement. He claimed that six Indians were wounded, two killed. Berthrong, *Southern Cheyennes*. The date of the engagement was June 3, 1865.—S.L.

[21] That their forecasts were short of the mark by more than one month is made clear by the subsequent events at Platte Bridge.—S.L.

safely. The river had been falling for two days, and we now found a ford and crossed to the south bank, where we hid in a willow thicket. The wagon train soon came up the road, and we saw cavalry guarding the wagons. It was now nearly evening, and when the train had come quite close to where we lay, the wagons were corralled and the teams unhitched. The teamsters now unharnessed the mules and drove them down to the river to drink. As soon as the herd reached the bank, we rode out of our hiding place and charged. The teamsters rushed back toward the wagons, and the cavalry opened fire on us, but their shooting was poor and the range was too great for them to do us much harm anyhow. The warriors were after plunder and paid no attention to the soldiers.

When the Indians charged out of the thicket, yelling and shooting and waving their shields and lances, the bell mare started up the river as hard as she could go, with all the mules tearing after her. We swept after the stampeded herd in a cloud of dust and powder smoke, every warrior urging his pony to top speed. One man on a very fast horse outdistanced all the rest of us. He circled around the herd and, rushing up alongside of the bell mare, caught her by the head strap. He swerved her toward the river, forced her into the water, and soon had her swimming toward the north bank; and all the mules piled into the river at her heels, urged on by the warriors in their rear, who were still yelling and shooting.

In five minutes the whole affair was over and we were driving the captured herd up the north side of the river. We had not had a man or horse hurt and had taken two hundred and fifty as fine mules as you ever saw—big strong fellows, many of them branded U.S. The bell mare had turned the trick in our favor. If she had run toward the wagons where the troops were we would probably have lost the herd, but when she turned up the river and away from the camp she handed the entire herd over to us. The mules would follow the mare wherever she led, no matter how frightened they were. These mares were kept with most of the wagon trains in which mules were employed. White mares were the best, because the mules could see a white mare at night, and if a stampede occurred they would all stick close to the mare instead of scattering and becoming lost in the dark.

We returned up the river and rejoined the women and boys. Next morning we started for home, having taken all the stock we could handle without difficulty. On the way home the horses and mules were divided up, the medicine man getting the largest share. We had induced this man to accompany our party by promising him a large share in the plunder. He came along to tell the warriors how to paint. War paint was not mere display, as so many people appear to believe, but was a sacred charm employed to protect the warrior from wounds and death. This medicine man instructed our party in the proper manner of putting on their paint, and the result was that the party captured over three hundred fine horses and mules without having a man or pony injured. Only a warrior who owned a shield or war rig was permitted to paint. The shields and war shirts had sacred qualities. Many men had shields but only a few of the bravest were allowed to make war shirts. A man who owned a war shirt might lend it to a friend, but the man who borrowed the shirt had to show uncommon bravery while he was wearing it. If he did not he was "talked about" and shamed. With these war shirts went a number of rules which the wearer was compelled to obey. One of these rules was that if a man ran away with the wife of another man who was the owner of a war shirt, the husband must not show anger or take away the horses of the man who had stolen his wife. I remember the case of a friend of mine, a Northern Cheyenne, still living, who had a war shirt made for him those days. The same day that the shirt was completed, my friend's wife ran off with a young man, and nothing could be done about it. My friend sent word to the young fellow to come over with his pipe and they would smoke, as a sign that everything was all right between them. This rule was one of the main reasons why very few men wore these shirts.

We found the big village encamped on Lodgepole Creek, a branch of Powder River, and as soon as we came in we heard the news about the breaking away of the Sioux prisoners. These Sioux were friendlies who did not wish to join in the war. All through the winter part of these Sioux had been encamped on the north bank of the Platte, about ten miles below Fort Laramie, and Charlie Elliston was in the camp with a body of armed Indian soldiers, keeping order. In March about 150 more lodges of Sioux and 90 lodges of Northern Arapahos came to this camp and also surrendered, and in April Little Thunder joined the friendly camp with sixty lodges of Brulé Sioux. In May, Two Face and Black Foot, Oglala Sioux leaders, made up their minds to surrender. Mrs. Eubanks and her child had been captured by the Indians during the raids of 1864 and were still in the Sioux camp. In order to show their friendliness, Two Face and Black Foot bought these prisoners from their captors at a large expense and brought them to Fort Laramie. At this time there were two colonels at Fort Laramie, Colonel [Thomas] Moonlight, commanding the district, and Colonel Baumer, commanding the fort. Both of these officers were hard drinkers, and William Rowland, who was inter-preter at the post then, told me in later years that Moonlight and Baumer were both drunk when these two Sioux chiefs came in with the woman and child whom they had ransomed. Which of the colonels issued the orders I do not know, but what happened was this. Two Face and Black Foot were ordered under arrest and were ill-treated by the soldiers, and shortly afterward they were taken out-side the fort and were hung up in artillery trace chains. This outrage was committed by these two officers while they were drunk and in no condition to listen to any evidence. They ordered the chiefs hung with the idea of punishing the Indians who had captured and mis-treated Mrs. Eubanks, but, as I have said, these two Sioux were not the captors but the ransomers of the woman and her child. A few weeks later Moonlight and Baumer were both forced to leave the army, not because of the hanging of Two Face and Black Foot but because of their general incompetence and drunkenness.

By the first of June there were some two thousand "friendlies" in the camp near Laramie, most of them Brulé or Spotted Tail Sioux,[22]

[22] In subsequent years, George E. Hyde revealed his impatience with those (notably Charles A. Eastman, himself a Sioux) who had Spotted Tail as chief of

a few Oglala or Red Cloud Sioux, and about ninety lodges of Northern Arapahos. These Indians were all against the war; the chiefs constantly gave information as to the location of our hostile camps and the plans of our leaders, and many of the young men in this camp offered to join the soldiers in fighting us. But General [G. M.] Dodge, commanding the department, did not trust the friendlies over much, and now he issued an order that the Sioux should all be removed to Fort Kearny on the lower Platte. This order alarmed the Sioux, for Fort Kearny was in the country of their bitterest foes, the Pawnees, and they did not doubt that when they had been taken to Kearny, and there disarmed, that the Pawnees would make an attack on them. They therefore made strong objections to being sent east, but the officers would not listen to them, and on June 11 the Sioux, one thousand five hundred of them, men, women, and children, were started on their long march, guarded by cavalry under the command of Captain [W. D.] Fouts of the Seventh Iowa Cavalry.

I have the story of what followed from the Indians themselves. The Indians were not even disarmed, as they were known to be perfectly friendly, and the only fear the officers entertained was that the band might attempt to run away. As soon as the fort was left, however, the soldiers of the escort began to ill-treat the Sioux, and that evening when camp was pitched the officers and soldiers came in among the lodges, picked out a number of young Sioux girls, and took them to their own tents for the night. This made the Sioux furious, and when the same thing was repeated on the following night the Indians held a night council in secret and decided to fight. On the evening of the fourteenth the Indians and their guards reached Horse Creek, fifty or sixty miles east of Laramie, and went into camp here for the night. The soldiers with their wagon train crossed the creek and camped on the east bank, while the Sioux pitched their

the Brulé Sioux at this time. He was a leader but Little Thunder was chief. (Hyde, *Spotted Tail's Folk*, 102.) Little Thunder was present at the Grattan massacre in which the young Lieutenant J. L. Grattan and his entire command, with the exception of one trooper, were annihilated in 1854 near Fort Laramie. See Hyde's note 24 *infra.*—S.L.

lodges on the west bank, picking out a place that would be easily defended. There was a big willow thicket near the lodges, in which the women and children could hide.

In the morning reveille was sounded while it was still dark and the wagons with most of the troops marched soon after, intending to halt farther down the road to give the Indians time to close up in rear of the wagon train. Meantime Captain Fouts with a few men recrossed Horse Creek, to inspect the Sioux camp and hurry the Indians up. The Indians had their plans all laid. The women and children were hiding in the thicket, and when the officer and his men rode up the warriors came out of the lodges with their bows and guns concealed under their blankets. The intention was to take vengeance for the ill-treatment of the Sioux girls by killing Fouts and all his men, but some young men were too hot-headed to wait and they drew their weapons and opened fire while the officer and his men were still some distance off. The other warriors at once followed suit, and at the first fire Captain Fouts and three or four men fell dead and most of the other soldiers were wounded. The troopers did not fire a shot, but wheeled about and galloped off down the road.

The Sioux now packed their ponies in all haste (everything having been already packed up inside the lodges so that no unnecessary delay would prevent their moving at once). They then started for the Platte, which was about two miles from their camp. They had no time to take down their lodges, but left most of them standing. On reaching the river, the women and children began to swim across, taking the pack ponies with them, but the warriors remained on the southern bank with their war ponies. Pretty soon they saw the soldiers who had been with the wagon train coming up the road. There were about one hundred troopers and two or three officers. They advanced toward the Sioux, evidently intending to charge them, but about halfway to the river they halted and dismounted. The Sioux at once made a charge, all on horseback, and the officers, seeing that their party would in another minute be completely surrounded, ordered their men into the saddle again and beat a hurried retreat back across the creek. The warriors chased them down the road and up to the wagons. These had been hastily formed into a corral, inside which the troopers now sought refuge. The Sioux remained for some time, keeping the whites at bay, to give the women and children an opportunity to cross the river without being attacked. As soon as the crossing had been made, the warriors withdrew and crossed the river after the women and children. The whole outfit then struck north through the sand hills, making for the Black Hills.[23]

As soon as the Indians were gone, messengers were sent down the road on the gallop to Camp Mitchell, about twenty miles east of Horse Creek. From this station a telegram was sent to Fort Laramie to inform Colonel Moonlight of what had occurred. Moonlight at once mounted three companies of cavalry and set out in pursuit of the fugitive Sioux. He marched down the north bank of the river to the point at which the Indians had crossed, then struck north through the sand hills, following their trail. On the evening of June 18 he encamped one hundred miles northeast of Laramie, and on the following morning after marching twenty miles farther north, he made camp on Dead Man's Fork, east of Spoon Butte, on the present Wyoming-Nebraska line. The country here is rough and hilly with some pine timber, and the camp was pitched in the valley of the Dead Man, with steep cut-banks closing in on it at either side.

Meantime the runaway Sioux had moved slowly northward through the sand hills, not supposing that they would be pursued. Near Spoon Butte they fell in with a war party of hostile Sioux, who joined them; and here they discovered that Moonlight was following their trail. They moved farther north at once, but kept out scouts in the rear to watch the troops. So, when Moonlight's men encamped in the valley of Dead Man's Fork on the morning of June 19, the Sioux scouts were watching from the hills. No experienced officer would have camped his men in such a trap; but Moonlight not only did this but he permitted the men to unsaddle and turn their horses out to graze. Some California officers who had seen Indian service before protested to the Colonel, but he would not listen to them, so

[23] Hyde, *Spotted Tail's Folk*, 104–105, gives details of this fight from both Indian and official sources.—S.L.

they contented themselves by seeing that their own troop's horses were securely picketed close to camp.

Meantime the Indian scouts had reported to the chiefs, and now two hundred picked warriors were selected and sent down to get the cavalry horses. This was in broad day, mind you, at ten or eleven in the morning. The soldiers were eating breakfast, when all at once the two hundred warriors swept over the bluffs and down into the narrow valley, yelling and shooting and waving their shields and lances to frighten the herd. The loose animals stampeded at once, and many of those which were picketed and hobbled in the camp broke free and joined in the rush. Following close after the running animals, the warriors swept by the camp, turned the herd, and drove it over the bluffs. About one company of the troops had saved their horses, and now these men mounted and set off in pursuit of the Sioux, but over the bluffs they almost fell into a trap which the Sioux had set for them among the hills; and seeing their danger just in time, the soldiers turned at once and rushed back to camp without attempting to fight.

The troops set off for Fort Laramie at once. Moonlight and most of his men were on foot; they had to carry their own saddles and equipment, and walking in cavalry boots among the sand hills is not pleasant. To make matters worse, the men were nearly out of rations, and water was to be found only in tiny trickles and pools about twenty miles apart, and even this was so brackish that it could hardly be swallowed. It was a very savage and footsore band of Indian fighters that finally straggled into Fort Laramie, and neither men nor officers forgave Moonlight for what he had led them into. His political pull saved him from a court-martial, but he was soon after relieved of command and mustered out of service.

The fugitive Sioux fled north to Bear Butte in the Black Hills, but even after what they had been through they were unwilling to join our hostile camp; and in July, after Moonlight and Baumer had both been mustered out of service, these same Sioux returned to Fort Laramie and again surrendered.

When our Cheyenne war party reached the hostile village on the

Lodgepole branch of Powder River, we found that other parties had come in ahead of us with plunder, and the following day Young-Man-Afraid-of-His-Horses came in with a big Sioux party which had taken much plunder on the Platte. This Sioux leader belonged to the same soldier society that I did, and the night that his party came in he gave a big feast to our society. I knew him very well in those days but never saw him after 1865. One night soon after we reached the village, all of the soldier societies held a great Shield Dance. A huge fire was started in the center of the camp and perhaps a thousand [Indian] soldiers joined in the dance around the fire. Meantime the chiefs of all the tribes were holding a war council, and in the middle of the night the headmen of the soldier societies announced to their warriors that the chiefs had decided to make a grand raid at Platte Bridge which the different war parties had visited and reported to be the best place for making a strong attack. The chiefs also announced that no more small war parties would be permitted to leave camp at present, and that the Crazy Dog Soldiers had been selected to police camp and see that orders were obeyed. Next day the Crazy Dogs sent through the camp some criers who announced that any young men who attempted to make up war parties would be severely quirted and would have their war ponies shot.

We moved camp from day to day, advancing slowly up the Powder. Everyone was busy preparing for war; all the charms worn in battle were being repaired, new eagle feathers were put in the war bonnets and on the shields, war shirts were put into perfect condition, etc. It was believed that if a man went into battle without his charms, war bonnet, etc., in perfect condition, he would be sure to get killed. All this repair work had to be done with the aid of the medicine men, who knew the proper ceremonies, and these men had to be given feasts and presents by the warriors who asked their assistance. At last we reached the Crazy Woman's Fork of Powder River, the point from which our grand war party was to set out; and here we encamped for several days while the final preparations were being made.

We were camped with the lodges set in a great circle, and the day before we started there was a grand war parade. That day all of the soldier societies held dances and everyone was painted and dressed in full war rig. Even the war ponies were painted and had their tails tied up and ornamented with eagle feathers. The warriors formed up outside the circle, each society in a separate band, the bravest men in front, two abreast, but in the rear rank there were four men abreast. The societies of each tribe formed in separate bands. The Crazy Dogs being accounted the bravest, were in front of all others, while the Dog Soldiers brought up the rear. When all were ready, we rode into the village and around the great circle of lodges, each band singing its own war songs. The old men, women, and children stood in front of the lodges, also singing. That night we danced until nearly morning, and at daylight we marched. The ponies had been herded inside the circle of lodges during the night, and in the morning each warrior caught his best pony and mounted. We made a short march and halted early, to give everyone time to come up.

This march to Platte Bridge was conducted just as the expeditions of olden times were. The Crazy Dogs still acted as police; they led the march and kept order in the column. About two hundred women came with us, the rest remaining at the village. In our camp each soldier band camped by itself in a separate group. In the morning the men of each band formed up in column. Each society had its appointed place in the column. The chiefs went to the head of the column, to lead the march, and behind them was a party of Crazy Dogs, acting as advance guard. Behind the column came another group of Crazy Dogs, serving as rear guard. The chiefs of all the four tribes rode ahead, bearing the war pipes. When we came to water these chiefs halted and sat down; then the column broke up and everyone drank, watered their ponies, and sat down to rest and smoke. In the evening, at the end of the march, the chiefs selected the camping place.

Old Platte Bridge was at the place where the city of Casper, Wyoming, now stands; indeed, this city is named after one of the officers killed in the fight we now had with the troops. When we drew near the bridge, the pipe bearers (as the chiefs were called) selected a party of scouts and sent them forward to see how things were at the bridge. Meantime our column went into camp on the head of a small stream which flows into the Platte from the north (now called Casper Creek, I believe). Toward evening the scouts returned and the pipe bearers sent three criers through the camp (three old men, one Cheyenne, one Arapaho, and one Sioux) to announce the news the scouts had brought in. There were fully three thousand warriors in this camp, the biggest war party that I ever saw, and perfectly organized. The criers also announced that no singing would be permitted that night and that anyone who started a war song would be severely "soldiered" by the Crazy Dogs, who still acted as police.

At dawn next day (July 25) ten more scouts were selected and sent out toward the bridge. They moved down the creek on which we were encamped. We then formed in column. The Crazy Dogs got in front of us and on both flanks, and the Dog Soldiers in our rear. They crowded us up into one big mass and held us so, to prevent anyone from slipping away. The pipe bearers formed up in a long line ahead of the column. I remember seeing in that line Red Cloud and Old-Man-Afraid-of-His-Horses with their scalp shirts on. We then started, the soldiers ordering us to walk our ponies, for if we moved faster a great cloud of dust would have arisen and might had warned the troops of our approach.

Old Platte Bridge spanned the North Platte just west of Casper Creek, the little stream on whose head our camp was located. This bridge had been built in 1859 and was much used by the emigrants, freighters, and the stage coaches in earlier years, but in 1865 the stage company no longer used this route and the bridge was mainly of service to the emigrants and the military trains. At the south end of the bridge was the military post, a stockade, the abandoned stage station, and the office of the Overland Telegraph Company. The road came up the south bank of the river, crossed at the bridge, and went on up the north bank toward the Sweetwater. At this point the Platte Valley was very wide, with high bluffs closing it in on the north and south.

When we had advanced some miles, we halted behind a hill which formed a part of the line of high bluffs on the north side of the valley. Now medicine making began, and everyone was told to get ready for a fight. Every man who had a war bonnet, shield, or other sacred object had to go through certain ceremonies. A man with a war bonnet would take it out of its bag and hold it up, first to the south, then to the west, to the north, and to the east, and then put it on his head. A shield was taken from its case and held in the right hand. It was then dipped toward the ground and shaken four times, held up toward the sun and shaken four times, and then placed on the left arm, where it was carried in battle.

While these ceremonies were being gone through with, some men who had field glasses were permitted to go up on the hilltop to see what the scouts were doing. These scouts had been instructed to attempt to draw the troops into the hills, where we could surround them. The scouts were now seen approaching the northern end of the bridge, and soon a body of troops was discovered coming across the bridge with cannon. The scouts began to retire toward the bluffs, drawing the soldiers after them. On the hilltop were the chiefs, Red Cloud, Old-Man-Afraid, Roman Nose, and some others.[24] Roman Nose now called out to the mass of warriors behind the hill that soldiers were crossing the bridge. The warriors, jammed into a dense mass and held where they were by the Crazy Dogs and Dog Soldiers, waited impatiently. Soon the distant boom of a cannon was heard, followed by the plup! plup! of rifles, and the dense mass of warriors

[24] These statements of Bent's about the "chiefs" who led this grand war party, are very enlightening; I have never believed Red Cloud was a real chief at this date, but a leader of the warriors. The Sioux at Red Cloud Agency in 1874 stated emphatically that R.C. had been put in his position of head chief by the whites. They said to the commission that Old-Man-Afraid was the man they most looked up to—he was formerly their "brave man." Now Old-Man-Afraid, says Bent, was with Red C. among the "chiefs" who led this party in 1865, and he now says Roman Nose was also one of these chiefs. Bent insisted always that Roman Nose was not a chief at all, but only a "brave man" and war leader. So these "chiefs" who led the party at Platte Bridge were not real chiefs, who were peace officials, but were leaders of the warriors.—G.H.

This analysis is supported in Hyde's later researches, as given in *Red Cloud's Folk* (1937), 139–40.—S.L.

surged forward. The Crazy Dogs attempted to beat them back with their quirts and war clubs, but the men were now too excited to pay any heed to the soldiers. They broke through the line of Crazy Dogs and rushed up to the top of the hills where Roman Nose and the other leaders were standing. Everyone was talking at once and the excitement was intense. From the hilltop we could see our ten scouts retreating toward us, followed at some distance by a troop of cavalry with some cannon, and infantry formed up on each side of the guns. The chiefs induced the warriors to keep down behind the hilltop so as not to show themselves on the skyline, and here we waited, watching the scene in the valley below. The scouts kept circling in front of the troops, slowly retiring toward the hills where we lay, but the soldiers appeared to be suspicious and were advancing with extreme caution. As they came near to the hills they moved more and more slowly, and at last they halted and would come no nearer. The scouts tried all manner of tricks, but it was useless, and about noon they gave it up and rode into the hills to join us. Everyone was greatly disappointed, but the leaders said that we would try again the following day.

The Crazy Dogs and Dog Soldiers now set to work and forced the warriors to form into a dense column again. They then marched us back up the creek and to camp. That was a bad night. We were all discouraged and the soldiers would not permit any singing or even much talking. Toward day another party of scouts was sent out, my younger brother Charlie accompanying them. After dawn we all formed up again, but this time we were divided into three parties. One body of warriors went down the creek, while another party, which I was with, moved farther west and hid behind the hills about due north of the bridge. These two parties were rather small ones. The third party was our main body, and it moved up behind the bluffs to the northwest of the bridge and west of the party which I was with. This day we were not held behind the hills by the Crazy Dogs but were permitted to go up to the hilltops.

I think it was about nine in the morning when we saw a body of cavalry march across the bridge and turn west along the road which ran between the river and the line of bluffs behind which we were concealed. When these troops appeared the warriors crowded up to the hilltops and sat there on their war ponies watching. I have always thought it strange that the troops did not see us and retreat back across the river at once, but they continued their advance without showing any signs of alarm. They passed the hills on which the party I was with stood watching them and moved on up the road. We were now nearer to the bridge than the troops were, and some of the warriors wished to make a charge, but the leaders urged them to wait. Moving slowly up the road, the cavalry presently came opposite the high hills behind which our main body lay; and then all at once we saw a couple of thousand mounted warriors swarm over the tops of the hills and sweep down into the valley.

We heard the distant yells and shots and saw the soldiers halt and break ranks. The Indians were half a mile or more away yet, but the troops were instantly thrown into confusion, and in another moment they had turned and were galloping back along the road, every man for himself. Our leaders now let us go and we rushed over the bluffs and down into the valley, to cut the soldiers off from the bridge, while at the same moment the third party, hiding behind the hills east of us, also charged out and raced for the bridge. The hills and valley were now alive with warriors, charging on the troops from the northwest, from the north, and from the northeast. As our party began its charge, I saw a company of infantry rush out of the stockade and start across the bridge on the run, and at the same time a cannon was brought out and swung into position; both infantry and artillery then opened fire on us in an attempt to cover the retreat of the galloping cavalry, but the men fired in such a hurry that they did us no injury. In fact, we were most of us still far out of range of rifle fire.

The troopers had only covered about half of the distance back to the bridge when our party ran into them, striking them on the left flank. Several hundred warriors on swift ponies were right at their heels and they had no time to stop and face us. As we rushed in among them, the air was thick with dust and powder smoke; you could not see a dozen yards and the shots and yells deafened the ears. As we went into the troops, I saw an officer [Lieutenant Caspar Collins] on a big bay horse rush past me through the dense clouds of dust and smoke. His horse was running away with him and broke right through the Indians. The Lieutenant had an arrow sticking in his forehead and his face was streaming with blood. He must have fallen soon after he passed me, for he dropped right in the midst of the warriors, one of whom caught his horse. I saw soldiers falling on every side. A few broke through and reached the infantry at the bridge; the infantry then ran back across the bridge and the cannon opened fire again. I do not think that more than four of five of the troopers succeeding in escaping. The road for a mile or more was dotted with dead bodies, and at the point where our party struck the troops the bodies of the men and the dead horses lay in groups.

Part of the warriors now attempted to rush the bridge, but the cannon was posted to sweep this clear and no one could get across here. The river was very high, but eight or ten warriors swam their ponies across below the bridge and made for a ranch which stood by the roadside. There were some cavalrymen at this ranch, but when they saw the Indians attacking Lieutenant Collins' men, they left the ranch and marched up the road toward the stockade at the bridge end. This little party of warriors, after swimming the river, charged the cavalry and drove them up the road and into the stockade. High-Back-Wolf, a very brave Northern Cheyenne, rode up to an officer and struck at him. The officer had a saber in one hand and a pistol in the other. He fired the pistol in High-Back-Wolf's face and the warrior fell off his pony dead. But the Indians think the officer's ball missed him and that he was struck by a rifle shot from the stockade.

The soldiers kept firing on us with their cannon. The whole valley on our side of the river was swarming with warriors, but they did not like the big guns and most of them retired behind the hills again. Here they were sitting on their ponies, excitedly discussing the fight, when all at once some men who were on the bluffs called out that Indians down in the valley were signaling that more soldiers were coming down the road from the west. The warriors at once rode over the hills again and down into the valley. We rode at top speed, every-

219

one eager to get into the fight. About five miles up the valley we came upon the fight. Many Indians were already on the ground and had the soldiers surrounded in a little hollow near the river bank. As far back along the road as you could see, the valley was alive with warriors, all hurrying up to join in the fight.

When the Indians I was with came up, the soldiers were already fighting a large body of warriors. The troopers had dug rifle pits around the corralled wagons and had also piled up their mess chests, bedding, etc. under the wagons. Some men were in the pits, others behind the barracade under the wagons, and a few sharpshooters were in the wagons, firing through holes cut in the canvas tops. Just as we came up, the Indians made a charge and ran off all the mules belonging to the train. (The soldiers had no horses. They were dismounted cavalrymen and were going east in the wagons.)

This fresh body of troops had come down the road from some post farther west. They did not know that a fight was in progress, but were simply on the march, going east under orders. They had a wagon train with them. They did not know that any Indians were about until they reached a point about five miles west of Platte Bridge, at which point the road crossed a hill. When they came to the top of this hill they had a view of the valley as far as the bridge, and here they saw that the valley was full of Indians and that a fight was going on. Soon after they were themselves discovered, and the Indians began to gather in their front. The troops then retreated back across the hill and to a bare sandy hollow on the river bank, where they corralled the wagons and prepared to fight.

When the Indians I was with came up, the soldiers were already fighting a large body of warriors. The troopers had dug rifle pits around the corralled wagons and had also piled up their mess chests, bedding, etc. under the wagons. Some men were in the pits, others behind the barracade under the wagons, and a few sharpshooters were in the wagons, firing through holes cut in the canvas tops. Just as we came up, the Indians made a charge and ran off all the mules belonging to the train. (The soldiers had no horses. They were dismounted cavalrymen and were going east in the wagons.)

These men held out against a huge force of Indians for about half an hour. At first there were no leaders on the ground and the Indian attack was not well organized. The little bare basin in which the wagons were corraled was surrounded by hillocks of sand. The warriors crawled up behind these knolls and fired on the wagons from all sides, but the soldiers, especially the good shots in the wagon beds, kept up a heavy fire and prevented the Indians from closing in. One teamster got down to the river bank, and buckling his revolver around his head by the belt he swam the river and reached the bushes on the other bank safely. Only a few of the Indians saw him or he would have been killed in the water. Presently Roman Nose's brother got into the water and swam after the white man. Reaching the bushes, the teamster turned and opened fire on his pursuer; one shot struck the Indian in the head killing him while he was still in the water. The teamster then got away. He was the only man to escape.

The Indians were now nearly all dismounted, firing from behind the hillocks; but presently the leaders came up—Roman Nose, Bear Tongue, Twins, and some other brave men. They called out for everyone to get ready for a charge. "We are going to empty the soldiers' guns," they said. These men all had war bonnets and shields. They rode out and began to circle around the wagons, riding very fast. The soldiers under the wagons fired many shots at them, and those in the wagons fired a few, but the warriors were not touched, for they all had very strong charms. Presently these riders gave the signal and the Indians all charged straight for the wagons, most of them preferring to go on foot. It was all over in a minute. I ran down from where I had been watching, and when I reached the wagons the Indians were still shooting at the men under the wagons. Three men had been killed in the wagons. A fourth was thrown out and shot on the ground. The Indians, following their usual custom, took no prisoners. I counted twenty-two bodies. Eight warriors were killed here and many more were wounded. There was nothing in the wagons but the bedding and mess chests. I never saw a printed account of this fight except one newspaper version which alleged that the soldiers were unarmed and were massacred by the Indians, who tied some of the men to the wagon wheels and burned them alive. This is all nonsense. The Plains Indians never tortured prisoners, they never took men prisoners but shot them at once, during the fighting. As to the soldiers being without arms, they were very well armed and put up a hard fight. They stood off a thousand warriors for a least half an hour. Lieutenant Collins and his men, on the other hand, were killed in a few minutes and with practically no loss to the Indians.[25]

After this second fight we all rode back to camp, everyone talking and greatly excited. It was now nearly evening and we had been fighting all day. In the morning we broke up into small war parties and these went out in different directions to raid the roads. More of the Indians, however, returned at once to the village on Powder River, taking no part in the little raids that followed. I went back to the village with the main body.

[25] George Bent's eye-witness account of the Battle of Platte Bridge, as here given, has never before been published, although historians have often cited his many letters, detailing events, to George E. Hyde. In general, the white casualties are more extensive in Bent's account than in the accounts left by white survivors, some of which were drawn upon by Hyde, *Spotted Tail's Folk*, 106; *Red Cloud's Folk*, 123–26 (in which Hyde Speaks of Bent's accuracy as sustained by official accounts); Grinnell, *Fighting Cheyennes*, 228–29; Berthrong, *Southern Cheyennes*, 248–49; Agnes Wright Spring, *Caspar Collins*, 82–94; and J. W. Vaughn, *The Battle of Platte Bridge*, which is the most recent, extended account of these events.—S.L.

CHAPTER EIGHT

POWDER RIVER

T HE EASE WITH which the Indians had carried out their great
raids during the winter of 1864–65 had caused an outcry in the
West against the generals who then commanded the troops in the
Plains. Everyone demanded a change, the newspapers declared that
the kid-glove generals must go and that a rough-and-ready Indian-
fighter was what was needed in the Plains. The Overland Stage
Company was particularly active in exerting pressure on the War
Department, and the result was that late in the winter Brigadier
General P. E. Connor was brought east and put in command of the
troops along the Platte. The people hailed Connor's appointment
with delight. He was a Mexican War veteran who had reentered the
service again in 1861 as colonel of a California cavalry regiment.
With his regiment he was soon sent to Nevada, where the Indians
were causing trouble, and in the winter of 1862–63 he took the field
against the Paiutes, surprised a large camp on Bear River, Utah,
January 29, 1863, and in the ensuing fight killed 278 Indians, including many women and children. This slaughter of the Paiutes, which
closely resembled the Sand Creek Massacre in which our people were
butchered a year later, made Colonel Connor the hero of the frontiersmen in Nevada, Utah, and California. Thereafter nothing was
too good for him. He was soon promoted to a brigadier general, and
a year later was put in command of all the troops in the Plains.[1]

[1] Bent neglects Major General Grenville M. Dodge, Connor's superior. He
knew only that Connor commanded in the field.—G.H.
The reorganization of army commands on January 30, 1865, placed Major

223

General Connor soon became as popular in Colorado and Nebraska as he had been farther west; the Overland Stage officials were especially pleased as the new General assured them that the line would be so strongly guarded that the Indians would be unable to make any serious trouble. He also let the public know that he was planning a campaign in the heart of the Indian country which would keep the warriors so busy near home that they would be unable to make raids along the roads. This plan for operations on a large scale in the Indian country was worked out in the early spring of 1865. [Major] General [Alfred] Sully with a strong column of cavalry was to march from the upper Missouri west to the mouth of Powder River, build a fort in that vicinity and then move up Powder River. At the same time General Connor was to march from Laramie north to the head of the Powder and build a fort; then proceed down Powder to meet Sully. Thus our hostile camps would be caught between the two columns and would be struck such a blow that they would be only too glad to keep the peace thereafter. This plan, however, fell through, as Sully failed to take the field; and it was then decided that Connor should deal with us single-handed.[2]

General Connor's first task was to put the Overland Stage into good running order and to detail troops to protect the line from raiders. This work was done in April and May; the roads were now declared safe and everyone was greatly pleased with the vigorous action of the new commander. But now, in the middle of May, the Indians broke up their winter camp and began to raid, as I have told

General John Pope in command of "the Military Division of the Missouri, including the Department of the Missouri and the Northwest, headquarters at St. Louis." General Orders No. 11, as cited in Jones, *The Civil War in the Northwest*, 191. Dodge thus served, as commander of the Department of the Missouri, under Pope. —S.L.

[2] Pope's plan was for Sully to move west from Fort Pierre, on the Missouri in present central South Dakota, and for Connor to march north from Fort Laramie, to engage the Indians on the Wind and Bighorn rivers, a location which was incorrect at the time because of faulty information gathered by Colonel Thomas Moonlight. Berthrong, *Southern Cheyennes*, 245–46.—S.L.

in the preceding chapter, and it was now seen that General Connor was as helpless in dealing with the raiding parties as [Brigadier] General Mitchell and the other officers whom he had superceded had been. The Indians soon had the roads tied up as badly as ever; then, toward the close of July, we made the great raid on Platte Bridge and wiped out two troops of cavalry. The Indians had never before shown such boldness in their attacks, and there was now a general slump in Connor stock.

The General, however, insisted that the raiding would stop immediately, as soon as he could march his columns into the Powder River country and alarm the Indians by threatening their camps. The Civil War was now ending and whole brigades of cavalry were soon set free for service against the Indians. The General, having been given a free hand, now called for large reinforcements of cavalry, at the same time sending in requisitions for great quantities of supplies to be sent up the Platte at once. Indeed, Connor's demands grew to such proportions that at length, in July, the War Department became alarmed and informed the General that the mere expense of transporting the supplies he had ordered was costing two millions a month, not counting the cost of the supplies themselves or the pay of the troops. He was therefore ordered to cut down on his requisitions and to get his columns into the field at once. At first it had been supposed that the columns would move in April, but now it was the end of July and no move had yet been made.

If the Indians had continued their raids I do not believe that Connor could have moved at all. His attention would have been entirely taken up in guarding the roads. But at the end of July the Indians stopped raiding and collected in their camps in the Powder River country, to hold the usual summer medicine ceremonies. This gave the General a breathing space, which he employed in making his final preparations, and early in August actually got his columns started. The plan of the movement that now began was as follows: The first column, commanded by Colonel [Nelson] Cole, was to march from the lower Platte to the Black Hills, around the northern side of the hills, and thence west to Tongue River, where he was to meet Connor's column near Panther Mountain. Colonel [Samuel] Walker with the second column was to march from near Fort Laramie straight north, right through the heart of the Black Hills, and join Cole's column on the north side of the hills. The General with the main column was to march from the Platte, above Laramie, north to the head of the Powder, establish a post there, and then march down Tongue River to the meeting place where Cole and Walker were to join him. The troops were to attack the Indians wherever met, and as the columns were to converge from different directions it was supposed that the Indians would be caught between them in such a way that they would find it very difficult to escape without being forced to fight at a great disadvantage. Having explained these movements of the troops, I will now return to the Indians and recount what they did after returning from the Platte Bridge fight.[3]

As I have said, part of the warriors broke up into small raiding parties after the big fight, but the main body returned at once to the village at the mouth of Crazy Woman's Fork of Powder River.[4] Here at this village the Indians all made medicine, the Sioux holding a sun dance and the Cheyennes going through the Medicine Arrow ceremony. After this the Northern Arapahos left and moved west to Tongue River, the Cheyennes and Sioux remaining on the Powder to hunt. We moved down Powder River, toward the north, and as soon as the medicine-making was over some small war parties set out to make new raids along the roads. Meantime Connor had taken the field, and unknown to us he was now approaching the head of Powder River. On August 11 he reached the point on Powder River where the Indians usually crossed. This was a favorite wintering ground of the Indians, and the General at once decided that the place was a good one at which to establish his post; he therefore set his men to work and soon had the new fort well under way. He called

[3] Bent's description of Connor's strategy is accurate in most details (see Berthrong, op. cit., 249–50). The movements started July 30, 1865.—S.L.

[4] Located in northwestern Wyoming, where Crazy Woman Creek empties into the Powder.—S.L.

the place Cantonment Connor, but the post was later known as Old Fort Reno.[5]

The trail used by the Indians in going south to the Platte to make raids ran just west of the new post. Connor had a large number of Pawnee and Omaha scouts with him, and while the fort was being built he set these warriors to watch the trail. The scouts were very skillful at this kind of work and during a week or so they caught several of our small raiding parties returning from the Platte and punished them pretty severely. My step-mother was with one of these war parties.[6] This party went up the Platte clear into the mountains, taking a great deal of plunder, and then started back for Powder River. They passed quite near to Connor's Fort without seeing any soldiers, but the next day, about fifty miles north of the fort, they ran into the Pawnee scouts. My step-mother and four men were riding some distance ahead of the others when they saw a few Pawnees on a hill far to the front. The Pawnees had disguised themselves so as to appear like Cheyennes or Sioux, and they now signaled with their blankets, "We are friends; come nearer." So the Cheyennes rode forward without suspecting any danger; but when my step-mother and the four men she was riding with had come quite close to the hill, a large body of Pawnees suddenly charged over the hill and attacked them, while at the same time a company of cavalry appeared off to one side and also attacked the Cheyennes. My step-mother and her four companions were overtaken and all killed, but the rest of the Cheyennes threw away their plunder and made their escape. The Pawnees claimed that they killed twenty-four Cheyennes in this fight, but this is not true. They may have killed twenty-four Indians in some other fight about this time, but this was the only Cheyenne war party they caught, and there are men still living who were with this party and who know that only five people were killed.

[5] Fort Connor was located on the east bank of the Powder, Reno slightly north, on the west bank.—S.L.

[6] Yellow Woman, the younger sister of Owl Woman, mother of Julia Bent, George's half-sister. H. L. Luebers, "William Bent's Family," *Colorado Magazine*, January, 1936.—S.L.

By setting traps in this way, the Indian scouts managed to catch three or four war parties returning from the Platte, killing some of the warriors and capturing a great deal of plunder.[7]

There were two big Indian trails near Connor's Fort. The one on the west side of the river was very large and plain; it was the trail our great war party had used in going to Platte Bridge and returning, and it is a strange thing that Connor did not follow this trail up with his column. At this time we were camped on the river not very far north of the troops, and as we did not know at the time that any soldiers were on Powder River, our camp might easily have been surprised. If he had used his Indian scouts in a proper way, instead of setting them to hunting for small war parties, he could easily have learned the location of our camps. The General's plan, however, was to march to Tongue River, and as soon as his post was put into some condition for defense, he detached some troops to garrison the place and with his wagons and the rest of his men marched west toward the Tongue. Old Jim Bridger acted as guide. The sharp-eyed Bridger soon declared that he could see a smoke far away to the front toward Tongue River. As Tongue River was still fifty miles away and the officers even with the aid of their glasses could see nothing, they expressed their doubts as to the truthfulness of Bridger's report; but the old man fell into a rage, called them a set "of damned paper-collared soldiers," and made such a row that the General hastily ordered the Pawnees to go on ahead and investigate. Connor encamped on Peno Creek to await the return of the scouts. When they came back they reported that a large camp of Northern Arapahos was on Wolf Creek, a small tributary of Tongue River, right where Bridger had seen the smoke rising.

Leaving his wagons at the camp on Peno Creek, the General took 250 cavalrymen and 80 Indian scouts and, setting out westward, marched all night. His intention was to attack the Arapahos by sur-

---

[7] The deaths of the five Cheyennes occurred on or about August 16, 1865. Brigadier General Connor in a letter of August 19, 1865, to General G. M. Dodge said that his Pawnee scouts had killed the whole party. Grinnell, *Fighting Cheyennes*, 206–207.—S.L.

prise at dawn, but the country was so rough and the trail so much encumbered with fallen timber that the troops were much delayed, and dawn came while they were still some miles from the Arapaho camp. About nine o'clock, while the column was moving up a little ravine, an officer from the advance guard rode back and cautioned the men to make no noise. He reported that the Arapaho camp was just ahead and that the troops would come in sight of it as soon as they left the ravine. He had seen the village and a great herd of ponies grazing near at hand; the Indians appeared to be on the point of breaking camp, and some had already taken down their lodges and were moving away. Having received this report, Connor placed himself at the head of the column and at once ordered an advance.

The Arapahos were taken completely by surprise when the soldiers rode up out of the ravine, formed in line and charged. The Pawnees and Omahas made straight for the pony herd, cutting the Arapahos off from their mounts, and then the soldiers dashed in among the lodges, firing right and left. The Arapahos fought fiercely but were pressed back from one group of lodges to another, and finally were driven out of the village. They retreated up Wolf Creek, closely pressed by the mounted troops.

The fight now appeared to be over, and the Pawnees scattered through the village to plunder. They had taken about six hundred ponies and had captured a number of women and children, including two young girls, who are old women now and from whom I recently secured an account of this affair. Part of the ponies, however, had been run off by some Arapaho warriors. The men made a wide circuit to avoid the Pawnees and finally rejoined the retreating warriors on Wolf Creek. Connor and his men were still eagerly pushing on after the fleeing Arapahos when these men arrived with the horses. The Arapahos, nearly all on foot, had found it impossible to make a stand against the cavalry, but now about half of the men secured ponies, and the minute they were mounted they turned on the troops and charged like a whirlwind, driving the soldiers back down Wolf Creek in confusion and pursuing them in among the lodges. Here the troops dismounted and held the Indians off, but the Arapahos circled all around the camp, shooting and yelling and making dashes at the herd which the Pawnees had taken. It was now noon and the famished troopers were eating dried buffalo meat, which was found in great abundance in the lodges. The horses were worn out after the hard night march and the long fight, and many of the men put their saddles on captured Indian ponies; but the moment they attempted to mount, the half-wild animals began to buck and kick. For a while the air was as full of cavalrymen as it was of bullets and arrows, and the Pawnee scouts sat on their sleepy ponies and laughed.

At last everyone was safely mounted; the lodges were fired and the flames leapt up as the troops marched out of the village. The Pawnees went ahead with their prisoners and the captured herd, while the troops attempted to push back the infuriated Arapahos, who circled and charged, drew off, reformed, and charged again. Hour after hour the fight went on, the Arapahos making charge after charge in the hope of recapturing their women and children and the herd. The troops were running out of ammunition, darkness came on, but still the Indians hung on the rear of the column, making a fresh charge every few minutes. At last, about midnight, the Indians fired a final fusillade and sullenly withdrew. The weary troops continued the march until dawn, when they reached the camp on Peno Creek. They had been in the saddle, marching and fighting almost without a pause, for two nights and one day, with little to eat during most of the time except the jerked meat they had found in the captured village.[8]

This fight with the Arapahos was the only successful one the troops had with the Indians during the whole campaign. A few days

[8] This fight took place after Connor had left the fort named for him on August 22. The Arapahos he and his Pawnee scouts engaged were Black Bear's northern band. Little Horse of the Northern Cheyennes and his wife, who were on their way to visit the Northern Arapahos, are quoted by Grinnell as having brought the warning of the approaching troops, at first unheeded, then acted upon, hence the break-up of the camp. Panther, Little Horse's brother-in-law, himself incredulous at the warning, was killed in the village. Grinnell, *Fighting Cheyennes*, 210–211. Berthrong, *Southern Cheyennes*, 252, credits the Pawnees with taking sixty scalps, and Connor's troops with one thousand ponies.—S.L.

later the Arapahos visited Connor's camp and he made a sort of peace with them, returning the captured women and children. He also wished to return the ponies, but the Pawnees declared that they had been promised all of the horses and other plunder they might capture during the expedition. Howling Wolf, a Cheyenne, was present at this talk, and he tells me that the Pawnees claimed that they had captured all of the ponies and that the animals therefore were their property. He says it was so: the soldiers did not capture any of the animals, and also all of the women and children were taken by the Pawnees. After arranging this peace with the Arapahos, Connor marched his column down Tongue River, to meet Colonel Cole's column at Panther Mountain.

While Connor was operating on Tongue River our big village of Cheyennes and Sioux was encamped on Powder River, not far north of the new fort. We did not see any of Connor's troops, but in August had a little fight with Sawyers' "road-building" expedition.[9] This man Sawyers had worked a smooth swindle on the War Department. He wished to take a party of emigrants (miners) to Montana by a new route through the hostile Indian country and wished to secure aid and an escort of troops to guard his party. As the government did not give aid or escorts to private parties, [Colonel Samuel] Walker pretended that he was going to build bridges and open up a new road which would be of great value to emigrants, and by exerting political pull he succeeded not only in securing a strong escort but also rations, tools, and other supplies for his party. Sawyers assembled his emigrants at Sioux City and the government sent a steamboat up the Missouri with the troops, supplies, and guns. The expedition marched

[9] James A. Sawyers and his surveying and emigrant party lost an advance scout, Nathaniel D. Hedges, on August 13, to the Cheyennes. Between five hundred and six hundred Dog Soldiers and Crooked Lances of the Southern Cheyennes, Dull Knife's Northern Cheyennes, and Oglala Sioux under Red Cloud attacked and harried the party for the next two days. Colonel Samuel Walker, whom Bent describes here, was in command at this time of a column sent north from Fort Laramie by Connor, to rendezvous with him later. There had been no news of his command since its departure. Grinnell, *Fighting Cheyennes*, 212; Berthrong, *Southern Cheyennes*, 253–54.—S.L.

on June 13 from the mouth of the Niobrara. Sawyers, who now called himself "Colonel," commanded the gold seekers, whom he styled "road builders." They had eighty wagons loaded with supplies and tools, mostly supplied by the War Department. The escort, commanded by Captain Williford,[10] was made up of two companies of U.S. Volunteers (ex-Confederate soldiers, enlisted in the prison camps to serve in the Indian country), and a troop of the First Dakota Cavalry, with two howitzers. The party moved up the Niobrara, not troubling themselves about road building. From the head of the Niobrara they struck up Cheyenne River and passed north of Pumpkin Buttes, making for Powder River, where they knew General Connor intended to build a fort; but they were now far north of the fort, and they soon found that the country between them and Powder River was so rough that it was impossible to take wagons through it. They therefore turned back, but soon lost their way; and while they were wandering about near Pumpkin Buttes they were discovered by a party of our warriors.

The Indians kept this train corralled four days, fighting most of the time, but the warriors did not make a serious attack, only desiring to secure some plunder. After one of the attacks Sawyers and Captain Williford came out of the corral to hold a talk and I went forward with one of the Cheyenne chiefs to meet them. I acted as interpreter.[11] During the talk one of the whites mentioned that General Connor was about to build a fort on Powder River; in fact, the post had already been built, but Sawyers and Williford did not know this. This was the first we learned of the government's intention of building such a post, and the Northern Cheyennes were very angry when they heard the news, as the post was to be established right in the heart of their hunting grounds. At the close of the talk Sawyers offered to buy off the Indians, promising to give them a wagonload of goods if they would stop attacking his outfit. The chief agreed to this and the goods were handed over; but later on another band of Cheyennes came up, and as they had received no share of the

[10] Not otherwise identified by either Bent or Grinnell.—S.L.
[11] Charles, George Bent's younger brother, accompanied him in this parley.—S.L.

goods, they made a second attack on the wagons and kept them fighting about two days longer.[12]

After this the Indians moved away and the wagon train wandered around in the rough country for some days, finally discovering Connor's Fort. Here a new escort of cavalry was secured and the train went on west to Tongue River, but when the party reached the vicinity of the Bighorn Mountains they ran into the Northern Arapahos, who were very angry because of the recent attack Connor had made on them. The Arapahos forced the train to corral again and fight, and this time the attack was serious. Sawyers, however, managed to get a messenger through the Indian lines, and this man made his way to Connor's camp on Tongue River. The General sent more cavalry to help the "road builders" out, and on the appearance of this force the Indians withdrew and the party moved on again toward the northwest, finally reaching Virginia City without any further accident.[13]

The next fights we had, and the only ones that amounted to anything during this whole campaign, were with Colonel Cole's and Colonel Walker's columns. Cole marched from Omaha above the mouth of the Platte on July 1 with about 1,500 men, mounted as cavalry, a number of howitzers, and a very large wagon train. Neither Cole nor his troops had served in the Plains before; they were brought up from Missouri to take part in this Indian expedition, and from the very beginning of the column's march everything was mismanaged. The horses and mules were also from Missouri and required special care to bring them through a hard march in the Plains; but no such care was given them, and from the lower Platte to the Black Hills the column's trail could have been followed by the carcasses of dead horses and mules. This column moved up to the northern side of the Black Hills, as it had been rumored that our hostile village was in that vicinity; but arriving near Bear Butte, Cole found

[12] Grinnell, quoting Sawyers, does not identify the dissenting Indians in the second attack. Berthrong identifies them as Sioux. Sawyers says George Bent at this time was wearing a staff officer's uniform, evidently plunder.—S.L.

[13] The Arapaho attack under Black Bear occurred on the Tongue River on August 31, 1865.—S.L.

that there were no Indians in that whole region, so he continued his march around the northern side of the hills and west toward Powder River.

Meantime Colonel Walker with the Sixteenth Kansas Cavalry, six hundred men and a large train of pack mules, had set out to march from near Fort Laramie straight north to the Black Hills. Neither Walker nor his regiment had any heart for Indian fighting. The men claimed that their time of service had expired, and just before the order to march was received, they mutinied and refused to obey orders. A number of howitzers loaded with grapeshot and trained on their camp by General Connor's order, soon, however, convinced the Kansas men that their term of enlistment was not yet ended. But it was with no good will that the regiment marched, and both men and officers appear to have made up their minds to see as little of the Indians as possible. They marched north past Rawhide Butte and through the Black Hills, came upon Cole at the northern edge of the hills, and joined his column in the march west toward Powder River. The two columns mustered over two thousand mounted men, a very strong force for those days, with a number of howitzers and a long train of wagons and pack mules.

From the Black Hills the troops moved down the Little Missouri into southwestern North Dakota, then turned up Box Elder Creek and from the head of that stream moved west to Powder River, in Montana. From the point where the columns reached the Powder the valley of that stream was shut in on both sides with very high and rugged bluffs, and great difficulty was experienced in getting the wagons down into the valley. This task was at length performed and on August 29 the whole command was encamped in the valley. A detachment of cavalry was now sent west toward Tongue River, to find the supply camp which General Connor had intended to form at Panther Mountain, but Connor had not yet reached that point, and the cavalry returned to the camp on Powder River with news that no trace of the General's column had been seen. Cole and Walker now did not know what to do. Cole was inclined to march up the Powder in hope of finding Connor's new fort, but Walker had another plan. Both commanders appear to have been considerably alarmed by this time. They were both new to the Indian country; they had no good guides and had to depend mainly upon maps which they did not entirely trust; and now they found themselves in the heart of a trackless and savage wilderness, several hundred miles from any known settlement or base of supplies. To add to their alarm, on September 1 their camps were suddenly attacked by the Sioux.

These Sioux were not the ones who had been camping with the Cheyennes all spring and summer but were Missouri River Sioux—Minniconjous, Sans Arcs, Hunkpapas and Blackfoot-Sioux. They had discovered the trail of the columns on the Little Missouri and, three hundred strong, they had followed the trail to the Powder, where, on the morning of the first, they went down into the deep valley, surprised the troops and stampeded part of the cavalry herd. The Indians, however, found it difficult to get up out of the valley quickly, the high cliffs on both sides of the river being impassable except at certain points. The troops were quickly in the saddle and set off in pursuit of the raiders; the Indians split up into several bands, each making off in a different direction; but they had to herd the captured horses ahead of them and could not retire with much speed, and the troops soon came up with several of the bands. Little fights were fought on both sides of the river. The Indians, having but few guns, were unable to make a stand and beat off their pursuers. The troops recaptured some of the stolen horses, but the Sioux succeeded in getting away with most of them, and at one point they set a trap for a detachment of cavalry, killing one officer and six men.[14] This was the old, old scheme of inducing the troops to pursue a few warriors to a point where a larger body was in hiding. It worked very well, as the soldiers were all new to Indian fighting and rode into the trap without any suspicion.

This raid greatly disturbed both Cole and Walker, as they feared that the Indians, having now located their camp, would soon return

[14] This apparently was the detachment led by Captain E. S. Rowland of the Second Missouri Light Artillery. He was saved by the arrival of Cole's column, but all of his men were lost. Berthrong, *Southern Cheyennes*, 254.—S.L.

in great force. The night was spent in watching. In the morning, September 2, a large smoke was observed far to the north, near the mouth of Powder River. This was probably from an Indian camp, but Colonel Walker believed that General Connor was up there, and informed Cole that he intended to march his command in that direction. Cole would not agree to this, so Walker marched alone; but Cole soon became alarmed at being left behind, broke camp in haste, and followed in the rear of Walker's march. That day a long forced march was made down Powder River. The weather was extremely hot, and the horses and mules, already in very bad condition, broke down by hundreds. During the day a party of the Second Missouri Regiment strayed from the column to hunt game and were surprised by a small party of Indians who killed two soldiers and drove the rest back to the column. Two warriors were reported killed.

That night the troops camped at a point where the high cliffs on both sides of the valley were very close together. Walker's men camped in advance with Cole's column in the rear. During the night there was a sudden drop in temperature and a storm of cold rain set in. When day dawned, the camps were strewn with the carcasses of mules and horses which had died of cold and exhaustion at their picket lines during the night. The two commanders now gave up the plan of marching to the mouth of the river and decided to turn back toward the south. The columns were now in such a condition that they could hardly move. They crawled back up the river a few miles and went into camp in the first timber they came to, in the hope that this shelter would save the horses and mules. During the night of September 2 and the following morning Cole lost two hundred and twenty-five horses and mules. Walker made no report, but his loss was probably in proportion.

The situation of the two commands was now truly alarming, and the only hope was to reach Connor's Fort, the position of which was not known; indeed, it was not even certain that any post had been established. Supplies were running low; the men were inexperienced in hunting and did not dare to go out to hunt for fear of the Indians. The grain-fed horses and mules, having had nothing but grass during several weeks of hard travel, were now dying by scores every day. The officers did not even know how to get good grass for the poor animals, and the Sioux have told me that, when they visited these camps after the troops had withdrawn, they found great holes in the ground which the starving horses and mules had pawed in their attempt to find something to eat. This day, September 3, the troops remained in camp among the timber, burning wagons, harness, saddles, and even boxes of ammunition. There were no longer enough teams to draw the wagons, and many of the cavalrymen were on foot. On September 4 the columns moved a short distance up the valley to get grass for the animals. More wagons and supplies had to be abandoned, and as soon as the new camp was reached a company of cavalry was sent back to burn the wagons and their contents. These troops were now attacked by one hundred Sioux, who drove the soldiers back to camp, and that evening, six hundred strong, the Indians attacked the camp itself, in an attempt to run off the herds; but the horses and mules were now too weak to run, even when alarmed by Indians, and as darkness was coming on fast, the warriors soon withdrew.

During all this time our big village of Cheyennes and Sioux was on the west side of Powder River, just above the mouth of the Little Powder. I do not believe this village was more than thirty miles north of the point at which Cole and Walker first struck the river on August 29, but we had no idea that such a strong force was in our vicinity, and it was only after the troops began their retreat up the river and came within a few miles of us that we learned of their approach. Early in September a small war party of Cheyennes and Sioux left camp and moved down Powder River, and they had only gone a few miles when they discovered Cole's and Walker's camps in a bend of the stream. The Cheyennes remained to watch the troops while two of the Sioux rode back to the village to give the alarm. The soldiers were reported in such force that the Indians were alarmed, and the women at once began to pack up and get ready to move camp.

In the morning a large body of warriors left camp about dawn and rode down the river. Woman's Heart was with this party and tells me that they had only got a short distance from the village when they met the war party, which had been watching the soldiers' camps all night. These Indians reported that the soldiers were just beyond the next bend in the river and were coming up in great force, toward the village. This news was sent back to camp, and now a second large party of warriors mounted and started down the river. This was the party I accompanied, and the sun was already up when we moved. Other bands set out after us, and the whole valley on both sides of the river was full of warriors, all going down to meet the troops.

In this vicinity the river flowed in great bends between its two enclosing lines of high bluffs. The country was very rough and difficult to traverse, and if you attempted to ride along the valley you had to cross the river every little while; at almost every bend the steep bluffs came down to the river's brink, forcing you to cross the stream, and in these bends were dense tangles of bushes and trees through which you had to force your way. Presently we heard firing off ahead, and hurrying forward we rode up on a hill and came in sight of the troops in one of these thicketed bends, engaged in fighting the advance parties of warriors. Both the Indians and soldiers were shooting and yelling and the troops were firing the howitzers at Indians who had gathered on the hills. The wagons had already been corralled, and the troopers had formed a hollow square, like this:

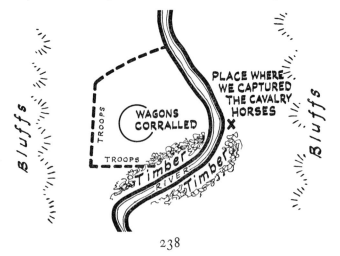

238

Our party was on the east side of the river, and just as we rode up on this hill and came in sight of the troops we saw two companies of cavalry come out of the timber on our side of the stream and make for a high hill. Our men set up a yell and started for the soldiers, who turned around at once and went back into the timber at a gallop. We were right behind them when they reached the trees and bushes. At this point the river bank was very high and steep; it was impossible to get horses down the bank without losing considerable time, and the soldiers had no time to waste. When they came out on the open bank they saw a swarm of warriors riding down from the hills on the other side of the river, and seeing that they would be cut off from the rest of the troops in a few moments more, the men now abandoned their horses and, jumping down the bank, waded across to the other side. When our party charged into the timber, we found eighty cavalry horses tied to the bushes, with their saddles and all equipments still on them. The saddle pockets were full of cartridges, and the blanket rolls were tied back of the saddles. These horses were so lean and broken down that the warriors did not even quarrel over the division of them, although they had a fierce wrangle over the saddles and other equipments. When we came to the open river bank we saw the troops on the other side, drawn up in lines around their camp and the corralled wagons, and a great body of Indians charging up and down along the lines.

We crossed over, and now Roman Nose rode up on his fine white pony, wearing his famous war bonnet that nearly touched the ground even when he was mounted, and with his face painted in a peculiar way, to protect him from bullets. As soon as he came up he called out to the warriors to form a line and get ready for a charge, as he was going to empty the soldiers' guns. The Indians formed a long line from the river nearly to the bluffs and sat on their ponies facing the troops. Roman Nose then put his pony into a run and rode straight out toward one end of the line of troops. When he was quite close he turned and rode at top speed straight along the front, from the river clear to the bluffs, the troops firing at him at close range all the way. Reaching the bluffs, he turned and rode back along the line

239

again. In this way he made three, or perhaps four, rushes from one end of the line to the other; and then his pony was shot and fell under him. On seeing this, the warriors set up a yell and charged. They attacked the troops all along the line, but could not break through anywhere. The trouble was that the Indians had very few guns, and armed only with bows, lances, and clubs they could not stand up to the well-armed troops for any length of time. The troops now opened up with their howitzers, and the Indians, who did not like the big guns, began to retire to the hills. They collected on the hilltops in great numbers and the troops attempted to drive them away by shelling the hills; but most of the shells went too high, and the only Indian hit was a very old man named Black Whetstone, who was smoking his pipe away off behind the hills when a shell came over and killed him.[15]

After this fight the Cheyennes left the Sioux on Powder River and moved east toward the Black Hills. Cole and Walker continued to move slowly up Powder River, and on September 8 they were attacked near the mouth of the Little Powder by about two thousand Sioux, who compelled the troops to corral their wagons and fight for some hours. No Cheyennes were present and I cannot give an account of this affair. That night another storm came on and in the morning the soldiers found hundreds of their horses and mules dead at the picket lines. Nearly all of the wagons that were left were now burnt, and the soldiers, most of them on foot, clad in rags, and with very little to eat, continued their slow movement up the river. The Sioux hung on their flanks and rear, harassing them all the way. If the Indians had had enough guns they could have closed in and annihilated the whole column. How poorly armed the Indians really were is shown by the fact that Colonel Walker mentions it as a notable thing that on September 10 the Indians had "four or five good mus-

---

[15] George Bent's graphic account must be considered a classic for this, one of the great representative engagements between white and Indian troops on the Plains. All subsequent histories owe something to it: Hyde's in *Red Cloud's Folk*, Grinnell's in *The Fighting Cheyennes*, Berthrong's in *The Southern Cheyennes*. The numbers of Indians, not clearly stated by Bent, may have aggregated one thousand.—S.L.

kets." There were little short of a thousand warriors present this day, and only four or five had good guns.

While these events were occurring on Powder River, General Connor's column was moving down Tongue River, with the purpose of meeting Colonels Cole and Walker near Panther Mountain. Arriving in that vicinity and finding no trace of the troops commanded by these officers, Connor went into camp and sent a detachment of Pawnee scouts to Powder River, to hunt for Cole and Walker. On September 11 the Pawnees returned to camp, reporting that they had failed to find any troops on Powder River, but that they had discovered a camp where hundreds of cavalry horses and mules lay dead on the ground, and where there were many huge piles of ashes in which were the debris of burned wagons and equipments.

When Connor received this report he became greatly alarmed for the safety of the columns under Cole and Walker, and breaking up his camp he marched rapidly back up Tongue River, making toward Fort Connor, while at the same time he sent another party of Pawnees over to Powder River, with orders to find Cole and Walker and guide them to Fort Connor. The Pawnees were driven back by hostile Indians; but they set out again and finally succeeded in finding Cole and Walker, whom they guided up Powder River to the fort. General Connor reached the post shortly afterward and found Cole's and Walker's troops encamped there, most of the cavalry without horses, the men nearly barefooted, clad in rags, and so demoralized by the hardships they had endured that they were totally unfit for further service. The troops were therefore loaded into wagons and hauled back to Fort Laramie, where they were mustered out.

For some reason the disaster that had overtaken Cole's and Walker's columns was concealed, and General [Grenville M.] Dodge, commanding the Department of the Missouri, issued a report in which he stated that Cole and Walker, when they reached Powder River, had discovered large bodies of Indians camped on the river above them. Turning up the river, the troops attacked and defeated the Indians with heavy loss. The Indians then fled up the river, the troops pursuing them and defeating them again. Day after day the troops continued their victorious advance, punishing the hostiles so severely that at last they scattered in every direction and made their escape. The columns then marched to Fort Connor in triumph. In this report is no mention of the loss of horses, mules, and wagons. The truth, however, was known to the officers of General Connor's command, who soon let the cat out of the bag, and threw all the blame for the failure of the expedition upon Colonel Cole. The result was that a year or two later, Cole issued a very long report in which, for the first time, the whole truth was given. This report shows that, from the time they first reached Powder River, Cole's and Walker's columns made no attempt to attack the Indians; that the march up Powder River was a retreat, that toward the end of the march the troops were nearly in a panic, and that they were probably saved from perishing of starvation by the arrival of Connor's Pawnees in their camp.[16]

When the Cheyennes left the Sioux on Powder River, after Roman Nose's fight with the troops, they moved east toward the Black Hills, in which direction the Northern Cheyennes said that buffalo were very abundant. We camped on the head of the Little Missouri, where antelope were found in great numbers. There was a kind of weed or forage plant that grew along this river which the antelope were very fond of, and the Indians believed the animals collected along this stream to feed on this plant. We moved slowly eastward, camping wherever game was abundant. We came in sight of Medicine Pipe Mountain, the sacred mountain of our tribe, from which Sweet Root Standing had brought the Medicine Arrows in ancient times. The mountain was far away in the Black Hills toward the east. All the Cheyennes went up on a hill and stood there, gazing at the mountain and praying. Few of the Southern Cheyennes had seen the mountain before. Near here the Cheyennes went out hunting one day and charged into a buffalo herd. While they were killing the animals a large body of Sioux hunters rode into sight and charged into the other side of the herd. The Cheyennes and Sioux came together in the

[16] Cole to Grant, February 10, 1867, O. R. I: Vol. 48, Pt. I, 366–80, as cited in Berthrong, *Southern Cheyennes*, extracted also in Grinnell, *Fighting Cheyennes*, 213, 213n.—S.L.

middle of the herd, and a violent quarrel broke out between the two tribes. For a while it looked as if a fight were about to begin, but the trouble was smooth over by the chiefs.

The Northern Cheyennes now left us and moved back toward Powder River. One of our bands, Black Shin's Sutais, moved back with the Northern Cheyennes as far as the Little Missouri (Antelope-Pit River), and here they went into camp with some Northern Cheyennes and remained all winter, pitting antelope. Roman Nose, the famous Northern Cheyenne warrior, remained with this band during the winter, and came south with them in 1866. Meantime, as soon as the Northern Cheyennes had left us, we Southern Cheyennes broke camp and started on our return home to the south. The people were homesick. They had been up north now for nearly a year, fighting most of the time, and were anxious to return home. We reached the Platte about October 20 and made some raids along the road, capturing trains loaded with goods for Denver.

Leaving the Platte, we moved south and went into camp on Solomon's Fork. Here the Dog Soldiers remained, for this was their country; the rest of us continued on southward. On the Smoky Hill we were surprised to find a new stage line running. This line had been established in the summer and fall of 1865, from the Missouri River to Denver. We made a raid and ran off a lot of stock, but the warriors failed to capture any of the stations. These stations were of a new type. They were dugouts made like storm cellars, with the sod-covered roofs rising only a few feet above the ground. Loopholes were cut in the wall just at ground level, and the station hands standing inside with only their heads above ground could fire out through the loopholes without exposing themselves at all. It was a fine arrangement, and the Indians, seeing that they could not "get much change" out of the stage hands, soon gave up attacking these places.

Leaving the Smoky Hill, we crossed the Arkansas in December, just about at the point where Dodge City, Kansas, now stands, and arrived near the Cimarron about Christmastime. Here we found Black Kettle with his band of Cheyennes, and the Kiowas, Comanches, and Prairie Apaches all camped near each other.

CHAPTER NINE

HANCOCK, CUSTER, AND ROMAN NOSE

As I HAVE TOLD in an earlier chapter, in January, 1865, a council of chiefs was held in the hostile camp and it was decided to move north of the Platte and spend the winter with the Northern Cheyennes and Red Cloud's Sioux on the Powder River. A part of the Southern Cheyennes, however, were opposed to this plan and elected to go south of the Arkansas River and winter with the Kiowas, Comanches, and Prairie Apaches. There were about seventy lodges of these people and Black Kettle was their principal leader. The same day that the big hostile village started for the north, these seventy lodges of Cheyennes started south, and I went around among their lodges to say goodbye to Black Kettle, Little Robe, Bear Tongue, Red Moon, and many other dear friends. A number of these people were on foot. They had few lodges and but little clothing, as their ponies, tepees, and most of their personal property had been taken or destroyed by the soldiers during the Sand Creek Massacre. However, they had robes to wear and to sleep in, and as buffalo were plentiful in this country they did not lack for food.

The Kiowas, Comanches, and Apaches were wintering on the Cimarron, about twenty miles south of Bluff Creek, and toward the end of January or early in February Black Kettle and his seventy lodges of Cheyennes joined them. The Cheyennes were received with great friendliness and sympathy and were given many presents, as it was the custom among all the Indians to give freely to visitors from other tribes. All were given horses and bridles, and also lodges. The chiefs of the three tribes called the poorest of the Cheyennes to the center of the village and gave them lodges just as they stood, with beds, kettles, dishes, and everything complete. The Kiowa chief, Black Eagle,[1] gave Black Kettle a fine lodge of buffalo skin, with three beds and bedding, riding and pack saddles, bridles, lariats, and all the kettles and dishes. The Comanches were especially rich in horses at this time, and they presented many fine animals to their Cheyenne friends. These were glorious days, dear to memory.

Most of the Cheyennes were very bitter against the whites on account of the treachery at Sand Creek and they wished to stir up the Kiowas and Comanches to war. The Kiowas and Comanches were already disturbed because of an attack by soldiers and Indian scouts under Kit Carson on a Kiowa camp in November, 1864.

The Kiowas, Comanches, and Prairie Apaches had gone into winter camp on the South Canadian, near the mouth of a stream now known as Kit Carson Creek, in Hutchinson County, Texas. With the intention of cleaning out these camps, Carson set out from Fort Bascom, New Mexico, with 336 cavalry, some artillery, and 75 Ute and Jicarilla Apache scouts. Marching down the Canadian he came first on the Kiowa camp, which was farther up the stream than the camps of the other two tribes. Most of the warriors in the Kiowa camp were away at the time. To-ha-san (Little Mountain), one of the most famous of the Kiowa chiefs, but then an old man, was in charge of the village. Intending to surprise the camp at daybreak, Carson pushed forward his Ute scouts to stampede the Indian ponies and throw the village into a panic. Some Kiowa herders discovered the Utes as they crept up through the grass and bushes and the camp was warned. The Indian scouts and soldiers charged on the village and drove the Kiowas out of the camp, the few warriors bravely covering the flight of the women and children to the camp of the Comanches and Apaches some miles below. Iron Shirt, a famous Kiowa chief was killed in front of his lodge. He took his name from the fact that he was possessor of a coat-of-mail, a relic of the old days of the Spanish

---

[1] Grinnell, *The Fighting Cheyennes*, 270, identifies Black Eagle in 1867 as a young chief of the Kiowas, which means that in 1865 he may just have been emerging as a war chief of the Kiowas.—S.L.

conquistadores, who penetrated into this region many years ago. The fleeing women and children alarmed the larger camp some miles down the river and warriors from these camps hurried to To-ha-san's village, where the soldiers were now burning the lodges and buffalo robes, and destroying the winter supply of meat. These warriors attacked the troops so fiercely that Carson was forced to retreat, the Indians pressing him closely all day. But for the coolness and skill of Carson and his Indian scouts the retreat would have become a rout and few would have escaped. The main camp, which it had been Carson's intention to destroy, was not even attacked, the Kiowa pony herd was unharmed, and only about 150 lodges and the store of buffalo robes and winter meat were destroyed. The Kiowas lost five persons killed, two of them being women. The Kiowa Chief To-ha-san was a great friend of my father's and was also well known to Kit Carson, who had met the Kiowa chief while in my father's employ.[2]

As as result of this fight, the three tribes broke up their winter camp on the South Canadian and moved north to the Cimarron, and it was here that Black Kettle and his Cheyennes joined them soon after. A few days following the arrival of the Cheyennes, the chiefs of the Kiowas, Comanches, and Apaches told Black Kettle that they would not hold a war council at that time, but would wait until the ponies were fat in the spring and then would consider making raids on the Arkansas and Smoky Hill roads.

At this time all things indicated that a general Indian war would break out on the southern plains in the spring of 1865. The Confederate authorities in Arkansas and the Indian Territory were scheming to stir up the tribes and arrange for a great Indian council in the

---

[2] In the Kiowa year count, a painted-skin record, 1833–1888, the period here is identified as "muddy travel winter, the time when the Kiowas repelled Kit Carson." James Mooney, "Calendar History of the Kiowa Indians," *Seventeenth Annual Report*, Part 2, Bureau of American Ethnology, 1893. The engagement took place at the camp of the Kiowas and some Comanches on Red Bluff on the north side of the South Canadian River between Adobe Walls and Mustang Creek. Carson's command consisted of troops and some Ute and Jicarilla Apache allies. Most of the Kiowa warriors were away at the time, those remaining in camp being under old Chief Dohasan. Carson lost two soldiers killed and twenty-one wounded. Mildred P. Mayhall, *The Kiowas*, 163–64.—S.L.

spring to urge the Kiowas, Comanches, and other tribes to join the Confederates in an attack on the Kansas border. These plans were spoiled by Colonel Jesse H. Leavenworth, who succeeded in reaching the Indians before the agents of the Confederates could open up negotiations. Colonel Leavenworth was a graduate of West Point and son of General Henry Leavenworth of the United States Army. Appointed agent for the Kiowas, Comanches, and Apaches in 1864, in February, 1865, Leavenworth sent runners out from Council Grove to visit the three tribes in their camps on the Cimarron, urging the Indians to keep the peace and make no raids and to arrange for the chiefs to meet him in council. Colonel James H. Ford commanded the troops along the Arkansas River at this time. He had concentrated a large force at Fort Larned with the intention of attacking the Indians on the Cimarron. Agent Leavenworth appealed to Ford to hold off his campaign until a council could be held with the tribes, saying he felt certain that the Indians would make peace. By great effort, and by appeals to influential friends in Washington, Leavenworth succeeded in stopping the march of the troops. He then held a talk with the head men of the tribes, who agreed to meet the government commissioners on Bluff Creek in October, 1865, to make a new treaty of peace. Through the efforts of my father and Mr. Thomas Murphy, superintendent of Indian Affairs, a similar agreement was made by the Cheyennes and Arapahos. Thus another war was averted.

The President appointed a commission to negotiate a treaty with the tribes. This commission was made up of Major General [John B.] Sanborn and [Major General William S.] Harney, Colonel Leavenworth, Judge [James] Steele, Kit Carson, Superintendent Murphy, and my father. They met the Indians on October 12 at the mouth of the Little Arkansas, near the present town of Wichita, Kansas. The Wichita Indians were living at this point in 1865, having taken refuge there during the troubles in the Indian Territory caused by the Civil War.

General Sanborn opened the council by telling the Cheyennes how sorry he was for the Sand Creek Massacre; he then offered to give (out of their own lands) 320 acres to each chief and 160 acres to each

woman or child who had lost parents in the massacre. All the rest of
the lands which had been recognized by the treaty of 1861 as Cheyenne territory was to be ceded to the government by the Indians. This
country embraced the eastern half of Colorado, a large part of western Kansas, and parts of Nebraska and Wyoming. Black Kettle,
speaking for the Cheyennes, refused this offer and objected to making
any land cessions because there were only eighty lodges of Southern
Cheyennes present at the council, the rest of the tribe (400 lodges)
being north of the Platte. He also reminded the commissioners that
there were only 190 lodges of Southern Arapahos present at the
council; the last time that tribe had been together there were 390
lodges. The other 200 lodges of the Southern Arapahos were up
north with 400 lodges of Southern Cheyennes. For this reason, Black
Kettle said, he did not wish to make any agreement as to land, knowing that it would cause trouble when the rest of his people and the
Southern Arapahos returned from the north. Black Kettle said: "I
have always been friendly to the whites, but since the killing of my
people at Sand Creek I find it hard to trust a white man." Then he
had his wife brought in and showed Generals Harney and Sanborn
the wounds she had received at Sand Creek, when after she was
wounded and lay on the ground the soldiers shot again and again into
her body. The commissioners found nine wounds on the woman's
body. Black Kettle so impressed General Harney that he presented
him with a fine bay horse. Black Kettle gave me this horse the next
year when I married his niece Magpie (Mo-he-by-vah).

Little Raven spoke for the Arapahos and was shrewd enough to
remark that the lands offered by the commissioners to his tribe were
north of the Platte and had already been given in treaty to the Sioux,
while the lands offered south of the Arkansas belonged to the Kiowas
and Comanches; he said that if his people accepted these lands and
moved upon them they would at once become embroiled with the
tribes to whom the lands rightfully belonged.

It was always easy to induce Indians to sign a treaty, even if they
did not like its provisions, and on this occasion the chiefs were finally
won over and the treaty was signed on October 14. The Cheyennes

who signed were Black Kettle, Seven Bulls, Little Robe, Black Whiteman, Eagle Head, and Bull that Hears; for the Arapahos, Little Raven, Storm, Big Mouth, Spotted Wolf, Black Man, Chief in Everything, and Haversack. The Prairie Apaches wished to leave the Kiowas, with whom they had been living for many years, and on October 17 they signed a treaty by which they were joined to the Cheyennes and Arapahos. This little tribe is now generally known as the Kiowa Apaches, but my father, and all the old fur traders, always called them Prairie Apaches. They never had any connection with the Apaches of Arizona, and, in fact, originally came from the far Northwest. They first met the Kiowas near the Black Hills of Dakota over two hundred years ago, and from that time on they lived and associated with the Kiowas and moved south with them. It was said that the Apaches quarreled with the Kiowas in 1865 and this was the reason they wished to leave that tribe and live with the Cheyennes and Arapahos. But the real reason was that the Apaches were very much attached to the country near the Arkansas River, and as the Kiowas and Comanches were moving farther south, away from the river, the Apaches wished to leave them and join the Cheyennes and Arapahos who lived near this river.

This treaty of October 14, 1865, was called the Treaty of the Little Arkansas. Though only one-sixth of the tribe was present, the Southern Cheyennes gave up all their lands between the Arkansas and Platte rivers, and while still permitted to hunt in that region, agreed to settle on a reserve to be established for them south of the Arkansas. The Indians were not to go within ten miles of any main traveled road, post, or station without permission. These were the main provisions of the treaty, and it was easy to see that trouble would result from any attempt to carry them out.[3]

As I said at the end of the last chapter, the Southern Cheyennes who were returning from the north had reached the Arkansas River.

[3] Bent's statement of the treaty provision is roughly accurate, but his father's presence and request that the Cheyennes and Arapahos sign the treaty had much to do with its acceptance. Berthrong, *Southern Cheyennes*, 242.—S.L.

The band I was with at this time was under Little Wolf (Honi-a-ha-ka). He was a Southern Cheyenne and must not be confused with the famous Little Wolf, the Northern Cheyenne chief. The latter's name was really Okohm-ha-ka, meaning Little Coyote, though he was always called Little Wolf by the whites, a mistake in translation. Just north of the Smoky Hill River we met runners from Black Kettle's camp who informed us that Black Kettle's Southern Cheyennes, Little Raven's Arapahos, and Poor Bear's Prairie Apaches were all camped on Bluff Creek, and that three outfits of white traders were there. On receiving this news, many runners from our band left for the south in advance of our main body. They went on foot, for by this time our ponies were very poor.[4]

When we arrived on Bluff Creek I found my father trading there in the Cheyenne village. This was the first time I had seen him since my visit to his ranch just after the Sand Creek affair. Little Wolf and my father were dear friends. We now learned for the first time that the southern tribes had signed treaties on the Little Arkansas and peace had been again made. The Kiowas and Comanches were in winter camp on the Cimarron, twenty miles south of Bluff Creek, at the same place where they had been in camp the winter before when Black Kettle and his eighty lodges joined them. We found everything peaceful on the Arkansas. This winter To-ha-san, or Little Mountain, the famous head chief of the Kiowas, died. He had led the tribe for over thirty years. Satanta (White Bear) and Kicking Eagle (often called Kicking Bird)[5] became rivals for the vacant leadership; but neither was strong enough to gain the title, and the result was that for many years the Kiowas were divided into factions and could never be brought to act together.

In February, 1866, came Captain G. A. Gordon and Lieutenant

---

[4] The precise time of this southward movement is not clear, but it apparently occurred in mid-winter, 1865–66. But in the middle of February, 1866, Major Wynkoop and Agent J. C. Taylor went with a company of cavalry to meet with the Indians on Bluff Creek, where on February 25 they found Medicine Arrows and Big Head, two important leaders of the bands that had come south. Berthrong, *Southern Cheyennes*, 258.—S.L.

[5] Tay-nay-angopte.—S.L.

A. E. Bates, with four companies of cavalry, escorting Major Wyn-koop, our new agent, with a train of annuities. Here were camped on Bluff Creek, about forty miles southeast of Fort Dodge, Black Ket-tle's Cheyennes and Poor Bear's Apaches; and Big Head and Rock Forehead had come in with some Dog Soldiers. The Arapahos, under Little Raven and Big Mouth, were camped about forty miles down the creek from us. Wynkoop held a council with the Cheyenne lead-ers who had not been present when the treaty was signed in 1865 and attempted to get them to agree to the terms of that treaty; but Big Head and Rock Forehead refused, the Dog Soldiers' band being still very hostile. All that they would say was that they would retain their country on the Smoky Hill and Republican where they had lived so long, and that they did not want any railroad through the country. The surveys for the Kansas Pacific railroad were then being made through the Smoky Hill hunting grounds. During 1866 and the following year Agent Wynkoop gave his best efforts towards gaining the consent of the Dog Soldier to the building of this new road through their country.

Mary Fletcher, a young white girl captured by Sand Hill's band of Cheyennes on the North Platte in August, 1865, was given up to Wynkoop at this council on Bluff Creek. She was about sixteen years old when captured near Fort Halleck, her family being from Miners-ville, Henry County, Illinois, and they were on their way west with a wagon train when attacked by the Cheyennes. I received a letter from her some years ago and she told me that despite reports to the contrary she was well treated by her captors. Sand Hill's wife, a Sioux woman, still living, was very kind to her while she was with this band. When Sand Hill reached the winter camp on Bluff Creek he sold this girl, after the Indian fashion, to John Smith, then trading in the camp for Morris & Hanger. Smith turned her over to Wyn-koop when the latter arrived with the annuity train. In her letter Mary Fletcher told me that she was married and the mother of six children. She also said that she had put in a claim against the Chey-ennes, but, as she had already been well paid years before, the Indian Department dismissed her claim.

Soon after Wynkoop's visit to our camp, a small party of Cheyennes moved up and camped near Fort Dodge. One day a trader named Boggs came to this little camp and found out that one of the Cheyennes had ten ten-dollar bills. Boggs produced eleven one-dollar bills and persuaded the Cheyenne to make a trade. It must be remembered in those days the Indians had little idea of the value of money, especially paper money. I have already told of the capture of the army paymaster's cash box at Julesburg, and how the Indians threw the bundles of banknotes in the air and laughed as the wind whirled the paper down the valley. When this Cheyenne man learned how he had been cheated, he started after Boggs; but the trader had decamped. With four companions, the angry Indian set out in chase and ran Boggs into Fort Dodge, where he took refuge under the protection of the troops. On their way back to camp, the Cheyennes ran across Boggs' young son, four miles east of the Fort, and acting on the Indians' idea that revenge on a member of the guilty man's family is as good as vengeance on the man himself, they killed the boy. This affair caused much excitement at the time. But it was little things like this that caused so much bitterness between the Indians and whites and led to hostilities, the original cause of which was lost in the bloody deeds which followed. What the Indian did to the white man was shouted by every newspaper in the land, but what the white man has done to the Indian has never been told. Except for a few small disturbances like the one above given, all was quiet in the south in 1866, and the Cheyennes were at peace.[6]

[6] Bent, who probably did not have from his father, William Bent, all of the details, here greatly telescopes events. In March, 1866, some four hundred Cheyenne, Arapaho, and Brulé Sioux warriors were preparing to raid for horses and mules on the Butterfield Overland Dispatch route. The Dog Soldiers among the Cheyennes were asked by Little Robe and Edmond Guerrier, who came to their camps, to talk with Wynkoop. On April 4, the soldier societies and Little Robe, who had been in the north when the Treaty of the Little Arkansas was signed, now gave their assent to it. Wynkoop subsequently reported all at peace, but increasingly the Indians began to stand out against the cession of the Smoky Hill country, and meantime ratification of the treaty was held up in the U.S. Senate. On August 14, Wynkoop held council at Smoky Hill with eight Cheyenne chiefs, who, in exchange for a requested six

It was in the spring of this year that I married Black Kettle's niece, Magpie, and went to live in that chief's lodge, where I made my home until the summer of 1868. Black Kettle had two wives, one of whom was a captive Ponca woman. He had no children of his own. He was very fond of my wife and her brother, Blue Horse, and treated them as his own children. These were happy days for us. Black Kettle was a fine man and highly respected by all who knew him.

In the middle of August, 1866, the agent distributed goods to the Cheyennes at Fort Ellsworth, on the Smoky Hill River. Black Kettle was there, and so was the famous Roman Nose, who had come down from the North a little while before with Black Shin's Sutaio, which band had remained up north to pit antelope during the winter of 1865–66. In September more goods were distributed to the Cheyennes at Fort Zarah, on the Arkansas just north of Great Bend, Kansas. This was a dull year, but in November an incident occurred that almost brought on war. Several lodges of Cheyennes were encamped near Fort Zarah, and my father was trading in this camp. The main village of the Cheyennes at this time was sixty miles south of the Arkansas. A young Dog Soldier named Fox Tail, son of Rock Forehead, procured some whisky and in a drunken quarrel killed a Mexican herder in my father's employ. This affair caused great excitement, and attempts were made to arrest Fox Tail. The little band of Cheyennes broke camp and moved south to join the rest of the tribe. The agents and army officers told the chiefs that if Fox

hundred ponies, supplies, and the restitution of two Cheyenne children taken by the troops at Sand Creek, promised to hold their young warriors in check.

However, in August parties of Cheyennes began visiting Fort Wallace and the stations on the Smoky Hill road, led by Roman Nose and Spotted Horse, threatening violence unless the Smoky Hill country were abandoned in two weeks. Talks with the Indians began on October 16, at which time Senate amendments to the Treaty of the Little Arkansas were to be accepted by the Indians. During these negotiations, liquor brought in by a trader had its influence on George Bent's brother, Charles, who, now an acknowledged leader among the Cheyennes, threatened to kill his father and his brother. William Bent sold his store of goods and gave up negotiations.

Councils were resumed at Fort Zarah, November 13–14, and the Indians accepted the Senate amendments. Berthrong, *Southern Cheyennes*, 259–65.—S.L.

Tail was not given up to justice the whole tribe would be held responsible. Black Kettle and the older chiefs were willing to do what they could, but Fox Tail had fled north and was out of reach. The head men and members of the warrior societies positively refused to consent to the surrender of the young Indian, maintaining that if Fox Tail had been killed by the Mexican no one would have thought of putting the Mexican on trial or punishing him. This affair hung fire during the winter of 1866–67. Meantime the war prophets of the frontier were very busy and several exaggerated stories of Indian outrages were sent in to General Winfield Scott Hancock, now in command of the Department of the Missouri. Fresh from the great battle fields of the Civil War, and with no knowledge of Indians or their customs, he easily fell victim to the gossip of the frontier alarmists, taking seriously the assertions he heard that the Indians were bent on beginning war "as soon as grass was up in the spring."

At this time the Kansas Pacific railroad had been completed as far west as Fort Riley, and preparations were being made for pushing the road up the Smoky Hill through the heart of the Cheyenne hunting ground. As the Cheyennes, particularly the Dog Soldiers, still opposed the construction of this line, the situation was one that required delicate handling by a man who understood Indians thoroughly. Such a man would have visited the frontier army posts, talked with the Indians, and found out what truth was in the stories that the Cheyennes were preparing for war in the spring. General Hancock, however, remained at this headquarters, and believing the stories that came to him soon became convinced that the Indians were planning trouble. Apparently he made up his mind to act against the Cheyennes in a rough soldierly manner and frighten them into keeping the peace. But little he knew of the trouble he was to bring about. Upon the authority of Captain [Henry] Asbury and a man named Jones,[7] the commandant at Fort Dodge, Major Douglas,[8] had made a report to General Hancock charging the Kiowas, Comanches, and Cheyennes with numerous raids and outrages. According to Jones,

[7] F. F. Jones, interpreter and guide at Fort Dodge.—S.L.
[8] Major Henry Douglass, commanding officer at Fort Dodge.—S.L.

a trader named Tappan had been assaulted, Major Page had been threatened, stock had been run off, the stages stopped and passengers bullied; Jones himself had been fired on, and, worst of all, a Kiowa war party had come in with two hundred stolen horses and the scalps of seventeen Negro cavalrymen and one white man, the fruits of a raid into Texas. Later on, Tappan and Major Page appeared before Major Douglas and declared under oath that none of the statements made by Jones and Asbury were true. For some unexplained reason Major Douglas failed to communicate this later information to General Hancock, who in the meantime had called for reinforcements and was busy organizing an expedition to punish the Indians. The statement about the scalps of the seventeen Negro cavalrymen should have deceived no one who knew anything about Indians. The Plains Indians never took a Negro's scalp, and the records of the War Department contain no mention of a fight in Texas in which seventeen Negro cavalrymen were killed at this period.[9]

Hancock's expedition, however, left Fort Riley in the latter part of March and arrived at Fort Harker about April 1; then moved to Fort Larned over the stage road by way of Fort Zarah, reaching Fort Larned about April 7.[10] Hancock's force was made up of 1400 men, cavalry, infantry, artillery, and a pontoon train. At Fort Zarah the troops were joined by Colonel Leavenworth, agent for the Kiowas and Comanches; and at Fort Larned by Major Wynkoop, agent for the Cheyennes and Arapahos. Wynkoop informed General Hancock that he had sent runners to the Cheyennes asking that the headmen meet the expedition at Fort Larned on April 10, and he urged

[9] There were higher level considerations of the troubles current and impending, for General William Tecumseh Sherman, commanding officer of the Military Division of the Missouri, had made a personal inspection of the area in conflict in the summer of 1866, with subsequent proposals for relocating the Cheyennes south of the Arkansas and east of Fort Union, the Sioux to be relocated north of the Platte and west of the Missouri. But the Sioux annihilation of the Fetterman command on December 21, 1866, on the Bozeman Trail near Fort Phil Kearny, and Cheyenne disturbances in the south, caused him to abandon hope. Robert G. Athearn, *William Tecumseh Sherman and the Settlement of the West*, 59–99.—S.L.

[10] The date was April 9, 1867.—S.L.

255

Hancock to wait for them to come in, saying that the charges that had been made against this tribe were mistakes and the rumors of war unfounded, and that everything could be fixed up in a friendly way if gone about in the proper spirit. The General consented to wait at Larned for the chiefs to come in for a talk.

On the evening of General Hancock's arrival, four Sioux came to the fort and showed papers signed by Colonel Maynadier,[11] commandant at Fort Laramie, setting forth that these men were friendly Oglalas who had been permitted to go on a hunt. These Sioux men informed the General that their band and the Dog Soldier band of Cheyennes were camped together on Pawnee Fork, about thirty miles northwest of Fort Larned. On April 9 a furious snowstorm, with a gale of wind, came on and continued until ten o'clock that night, eight inches of snow falling. Next day, the time set for the council with the Cheyenne chiefs, runners came in to announce that the Cheyenne leaders were on the way, traveling slowly on account of the snow and the poor condition of their horses. General Hancock gave as his opinion that the Indians were not acting in good faith and did not intend to come in. On the twelfth, Tall Bull, White Horse, Bull Bear and Little Robe, the headmen of the Dog Soldiers, arrived at the fort accompanied by some Arapaho and Sioux chiefs. Hancock had a great fire built outside the fort that evening and held the council with the chiefs, all of the officers of artillery, cavalry, and infantry attending in full dress uniform. The General intended to impress the Indians by this night council around the big bonfire, but as this procedure was contrary to custom the chiefs came to the conclusion that Hancock was either a man who did not know anything or else had made up his mind to treat them badly.

The General opened the council by turning over to the chiefs an Indian boy who had been captured at Sand Creek and was supposed to be a Cheyenne boy whose return the Cheyennes had often demanded. Each chief in turn took the boy in his lap, but none of the

[11] Henry Eveleth Menadier, in all probability, but it is difficult to reconcile his presence at Fort Laramie at this time from his army record, which has him serving as colonel of the Fifth Volunteer Infantry until August 30, 1866.—S.L.

Cheyennes could recognize him. Finally one of the Arapahos announced him to be an Arapaho boy, the son of Red Bull. His mother had been killed during the Sand Creek fight; then the boy's grandmother took him and they were both hiding in a hole in the bank of the creek when discovered the day after the fight by a soldier named Wilson. Two little Cheyenne girls, sisters, were captured at the same time, and Wilson took one of the little girls and the Arapaho boy and exhibited them in a circus called the Wilson & Graham Circus. The Indians had often demanded that those children be returned to them and the government detailed an officer to trace them. The officer finally found them in the Wilson Circus. One night after the performance, he ran behind the scenes with some local officers and secured the little boy; but in the confusion the girl was spirited away by the showmen and neither she nor her sister were ever found again. This Arapaho boy had been named Tom Wilson by the showmen, but the officers called him Graham Wilson. After he had been recognized by the Arapahos at the council, General Hancock turned him over to Agent Wynkoop to be returned to his relatives. He is now known as Tom Whiteshirt and lives about forty miles from Colony, Oklahoma.[12]

After the boy had been turned over to the agent, General Hancock made a long speech. But he did not know how to talk to Indians and the chiefs did not understand him at all. Little Robe told me afterwards that he could not make out what Hancock was driving at; and even the interpreters, John Smith, Dick Curtis, and Ed Guerrier, with all of whom I talked afterwards, said that they did not know what Hancock meant. He asked why more chiefs were not present and particularly why Roman Nose was not there. Now Roman Nose was not a chief. While he was one of the bravest and best known warriors on the Plains, not being a chief, he had no right to attend a council of this nature. Hancock, however, like most of the whites, believed that Roman Nose was head chief and saw in his failure to attend a hostile sign; the General therefore announced that he would start next day and march his troops to the Cheyenne village. The

[12] The time here is 1906.—S.L.

chiefs objected to this. Tall Bull told the General that nothing could be gained by such an act; that both sides could say all that was necessary where they were; that if the soldiers marched near the village the woman and children would naturally think that another massacre was to take place and they would all run away. This reply of Tall Bull only convinced the General that the chiefs were acting in bad faith. He persisted in his intention of marching to the Indian village, and the council thereupon broke up.

The next day the troops marched about twenty-two miles toward the Indian camp, most of the chiefs accompanying the officers, much worried by the turn of affairs. The troops went into camp at what they supposed to be ten miles from the Indian village. Hancock sent word by Pawnee Killer, a Sioux chief, for more of the leaders to come and see him in the morning. He persisted in his demand that Roman Nose be present. Hancock set the time for the chiefs to arrive at his camp, but as the Indian village was farther off than he supposed, the Indian leaders did not arrive on time, and the General, taking this to be another sign of bad faith, at once resumed his march toward the Indian encampment. This was on April 14.

Meanwhile the Indians in their turn had become much alarmed. The approach of a large body of troops, the General's threatening attitude and speech, the council in the open field at night, had convinced the chiefs and people that an attack was impending. Everybody in the village was greatly excited, and at last a body of warriors mounted and set off to meet the soldiers. It was about noon when this force of warriors came in sight of the column. At their appearance Hancock's suspicions were again aroused and he ordered the troops to form to meet the Indians, the cavalry coming into line at a gallop with sabres drawn and the artillery unlimbering. When the Indians saw this they halted. Agent Wynkoop rode forward alone to reassure them and brought back to a point between the two lines a large deputation of chiefs and headmen, including Roman Nose, who carried a white flag, Bull Bear, White Horse, and Gray Beard of the Cheyennes, Pawnee Killer, Bad Wound, Tall Bear, and some other Sioux. Hancock and his staff rode out to meet them. The General

258

inquired for Roman Nose and riding to him asked him sharply if he wanted war. Roman Nose replied, through an interpreter, that if the Indians wanted war they would not come so close to the big guns. Hancock, still persisting in his opinion that Roman Nose was the head chief, asked Roman Nose why he had not come to the council at Fort Larned, to which Roman Nose replied, "My horses are poor, too weak to travel, and every man who comes to me tells a different story of your intentions." Hancock then abruptly dismissed the party, saying that it was too windy to talk in the open and that he would move up and camp near the Indian village. This alarmed the Indians more than ever; they could not understand his intentions and many believed that he wanted to surround the village and capture or kill all the people; as they had done nothing they could not see why he should do this.[13]

After a march of about ten miles, the village of three hundred lodges was sighted in a beautiful grove on the banks of Pawnee Fork. As the troops drew near, Roman Nose, very angry and with his usual fearlessness, announced to the Indians that they must get ready for a fight, as he intended to ride out and kill Hancock at the head of his troops. "This officer," he said, "is spoiling for a fight. I will kill him in front of his own men and give them something to fight about." Many Indians present at this time have told me that Roman Nose was determined to kill Hancock, and the chiefs were so alarmed that they sent Bull Bear to ride out with Roman Nose and prevent him from carrying out his intention. They felt that if Hancock was killed the troops would slaughter a great many women and children, as the ponies were in such poor condition that the warriors would not be able to fight the soldiers and the others could not get away. The Cheyennes say now that it would have been better, after all, if Roman Nose had been permitted to kill the General, as Hancock was so conceited that he would not listen to anyone and this caused all the trouble that followed.

[13] Lieutenant Colonel George Armstrong Custer, who was with Hancock's command and met with the Indians between the lines, gives a graphic account of this tense incident in *My Life on the Plains*, 34–35.—S.L.

Ed Guerrier was present as interpreter for Hancock when Roman Nose and Bull Bear rode up. Guerrier and Roman Nose were friends, and the wife of Roman Nose was a cousin of Guerrier. Roman Nose wore his famous war bonnet and looked Hancock right in the eye. The General inquired why the women and children were leaving the village, saying that it looked to him like treachery. Roman Nose replied, "Are not women and children more timid than men? The Cheyenne warriors are not afraid, but have you never heard of Sand Creek? Your soldiers look just like those who butchered the women and children there." Roman Nose then turned to Bull Bear and told him to ride back to the Indian line, as he might get killed, saying he was now going to kill Hancock. Instead of doing this, Bull Bear, who had a great deal of control over Roman Nose, suddenly grabbed the bridle of his friend's horse and led him away. He persuaded Roman Nose to give up his idea for the sake of the women and children; but General Hancock had a close call.

The General now sent orders to the chiefs to bring back the women and children who fled from the village on the approach of the troops. The chiefs sent back word that they were too frightened and could not be brought back. On receiving this reply, Hancock sent Ed Guerrier into the Indian camp to report to him if anything took place there. By this time it was dark, and Guerrier saw that the Sioux, both men and women, had all slipped away and that the Cheyennes were preparing to leave. The people were convinced that Hancock intended to attack the camp. When the troops had marched up near the village, the Cheyennes wished to fight them and requested the Sioux to join. The Chiefs of the Sioux said that the ponies were too weak and the soldiers were now so near that if a fight was started many women and children would be killed before they could get away. So the idea of fighting had therefore been given up, and when Guerrier arrived, the Cheyennes were abandoning the village. Guerrier's orders were to report at once if he saw anything of importance taking place in the village; but his sympathies were always with the Indians and he did not hurry to report. When he did make his report most of the Indians had slipped away. Cavalry under

[Lieutenant Colonel George Armstrong] Custer was thrown around the village to prevent the escape of the Indians. But it was now about ten o'clock at night and the Indians were all gone. The soldiers had the run of the Indian camp during the night and ransacked it thoroughly.

When morning came a search of the camp revealed an old Sioux man and his decrepit wife, who had been overlooked in the flight of the Sioux; in the Cheyenne village a sick girl was found. The military afterward reported that this girl was a white captive who had been outraged by the Cheyennes before they abandoned the camp. She might have been outraged, but not by the Indians, for she was a half-witted Cheyenne girl, forgotten by her people in their hurry.

The Indians knew there would be war now. They made all haste north toward the Smoky Hill, breaking up into small bands to elude the cavalry which they knew would be sent in pursuit. They crossed the stage road in the vicinity of Lookout and Stormy Hollow stations, just west of Fort Hays. At Lookout the Sioux burned the station and the hay stored there, ran off eight horses and four mules, and in the fight killed two men. At Stormy Hollow the Indians ran off some stock and fired a few shots but made no determined attack on the station. They crossed the stage road in small bands headed north, Custer and his cavalry in pursuit, with Ed Guerrier and Bill Comstock as guides and some Delaware Indian scouts.[14] Guerrier said the trail was hard to follow, as the Indians had no lodgepoles dragging. When they fled from the village the Indians left their lodges standing and took only what property they could hastily pack on their ponies. For this reason they traveled fast and left little trail. Indians could always travel faster with packs than with lodgepoles dragging. When traveling with poles dragging the Indians used mules, if possible, as they were stronger than the horses and stood the work better. Five poles on each side of a pack saddle made a good load for a strong animal and left a plain, well-marked trail.

Guerrier says that Custer ordered him to go on ahead and if he

[14] "Wild Bill" Hickok was also one of the scouts on this march. Custer's admiring description appears in *My Life on the Plains*, 44–45.—S.L.

met any Indians to tell them that Custer would not harm them but only wished to have a talk. Of course Custer only wanted to trap the Indians and take a lot of prisoners. Guerrier was riding three miles ahead of the cavalry when he saw a Cheyenne who had come back after some ponies which had escaped during the night. The Indian was some distance away, in a ravine, and Guerrier signaled him "get away, soldiers coming." So the Indian ran down in the creek with the ponies. Guerrier then rode in another direction and when the soldiers came up with him he told Custer that the Indians had all scattered and he wanted to know which trail to follow. Custer said to follow the trail that went due north. Although their ponies were poor and they had their women and children, Custer never got near the Indians. When he found that he could not overtake them he put into Fort Hays for supplies and from there went on to Fort Harker. Custer never even saw any Indians after he started his chase.

Meanwhile General Hancock, still at the Indian camp with his artillery and wagons, was doing nothing. On the 19th of April he burned the camp, despite the protest of Agent Wynkoop; he kept about forty lodges to issue to the Indian scouts at Fort Dodge and burned 110 Cheyenne lodges and 140 lodges in the Sioux camp. A thousand buffalo robes, hundreds of parfleches, headmats, lariats, and in fact all the camp property was destroyed except some turned over to the quartermaster. Hancock then marched his force to Fort Dodge.[15]

The Sioux with the Dog Soldiers were Pawnee Killer's band.[16]

---

[15] In the storm of criticism which followed the news of the burning of this camp and the resultant Indian war, Hancock and Wynkoop and Leavenworth engaged in a wordy battle in the newspapers. Hancock insisted that the Cheyennes had been hostile, but admitted that the Sioux were at peace. When taken to task, then, for burning the Sioux lodges, he declared that he could not distinguish between the two. But the two tribes were camped in separate circles, and in the list of property destroyed Hancock's adjutant gives a separate list for the Cheyennes and the Sioux, thus disproving Hancock's statement. He also said that he did not give orders to burn the camp until he received word from Custer of the killing of the two men at Lookout Station; but Wynkoop proved that Hancock had ordered the camp burned the day after the Indians abandoned it, at which time Wynkoop entered a written protest.—G.H.

The mother of White Horse, one of the Dog Soldier chiefs, was an old woman deaf and dumb and partly demented. She was left behind in the panicky flight of the Indians and it was thought that the soldiers had killed her. But, after the village had been burned, some Indians came back to look for their ponies, which had been left running loose near the camp, and they found that someone had put the old woman in a safe place and she was unharmed.

Hancock had boasted to the Indians that he had come prepared for war; now that the Indians had slipped away, he found it beyond his powers to strike a blow. The Cheyennes and Sioux had no trouble in eluding the troops. The only Indians killed during Hancock's campaign were some young men from Black Kettle's village who were with a party visiting in the Dog Soldiers' camp at the time. When the Indians stampeded and abandoned their camp, these six young Cheyenne men set out on foot for the Arkansas River. The young men, all of whom I knew well, were: Lone Bear, Plenty of Horses, Big Wolf (or Burnt All Over), Wolf Walks in the Middle, Pawnee Man, and Eagle Nest.[17] They started at nightfall to go on foot to their own village, then on the Cimarron River, about ninety miles south of the Arkansas. By traveling rapidly all night, the young men reached a point near the Cimarron crossing of the Arkansas just at daybreak. Here they stopped to rest on a hill near Anthony's Stage Ranch on the Arkansas River road, or Santa Fe Trail, west of Dodge City. Presently, as they sat there smoking, soldiers appeared riding toward them. The young men got up to hide from these soldiers and then saw another party of soldiers coming from another direction. Lone Bear shouted "Let us make for the river above the station." They

[16] Most of the accounts, including Hyde's, do not identify the Sioux who were with the Cheyennes at this time. They were Southern Oglalas, for the most part, their principal chief being Little Wound, their war leader, Pawnee Killer.—S.L.

[17] Grinnell, *Fighting Cheyennes*, 254, gives the list with some variants in the English rendering of the Indian names, which he, however, gives in Cheyenne form in his notes. That this Grinnell list may be Hyde's (from George Bent) is indeed possible, for Hyde speaks in his letter of May 11, 1967, to me of his work "on Grinnell's *Fighting Cheyennes*," for which he was research assistant. How much of Grinnell's book was Hyde's may never be known.—S.L.

started in that direction and the soldiers, seeing them, started in pursuit, overtaking them just as they reached the river bank. Here were some scattered cottonwood trees, with much brush and high grass. Pawnee Man and Wolf Walks in the Middle ran up the bank a short ways and laid down in the grass. The others crossed through the river to a small island and made a stand behind some sandbanks. The two troops of cavalry (under Major Cooper and Lieutenant Berry)[18] dismounted on the river bank and opened a hot fire on the little party on the island. The two Cheyennes hiding in the high grass were close to the soldiers' picketed horses, and Pawnee Man suggested that they rush out and mount two of the horses and get away. But Wolf Walks in the Middle said "No we may choose poor horses and the soldiers will follow and kill us both. Rather let us crawl farther down the river and hide till night comes." This they did and saved their lives. Meanwhile the Cheyennes on the island were making a brave stand, but the fire of the soldiers on the bank was so hot that Lone Bear called to the others "We must get out of this or be shot down." Jumping out of the sand pits, they made a rush across the shallow stream to the other bank. Just as they reached there Lone Bear was shot down and fell against the river bank. Plenty of Horses, the nearest man to him, ran over and picked up his quiver of arrows. The soldiers were firing fast and crossing after the Indians through the shallow water. They dragged Lone Bear's body to the bank, the three young Cheyennes retreating before the soldiers. Eagle Nest started running for some sand hills a mile away from the river. Plenty of Horses called to him to come back, to stick with the others. But he kept on, and several soldiers started after him and killed him just as he reached the sand hills. Plenty of Horses and Big Wolf fought their way up the river bank through the heavy brush and high grass, the soldiers not daring to rush in on them. Once Big Wolf was shot down; but Plenty of Horses stayed by him and,

[18] Custer identifies Cooper as Colonel Wickliffe Cooper, second in command of the Seventh Cavalry and in command of this detachment. Lieutenant Berry is not otherwise identified. Custer, *My Life on the Plains*, 66.—S.L.

all bloody, they fought and hid till darkness came and they were saved.

Six men on foot against two troops of cavalry. I was in Black Kettle's camp when Plenty of Horses, Big Wolf, Pawnee Man, and Wolf That Walks in the Middle came in and told the story of the fight. Three months after this fight I was with a war party of fifty Cheyennes under Lame Bull and we came to the very spot where Lone Bear was killed and dragged up on the bank by the soldiers. His bones were there then, though scattered by the wolves. In 1868, at Fort Lyon, I met Captain Berry who, with Major Cooper, was in command of this fight. He had Lone Bear's beaded belt and pistol and quiver, and proudly showed them to me. I told him that he had killed a very brave man. I knew Lone Bear very well and he was a fine warrior.[19]

This Anthony who kept the stage ranch at the crossing near where the fight took place was a relative of Susan B. Anthony, the famous temperance advocate so prominent some years ago, and it was one of her great sorrows that this man sold whisky on his ranch. His place was well known in those days.

I have often been asked what the Cheyennes called Hancock. They had no name for him, merely referred to him as the "Officer who burned the Dog Soldier camp on Red Arm Creek." In the summer of 1847 my father's train, encamped on this creek, was attacked by a war party of Comanches under a chief named Red Arm or Red Sleeve. In the fight this chief was killed, and John Smith and Thomas Murphy, long employed by my father, both claimed that they shot

[19] Major Cooper's report of this fight on April 19, 1867, shows how careless the army officers were in handling the facts of these Indian fights. He says that these six Cheyennes refused to surrender and "as they fought to the death, all that were first discovered—viz., six—were killed." He says that on examining the bodies of the dead "they proved to be Cheyennes and Sioux on the warpath, probably spies." The captured property included "one rifle, one pistol, two bows and quivers, three blankets, one pair of moccasins, one belt, and one powder flask, and one chief's headdress." Strange to say, on April 21st Major Cooper was ordered to Fort Dodge, and "positive instructions must be given to Lieutenant Berry that friendly Indians must not be molested."—G.H.

him off his horse. The Cheyennes knew this chief well and say that in battle he always wore a buckskin shirt with the sleeves stained red. Hence the Indians named this stream after this Comanche chief. The whites called it Pawnee Fork.

The force of 1400 men that General Hancock brought into the field to "chastise the Indians if they misbehaved" thus only succeeded in killing two young men during a campaign in which the troops wore themselves out. Hancock's campaign was over but the trouble he stirred up had just commenced and many innocent lives were lost before peace was again made.[20]

[20] A battle in the press between Hancock and the Indian agents, Wynkoop and Leavenworth, followed this foolish campaign. These letters can be found in the daily press of that period, *The Army and Navy Journal,* and the *Report of the Commissioner of Indian Affairs* for 1867.—G.H.

CHAPTER TEN

MEDICINE LODGE

THE STORIES THAT during the winter of 1866–67 the Indians were planning to begin war in the spring were untrue. The winter camps of all the tribes had white traders in them that winter. If the Indians had been plotting an outbreak, these traders would have been the first to learn the facts and would soon have packed up their outfits and left the camps. During this winter the Kiowas and Prairie Apaches were in camp on Bluff Creek, and Charlie Rath and I were in this village trading for buffalo robes. I was staying in Kicking Bird's lodge, and Rath in Satanta's. These two men were the most important Kiowa chiefs. Traders always stayed in the lodges of prominent chiefs, and these men protected the traders and were responsible for the trade goods which were stored in their lodges.[1]

After trading in the Kiowa village for about two months, I moved back to Black Kettle's Cheyenne camp, twenty miles east of the Kiowa village. I had been in this camp about three weeks when news was brought in of General Hancock's march toward Fort Larned. The Cheyennes could not understand what Hancock intended to do and

[1] General William Tecumseh Sherman, commanding the Military Division of Missouri, became convinced, less from what was happening in the south in December, 1866, than from information on the killings on the Smoky Hill road the previous summer, that the Cheyennes, as well as the Sioux, who had annihilated Brevet Lieutenant Colonel William Fetterman and his command near Fort Phil Kearny, "must be exterminated, for they will not settle down." Early in December, Major General Winfield Scott Hancock decided upon a spring campaign against the Cheyennes. Custer, *My Life on the Plains*, 27–28; Berthrong, *Southern Cheyennes*, 268.—S.L.

were a great deal alarmed by the reports of such a large body of troops in the vicinity. In fact, when Hancock made his appearance in the field, everyone in the Indian country began to fear trouble. I was trading for David Butterfield at this time, and he promptly sent word to me to send in the wagons with all the goods and robes I had on hand. He was sure that trouble was coming.[2]

In the meantime Indian runners were coming in with reports of the large body of troops at Fort Larned, and finally Black Kettle called a council, as he was getting much disturbed.[3] I was not present at the council, but was married to Black Kettle's niece and living in his lodge. After the council Black Kettle came in and told me that it had been decided to move farther south. He said that it looked as if the Indians would have trouble with Hancock's troops and he wished to keep out of it. That day the women packed up everything, and on the next day we started south. The Comanches, Kiowas, and Apaches also moved south, as they, too, thought Hancock's actions were war-like and wished to get out of the way before it was too late. Our village moved down to the north fork of the Canadian, and here we found a Comanche camp under chiefs Ten Bears and Tall Hat. In this camp were two white traders who had not yet heard of Hancock's march. I knew both of these men very well; they were Bill Mathison and Phillip McCusker. Mathison was the original "Buffalo Bill."[4] He was called by this name long before William F. Cody adopted it. McCusker was trading for a man named Meade, and Mathison owned his own outfit. They had acquired in trade about all the robes the Comanches had, and as spring was coming on they were almost

[2] Butterfield, formerly operator of the Overland Dispatch stage line, was selling arms and ammunition to the Indians, for which activities his Indian trading license was threatened.—S.L.

[3] This council seems quite unrelated to the council attended by Tall Bull, Bull Bear, White Horse, Little Robe, and ten other Cheyenne headmen with General Hancock at Fort Larned on the evening of April 12, 1867. Custer, *My Life on the Plains*, 29–32.

[4] There were several "Buffalo Bill" claimants; the one here and subsequently referred to was William Mathewson.—S.L.

ready to move with their trains to the Big Bend of the Arkansas, where their headquarters were. When I told them that General Hancock was in the field with a big force of troops, they realized that trouble was likely to start at any time, so they decided to move for the Arkansas at once. All this goes to show what the Indians and Indian traders thought of Hancock's movements. Our bitter experience with troops in the past served to make us hunt for cover when we learned of the arrival of Hancock's force at Fort Larned.

Black Kettle's band stopped at this Comanche village for a few days and traded all their spring robes to these two traders for sugar and coffee. We then moved on south to the south fork of the Canadian. Here two runners came in, and Bear Tongue and Snake, two of the camp criers, rode through the Cheyenne village announcing that the runners had brought bad news. These runners were Iron Shirt and his brother Riding on the Cloud, and they told us that Hancock's troops had burned the Dog Soldier and Sioux village on Pawnee Fork and that there had been a fight with troops at Cimarron Crossing, in which fight Lone Bear and Eagle Nest had been killed.[5] The two criers called out this news through the village and there was great excitement. That night the Cheyennes held a council and in the morning we broke camp and moved south to the Washita River. When we reached that stream we found all the Arapahos there in one big village under the head chief, Little Raven. The Caddos were there also, this being their home country. Their chief was called Jim Pockmark. These Indian villages were strung out along the Washita for a long distance.

We remained on the Washita about three weeks, and then the camps scattered to hunt. The buffalo herds were farther west, so Black Kettle moved in that direction, up the Washita, while the Arapahos moved northwest to the Canadian. The Caddos stayed where they were. When we got to the head of the Washita, we were joined by all the other bands of the Cheyennes, except the Dog Soldiers, who were up north in their own country on the Republican and

[5] The army detachment reported killing six Indians on April 19.—S.L.

Smoky Hill rivers. As soon as the Cheyenne bands came together, war parties were made up and started north on raids, as war had already been begun by Hancock.

I went with a party of about seventy-five warriors led by a medicine man named Lame Bull. We went towards Cimarron Crossing, which was a great camping place for wagon trains moving between New Mexico and the States. When we reached the Crossing we found the skeleton of Lone Bear on the river bank. Eagle Nest had been killed by the soldiers back in the sand hills away from the river, but we could find no trace of his body. That evening we attacked a mule train going west and took about fifty head of mules. Next day we left the Arkansas and started west along the Cimarron route toward New Mexico. Soon we saw a mule train coming east. Our party hid in a ravine near a spring, or water hole, to wait until the mules were turned out to water and graze. The trains on this route always stopped at the watering places, and we knew that when the mules were turned out we would have a good chance to run them off. But, as so often happened, some of the warriors could not wait until the right time. They broke away from the rest of us and made a charge at the herd. The white bell mare saw them coming, instinctively turned and ran for the camp, and of course all the mules followed her. Our main party was still hiding in the ravine, but when we saw the mules turn we made a rush for the herd. The men with the train opened fire on us to turn us away from the mules; but we kept on and cut off twenty-two mules and four horses before the herd reached the wagons. Howling Wolf, who is still living down here, made a rush for the white bell mare, knowing that if he cut her off and turned her the mules would all follow and we would get the whole bunch. Before he could turn the mare he was shot through the thigh and gave up the chase. Two years later I met the boss of this train in Colorado and drank with him. He told me that this big wagon train had been hauling government supplies to Fort Union, New Mexico, and they were on their return trip east when our war party struck them.

Lame Bull now decided that we should return to the village with all the mules and horses we had captured. The Cheyennes were in camp on the north fork of the Red River. I don't believe the Cheyennes had ever camped so far south before; but the troops were forcing us farther south every year. The Red River was in the Comanche country, and the north fork was a favorite camping place for the Comanches and Kiowas. The creeks that come into the north fork from the north, west of the Sweetwater, were well timbered with cottonwood and contained plenty of good water. The Comanches and Kiowas liked to make their winter camps along these creeks. In the cottonwood groves one could see the stumps where the Indians had cut down the trees so the horses could feed on the bark and small twigs in the winter. These cottonwood trees were more abundant here than anywhere else on the Plains, and many of trees were of great size. There was always good water in the creeks and fine grass in most of the valleys. The Red River heads in the Staked Plains.[6]

We found that another war party had returned to the village ahead of us, a larger party than ours. They had been raiding along the Arkansas River, about sixty miles east of Fort Larned. They had captured and destroyed two wagon trains, plundering them of goods of all kinds and running off all the horses and mules. In the second of these trains the war party found a lot of whisky, and after capturing this train decided to start for home. That night they camped in the sand hills on the south side of the Arkansas, and all except a few of the youngest warriors got drunk on the whisky. In the morning a large number of the warriors were still drinking. Lean Bear, a very fine man, was leader of this band. He began to get much worried over the condition of his party. They had been very careless and had made several mistakes after starting for home and had left a plain trail. Lean Bear began to fear that soldiers might find the trail and strike his party while the men were still drunk. He ordered a number of soldiers of the Bowstring Society to stop the drinking and make everybody pack up and get ready to move. Lean Bear afterward told me that many of the warriors were so drunk that the Bowstring men

---

[6] The location of this camp could have been almost anywhere west of the Wichita Mountains in southwestern Oklahoma and the area slightly south of present Pampa, Texas, but probably was in the vicinity of present Sentinel, Oklahoma.—S.L.

271

had to lift them on their ponies and tie them with ropes. The younger warriors looked after the captured mules and horses, and the party finally moved out from the sand hills. They had to go very slowly to keep the drunken warriors from falling off their horses. Luckily they were not followed by the troops and reached the village in safety.

While we were making these raids along the Arkansas and Cimarron routes, the Dog Soldiers and Sioux were busy on the Platte and Smoky Hill roads. The troops had not bothered us much, as they were giving most of their attention to the Dog Soldiers and Sioux. It soon became clear to the authorities that the soldiers could do little to stop the raids of these bands. The troops did not dare take the field in small detachments, and the Indians had no trouble in avoiding the large columns moving slowly across the country, encumbered with wagon trains hauling their supplies. The whites greatly exaggerated the size of these war parties raiding on the Platte and Smoky Hill. The Indians always preferred to raid in small bands, so that when stock was captured there would be but few men among whom to divide the animals.

A cavalry column under General [George Armstrong] Custer was sent into the field to operate against these bands, but the Indians had no difficulty in avoiding Custer's command, and the raids went on. Custer left Fort Hays on the Smoky Hill in May and moved north, examining the country carefully, but he saw no Indians. Reaching the Platte he went into camp near Fort McPherson (old Fort Cottonwood or Cottonwood Springs) and near Jack Morrow's Ranch. Here Pawnee Killer and Turkey Leg came in and had a talk with Custer. Guerrier was still with Custer as scout and trailer. He left him in July. Pawnee Killer was an Oglala Sioux headman; Turkey Leg was a Northern Cheyenne who generally traveled with about fifty lodges of his own followers and lived alternately with the Southern Cheyennes and the Northern Cheyennes. He moved back and forth, sometimes living with the Dog Soldiers and Brulé Sioux on the Republican and sometimes with the Northern Cheyennes and Oglalas on the Powder River. Turkey Leg and Pawnee Killer were great chums and their bands moved together a great deal of the time. As

272

they often crossed the Platte going north and south, they were frequent visitors at the forts in this neighborhood and both men were very well known to the army officers. While Pawnee Killer was very wild, Turkey Leg was friendly and preferred to keep peace with the whites. After the talk with Custer, Turkey Leg saw clearly that the war was likely to continue all summer south of the Platte, and wishing to keep his band out of trouble, he left Pawnee Killer and turned to the north. Following his talk with Pawnee Killer and Turkey Leg, Custer started on his return trip to the south. The troops moved through Jack Morrow's Canyon, some miles west of Fort McPherson. All along the south side of the Platte in this country are high impassable bluffs, and the only way to reach the plains south of the river was through one of the numerous canyons that started at the edge of the prairie and cut down through the bluffs into the valley of the Platte. Jack Morrow's Canyon (now known as Morin's) was one of the largest of these and was a real gateway through the bluffs. From time immemorial this canyon had been the path taken by the buffalo in their movements north and south, and it was a well-known Indian route. It had been used by General Mitchell in the winter of 1864–65 on his march south to the Republican.

When Custer reached the Republican River his wagon train was attacked by a party of Dog Soldiers and some of Pawnee Killer's Sioux, for Pawnee Killer had come south immediately after parting with Turkey Leg. Custer claimed that his troops killed a number of Indians in this fight, but he was wrong. Two Crows and Yellow Nose, both still living, were in the fight, and they say that the Indians had two or three horses shot, but no warriors were killed.[7]

Failing to locate the Indian villages, Custer soon left the Republican and started north again. He took a more westerly route this time and struck the South Platte near Fort Sedgwick (old Julesburg) in the northeast corner of Colorado. Here Custer learned that while he

---

[7] Custer, *My life on the Plains*, 79–85, describes the fight and Pawnee Killer's bland offer to parley afterward, as well as the repeated efforts of the Indians to break the parley conditions. Captain Louis McLane Hamilton, grandson of Alexander Hamilton, himself almost entrapped with his detachment while pursuing the Indians later, extricated his command without loss.—S.L.

had been on the Republican Lieutenant [Lyman S.] Kidder, with
ten men and a Sioux guide, had been sent out from Fort Sedgwick
with new orders for him.[8] As Custer had never received these orders
nor seen any signs of Kidder and his men there was a good deal of
anxiety for the safety of Kidder's party. Having received new orders
and supplies, Custer again set out from the South Platte to march to
Fort Wallace on the Smoky Hill. Crossing the Republican, Custer's
column reached Beaver Creek, and here, in a little hollow, they
found Lieutenant Kidder and all his men lying dead among the tall
grasses.

The death of Kidder and his men has always remained much of a
mystery to the whites. In later years army officers questioned the Indians about this affair, but the Cheyennes would not tell what really
happened as they were afraid the government might punish them,
and even today old men who took part in the Kidder and other fights
do not like to speak about them to white men. I have often talked this
fight over with Good Bear and Two Crows, both of whom are old
men now. They are Dog Soldiers, and took part in this battle. They
say that a band of Sioux under Pawnee Killer and Bear Raising Mischief were camped on Beaver Creek, and near this Sioux camp were
a few lodges of Cheyennes, numbering twelve warriors in all, under
the leadership of Howling Wolf, Tobacco, and Big Head. This was
a hunting camp, not a war party. The weather was warm and buffalo
were plentiful. One day most of the Sioux warriors went off hunting
buffalo. The Cheyenne men were lying around camp in the shade of
the lodges, the women gossiping and sewing or cooking. Suddenly all
was excitement. Sioux hunters came in sight riding fast. As they
rushed past the Cheyenne lodges they shouted, "Hurry and gather
your horses, all you Cheyenne men. Soldiers with pack mules are
coming." Good Bear says that the Cheyenne ponies were picketed
close to the lodges, so they were the first to get mounted. They rode

[8] The orders were General Sherman's, for Custer to take up a new base of
operations at Fort Wallace at the junction of Pond Creek and the south fork of the
Smoky Hill River in northwestern Kansas. Kidder left Fort Sedgwick in northeastern
Colorado, June 29, 1867. Grinnell, *Fighting Cheyennes*, 260.—S.L.

out swiftly and soon found the soldiers. Seeing the Cheyennes coming, the soldiers took alarm and dismounted, taking refuge in a little grassy hollow near the creek. The Cheyennes rushed up and circled around them, riding fast and shooting as they rode. Now the Sioux warriors came up and dismounted from their ponies, as the Sioux usually preferred to fight on foot. They began crawling in toward the little hollow from all sides, the Cheyennes still circling around and shooting. Good Bear and Tobacco each had a pony shot under him. The soldiers' horses and mules were soon killed. With the soldiers was Red Bead, or Red Drop, a Sioux guide. I think he was the first Plains Indian to act as scout and guide against his own people. He was badly scared, and all during the fight kept calling to the Indians to let him out, telling them that he was a Sioux. The Sioux taunted him for being with the soldiers and would show him no mercy. The soldiers shot wildly and the fight lasted only a little while. No Cheyennes were hurt in the fight, but two Sioux were killed. One of them, Yellow Horse, I knew well. He had been made a chief a short time before this, and his sister was married to John Smith, who was interpreter at Fort Laramie a long while ago.

About June 25, a few days before the Kidder fight, a war party of about two hundred Cheyennes and some Sioux attacked a station a few miles west of Fort Wallace and ran off a lot of stock belonging to the Overland Stage Company. Two companies of the Seventh Cavalry came out from the Fort to attack the Indians. The Cheyennes fell back a little way, then suddenly turned on the soldiers and drove them back toward the fort. A company of infantry was hurried out to support the two troops of cavalry. The Indians at this time were mainly armed with bows and lances. It was reported by the whites that Roman Nose was in command of this war party but this statement is incorrect. The officers imagined that Roman Nose led the Cheyennes in all these fights during this period, and they were generally wrong. While the Cheyennes were fighting the troops at Fort Wallace, Roman Nose was miles away in the Dog Soldier village on Beaver Creek. When the Cheyennes turned on the soldiers and charged in among them the troops were thrown into confusion and many men were killed and several cavalry horses captured by the Indians. Bear with Feathers, a brave man, tall and strong, struck a soldier with his lance and knocked him off his horse. Big Moccasin, another great warrior and a powerful man, knocked the bugler off his horse and then, without dismounting, picked him up from the ground and carried him off. Big Moccasin turned this soldier over to Long Chin, an old man who was with the war party. Long Chin had lost a son in a fight with the soldiers a short time before, and he promptly killed the bugler with a war club. Corporal Harris afterward claimed that he killed Roman Nose in this fight, but the man he referred to was a Sioux, who was riding a fine gray horse.[9]

Custer's summer campaign on the Republican and Smoky Hill proved a dismal failure. He was not able to strike the Indians and could not even protect the lines of travel. All through June, July, and August the Indians continued to raid in Kansas and Nebraska, easily avoiding the large bodies of troops sent against them and attacking the small detachments. At this time the Union Pacific had been completed as far west as Julesburg at the forks of the Platte. The stage line was still running from the end of the track to Denver, and thence on farther west. In August the Cheyennes went so far as to derail a train on the Union Pacific, near Plum Creek Station, Nebraska.

As I have said, after the conference with Custer on the Platte in June, Turkey Leg and his band of Northern Cheyennes moved for the north to get out of the way of the troops. Early in August he started south again, intending to rejoin his friend Pawnee Killer on the Republican. Turkey Leg's band struck the Platte near Plum Creek, and about four miles east of the railroad station a party, under the direction of Spotted Wolf, took out a culvert and ditched a westbound freight train. This train came along in the night, and when it went off the track the Cheyennes killed as many of the train crew as they could find. Then they broke into the boxcars and began plun-

[9] *Harper's Weekly* for 1867 has an account of this fight.—G.H.

The War Department, 1867, has the Indian attacking party at five to six hundred warriors, but Bent's figures are probably more accurate.—S.L.

dering. When daylight came the goods were strewn over the ground: bolts of silk and calico, sacks of flour, sugar, coffee, &c; boxes of shoes, barrels of whisky, and all kinds of stuff. The Indians broke in the head of a whisky barrel and many of the warriors got very drunk. Taking hold of the end of a bolt of calico or silk, a young man would mount his pony and gallop wildly across the prairie, the bolt of cloth bounding and leaping behind while unrolling in great billowy waves. Other riders tried to ride over or on this streaming ribbon of silk or calico. Some took hot coals from the engine and scattered them in the empty boxcars, setting the train into a blaze. After packing as much of the goods as they could on their ponies, the Cheyennes moved on south toward the Republican.

Near this stream they met a band of Sioux, and a few days later the Cheyennes and some Sioux came north with a lot of pack ponies to secure another load of plunder from the wrecked train. They did not think there was any danger and so brought with them a number of women and children to help collect the plunder and pack it. But in the meantime news of the wrecking and plundering of the train had been telegraphed all along the line, and a company of Pawnee scouts had been hurried to the scene on a special train. These Pawnees, under Major Frank North, arrived at Plum Creek just before Turkey Leg's band and the Sioux returned for their second load of plunder.

The railroad ran along the north side of the Platte, while the old Overland Stage Road, then abandoned, ran along the south side. At this point Plum Creek comes into the Platte from the south. The old Plum Creek stage station stood on the east bank of this creek, over which the stage company had built a small bridge. The Plum Creek railroad station was on the north side of the river, about opposite the old stage station of the same name. The Pawnee scouts detrained at Plum Creek station and then crossed the river to the old stage station. These Pawnees were originally uniformed and armed just like cavalry, but soon got rid of most of their uniforms. When the Pawnees rode across the stage bridge, the Cheyennes and Sioux first thought they were white soldiers, but as they drew nearer saw they were their old enemies, the Pawnees. Turkey Leg's party had less than a hundred warriors, armed principally with bows and lances. Major North had fifty Pawnees, well armed with new Spencer repeating rifles and Colt's revolvers. These repeating rifles were entirely new to the Indians. The Pawnees advanced slowly, apparently not over-anxious for a fight. With a yell the Cheyennes and Sioux charged on them, and when the leaders were within a hundred yards the Pawnees gave their old enemies a volley. Firing shot after shot in rapid succession, the Pawnees drove the Cheyennes and Sioux over the bluffs and several miles back across the prairie, capturing many of the pack ponies and taking prisoner a Cheyenne woman and boy. Yellow Bull, a Northern Cheyenne recently here on a visit, told me that the Cheyenne woman escaped from the Pawnees the same day. The boy was turned over to the Cheyennes at the peace council on the North Platte in September of this same year, and he is still living up north. The Cheyennes call him Pawnee because of the fact that he was captured and held prisoner by that tribe.

While these events were taking place in Kansas and Nebraska, north of the Arkansas, most of the Southern Cheyennes, Arapahos, and all of the Kiowas and Comanches were camped south of the Arkansas in what is now Oklahoma. I have already told how I went with a party of Cheyennes on a raid to Cimarron Crossing. When we returned we found the tribe encamped on the north fork of the Red River. That evening Black Kettle came into my lodge bringing a Mexican named Salvatore, or Sylvester. This man had been living among the Cheyennes and Wichitas for some time, and was now working for William Griffenstein, or Dutch Bill, as he was called by the whites. The Mexican had been sent out by Colonel J. H. Leavenworth, the agent for the Kiowas and Comanches, with a letter from the Wichita village at the mouth of the Little Arkansas, where Wichita, Kansas, now stands. Sylvester had been in Black Kettle's camp for several days; but no one could read his letter until I came in from the raid at Cimarron Crossing. The letter asked the chiefs of the Cheyennes, Arapahos, Kiowas, Comanches, and Apaches to come in

and have a talk with Colonel Leavenworth regarding peace proposals.[10] After I read the letter, Black Kettle said he would go in to
see Colonel Leavenworth and asked me to go along with him. To
this I consented. The chief then sent a crier through the camp saying
the village would move next day to Lake Creek.

A Cheyenne war party had just killed a Wichita Indian. Some
Wichitas had made a raid into Texas, and on their way back with a
fine herd of stolen horses met the Cheyennes and a fight followed.
One Wichita Indian was killed. Black Kettle was now afraid that if
we went near the Wichita village to see Colonel Leavenworth the
Wichitas might attack us in revenge for this killing. Sylvester informed us that Buffalo Goad, one of the Wichita chiefs, had told him
that the Wichitas would not attack any Cheyennes coming in for a
talk with Colonel Leavenworth. Black Kettle was still suspicious of
the Wichitas despite the promise of Buffalo Goad, but being anxious
to see Leavenworth and arrange for peace he decided to risk the
dangerous trip through a country occupied by hostile tribes.

Next day the Cheyenne village moved to Lake Creek, and as soon
as the camp was settled our party started from the Little Arkansas
to see the agent. The party was made up of Black Kettle and his wife,
Lame Man and his wife, Lone Bear, Sylvester, and myself. No other
chiefs or headmen would go. It was considered too dangerous. Griffenstein, the Wichita trader, was married to a Cheyenne woman,
called by the whites Cheyenne Jennie. Lame Man was her stepfather and his wife was Cheyenne Jennie's mother. So, Lame Man
and his wife, went with our party merely to visit Jennie. Lone Bear
was not a chief, but was cousin to Black Kettle and went along with
him for company, willing to share the risks. Ever since the Chivington Massacre, in November, 1864, I had been with my mother's
people, the Cheyennes. During this period the border press, and even

---

[10] Although Berthrong, *Southern Cheyennes*, 290 n., states that Agent Leavenworth "was not responsible for the gathering of the Indians as Grinnell asserted in
Fighting Cheyennes, 270–73, basing his conclusions on George Bent to Hyde, December 17, 1913," the great detail which Bent gives here and in ensuing pages pro-
vides us strong reason to credit Leavenworth with an important, if not the only, role
in bringing the Indians together preparatory to the Medicine Lodge council.—S.L.

the magazines and newspapers of the East, had frequent references to brother Charles and myself in connection with Cheyenne war parties. The most malignant and senseless stories were told of us and really believed and widely circulated in the border towns and around the forts. Years later these outrageous stories were still being repeated. So, when I consented to accompany Black Kettle I knew my trip also was attended with considerable peril.[11]

After we had started, about ten miles from our village we struck a herd of buffalo. The thick grass had been eaten off close. For hours we rode through the great herd, and little did we think then that in ten years the last buffalo would be shot and skinned by the white hide hunters. In these days our gods were good to us. For several days we were on the road; then we came on a party of our enemies, the Osages, chasing buffalo. We rode right up to one of the chiefs, who had made a kill and was skinning the dead animal. He looked up at us with a knife in his hand. I spoke to him in English. "We are Cheyennes, on our way to the Wichita village to see the agent there." He spoke good English, told me his name was Pawhuska, and that he had just been made chief. While we were talking, another Osage came up and stood looking at us. Pawhuska told him to take us to his wigwam. The Osages did not use tepees. When we entered the wigwam the Osage directed his women folks to serve us dinner. Meanwhile Pawhuska came in with his load of meat, and we had fresh roasted ribs, coffee, and fried bread. After the meal many Osage men came in to look at us. I told them that Black Kettle was on his way to make peace with the whites and with all our enemies. They said this was good. Pawhuska told us that farther on we would meet the Sacs and Foxes, who were also our enemies. He said they were just moving to their new home in Indian Territory. After the dinner and talk

[11] [Colonel Nelson A.] Miles' *Personal Recollections*, 140–41, credits George Bent with being the leader of the Southern Cheyennes, and Charles Bent as head of the Northern Cheyennes and part of the Sioux. General G. W. Dodge, in this same book, writing in 1895, says that George Bent was killed in an engagement with troops under General Sanborn on the Arkansas in 1865, though Bent was then in the north, as we know. Inman, in *The Santa Fe Trail*, is also guilty of like misinformation. Even the government reports are full of such errors.—G.H.

we went on our way. Next day we met the Sacs and Foxes. Keokuk, son of the famous chief of that name, was now chief of the Sacs. We rode boldly into their camp. They had wall tents instead of tepees. Many of them could speak English, so I made a short speech and told them our business. The Sacs were quite friendly and gave us a big feast. Early that evening we moved on again. The buffalo were as thick as grass all the way, to within fifteen miles of the Arkansas. We had fresh meat every day on this trip.

Soon we came in sight of the Wichita village, and we sent Sylvester, the Mexican, to ride ahead and notify Colonel Leavenworth that Black Kettle was coming. The Arkansas River was high, but we managed to cross it without trouble. Colonel Leavenworth, Griffenstein, Meade, Phil Block, and a lot of other white men were on the bank to receive us. The Wichitas were sitting in a circle smoking; an old Wichita man and his wife, both with gray hair, were sitting apart to one side, crying. It was their son the Cheyennes had killed. Three or four Wichita chiefs, among them Buffalo Goad, then head chief, came up with Colonel Leavenworth, Griffenstein, and Meade and shook hands with all of us. Griffenstein and his Cheyenne wife took care of our party; we went to stay with them. We found Jesse Chisholm here with some Comanche chiefs, Ten Bears and Tall Hat among them.[12] They had arrived ahead of us to see the agent.

Next day the council was held. Colonel Leavenworth told us that [Major] General [William S.] Harney, with the Commissioner of Indian Affairs and a number of other big men were coming out to hold a council and make peace with all the tribes. He read us a long letter, which I interpreted to Black Kettle. The Chief told Leavenworth that he would take the news back to his people. Here Colonel Leavenworth employed me and said that as soon as he received notice from Washington he would engage me to go out and notify all the tribes of the place where the peace council was to be held and the time of meeting. Black Kettle now returned home, and I stayed on with

[12] Jesse Chisholm, best known for his association with the Chisholm Trail, was a part-blood Cherokee Indian, d. 1868. He had been carrying on extensive Indian trading operations in Indian Territory (present Oklahoma) and Kansas.—S.L.

Griffenstein and his wife, Cheyenne Jennie. When Agent Leavenworth received the letter from Washington notifying him of the date and place of the meeting of the peace commission with the Indians, he induced Griffenstein to move down to Jesse Chisholm's ranch on the North Canadian to meet some chiefs there. He then gave me my instructions, and I set out with Griffenstein's wife. This woman, Cheyenne Jennie, was an invalid, and always traveled in an army ambulance which her husband had bought for her. She was a fine woman and had often succeeded in recovering white captives from the Comanches, Kiowas, and other tribes. She did more good work in fostering peaceful relations between the Indians and the whites than many an official or high commissioner sent out by the government.

The first village we visited was Little Raven's Arapaho camp on the Cimarron. I had him send out a crier to call all the chiefs and headmen of the soldier bands together in the center of the camp. Then I read and interpreted the Commissioners' letter to them. The letter said that all the chiefs of the five tribes were to meet Superintendent of Indian Affairs, Thomas Murphy, at Fort Larned to select a place for the great council. The next camp we came to was Black Kettle's, on Wolf Creek. I told Black Kettle to call the chiefs and headmen to the big lodge in the center of the camp circle, and there I read the letter to them. My brother Charlie was in the camp and also read the letter to the chiefs. After visiting Black Kettle's camp I went to the camps of the Kiowas and Comanches and brought back to Fort Larned Black Kettle and a few other Cheyenne headmen, a good many Arapahos, a small party of Kiowas and Comanches, and several Prairie Apaches.

At Fort Larned we held a talk with Leavenworth and it was decided to hold the big council on Medicine Lodge Creek, south of the Arkansas, where for many years the Kiowas had held their annual Medicine Lodge. Congress had appointed this commission to come out and make peace with all the Indians then hostile and, if possible, to remove the causes of war. This commission consisted of N. G. Taylor, then commissioner of Indian affairs, Senator John B. Henderson, John B. Sanborn, Samuel F. Tappan, and Generals W. T. Sherman, William S. Harney, Alfred H. Terry, and C. C. Augur.[13]

The council opened about October 16 at Medicine Lodge Creek, about seventy miles southwest of Fort Larned. Thomas Murphy, the superintendent of Indian affairs, was the man who had charge of getting the Indians to the council, and he gave out the presents to the Indians when the council opened; in fact, he practically managed the affair. The Commissioners had an escort of two hundred cavalrymen, and the drivers of the wagons, which numbered one hundred and sixty-five, six mules to a wagon, with all the camp followers brought the number of whites up to fully six hundred. They had over twelve hundred horses and mules with them.

The great camp was in a beautiful hollow through which flowed Medicine Lodge Creek, with its lovely wooded banks. This was a favorite place for the summer medicine-making of the Indians and also for their winter camps. At the head of the camp were the Arapahos, under Little Raven, with about one hundred and seventy lodges; next, in a fine grove, were the Comanches, with one hundred lodges, under Ten Bears and Silver Brooch; below them were the Kiowas, under White Bear, Black Eagle, Sitting Bear, and Kicking Eagle, with one hundred and fifty lodges; and next were the Apaches, eighty-five lodges, under Poor Bear. The council grounds were in the center, in a grove of tall elms. Across the creek from the council grounds was Black Kettle's camp of sixty lodges. The remainder of the Cheyennes were camped several miles away on the Cimarron river, and when they moved in later on they brought the number of Cheyennes lodges up to two hundred and fifty. About six persons are calculated to a lodge, so some idea can be gained of the size of the camp. Fully five thousand Indians were encamped here, each Indian village being pitched in a circle.[14] Thousands of ponies covered the

[13] The act creating the peace commission was of Senator John B. Henderson of Missouri's authorship, passed by Congress July 20, 1867.—S.L.

[14] Bent's estimate of the total number of Indians present squares with Superintendent Murphy's. Drawing upon the eye-witness accounts of the newspaper correspondents present (Henry M. Stanley, later to gain additional fame in Africa), Douglas C. Jones has given a vivid description of the encampments, the sights

adjacent hills and valleys near the camp and great was the excitement. The crowd of white camp followers quickly brought down the wrath of Satanta (White Bear) on their heads by the wanton killing of buffalo near the camp. He protested so vigorously against this unnecessary slaughter that the commission ordered the arrest and confinement of several of the wrongdoers. I was married to Black Kettle's niece and we made our home in the Chief's lodge. A big wagon train with supplies for the camp was corralled near Black Kettle's village, guarded at night by Arapaho and Apache camp police. Black Kettle, Little Robe, Superintendent Murphy, Agent Wynkoop and I were eating supper one evening in the Cheyenne village when Roman Nose and Gray Beard, with an armed party of Dog Soldiers, came charging up to the train. The Arapaho and Apache guard ran out to meet them, but nothing happened. Roman Nose and Gray Beard brought their party to our camp and stayed with us for two days. Murphy and Wynkoop had a talk with them and they took the news to their camp on the Cimarron and later joined the great council. I mention this because the report was circulated by newspaper correspondents that Roman Nose had charged on the camp to kill Wynkoop for telling Hancock the location of the Dog Soldiers' camp the previous spring. This was untrue, but was in line with the usual misstatements about Indian affairs. The Dog Soldiers were at the head of the peace party at this council, and Bull Bear, Tall Bull, and White Horse, the Dog Soldiers' leaders, were signers of the treaty, as well as Black Kettle, Little Robe, Whirlwind, Plenty Birds, and others. The Cheyennes signed the treaty of October 28, 1867. John Smith and Charlie Bent acted with me as interpreters.[15] The Kiowas, Comanches and Apaches signed this famous

and scenes and sounds during the days of the great treaty council in his *The Treaty of Medicine Lodge.*

[15] Seven languages were used by the principals at the council, and of these Comanche was the *lingua franca* of the Indians present. The master of the latter, among the interpreters, was the plainsman, Phillip McCusker, who had married a Comanche. McCusker also knew both Kiowa and Kiowa-Apache. Bent does not mention his brother-in-law, Edmond Guerrier, who was present and identified as an interpreter; nor does he mention his sister, Julia, who was not one; Fishermore, a

treaty on October 21, 1867. Among the signers for the Kiowas were Satank (Sitting Bear), Satanta (White Bear), Black Eagle, Kicking Eagle (also called Kicking Bird), and Stumbling Bear; for the Comanches, Ten Bears, Painted Lips, and Silver Brooch; and Wolf's Sleeve and Poor Bear for the Apaches. Phillip McCusker, who died in 1885, was interpreter. I recall that Major [Joel H.] Elliott, who lost his life in the attack on Black Kettle's village a year later, was also present.

This was, in a way, the most important treaty ever signed by the Cheyennes, and it marked the beginning of the end of the Cheyenne as a free and independent warrior and hunter, and eventually changed his old range, from Saskatchewan to Mexico, to the narrow confines of a reservation in Oklahoma.[16]

Kiowa, was named by some of those present as an interpreter; Mrs. Margaret Adams, the daughter of the French-Canadian trader, John Poisal, and an Arapaho woman, interpreted for Little Raven of the Arapahos. The Bent brothers and John Smith handled Cheyenne interpreting; William Bent was not present for the council. Jones, *Treaty of Medicine Lodge*, 104–109.—S.L.

[16] What the Cheyennes agreed to at Medicine Lodge consisted of promises of peace, the right of emigrant travel through the Plains, safety of the railroads, the cession of their lands in Kansas, and a further restriction of reservation lands formerly granted them in 1865 to those bounded by the 37th parallel and the Cimarron and Arkansas rivers. The grant of land in severalty (320 acres), like other provisions of the treaty, became abortive. Berthrong, *Southern Cheyennes*, 298–99.—S.L.

CHAPTER ELEVEN

THE DEATH OF ROMAN NOSE

THE GOVERNMENT HAD expected a great deal of good to come from the signing of the treaty at Medicine Lodge. Peace was now thought to be assured, but it soon became clear that trouble was likely to crop up again before long. Everywhere, the Indians found the whites invading their country, building houses, breaking up and planting the soil, opening new roads, and wantonly slaughtering the game on every side. The Cheyennes, especially the wild Dog Soldiers, resented this unwarranted invasion of their hunting grounds, and whenever the Indians and whites met there was the prospect of trouble.

Immediately after the close of the Civil War the governor of Kansas had opened a campaign of advertising with the object of inducing settlers to come to Kansas.[1] This movement proved very successful; all the best lands in the eastern part of the state were soon taken up, and the settlers then began to crowd out into the Indian country to take up lands in the valleys of the Saline, Solomon, Republican, and Smoky Hill. As the Cheyennes and Sioux still occupied this region, it could easily be seen that sooner or later trouble would break out. Beside this swarm of settlers, Kansas had more than her share of the usual frontier riffraff, a floating population of ex-soldiers, Union and Confederate, many of the worst characters from both

---

[1] Samuel J. Crawford, an attorney from Garnett, held office as governor twice during the period, 1865–66, and 1867–68, and with a forward looking legislature advanced many programs of settlement and development. Frank William Zornow, *Kansas: A History of the Jayhawk State*, 121–24.

armies, and all kinds of frontier roughs who hung around the railroad camps and the new canvas towns that sprang up along the line. Large numbers of these men were grubstaked by the storekeepers, who supplied them with rifles and ammunition, wagons and horses, and sent them out in small parties to kill buffalo for the hides. Hundreds of these bands of white hide hunters were soon at work on the Kansas and Nebraska plains slaughtering the buffalo, ripping off the hides, and leaving the carcasses to rot on the ground. A favorite method with these men was to conceal themselves near some water hole or small stream where the buffalo had to come to drink. When first fired on, the buffalo usually did not run, but stood pawing the ground, staring stupidly at their companions that had been shot down. Thus lying in concealment, half a dozen hide hunters sometimes slaughtered a great part of the herd before the animals became alarmed and ran off. The Indians watched this butchery sullenly. The herds of buffalo were the very life of the Plains tribes, and it was not to be expected that they would for long remain quiet while these white hide hunters slaughtered the herds.

During the winter of 1867–68 part of the Cheyennes were in winter camp on the Pawnee Fork with the Kiowas and Comanches, not far from Fort Larned. The rest of the tribe camped with the Arapahos near Fort Dodge. At the Medicine Lodge council the Indians had been promised that guns and ammunition would be issued to them early in the spring of 1868, and expecting that this issue would be made at Fort Larned and Fort Dodge, the Indians remained at these places awaiting the issue. It was at this time that General Philip H. Sheridan visited the two forts and went through the Indian camps. The arms, however, failed to make their appearance, and at last the camps broke up and the tribes moved away, many of the men in sullen humor.[2]

---

[2] Major General Philip H. Sheridan replaced Brigadier General John Pope at Fort Leavenworth in September, 1867, taking command of the Department of the Missouri, under Lieutenant General William T. Sherman, commanding officer of the Division of the Missouri. Carl Coke Rister, *Border Command: Phil Sheridan in the West*, 40–44.—S.L.

In the latter part of 1867 the Cheyennes had trouble with the Kaws, who were then living on a reservation at Council Grove, in southeastern Kansas. About the first of June, 1868, a war party of about one hundred and fifty Cheyennes, under Little Robe, went out to raid the Kaw village. The game in that region had been slaughtered, and the Cheyennes, unable to procure any wild meat on the trip, killed some cattle belonging to white settlers. This caused a great deal of excitement and a hasty arming among the whites. Meantime news of the approach of the Cheyennes had reached the Kaws, who at once prepared for a fight. The Kaw agent, an ex-officer in a Kansas cavalry regiment, posted his Indians in the woods near the village, and as the Cheyennes advanced through the timber they were fired on from this ambush. The fight that followed, like most fights between tribes, did not amount to much. There was a great deal of wild shooting and yelling, charging and circling, but no one was seriously hurt, and after a few hours of this the Cheyennes withdrew.[3] On the way home the Cheyennes ran into a trail outfit driving a herd of Texas cattle to the north and, with the permission of the cattle men, killed some beef. This was later represented as a raid on the cattle herd and also created a great deal of excitement. The settlers complained to the War and Indian Departments, charging the Cheyennes with making depredations, so, when the annuities were issued in accordance with the provisions of the Medicine Lodge treaty, the promised arms and ammunition were withheld, to the great dissatisfaction of the Indians. The agents wished to keep the promise and issue the arms, but General Sheridan forbade it.[4]

That summer a large village of Dog Soldiers, with ten lodges of Sioux, were camped near Walnut Creek, not far from Fort Larned, and about August 2 a war party of two hundred set out from this

[3] The site of this fight was at Council Grove, Kansas, June 3, 1868, as Lieutenant Frederick H. Beecher reported to Sheridan on June 4. Berthrong, *Southern Cheyennes*, 301–302.—S.L.

[4] Superintendent of Indian Affairs Thomas Murphy, not Sheridan, issued the ban on the distribution of arms, and Agent E. W. Wynkoop carried it out in mid-July, but on August 9 reversed himself and so reported to Murphy on August 10. Custer, *My Life on the Plains*, 150–52.—S.L.

village to make a raid on the Pawnees, up in Nebraska. Most of the young men in the village, including the Sioux, went with this war party, and with them were four Arapahos, one being Little Raven's son. They crossed the Smoky Hill River near Fort Hays, and when they reached the Saline Fork the main body turned down this stream toward the settlements. Fearing trouble might come on with the whites, about twenty of the warriors continued on toward the Paw- nee villages. When the main party stopped to camp for the night two men, one a brother of White Antelope, who was murdered at Sand Creek, went toward the settlements and rode up to a settler's house to ask for something to eat. A man came to the door and ordered them away. The Indians, not knowing what he said, continued to ride toward the house, so the settler took a gun and fired on them. As the Indians rode away they came on a white woman and forced her to go with them to the camp. The men in the camp were annoyed at this, and taking the woman away from the two young men they re- turned her to her home. In the morning the party moved north again, and on the south fork of the Solomon were well treated by the white settlers. When near the north fork the Cheyennes came upon a body of well-armed white men who fired upon them. Skirting this party, the Indians rode on and attacked a settlement for revenge, though many of them opposed any clash with the whites. In fact only a part of the warriors engaged in this attack. Several white men were killed and two little girls captured. Most of the Indians in the party were bitterly opposed to any further raiding, so the whole band turned south. They had not proceeded very far when they ran into a force of cavalry, by whom they were pursued. The warriors who had the two little girls dropped them without hurting them and soon the war party split up, part turning north again toward the Solomon, the majority making for the village near Walnut Creek, while a few headed for Black Kettle's village near Fort Larned. Most of the Indians admitted at the time that it was a bad mistake to have made this raid; but the young Dog Soldiers were very wild and hard to control, and there was such provocation by the whites.[5]

[5] These raids spread terror all through Kansas and up into Nebraska, and at the

Meanwhile Agent Wynkoop had issued annuities, including a small amount of arms and ammunition, to the main body of Cheyennes at Fort Larned, ignorant of the outbreak which had just occurred. All the five tribes were here at Fort Larned and had a big council, at which General Sheridan was present.[6] I was present as interpreter. At the council, Wynkoop asked General Sheridan if he could issue arms to the Indians. Sheridan said "Yes, give them arms and if they go to war the soldiers will kill them like men." This I interpreted to the Cheyennes, and Stone Calf, a Cheyenne chief and great warrior, replied to Sheridan, "Let your soldiers grow long hair, so that we can have some honor in killing them." Sheridan smiled and said he was very sorry he could not accommodate him, as the soldiers would get lousy.

Though efforts were made to arrest the ringleaders of the Solomon and Saline raids, before anything could be done in the matter by the agents, troops were poured into the field, and, as usual in Indian wars, the innocent suffered with the guilty. Black Kettle knew that, though his band had nothing to do with the raids, trouble was coming, and, as soon as his people had secured their annuities, moved south to get away from the troops. I was with Black Kettle's band until we reached the crossing of the Arkansas. Here I left the Indians

---

time it was claimed that hundreds of settlers had been attacked or killed and the whole frontier threatened with destruction. Crawford, who at that time was governor of Kansas, gives the number of killed and wounded as about forty, and since the governor was a great Indian-hater, even his figures were probably exaggerated. —G.H.

[6] Sheridan was visited at Fort Dodge by Little Raven, Powder Face, and Spotted Wolf of the Arapahos during the first two days of September, 1868. We have only George Bent's statement that the Cheyennes, Kiowas, Comanches, and Prairie Apaches were also present (at Fort Larned). But in councils at Fort Larned on September 20, Generals Sheridan and William M. Hazen, the latter on loan to the Office of Indian Affairs, treated with the Kiowas and Comanches and arrived at agreement for the removal of the two tribes to the area of Fort Cobb in Indian Territory, which General Sherman conceived as a reservation for the Cheyennes and Arapahos and as a temporary territory for the other three Plains tribes who might be willing to keep themselves out of the hostilities then threatening to engulf the whole of the Southern Plains. Nye, *Carbine and Lance*, 68–72; Berthrong, *Southern Cheyennes*, 318–21.—S.L.

and went on to Colorado to visit my sister Mary and brother Robert. I never saw Black Kettle again, as in November General Custer surprised his village on the Washita and Black Kettle was killed. When I arrived at Fort Lyon with my wife, I found that war was on again. The War Department offered me ten dollars a day to go with the troops and act as chief of scouts. This I refused, as I preferred not to go against my own people. Here I met Bill Cody and Wild Bill Hickok, who were serving as scouts. Cody, or Buffalo Bill, is known to every one of the present generation; but Wild Bill was the more famous at this time. His name was James Butler Hickok, and he was one of the greatest characters of the frontier. Wild Bill was scout during the Indian wars, marshal of some of the toughest towns in the west, and, though one of the quickest men with a gun that ever lived, was shot in the head from behind by a cheap gambler in Deadwood City in 1876.[7]

I found my father living this summer at the stockade on the south side of the Arkansas at the mouth of the Purgatoire River.[8] He spent the last years of his life at this stockade trading for buffalo robes. Though he was one of the best known of the famous old fur traders, the Indians did not care to visit my father now, as there was no game in the vicinity and, on account of hostilities, it was dangerous to go there. My father sent out traders to the Indian camps, mule wagons carrying the trade goods and bringing back the robes. At the stockade he had built a robe press for making the robes into packs. Big ox teams hauled the robes to the Missouri River and brought back the trade goods to the stockade. Judge R. M. Moore was married to my eldest sister, Mary, and they were living here. The famous

[7] The invitation to George Bent was for Sheridan's winter campaign. William F. Cody was chief of scouts at this time for Brevet Brigadier General E. A. Carr, in command of the Fifth Cavalry. Hickock was guide and Charles B. Autubees was chief of scouts for Brevet Brigadier General W. H. Penrose, in command of a column of four companies of the Tenth Cavalry and one of the Seventh. Joseph G. Rosa, *They Called Him Wild Bill*, 87.—S.L.

[8] William Bent had leased to the army his stone trading post at the Big Timbers on the Arkansas on September 9, 1860, but as early as 1857 had constructed a temporary picket post at the mouth of the Purgatoire, which he greatly enlarged in the fall of 1860. Lavender, *Bent's Fort*, 333, 346.—S.L.

Old Bent's Fort was being used as a stage station and eating house. Bent's New Fort (old Fort Lyon) had been abandoned by the government in 1866 because the river had undermined the bank, and new Fort Lyon had been established twenty miles farther up the Arkansas. Tom Boggs, one of the old traders for Bent & St. Vrain, had a ranch near Fort Lyon, and living with him here were Kit Carson and wife, who were both in bad health. Carson had come up from Taos, New Mexico, hoping that a change of climate would improve his wife's condition as well as his own. He was one of my father's best men in the good old days of prosperity, though in later years he had been taken up by government officials and become famous. One day my brother-in-law, Judge Moore, went with me to call on Carson. Though we did not know it when we started, Carson's wife had died the day before. We talked with him for an hour about the good old days. Owing to bad health and the shock of the death of his wife, Carson was in poor spirits. He had a fine race horse, which he asked me to buy as we were leaving. After paying for the horse, Judge Moore and I left for home. Soon after, Carson's condition became so alarming that he was removed to Fort Lyon in order that he might have the attention of the post surgeon. He failed to improve and died May 23, 1868.[9] My father died almost a year later, at the stockade, on May 19, 1869, aged sixty years. Strange to say, his old partner, Ceran St. Vrain, died at his son's ranch, at Mora, New Mexico, in 1870, a year after my father's death.[10] Queer thing about this race horse, he strayed from my herd in 1870, and a soldier near Camp Supply caught and presented him to an army officer's wife. I sent

[9] Carson, colonel of New Mexico Volunteers during the Civil War, commanded Fort Garland, Colorado, from August 11, 1866, to November 22, 1867, as lieutenant colonel, retiring from service as brevet brigadier general on the latter date. He had already settled his family at Boggsville, two miles from Las Animas, Colorado, where Thomas O. Boggs had a ranch nearby. Carson had bought two pieces of land, one from Ceran St. Vrain and another near William Bent's picket post and ranch further up the Purgatoire. George Bent's chronology at this point is clearly doubling back, for his visit with Carson must have occurred in May, whereas his narrative immediately preceding deals with the fall of 1868. Estergreen, *Kit Carson: A Portrait in Courage*, 218 *passim*, 272–80; Lavender, *Bent's Fort*, 365–66.—S.L.

[10] October 28, 1870, in Mora, New Mexico.—S.L.

word to her that it was my horse, but she might keep him if she wished.[11]

Early in the summer of 1868 General Sheridan had announced his intention of driving the five tribes to their respective reservations in what is now Oklahoma, though, as a matter of fact, no arrangements had been made to put the reservations in shape to receive the Indians according to the Medicine Lodge treaty. The result of Sheridan's policy was to drive the Kiowas and Comanches into the war. About the time the Cheyenne war party was raiding the Saline Valley, the Kiowas and Comanches were having trouble farther south. A column of troops under General Sully ran into a party of Kiowas and Comanches and drove them toward the Cimarron River. When they reached the river, the Indians turned on the troops and drove them back. Next day they again attacked Sully, the fight lasting several hours, and on the following day made another attack on the troops. Though Sully reported victories on all three days he was glad to get back to Fort Dodge.[12]

In the latter part of August, William Comstock and Sharp Grover, who, with Richard Parr, were employed by General Sheridan as scouts, came into a Cheyenne camp for news. War was on long before

---

[11] This is a fact. Mrs. Roe, in *Letters of an Army Officer's Wife*, gives an account of this incident.—G.H.

[12] Brigadier General Alfred Sully with nine companies of the Seventh Cavalry and one company of the Third Infantry left Fort Dodge on September 7, 1868, for the Cimarron. John Smith, Ben Clark, and Amos Chapman, intermarried whites with the Cheyennes and Araphos and frequently used as interpreters, were scouts. The night of September 10–11, the army detachment encampment at the confluence of Crooked Creek and the Cimarron was surrounded by Indians, who the next day attacked the rear guard as the troops resumed their march, killing one trooper whom they were abducting and dropping another in flight. The scouts identified the Indians as Dog Soldiers. Retreating from the Cimarron Valley, the Indians again joined battle on Beaver Creek, an upper tributary of the Canadian River. Entrapped on September 13 on the Canadian, Sully finally extricated himself and returned to Fort Dodge. Berthrong, *Southern Cheyennes*, 318–20.—S.L.

The Indians whom Sully faced may have been a mixed force, with Kiowas and Comanches joined with the Cheyennes and Arapahos, or Cheyenne Dog Soldiers, but Bent's identification of them as Kiowas and Comanches is difficult to reconcile with the guides' statement that they were Cheyennes.—S.L.

these two scouts set out for the Cheyenne village, and troops were attacking the Indians wherever they met them, so the two whites were really spies and knew it. Yet in spite of this Chief Bull Bear, of the Dog Soldiers, took the two white men into his lodge and fed and protected them. Now, few white people understand the position of an Indian chief. There is no such thing as a "war chief," these so-called war chiefs being simply leaders of the warrior societies and not chiefs at all. Thus, Roman Nose was always called a war chief or head chief by the whites, though he never was a chief. A chief was a peace official. Many chiefs were famous fighters in their younger days, yet others who gained fame as wise leaders were never noted as warriors. Yellow Wolf, as he was called by the whites, or Yellow Coyote (Okohm-e-ho-wist), as his name should properly be translated, was a famous Cheyenne chief in the old days, and, though often a leader in horse raids against other tribes, was never noted as a fighting man. His son, Red Moon, was later a chief, but was never famed as a warrior. Nor was Dull Knife famous except as chief. Little Wolf, as the whites called him, or Little Coyote (Okohm-ha-ket), was celebrated as a warrior even before he became chief, and Stone Calf, too, was also a great warrior. A chief was the headman of the village, directed its movements, selected the camping places, and appointed the soldier societies to maintain order in the camp; he settled disputes and was just to all, else he fell into disfavor. He never took sides in village quarrels even when his own relatives were involved. To do so would bring him into contempt.[13] He dispensed hospitality to prominent visitors, one very good reason why a chief often had more than one wife, since one woman was physically unable to do all the work of a chief's lodge. In attacks on the village by enemies he often fought as a simple warrior, leaving the direction of the battle to others more skilful as fighters. In some of the hardest fights with white troops, chiefs fought like other warriors, ignorance of which fact often leads the whites into the error of crediting noted chiefs

[13] Karl N. Llewellyn and E. Adamson Hoebel, in *The Cheyenne Way: Conflict and Case Law in Primitive Jurisprudence*, reveal how elaborate the Cheyenne legal system was and the chiefs' responsibilities under it.—S.L.

Fort Benton

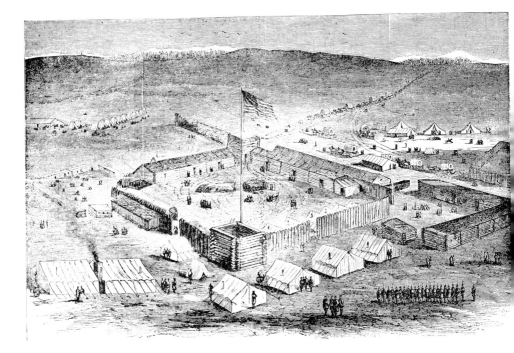

Camp Supply

Bull Train Crossing the Smoky Hill River, 1867

Medicine Lodge Peace Commission
From left to right: Generals Terry, Harney, and Sherman; unidentified
Indian woman; Commissioners N. G. Taylor; Samuel F. Tappan;
and General C. C. Augur.

Battle of the Washita. From George Armstrong Custer, *My Life on the Plains*, edited by Edgar I. Stewart

Little Bear, Hairless Bear, and Island

Cheyenne Prisoners at Fort Marion, 1876. From Cohoe, *A Cheyenne Sketchbook*, edited by E. Adamson Hoebel and Karen Daniels Petersen

Quanah at right

with undue skill in directing a battle. If an enemy came peacefully to the village, it was the duty of the chief to care for and protect the visitor so, when Sharp Grover and Bill Comstock came into the Dog Soldier camp, Bull Bear took them to his lodge. Though the Cheyenne men knew the whites were scouting for the soldiers, still they would not kill them in the hands of the chiefs. Bull Bear took them into his lodge and fed them, and after dark, accompanied by several other chiefs, escorted the whites for some distance away from the camp. Soon after the chiefs left the scouts, a war party returning to the village came on the two white men and a fight followed. Comstock was killed and Grover was wounded, but got away in the dark. When General Sheridan heard of this affair he accused the Indians of acting treacherously. That charge was absurd. These scouts came into the camp as spies and the Indians would have been justified in shooting them as soon as they entered the village. Sheridan also made the mistake of saying that this affair took place at Turkey Leg's camp; but, as I have said, it occurred at the Dog Soldiers' village.[14]

The war was now waged with great fury through all the middle Plains. Stations on the great overland routes were attacked, stock was run off and agents killed, and travel was practically abandoned during the late summer. Isolated settlers were attacked and driven off, and the detached settlements were deserted. The troops, as usual, were powerless, and Sherman himself said that "fifty Indians could checkmate three thousand troops." In fact, the troops could reach the Indians only when it suited the latter to risk an engagement, and this happened but seldom.

Early in September a train of ten wagons was captured near the Cimarron Crossing. The governor of Colorado telegraphed the War Department that the fifteen men with this train had been captured alive and burned to death, and this lie has been perpetuated ever since. The wagons were captured by a Cheyenne war party and the

---

[14] Grover's testimony was that, on being escorted from the camp by seven young warriors, he and Comstock were fired upon from the rear. Berthrong, *Southern Cheyennes*, 309.—S.L.

fifteen men were all killed while defending themselves. The Indians at that time made a practice of burning all the wagons they captured, as they could not take them away. Having set fire to the wagons, as an after-thought the Cheyennes threw the dead bodies of the train-men into the flames. Cheyenne Indians never torture prisoners. Harsh treatment of prisoners by captors was considered a disgrace to the tribe and was always resented as such. In a fight, the Cheyennes always killed the men at once, taking no prisoners except women, girls, and young boys, all of whom were invariably well treated and adopted into the tribe. About seventy years ago the Cheyennes killed a Shoshone man and dragged his body to the center of the village, where the women and children piled up a lot of sagebrush around the body and burned it up. This was the only previous case I ever heard of where the Cheyennes burned the bodies of any enemies. When the Cheyennes killed an enemy they laid him on the ground face down, as it was considered bad luck to leave a dead enemy with his face turned toward the sky. But I have seen them kill white men and not care how the bodies lay. Such was their bitterness against the whites. While with the Cheyennes up north in 1865, we had a fight with and killed some Crows. I remember well how an old Cheyenne man dismounted from his horse and turned the dead Crows over with their faces to the ground.

The battle customs of the Indians all originated in the old-time intertribal wars. In the old days a warrior never surrendered; if he could not make his escape he died fighting, and this was why Indians never tried to take full-grown men prisoners in battle. When the wars with the whites came, the Indians stuck to the old custom, asking no quarter and never giving it. It was only in the later 1870's that Indians occasionally surrendered in battle, usually due to the efforts of the Indian scouts serving with the troops, who called out to the hostiles that they would not be killed or mistreated if they stopped fighting and gave themselves up. Women and children taken in a fight belonged to the warrior who captured them and were usually adopted into his family, though he had the right to dispose of them in some other way if he saw fit. However, it was considered a disgrace to the tribe to ill-treat these prisoners. If they did not escape soon after their capture, they ordinarily became reconciled to their lot and were as proud of their adopted tribe as if they had been born into it. The Cheyennes were constantly at war with most of the other Plains tribes, and being daring raiders, they captured large numbers of women, girls, and young boys. The women and girls invariably married into the tribe, and many Cheyennes are descended from these captive women. For example, in 1837, in a fight with the Kiowas, a little girl about two years old was captured. She had evidently been taken earlier by the Kiowas in a raid on the whites. She grew up among the Cheyennes and is to all intents and purposes a Cheyenne woman, speaking only the Cheyenne language; but she has blue eyes and brown hair and is apparently of Irish descent. Black Kettle's wife was a captive Ponca woman; Dull Knife's wife a Pawnee woman, captured in 1854. A number of captive Mexican boys have been members of the Southern Plains tribes for many years. One is still among the Northern Cheyennes. Some years ago his relatives were traced and it was decided to return him to his friends in old Mexico. At that time he was a grown man, but at the railroad station he absolutely refused to go to Mexico and returned to the Cheyenne reservation. In 1858 Lean Bear captured Yellow Nose and his mother, a Ute woman. The mother later escaped and rejoined her people. In 1862 I saw her, living with the Utes; yet Yellow Nose, her son, became one of the most famous of Cheyenne warriors.

The war continued during the late summer and early fall of 1868, the Indians raiding where they pleased and the troops unable to strike them a blow. Major George A. Forsyth, of Sheridan's staff (he had accompanied General Sheridan on his famous ride from Winchester to Cedar Creek in 1864), had been authorized to raise a company of fifty scouts, men of the frontier more or less familiar with Indian warfare. With this force Sheridan expected to obtain great results. Although the company did a great deal of scouting and hard riding, they were for some time no more successful against the Indians than the regular cavalry.[15]

In the early part of September the Indians attacked a party of traders near Sheridan, Kansas, then the end of the Kansas Pacific Railroad, about thirteen miles east of Fort Wallace. Forsyth and his scouts happened to be at Wallace at the time and were at once sent out. They struck the fresh trail of the war party and followed it in a northwesterly direction toward the Arickaree Fork of the Republican River, across the Kansas line in northeastern Colorado. Meantime this war party had reached their village, which was made up of Dog Soldiers, under Tall Bull, White Horse, and Bull Bear, and a number of Sioux lodges, under Bad Yellow Eyes and Two Strikes (Strikes Twice); a few young Arapahos were also here with friends in the Cheyenne village. Two Crows and Good Bear estimate that there were between three hundred and three hundred and fifty fighting men in the Indian village; but I doubt if there were more than two hundred Cheyennes, for the reason that most of the Cheyennes were south of the Arkansas River at this time, where they had gone after the distribution of annuities at Fort Larned in August. A Sioux war party returning from a raid on the South Platte River discovered Forsyth's men. They watched the scouts and late in the day brought the news to their village. Messengers were sent over to the Dog Soldiers' camp with the news. In the meantime two Cheyennes who had been hunting buffalo came in and reported seeing soldiers about twelve miles up the Republican River from the Indian village. They had watched the scouts go into camp. By this time the warriors had made ready their war rigs and put on their sacred face paint. Criers rode through the village announcing that no small parties would be permitted to go out and attack the troops; all must wait and go out in a body, Sioux and Cheyennes; anyone attempting to steal out would be harshly punished. Finally the warriors started out, but Forsyth's force had moved about twenty miles away from the place

[15] Forsyth's force included, in addition to the scouts, Lieutenant Frederick H. Beecher, Surgeon John H. Mooers, and Arthur S. Grover, who had recovered from his wounds at the hands of the Dog Soldiers.—S.L.

in which they were seen by the Indian scouts. Night came down on the Indians and they had not located the whites. When it became too dark to go further, the chiefs gave orders to stop where they were. The warriors were directed to hold their horses and not stake them out. Then, when the morning star came up, everybody must be ready to start again.

But in spite of the strict orders Starving Elk and Little Hawk, Cheyennes, with six Sioux, all young men, mischievously agreed to slip out and find the whites. Starving Elk was a great friend of mine and he told me that his party scouted for a long time in the dark, trying to find the light from the camp fires of the whites. It was not until just before daybreak that they located the scouts. Even at this early hour Forsyth's men were moving about camp getting ready to start, and Starving Elk's little party startled them by making a rush toward the horses and mules. The white men opened fire on the raiders, but some of the stock stampeded and was swept off by Starving Elk and his friends. But these wild young men spoiled everything. The white men had their mules all packed, horses were saddled, and they were ready to move away.

Meanwhile the main body of the Indians had located the camp, and they appeared some miles away, on the low line of hills to the west, just following the clash of Starving Elk's party. Down onto the open plain the Indians surged. The scouts hurriedly mounted and raced for a small island in the dry bed of the Arickaree Fork, driving their pack mules with them. Now the scouts quickly dismounted and made breastworks of the packs and their horses while the Indians circled around. In the first moments of the battle, after reaching the island and while entrenching, the white men suffered heavily in killed and wounded, though, of course, the Indians did not know this.[16]

The Arickaree Fork of the Republican River at this season was practically dry; but here and there in the broad bed of dry sand were little pools of water. The sandy island on which Forsyth and his men

[16] Forsyth had gone into camp at sunset September 16, and at dawn on September 17 the initial action took place.—S.L.

had taken refuge rose several feet above the dry bed of the stream and was covered with a growth of tall grass, bushy willows and alders, and one cottonwood tree. The banks of the stream bed were well covered with high grass and willows in spots, the land on one side of the stream rising in a gentle slope to a line of low-lying hills about three miles away, while on the other side the land rolled off into the prairie.

Having reached this little island, now called Beecher's Island, the scouts tied their horses among the bushes and set hastily to work digging a line of rifle pits around the edge of the island. Colonel Forsyth was severely wounded, Lieutenant Beecher, a nephew of Henry Ward Beecher and second in command, was fatally wounded by bullets and arrows, and Surgeon Mooers was also fatally wounded. Besides these leaders, several of the scouts were also more or less severely wounded. The white scouts, fifty-three in the party, were all armed with the latest model Spencer seven-shot repeating rifles, the new Colt's army revolver, and they had loads of extra ammunition. As they were well protected on the island, it must be clear that the Indians, although they outnumbered the scouts, did not have all the advantage on their side. Some of the older Indians had old-fashioned heavy carbines and others had old-model Sharps rifles; but most of them were armed with lances and bows. There was no shelter for the Indians except near the banks of the stream, and this position could only be reached across the open prairie under heavy fire. The number of Indians engaged has always been grossly exaggerated by white writers.

The first charge on the island was not led by Roman Nose, as the whites seem to think. As a matter of fact, Roman Nose was still at the Indian village twenty miles up the Republican River. In a tumult of shouting and shooting, singing war and death songs, the Indians charged up the stream bed; many of the Sioux with streaming war bonnets of eagle feathers, the Dog Soldiers wearing their peculiar bonnets of crow feathers without a tail. Many of the warriors wore a war whistle, made from the wing bone of an eagle, hanging by a beaded cord of buckskin strung around the neck; these whistles warded off bullets when blown by the wearer in a fight. But the white men, with their new repeating rifles, poured such a hot fire into the Indians that the charge broke down before it reached the island. The rifle fire of those new repeaters was continuous and unlike anything the Indians had ever before experienced, yet, strange to say, was not especially damaging, though a number of ponies were killed. Instead of riding over the sandy island and stabbing and lancing the white men as planned, the Indians swept down the river bed on either side of the island. Wolf Belly, or Bad Heart, half-Cheyenne and half-Sioux, whose medicine was so strong that bullets could not harm him, headed this charge, armed only with lance and shield. He wore a breechcloth and a panther skin thrown over his shoulder. Unlike the others, he never faltered under the terrific rifle fire from the island and rode through the scouts and up the river bank, then turned and, to show his strong heart, charged back again through the entrenched whites. He was never struck by a bullet. In writing an account of this fight some years afterward, Major Forsyth called this man Roman Nose and asserted that he was shot and fell a little way from the rifle pits. Colonel Forsyth's account is entirely inaccurate, and since he was terribly wounded immediately following the panicky rush for the island, all his details were hearsay statements obtained months after the fight. Besides the many Indian participants, I have talked with a number of the white scouts present at this battle, particularly Jack Stilwell and Cole, the first sergeant. Stilwell could never understand how Wolf Belly escaped the hail of bullets, and thought that he must have been wounded. As Wolf Belly charged again and again to the breastworks, Stilwell told me, the whites thought he was insane. He was bullet-proof and died in the north in the 1870's. Though many ponies were struck in the charge, not a man was killed. In fact, only one Indian had been killed up to this time; this was Dry Throat, who was killed on the prairie while circling around the island. It appears that Jack Stilwell and a few other scouts, just how many is not certain, as the white narrators are not clear, were sent at the beginning of the fight to take a position at the lower end of the island. Instead of entrenching where directed, whether from lack of time or other reasons, but with good judgment, they took up a position in a hole on the river bank in the high grass. They were about forty feet from the main party, and as nothing but the dry bed of the stream lay between, there was no way for the Indians to creep up and cut them off, even had they been discovered. This party did a great deal of damage to the Indians, and owing to the smoke from the gunfire and the tall grass, their position was not discovered until late in the day. Weasel Bear, also called Ermine Bear or White Bear, and brother-in-law of White Horse, the Dog Soldier chief, in a mad rush on the island, rode close to Stilwell's party hiding in the hole on the bank. He was shot in the back just above the hips and fell from his horse in the grass not far from Stilwell's party. As the scouts were keeping up a heavy fire at this time and the smoke hung low, it was not noticed how Weasel Bear had been shot. Some time later White Thunder, son of White Bear, went down to carry off Weasel Bear and he, too, was shot by these scouts.

The Indians were disappointed in their efforts to reach the island, so a number of good shots were told to dismount and rush over into the high grass on the river bank where they might pick off some of the men on the island. By this time most of Forsyth's horses and mules had been killed, so they were in for a siege. Having loads of ammunition, which they used freely, it seemed possible they would hold off the Indians. Good Bear, brother of White Horse, and Prairie Bear and Little Man, a Northern Arapaho, ran swiftly on foot toward the bank, while a number of Cheyennes made a feint of charging on the island to draw the fire of the whites. These three men jumped into some little water holes on the low river bank, but their position lacked cover and they were exposed to the fire of the scouts. Prairie Bear and Little Man were killed soon after reaching the bank, both being shot in the head. Seeing this, a number of warriors on horseback shouted to Good Bear to get ready to dash back to the Indian lines. Making a pretense of again charging down on the island, a body of the mounted men drew the fire of the whites and Good Bear ran back without being hit.

Runners had been sent to the Indian camp to ask Roman Nose to hurry to the fight, but it was not until late in the day that he came. Because of the fact that a Sioux woman had used an iron fork in serving food to him at a feast a few days before, Roman Nose felt that his protective medicine had been so weakened that he was in great danger if he entered the fight. Tall Bull and White Horse and other Dog Soldier leaders knew this and talked with Roman Nose when he arrived. There was a great deal of excitement among the Indians as the news was passed that the great Roman Nose had come up. An old man rode up to the group of chiefs and reproached Roman Nose for not getting into the fight. Finally, as was the custom, one of the chiefs asked him if he would lead another charge. He instantly consented. Donning his famous one-horn war bonnet, he rode to the head of the Indian line. It was now late in the day. In this charge there were fewer warriors than in the one made in the morning. As they charged down on the island in a hail of bullets, Roman Nose rode near the scouts lying in the hole on the river bank and was shot in the small of the back as he passed. The others weakened under the hot rifle fire and again failed to ride over the whites. Roman Nose did not fall from his horse when shot, but turned and rode back to the Indian line. Here he got down from his horse and lay on the ground. No one knew he had been shot. Bull Bear and White Horse rode up and spoke to him. Then he told them. He said he did not see these men hiding in the grass, and up to this the Indians did not know there were any scouts fighting except on the island. Some women had now come up to look after the wounded, and Roman Nose was taken back to the camp. He lingered through the night and died at daybreak next day.

A small party under Cloud Chief crawled through the high grass to bring off the bodies of Weasel Bear and White Thunder, lying near the scouts' position on the river bank. With Cloud Chief went Black Hawk, Turkey Without Feathers, Two Crows, and Black Moon. This was dangerous work. The scouts fired when they saw the grass move and the Indians had to go slowly and carefully. Cloud Chief went first and carried a lariat. Turkey Without Feathers was struck in the shoulder by a bullet, but not badly hurt. Someone called to him in a low voice to go back but he refused. The man in the lead was in the most danger, as he had to push the grass aside as he crawled along. The others followed the trail he made. Then Black Moon was hit. Always Cloud Chief crawled in the lead. Presently they came on White Thunder and Weasel Bear lying close together. The bullets were still spitting around them whenever they moved. Here Cloud Chief was wounded in the shoulder. Except Two Crows, all of the party had now been wounded. The lariat was passed around White Thunder's foot and he was dragged away by those in the rear. Weasel Bear was still alive, and Two Crows, his brother-in-law, spoke to him. Weasel Bear told them that he had been shot in the hips and could not move his legs. They passed the lariat around his body and dragged him away. He was a heavy man and over six feet tall. Two Crows says that on account of his wounds they had to rest him frequently as they dragged him out. The scouts were shooting into the grass at them all this time.

A number of women had come up from camp with travois, and the wounded and dead were hurried back to the Indian villages. As they neared camp they were met by a large number of women and children and these followed the procession bearing the dead and wounded, the women wailing and crying over the dead. It was considered bad luck to wail over the wounded. In the old days, in mourning for dead relatives, Cheyenne women cut their legs with flint from ankle to knee, their arms from wrist to elbow. Arapaho women did the same. Kiowa and Comanche women cut cheeks and foreheads as well as legs and arms. Older women generally did this cutting for the younger women. The Cheyenne and Arapaho women used flint, and the Kiowa and Comanche women ordinarily used knives. I saw this cutting myself by women who had lost relatives in the Sand Creek Massacre. When ten years old I saw forty women relatives of Touching the Sky cut themselves and call on the Crooked Lances to avenge the death of their relative. The Cheyenne and Arapaho women sometimes also cut off the little finger at the first joint. So did the Kiowas and Comanches. I have seen Kiowa and Comanche women cut themselves all up: the legs, arms, cheeks and

304

forehead. The last time the Cheyenne women cut themselves was in the North in 1865.

The Indians kept the scouts closely besieged for two days longer, but on the third day word came that troops were coming, so they moved away. The whites give this fight much importance, but the Indians take it as an ordinary incident. There were nine men killed on the Indian side: Roman Nose, White Thunder (also called Old Lodge Skin), Weasel Bear (also called White Bear and Ermine Bear), Prairie Bear, Dry Throat, Killed by the Bull, all Cheyennes; Little Chief, a Northern Arapaho; Black Crow and Old Sioux Man, of the Sioux.

Meantime Jack Stilwell and Trudeau had succeeded in slipping through the Indian lines, and later on Jack Donovan and A. J. Pliley also got through. Stilwell and Trudeau made their way on foot to Fort Wallace, and Captain H. C. Bankhead, with a large force, at once started out to relieve Forsyth.[17] Of the other messengers sent out, Jack Donovan was lucky enough to run across Captain Louis H. Carpenter, who was then in the field with a force of Negro cavalry. Carpenter at once started for the Arickaree, where he arrived ahead of Bankhead and just in time to save General Forsyth's life. Forsyth had been very severely wounded; Lieutenant Beecher was dead; Doctor Mooers had been killed early in the fight; and more than half of the scouts were either killed or wounded. All of the horses and mules had been killed.[18]

When the Indians moved away they took the bodies of the nine dead warriors with them,[19] and these bodies were placed on scaffolds in the valley of the South Fork of the Republican. Here they were

[17] Stilwell enjoyed one of the most successful careers of all the western scouts, serving at Fort Sill until well after the close of the Plains wars.—S.L.

[18] Bent's account may be compared with Grinnell's in *The Fighting Cheyennes*, 282–92, in which Grinnell lists the same number of Indian dead, but places the Indian force at some six hundred. Forsyth's losses were six killed and fifteen wounded. He placed the Indian dead at thirty-two and the wounded at approximately one hundred. Berthrong, *Southern Cheyennes*, 313.—S.L.

[19] The date of the lifting of the siege was September 25, nine days after hostilities began.—S.L.

discovered by Captain Carpenter's troops while on the way to relieve
Forsyth, and Carpenter stopped long enough to pull the bodies to
the ground and leave them there. One of Carpenter's scouts identified one of the bodies as that of Roman Nose. The body was really
that of Killed by a Bull, a Northern Cheyenne. This body had been
put on a scaffold and a new lodge erected over the scaffold. His
medicine drum was hung over his head. Because of all these atten-
tions Carpenter and the scout made the mistake of thinking the body
was that of Roman Nose, just as Forsyth and his scouts mistook the
medicine man, Wolf Belly, for Roman Nose. The bodies were left
on the prairie for the wolves to eat.

Roman Nose was the most famous Cheyenne warrior of his
day. Although Little Wolf (Okohm-ha-ket), or Little Coyote, had
counted more coups, he was not as widely known as Roman Nose. As
a boy Roman Nose was called Sautie (the Bat); but when he became
a warrior he was given the name Woqini, meaning Hook Nose,
which the whites always interpreted Roman Nose. He had two
brothers and one sister; only one of these is still living, a brother,
Cut Hair, now at the Tongue River Agency. Contrary to the general
opinion, Roman Nose was never a chief, nor was he even the head
man of any of the soldier societies. He was a member of the Hi-moi-
yo-qis, or Crooked Lance Society, so called from the peculiar lance
carried by the leader. This society is sometimes called the Bone
Scrapers, from a peculiar piece of elk horn made in the shape of a
lizard and used in the dances of this society. I also belonged to the
Crooked Lances and it was at ceremonies of this society in the North
in 1865 that I first made the acquaintance of Roman Nose. At the
time of the great wars in the 1860's he was known as a great warrior
to all the Indians of the Plains, and his fame so spread to the whites
that they credited him with being leader in all the fights where the
Cheyennes were engaged. Thus he was reported as being one of the
leaders in the Fetterman battle near Fort Phil Kearny, in December,
1866, though at that time he was living quietly with the Dog Soldiers
south of the Platte. In the summer of 1866 he had come south with
Black Shin's Sutaio and Gray Beard's band of Dog Soldiers and he

never went north again. He liked the Dog Soldiers, who were the wildest and most aggressive fighters in our tribe, and he continued to live with them until his death. I knew him very well and found him to be a man of fine character, quiet and self-contained. All the Cheyennes, both men and women, held him in the highest esteem and talk of him a great deal to this day. Roman Nose always wore in battle the famous war bonnet which was made for him up North in 1860 by White Buffalo Bull (or Ice Bear), who is still living at Tongue River Agency and is one of the most famous of the old-time Northern Cheyenne medicine men. This war bonnet was the only one of its kind ever made. When a boy, Roman Nose fasted for four days on an island in a lake in Montana, and in his dreams saw a serpent with a single horn in its head. This was the reason White Bull came to make this peculiar war bonnet. Instead of having two buffalo horns attached to the head-band, one on each side, it had but one, rising over the center of the forehead; it had a very long tail that nearly touched the ground even when Roman Nose was mounted. This tail was made of a strip of young buffalo bull's hide, and had eagle feathers set all along its length, first four red feathers then four black ones, then four red feathers again, and so on, forty feathers in all. In making this famous war bonnet, White Bull did not use anything that had come from the whites: no cloth, thread, or metal. Usually war bonnets required little medicine-making when going into battle, but Roman Nose's bonnet was very sacred and required much ceremony. In taking it out of its hide case, it was held over a live coal on which was sprinkled a pinch of powder from a medicine root; then the bonnet was raised toward the sun four times, next unwrapped from its covering and held up to the north, west, south, and east, after which Roman Nose carefully put it on his head. With the war bonnet went sacred medicine paint for the face, which was, for the forehead, Indian yellow, red across the nose, and black across the mouth and chin. A strict set of rules of conduct went with the war bonnet: certain things Roman Nose was forbidden to eat; he must not go into a lodge where a baby had been born until four days had passed; and there were other rules. White Bull particularly cautioned Roman Nose never to eat any thing that had been touched by metal, and was told that if he neglected this rule he would be killed in his next battle. Most of the Plains Indians disliked eating food that had been touched by metal spoons, knives, or forks, as the medicine men believed that warriors who had eaten food touched by metal would, by some mysterious attraction, be shot by a metal bullet in the next battle. For this reason most Indian warriors preferred to use sharpened sticks in place of forks in eating.

Now, a few days before the Forsyth fight a feast was given by the Sioux to some of the prominent Cheyennes, and Roman Nose was one of the invited guests. While talking to the chiefs he forgot to warn the Sioux women not to touch his food with a metal fork or spoon. After the feast he remembered that he had neglected to make this request, as was always his custom. So he asked one of the Sioux chiefs to inquire of the women who had cooked the meal. One woman remembered having taken his bread from a skillet with an iron fork. This oversight destroyed the protecting power of Roman Nose's medicine. Certain purification ceremonies must be performed to restore this power, but these took some time, and before Roman Nose could start his ceremony word was brought that Forsyth's scouts had been discovered. And this was the reason why Roman Nose, always eager for battle, took no part in the fighting during the early part of the day. He firmly believed that his medicine was so weakened that he would be killed if he went into the battle; yet, when Bull Bear and White Horse came to him late in the day and begged him to lead a charge, he could not resist the temptation and went to his death. Roman Nose had never before been wounded except by an arrow in a fight with the Pawnees, yet he was always in front in battle and rarely had a horse shot under him. Roman Nose was killed in the prime of life; he was strong as a bull, tall even for a Cheyenne, broad-shouldered and deep-chested. His first wife was named Island and they had one daughter named Crooked Nose Woman. Both of these women are dead. His second wife was called Woman with White Child, and she also had a daughter by Roman Nose. Both of these are dead.

After the fight with Forsyth, the Dog Soldiers and Sioux moved to the south, intending to join the Southern Cheyennes south of the Arkansas River. They were in no hurry, but moved leisurely and went into camp on Beaver Creek. Meantime Major Eugene A. Carr, commanding the Fifth Cavalry, had arrived at Fort Wallace, on the Smoky Hill. The Major's regiment was in the field, up toward the Republican, and being anxious to join it, Carr took two companies of the Tenth colored cavalry as escort and set out from Fort Wallace to hunt for his regiment. These two companies, 120 men, were under the direct command of Captain Louis H. Carpenter. Marching to Beaver Creek, Carr and his escort examined this stream for fifty miles without finding any trace of the Fifth Cavalry.

A party of Cheyenne men, hunting buffalo, discovered the two troops of Negro cavalry near the Beaver and at once returned to the Indian camp with the news. In the Cheyenne village at this time was a medicine man named Wolf Man, sometimes called Bullet-Proof because in 1865, in a fight with Colonel Nelson Cole's column on Powder River, he had been struck by two bullets which did not even break his skin. Following this event, Wolf Man set up as a medicine man and claimed that by dressing young buffalo-bull hides in a secret manner, with the horns left on, he could make the wearers of these bull hides bullet-proof. He had convinced five young Dog Soldiers (Little Hawk, Bear with Feathers, White Man's Ladder, Broken Arrow, and Bobtail Porcupine) that if they followed his instructions the white men's bullets could not harm them. So, when the hunters rode into camp shouting that they had seen soldiers with wagon trains coming along the creek, Wolf Man felt that the time had come to prove the power of his medicine. He, therefore, sent a crier through the camp calling on the men not to attack the soldiers until he and his young men should show that the soldiers' guns were without power to harm them. The warriors were impatient and would not wait for Wolf Man and his "Young Bull Robes," as they were called in the camp. The war ponies were driven in while the fighting men were getting ready their war rigs and sacred paint, and they straggled out of camp toward the south side of the Beaver, up which Carr and

Carpenter were marching. An advance guard had been pushed ahead of the main party of soldiers, which was moving along slowly with the wagon train. As this scouting party moved forward it was suddenly charged by a number of warriors who had hidden themselves in a ravine near the stream. The Negro cavalrymen were forced over the steep bank into the creek, and the officer in command had a narrow escape for his life, his saddle slipping off as his horse took the jump. Soldiers from the main body rushed up and saved their comrades in the creek, but were themselves forced back on the main body by more Indians coming up.

The land on the south side of the creek was too rough for the wagons, so the column crossed to the north side, which was a gently sloping valley. Forming his wagons into two columns and deploying his troops as a screen between the wagons and the gathering Indians, Carpenter fell back from the creek to a little knoll on the grassy prairie. Here he hurriedly corralled his wagons in a circle, mules headed inside, and the troops rushed into the corral and dismounted. Dog Soldiers who were present told me that the wagons were corralled just in time, as the Indians were now strong enough to throw the column into confusion and do much damage. The soldiers formed their horses in columns of fours inside the circle, then crept up to the shelter of the wagons to hold off the Indians. Wolf Man and his young assistants rode up just as the troops corralled. The medicine man harangued the warriors and told them that his young men would ride four times around the troops and all might see that his medicine was so strong that it made the bullets of the white men harmless. Wolf Man, with a blanket thrown over his arm, rode to a small knoll, saying that when the time came he would signal with his blanket for the warriors to charge in and kill all the troops. The young men circled around the corralled wagon train, fifty yards away, brave enough in the shower of bullets. Broken Arrow and Bobtail Porcupine wore the sacred bull robes. Bear with Feathers rode first, on a spotted pony of great speed, the two wearers of the bull robes riding last of all. Before the first circle had been completed, Bear with Feathers had his horse killed under him and he hastily retired. Little Hawk, riding a claybank pony, was slightly wounded in the shoulder and his horse killed, and he, too, withdrew. The horse of White Man's Ladder was badly wounded but carried its rider off the field. Only the two bull robes were left and both riders and horses went down just as they completed the first circle. While the young medicine men were making this demonstration of Wolf Man's power, the main body of warriors had gone off to points where they could see all that was going on. When Broken Arrow and Bobtail Porcupine were shot down, many of the warriors moved away toward camp, disgusted by the failure of Wolf Man's promises. The Cheyennes say that, after Bobtail Porcupine was shot and fell from his horse, he sat up on the ground, and then a soldier went to him from the wagons. After the soldiers left, the Indians first picked up the body of Broken Arrow and found that he had been scalped by the Negro troopers. Bobtail Porcupine was not yet dead, but an artery in his neck had been cut with a knife. The Cheyennes still believe that Bobtail Porcupine was not badly wounded and that a vein in his neck was opened by the soldiers so that he would bleed to death. When the soldiers saw the Indians move away, they quickly pulled out, leaving a number of boxes of hardtack and bacon behind them. The Indians took the hardtack, but had no liking for the bacon. This affair took place on October 18, 1868.[20]

Two Crows tells me that after this incident on the Beaver the Dog Soldiers and Sioux held a council and decided not to go south to join the Southern Cheyennes but to stay where they were and make raids. Meantime Major Carr returned to Fort Wallace, where he assumed command of the Fifth Cavalry and a body of scouts, 450 men in all, and with this force he set out after the Indians, whom he hoped to find in the vicinity of Beaver Creek. On October 25 Carr ran into a small body of warriors, and a running fight started and continued for two days. This party of Indians were merely the rear guard following the village, and they put up such a bluff that Carr was completely fooled. He dismounted his men and advanced slowly

---

[20] Carr, reporting on April 7, 1869, seven months later, put the date of the battle at October 17, 1868.—S.L.

in skirmish line, thus permitting the screen of warriors to hold him in check until the women and children had time to move away with the village. At the end of two days Carr reached the spot where the village had stood and found nothing but a few broken down ponies and some lodgepoles and old buffalo hides, which he burned. He then marched back to Fort Wallace again, while the Indians broke up into small bands and attacked the railroad stations at several points west of Fort Hays, compelling the authorities to reinforce the railroad guards.[21]

There were no more important fights during the fall of 1868. Some Dog Soldiers and Sioux had a fight with the Pawnee, and I was at the Cheyenne village on the Smoky Hill when this party came in after the fight. The Dog Soldiers also had a skirmish with some troops near Fort Wallace that fall, and some Cheyennes ran off the mules belonging to Moore, the post trader at Fort Union, New Mexico. Moore tried to get me to go out and recover his animals, but I did not care to do it.

---

[21] On his return to Fort Wallace, Carr estimated he had captured 130 ponies, killed 20 Indians, and wounded others. Carr to Sheridan, November 1, 1868, Office of the Adjutant General, Letters Received, Carr, *Report.*—S.L.

CHAPTER TWELVE

BATTLE OF THE WASHITA

GENERAL SHERIDAN WAS now convinced that Indian campaigns in summer were barren of results and so determined on a winter campaign as the only means by which he could reach the hostiles. Early in November, 1868, he organized three expeditions to this end. One was under Major Eugene A. Carr, starting at Fort Lyon, Colorado, and operating from the North Canadian. Carr hunted Indians all winter and returned in the spring without finding any. Another column, the largest, was under General Sully, and consisted of eleven troops of the Seventh Cavalry, under General Custer, and five companies of the Third and Fifth Infantry, with twelve companies of the Nineteenth Kansas Volunteer Cavalry. This column operated from Camp Supply, a depot established at the junction of Beaver and Wolf Creeks in the Indian Territory, where were quartered a large body of men and hundreds of wagons. The Kansas Cavalry, twelve hundred men under Colonel Crawford, failed to arrive at Camp Supply at the time set by Sheridan for the expedition to start; in fact, they were lost in the snow in the canyons on the banks of the Cimarron River and their whereabouts were not discovered until after Custer started for the south. Then Sheridan had to send some white scouts from Camp Supply to extricate the volunteers, who lost most of their horses in the deep snow.

On November 23 Sheridan ordered Custer to take the field, which he did with eleven companies of the Seventh Cavalry and a force of white, Osage, and Kaw, scouts.[1] A great deal of snow had fallen and,

[1] Sully, who had demonstrated his lack of familiarity with tactics against the

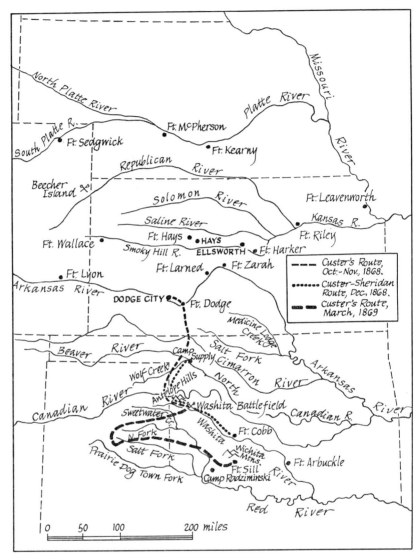

Legend

- ▬ ▬ ▬ Custer's Route, Oct.–Nov., 1868.
- •••••••• Custer–Sheridan Route, Dec., 1868.
- ▬■▬■ Custer's Route, March, 1869

Scale

0   50   100   200 miles

From George A. Custer, *My Life on the Plains*

CUSTER'S ROUTES, WINTER CAMPAIGN, 1868–69

in fact, it was still snowing when Custer's force started, the troops proceeding in a southerly direction.

Three days earlier, on November 20, at Fort Cobb, Indian Territory, Black Kettle and Little Robe of the Cheyennes and Big Mouth and Spotted Wolf of the Arapahos held an interview with General William M. Hazen, who had been assigned as superintendent of Indian Affairs for the Indian Territory. The tribes were becoming alarmed at the reports of the hostile intentions of General Sheridan. Black Kettle told General Hazen that his band was camped on the Washita, forty miles east of the Antelope Hills, and he assured Hazen that the Cheyennes and Arapahos south of the Arkansas were and had been peaceful. Hazen was sympathetic, but insisted that Black Kettle should deal directly with Sheridan, who was personally in command of the troops. This was a queer situation for Black Kettle (who was always for peace with the whites), as Sheridan had already taken the field against all the Indians south of the Arkansas.

On the morning of November 26 Custer claimed that he struck the trail of a war party of Cheyennes who had been raiding on the Smoky Hill. This party going to Black Kettle's village has made it appear that Black Kettle's band was hostile, though these Cheyennes were not of his band. A war party of Kiowas who had been against the Utes also passed through Black Kettle's village and one, at least, of this party stayed with friends in the Cheyenne camp and took part in the fight which followed. Custer kept on this trail all day and late that night the Osage trailers told him that he was close to the Cheyenne camp. In a grove of heavy timber on the bank of the Washita River, near the present town of Cheyenne, Oklahoma, Black Kettle's band, numbering forty-seven lodges, was camped, with two lodges of Arapahos and two of Sioux. I was not in Black Kettle's camp at this time, having left the Southern Cheyennes when they crossed the Arkansas River on their way south. My wife, Magpie, Black Kettle's niece, went with me on a visit to my people near Fort Lyon,

---

Southern Plains tribes in September, 1868, on the Cimarron, was ordered back to Fort Harker from Camp Supply by Sheridan and resumed his post as commanding officer of the District of the Upper Arkansas.—S.L.

Colorado. This probably saved us from the same fate that befell Black Kettle and his wife. Though Custer did not know it, Black Kettle's village was the farthest west of a series of Indian villages. About seven miles below Black Kettle was a big village of Arapahos, under Little Raven, and seventy lodges of Cheyennes; below these were villages of the Kiowas and Comanches.

Custer divided his command into four columns and arranged to have them charge from the four sides of the little camp just at dawn.[2] Of the fight which followed little can be said. Many of the Indians, men, women and children, rushed from the lodges to be shot down by exultant soldiers and in a short time the village was in the hands of the whites. Black Kettle and his wife, Medicine Woman Later, both rushed out of the lodge at the first booming of the guns. Black Kettle mounted a horse and helped his wife up behind him and started to cross the Washita River, but both the chief and his wife fell at the river bank riddled with bullets; the horse was also killed

---

[2] Custer's report says, briefly, that on the 26th of November, in twelve inches of snow, he struck the trail of a war party of about one hundred warriors. Leaving his wagons, tents, and other impediments under guard he followed the trail from daylight until 9 P.M. Taking an hour for refreshment, he continued the trail until 1:30 in the morning of the 27th, when the Osage trailers reported the village one mile away. The column then withdrew to a safe distance and the village was reconnoitered by the officers. He divided the command into four columns: Major Joel H. Elliott, with three companies, to attack in the timber below the village; Colonel Myers to move down the Washita and attack from above the village; Colonel Thompson to attack from an elevation north of the village; and the fourth column to charge from an elevation overlooking the village on the west bank of the Washita. At the first dawn of day the surprise was completed. The band struck up "Garry Owen" the moment the charge started. The Indians were caught napping. Ten minutes after the beginning of the fight the village was in the hands of the soldiers, but it took several hours to clean out the warriors posted in ravines and underbrush.—G. H.

Except for Elliott, Custer does not name fully some of those whom he assigned columns in the Battle of the Washita: Colonel Myers, Colonel Thompson, the former in position for attack on Custer's right, the latter on Elliott's left below the Indian village. Custer himself was with A, C, D, and K troops of the Seventh Cavalry, the Osages and scouts (including California Joe), and Colonel Cook (Captain Robert M. Cook) with forty sharpshooters. Captain Louis McLane Hamilton commanded one of the squadrons of the latter column, Colonel West the other.—S.L.

at the same time. Red Shin tells me that the soldiers rode right over Black Kettle and his wife and their horse as they lay dead on the ground, and that their bodies were all splashed with mud by the charging soldiers. Medicine Elk Pipe and Red Shin stood among the lodges and fought the soldiers until forced to get away into the brush to save themselves. Captain Louis M. Hamilton, whom I knew well, was shot off his horse as he charged through the village at the head of his company. He was killed right in front of Cranky Man's lodge and both Red Shin and Medicine Elk Pipe tell me that Cranky Man rushed out of his lodge and shot Hamilton. Cranky Man was killed fighting in front of his lodge, making no effort to get away. The warriors that escaped the first attack took a position in the ravines and brush to hold off the soldiers while the younger and more active women and children could escape and alarm the villages below. These warriors put up a desperate defense, and, though few in numbers, it was some time before they could be dislodged. Besides Captain Hamilton, three men were killed in the early attack on the village and three officers and eleven men wounded. Later there was a great deal of criticism of Custer because so many women and children were killed, which he claimed was unavoidable. Ben Clark, who was interpreter at Fort Reno for many years and died last year, was chief of scouts during this battle and saved the lives of a party of fugitive Cheyenne women, one of whom, then a young girl, afterward became his wife. He told me that during the fight a Mexican who used to live with my father came up with a little girl in his arms and asked the soldiers to save her. A sergeant took the child, then telling the Mexican to run, shot him in the back. Major Fred Benteen told of a personal fight he had with Black Kettle's son, who shot Benteen's horse from under him, and, refusing to surrender, was killed by Major Benteen. But Black Kettle had no children. This boy was Black Kettle's nephew and lived in Black Kettle's lodge, acting as herder for the chief. His name was Blue Horse, and he was about twenty-one years old at the time of his death.[3] My wife's brother,

[3] Custer, *My Life on the Plains*, 241–42, tells of Benteen's dilemma and the killing of Blue Horse, whom he presumed to be about fourteen years of age but eager to fight.—S.L.

317

then a young boy, was captured, and so was his mother. The large number of Cheyenne women and children were made prisoners and the camp and all its contents fell into Custer's hands. Even the pony herd was captured and destroyed.[4] Lieutenant E. S. Godfrey, with a company of soldiers, went out to bring in the pony herd, and after sending in the ponies under a small guard gave chase to some Indians escaping from the village on foot. Before Lieutenant Godfrey could overtake them the Indians ran into another pony herd and mounted and escaped.[5] Godfrey's company followed them until they saw in the distance a large Indian village, to which the Indians they were pursuing made signals of "enemy." The warriors from this large village rushed to the aid of their friends in distress, and Godfrey was hard put to make his escape back to the main body of troops.

Across the creek from where Godfrey's troops were being hunted Major Joel H. Elliott, with sixteen men, was not so fortunate. His party was cut off and killed to the last man, and many surmises have been made by the whites as to how these soldiers came to their death. While the warriors of Black Kettle's camp were holding off the

[4] Custer reported that he captured 53 Cheyenne women and children, and 875 horses and mules, about 800 of which were shot by the soldiers to prevent them from again falling into the hands of the Indians. He gives a list of captured property: 241 saddles, some very fine; 573 buffalo robes, 390 buffalo skins for lodges, 160 robes, 210 axes, 140 hatchets, 35 revolvers, 47 rifles, 535 pounds of powder, 1,050 pounds of lead, 4,000 arrows, 75 spears, 35 bows and quivers, 90 bullet molds, 12 shields, 300 pounds of bullets, 775 lariats, 940 saddlebags, 470 blankets, and the winter supply of buffalo meat.—G.H.

Custer's itemization in *My Life on the Plains* is less inclusive but gives the essentials George E. Hyde here cites. Major General P. H. Sheridan's General Field Order No. 6 of November 29, 1868, read by Custer to his troops after its delivery by California Joe, contained Custer's earlier compiled data. It acknowledged the loss of Major Elliott and Captain Hamilton and nineteen men, and claimed 103 warriors killed, including Black Kettle, and 53 women and children captured.—S.L.

[5] Custer's character sketch of California Joe and his ways are among the more attractive features of an otherwise sketchy, and sometimes misleading, book. It was California Joe, who had been "moving about in a promiscuous and independent manner," who reported ponies nearby and after half an hour came driving some three hundred of them in with the aid of two Indian women and a lariat used as a bull-whip. Custer, *My Life on the Plains*, 236–37, 245; Nye, *Carbine and Lance*, 84–88.—S.L.

soldiers so that the women and children could escape to the villages of the Cheyennes and Arapahos seven miles below, Custer sent Major Elliott with a party to cut off these fugitives. A large party of women and children ran to the bed of the Washita River and, wading in the water close to the high banks, started to make their way down to the other villages. The people having been taken by surprise in the first attack had very few clothes, and suffered severely in the bitter cold wading in the water. By keeping close under the high banks they escaped the bullets of the soldiers shooting at them from above. Three warriors covered the flight of these women and children, one being the Kiowa who stopped in Black Kettle's village the evening before on the return of the Kiowa war party from the raid on the Utes.[6] The other two men were Cheyennes, Packer (Sto-ko-wo) and Little Rock (Ho-han-i-no-o), a Cheyenne chief. Major Elliott's party followed this band of fugitives, trying to cut them off. The three Indian men fought very bravely to keep the soldiers from closing in. As they waded down the river they finally came to a bend in the Washita where the water was very deep, with steep banks on either side. Little Rock ordered them to get out of the river bed and strike across the prairie to reach the river below the bend. As soon as they struck the open ground the soldiers saw them and closed in. Little Rock, Packer, and the Kiowa stayed in the rear and fought off the soldiers. The soldiers charged on the three Indians, firing as they came on, and here Little Rock was shot in the forehead and killed. Packer tells me that Little Rock carried a muzzle-loading rifle, as well as bow and arrows. When he fell dead the Kiowa ran to him and picked up his quiver containing six arrows. Packer and the Kiowa had only two arrows apiece when Little Rock was shot. A Cheyenne woman, named White Buffalo Woman, and her sister and some children had been running so long that they were exhausted and

[6] The Kiowa was Eonah-pah (Trailing the Enemy), as identified by George Bent in a letter to Robert Peck, in James A. Hadley, "The Kansas Cavalry and the Conquest of the Plains Indians," *Kansas Historical Collections*, X, 441–42. His heroic flight, loosing arrows at various stands, is described in Nye, *Carbine and Lance*, 85–86; his later, peaceful exploits are briefly described in Nye, *Bad Medicine and Good: Tales of the Kiowas*, 233–43.—S.L.

stopped here on the prairie. A soldier came up to them and made motions for them to walk back toward Black Kettle's village, the soldier walking behind them. About this time a small party of warriors escaping from Black Kettle's camp rode out of the creek timber and seeing the soldier with the Cheyenne girls rode toward them. The soldier fired twice at the Indians, and then, White Buffalo Woman says, a cartridge stuck fast in his carbine. Bobtail Bear quickly rode up to the soldier and tomahawked him.[7] The rest of Elliott's men had continued on after Packer and the Kiowa, fighting behind their party of women and children, who had entered the river bed again below the bend. The warriors who had killed the soldier rode on after Elliott's party, still chasing the women and children down the Washita. Elliott was now cut off from Custer, and Bobtail Bear's party pushed him out onto the prairie right into a bunch of warriors coming to Black Kettle's aid from the big village of Cheyennes and Arapahos below. When the soldiers of Elliott's party saw that they were surrounded they turned their horses loose and took up a position in a small ravine in the high grass. Touching the Sky tells me that he got off his horse and crept up toward the head of the ravine. Seeing soldiers all lying down and firing wildly, he signaled to the other Indians to come up with their guns. Several more then crawled up and opened fire on the soldiers; as they were very close some of them were hit. The mounted Indians now commenced to close in while those on foot at the head of the ravine kept on shooting. Suddenly, Roman Nose Thunder, a Cheyenne, rushed in and counted coup on a private. Other accounts say that an Arapaho warrior was the first to rush in and count coup. However, the mounted Indians all charged in at the same moment, and the fight was over for Elliott and his men. The soldiers did not do much shooting for some reason, the Indians say, and the fight lasted but a short time. Two Arapahos were killed in this fight, though several other Indians were wounded. Packer and the Kiowa, with the Cheyenne women and children in

[7] Sergeant Major Walter Kennedy was Bobtail Bear's victim, but Grinnell has Little Chief of the Arapahos counting coup on him (*Fighting Cheyennes*, 303). —S.L.

the river bed, soon noticed that the soldiers were no longer shooting at them and came out to rest in the creek bottom while the warriors were killing Elliott and his men. Some of these women went over to where the dead soldiers lay. After killing Elliott, those warriors kept on to Black Kettle's camp and fought Custer again.[8]

During all this time the troops under General Custer were engaged in destroying Black Kettle's little camp. This village was the farthest west on the Washita, and when the Indians at the other villages heard the firing the herders ran the pony herds into camp and the fighting men got ready. Meanwhile the fugitive women from Black Kettle's camp began to arrive and told the story of the attack by the soldiers. Runners were sent with the news to the Kiowas and Comanches farther down the river. Men from these villages rode quickly to the battlefield, meeting on the way the women and children fleeing from Black Kettle's camp. Of these, Packer's and Little Rock's party was the last to come down the creek. Elliott lost his life and sacrificed his men by following these fugitives too far.

The Kiowas and Comanches came up and helped the Cheyennes and Arapahos fight Custer and toward night he was glad to fall back on his wagon trains.[9] He then marched back to Camp Supply, taking with him as prisoners the Cheyenne women and children, arriving there about December 1.[10] In this campaign he lost two officers and

[8] Tobacco, an Arapaho late-comer to the fight with Elliott, may have counted coup on the Major, as Grinnell (304) indicates, but Touching the Sky and Roman Nose Thunder, Cheyennes, had strong claims, the one to the final assault, the other to the actual killing of Elliott. Colonel Nye's assessment of Elliott's defensive strategy, notably his loss of field of fire, is that of a military man and one of the best students of Plains warfare. Tobacco lost his life in the act of victory. Nye, *Carbine and Lance*, 87.—S.L.

[9] Custer's reassembled forces at the village of Black Kettle had, by 3 P.M. on November 27, a stabilized situation, with the retreat of the Indian allies at each thrust made from the army lines. The risk to the baggage train and eighty men left by Custer on November 26 to safeguard it, should he continue longer, forced him to the decision to destroy the village and all but a few score of the Indian ponies. As night drew on, Custer moved downstream from Black Kettle's village to the now deserted villages well below it, then faced about and rejoined his train at 10 the next morning. Custer, *My Life on the Plains*, 257–59.—S.L.

[10] Custer says December 2. The Osages with his command had brought to him,

nineteen men killed and three officers and eleven men wounded.[11] I knew Major Elliott and Captain Hamilton well. I had met both those officers in 1867 at the council on Medicine Lodge Creek. They were present at this council with four companies of cavalry guarding the annuity goods. Thus, fourteen months later both were killed. I was living in Black Kettle's lodge at the time of the council, and we were camped on the south side of the creek, the officers being camped on the north side, directly opposite. Both these officers and Doctor Remick, with whom I went to school in St. Louis, used to come over to my lodge every evening and smoke with Black Kettle.

The Cheyennes lost eleven men, twelve women, and six children killed. The names of the men killed in the fight were: Black Kettle and Little Rock, chiefs; Bear Tongue, Tall Bear, Blind Bear, White Bear, Cranky Man, Blue Horse, Red Teeth, Little Heart, and Red Bird. Two Arapahos were killed in the fight with Elliott's men. Little Rock was over sixty years old when killed. Little Rock was no warrior, but was well liked by the whites around the army posts. Colonel Wynkoop, agent for the Cheyennes and Arapahos, employed him a great deal as a sort of a messenger.

Black Kettle was sixty-seven years old when he lost his life. I married his niece in 1866 and lived with him until the early summer of 1868, when I went to Colorado and never saw him again. He was a Sutai (plural Sutaio), a people who came to the Cheyennes from the northeast a long time ago and spoke the same langauge, but a different dialect. Though up to the middle of the last century the Sutaio camped apart from the Cheyennes, they have long been one of the tribal divisions. They brought the sun dance to the Cheyennes; also the buffalo-cap medicine, still regarded by the tribe with almost as great reverence as the famous Sacred Arrows. Black Kettle was son of Swift Hawk Lying Down, who was never a chief. He had three sons: Black Kettle, Gentle Horse, and Wolf; and one daugh-

---

during the return march to Camp Supply, the news of the Elliott tragedy, which they had evidently gained from observing the Cheyennes, whose positions they were to scout while Custer continued north to his base. Nye, *Carbine and Lance*, 90.—S.L.

[11] Captain Albert Barnitz died of his wounds en route to Camp Supply.—S.L.

ter, Wind Woman. When a young man, Black Kettle was a good warrior and led several war parties against other tribes. When the Cheyennes were at war with the Kiowas, Comanches, and Apaches, he took a leading part in the fights and led several pony-stealing expeditions against them. He and some other scouts located the hostile camp of the three tribes the day before the big fight on Wolf Creek in the summer of 1838. In the summer of 1848 he led the war party against the Utes. This party ran right into the Ute village without seeing it, and in the retreat Black Kettle's wife and another woman were thrown from their horses and captured. The Utes being close behind, the Cheyennes could not stop to assist these women, as they would all have been killed. Both were young women, and Black Kettle's wife, it is said, was fine looking. Mexican traders were induced to try to find these women, but they could get no trace of them and they were never heard of again. Black Kettle later married a Wotap woman (plural Wotapio). This was a small division of the Cheyennes, and is called the Cheyenne-Sioux band by the old people. This band was made up of Moiseyu and Cheyenne people, and the old Cheyennes say the Moiseyu were Sioux. The Moiseyu left the Cheyennes about 1815 and moved north of the Missouri. I know some old women still living whose mothers were Moiseyu, and these women still speak Sioux. When Black Kettle married into the Wotapio he went to live with his wife's people, as was the old custom. The chief of this band at that time was Bear with Feathers, and when he died in 1850 Black Kettle was elected chief.

The Wotapio were famed for the number of fine horses they owned, also for their fine large lodges. Everything they had was clean and of the best quality, and by the other Cheyenne bands they were called "Stingies," because they did not like to give away their things as presents like the others.

Black Kettle was one of the six signers of the Fort Wise treaty in 1861. The whites presumed to treat these six chiefs as the head chiefs of the tribe, and as this was against custom the Cheyennes refused to abide by the treaty. They called the signers of this treaty the "Six Chiefs," as a sort of nickname. The whites also wished to consider

Black Kettle as head chief, and this, too, was against custom. From the old days the tribe was governed by forty-four chiefs, and every four years new selections were made to replace those who had died or become too old. A son or relative did not take a chief's place. New chiefs were chosen for their ability, and the office was never hereditary with the Cheyennes. The whites have the wrong idea about Indian chiefs. Among the Plains Indians a chief was elected as a peace and civil officer and there was no such office as war chief. What the whites call war chiefs were only warriors of distinction. Roman Nose was never a chief, and Red Cloud, at the height of his fame, was only a distinguished warrior; when he was elected chief he lost most of his real power. Some of these so-called war chiefs were often headmen of the soldier societies, and when matters of importance came up the chief usually referred them to these warrior societies for settlement, and so they really had more power than the chief. But the Indian idea of a chief is not a fighter but a peace maker. About 1832 High-back Wolf, a great Cheyenne chief, ran out of his lodge to help some relatives in a village quarrel; he was stabbed to death. The Cheyennes said he deserved this; he was a chief and had no business to fight even in aid of his closest kinsmen.

After the destruction of Black Kettle's village on the Washita, the five tribes moved south to the Red River, on the Texas line, most of them making camp on the North Fork of the Red River. General Custer had taken his prisoners to Fort Hays, except one old woman, named Red Hair, who was taken to Fort Sill.[12] She was later sent out to the Indian camps to notify the Indians to come in to Fort Sill, though Custer did not wait for them to come in. The husbands and relatives of these prisoners waited on the chiefs of the tribes and asked that no war parties be sent out, as this would make the case of the prisoners worse; for this reason no raiding was permitted. Little Robe, Cheyenne, and Black Eagle, Kiowa, went to Fort Sill to see General Hazen, and asked how the prisoners could be released.

[12] Near present Lawton, Oklahoma; founded January 8, 1869, by Colonel B. H. Grierson of the Tenth Cavalry.—S.L.

Hazen told them that General Sheridan (called Three Stars by the Cheyennes) was coming and would talk to them. Little Robe and Black Eagle waited, and in a few days Sheridan arrived, with Custer and a lot of troops. They held council, and Sheridan said that the Cheyennes must give up two white women held prisoners in the Cheyenne camp. Little Robe told Sheridan to send some whites with him and he would turn the prisoners over to them. Little Robe then asked about the Cheyenne prisoners, and Sheridan said that if the Indians kept peace all summer the Cheyenne women and children would be sent to Camp Supply and liberated. He also advised the Cheyennes and Arapahos to go to Camp Supply, where rations would be issued to them. Little Robe told me that he intended to take the prisoners in, but Custer rushed his troops out to the villages and tried to make trouble before he could return with the white women. The ponies were so poor that the Cheyennes could not start war at this time even if they wished, and Custer knew it. Custer was tricky and did not have a very good name among the officers.

Following this talk with Sheridan Little Robe returned to camp, and soon afterward Custer marched up with his troops and camped near the Cheyenne village. Sand Hill met Custer and took him to the Cheyenne camp to get the two women prisoners. Together they rode up to the Medicine Arrow lodge in the center of the camp circle. Sand Hill told Custer to dismount and enter. He was all alone and entered the lodge followed by Sand Hill. Rock Forehead, the keeper of the arrows, made room for Custer right under the sacred arrows, which were hanging from a forked stick made for that purpose. Lighting his pipe, Rock Forehead held it while Custer smoked, telling Custer at the same time, in Cheyenne, that if he was acting treacherously he and all his command would soon be killed. When Custer had smoked, Rock Forehead took the pipe stick and loosened the ashes, then poured them on Custer's toes to give him bad luck. Custer then went out with his prisoners and joined his troops. Next morning he asked the chiefs to come to his camp for a talk; so a number of the men went to Custer's camp. While the Indians were standing around the camp among the soldiers, Custer ordered his men to close in on the Cheyennes, as he wished to capture a number of the warriors. My friend, Wolf Chief, now dead, said that he was standing among the soldiers when he heard the officers giving loud commands; then the soldiers rushed for their guns while the alarmed Indians ran for their ponies. A brave young Cheyenne, named Crazy Wolf, drew his knife and shook it in Custer's face, shouting "You are no man, but a coyote." Two very old men and a middle-aged one stood in the center of the camp, warming themselves at a fire, and did not move. The Cheyennes, having mounted their ponies, rushed through the line of soldiers. Crazy Wolf and Black Stone, both noted warriors, rode up to the three Cheyenne men standing by the fire and offered them their horses, urging them to escape. This the older men refused to do, and advised the young men to get away at once. So they, too, broke through the soldiers' line in a storm of bullets and escaped unharmed. The three older men made prisoners were Lean Face, Fat Bear, and Curly Hair.[13] Lean Face is the man called Dull Knife by officers and writers. As the Indians had been invited by Custer to come to his camp on a friendly visit, they considered this a most treacherous act and ever after had a great hatred for him.

These three prisoners were taken to Fort Hays. On May 10, 1869, Lean Face, eighty years old, and Curly Hair, fifty years of age, were shot down by the guard inside the stockade. A Cheyenne woman was also killed at the same time, and Fat Bear was badly wounded. The men had no arms except knives when the soldiers killed them. People in the East never heard much about these things.

In the spring the Kiowas and Comanches went into Fort Sill and made peace, and the Cheyennes and Arapahos moved into Camp

[13] The picture of these men, believed by Grinnell to have been made at Fort Dodge, Kansas, March 13, 1869, is reproduced in the present book (see list of illustrations). John Stands in Timber of the Northern Cheyennes, during a visit to Oklahoma in mid-1960, identified the men shown as Little Bear, Hairless Bear, and Island. The picture, reproduced in Grinnell's *The Fighting Cheyennes* (University of Oklahoma Press, 1956), opposite 302, again reading left to right, shows Curly Head, Fat Bear, and Dull Knife. The latter, in Bent's identification, would be Lean Face. Ē hyōph'stā, niece of Island, gave the names Younger Bear, Chief Comes in Sight, and Island. (John Stands in Timber, personal interview with S.L., at Norman, Oklahoma, July 18, 1960; Grinnell, *Fighting Cheyennes*, 308.)—S.L.

Supply. In the middle of the summer the women and children cap-tured when Black Kettle's village was destroyed were sent to Camp Supply and turned over to their relatives. The Cheyennes did not go to war again until 1874.

The result of this winter campaign was that in the spring the five tribes went in and settled on their new reservation, except some of the wilder bands of the Kiowas and Comanches, who remained out on the Staked Plains. The Dog Soldiers, the wildest of the Chey-ennes, were still holding on to their old hunting grounds on the Republican.

CHAPTER THIRTEEN

SUMMIT SPRINGS

URING THE WINTER of 1868–69 the Dog Soldiers made their
camp at the head of the Republican River and in the spring
moved farther south to Beaver Creek. With seven troops of the Fifth
Cavalry, Major Eugene A. Carr had been hunting Indians all winter
without finding any, and on May 10, 1869, he left Fort Wallace
with his command, headed north. He discovered indications of a
large village and sent out a scouting party to reconnoitre.[1] A returning party of Cheyenne hunters jumped this scouting party and drove
them back on the main column. The hunters brought the news to
the village, and so a body of warriors came out and put up the bluff
of attacking Carr's troops, to hold them in check while the camp was
being moved. Carr lost a few men and thought he killed some
Indians, but he was mistaken. He also supposed he was fighting the
main body of Indians, but it was only the rear guard holding him
back until night came. This was on May 15, 1869. Next day,
realizing that the Indians were getting away from him, Carr left his
wagons under a guard and pushed on. White Horse and Tall Bull
were the principal leaders of the Dog Soldiers at this time. Two
Crows, brother of White Horse, and Good Bear were with the Cheyennes that Carr was chasing, and they tell me that Tall Bull sent out
a small body of Indians to draw off Carr's advance guard in pursuit.

[1] Carr and the Fifth Cavalry were in camp on Beaver Creek on May 13, from
which point he sent out Lieutenant E. W. Ward and Buffalo Bill Cody, as scout; in
the ensuing action, Cody was wounded, but the furrow in his scalp was not enough
to take him out of action. Don Russell, *The Lives and Legends of Buffalo Bill*,
121–22.—S.L.

The advance guard chased this small body for some time, but for some reason became alarmed and stopped. Tall Bull was hiding in the shelter of a hill nearby with two hundred Cheyennes, waiting for the soldiers to come near his position so that he might dash out and cut them off from the main body and annihilate them. But the soldiers were too wary and gave up the chase, so when Tall Bull charged down on them they were ready and put up a determined resistance, fighting from behind their horses. The troops were better armed and held the Indians off until the main body of Carr's command hurried up to the rescue. The Indians succeeded in killing a large number of the horses and two of the men. The Indians now moved off and had no trouble in eluding the soldiers.[2]

Breaking up into small bands, they harried the settlements on the Solomon, even going so far as to pull up the railroad track at Grinnell's Station and dashed boldly through the settlements. Carr abandoned the chase and pushed on to Fort McPherson, Nebraska. Here he refitted his command, and, having procured the reinforcement of three companies of Pawnee scouts, returned to the Solomon and Republican rivers in the early part of July.

The Dog Soldiers and Sioux were camped at this time at the head of Cherry Creek, a small stream which flows into the Republican from the north. The soldiers were camped near the mouth of this creek, news of which was brought in by a small scouting party of young Dog Soldiers. A number of young Dog Soldiers went out to make a night attack on the camp, hoping to stampede some horses. This was on July 8, 1869. Yellow Nose, the Ute captive, then a young boy of about twenty, was in this raid and says that they charged the camp about midnight, yelling and shooting. White Horse, one of the Cheyennes, shot a Pawnee scout doing guard duty. Yellow Nose said that his war horse ran against a picket rope and

---

[2] The Indian losses reported by Carr varied from twenty-five to thirty warriors killed, but as with many estimates of the period, the figures were probably excessive, as Bent's testimony tends to make clear. Carr's own losses were four killed and three wounded. His command reached Fort McPherson, Nebraska, May 20. Berthrong, *Southern Cheyennes*, 340; Russell, *The Lives and Legends of Buffalo Bill*, 121–22.—S.L.

threw him in among the frightened cavalry horses. His arm was broken and his horse got away from him, leaving him on foot. He lost his lance and shield when he fell and could not find them in the dark. The cavalry horses were thrashing around wildly, making it very dangerous for Yellow Nose. The soldiers and Pawnee scouts were shooting and shouting, but Yellow Nose had no trouble in slipping through them, though at times they were very close. The rest of the Cheyenne party thought Yellow Nose had been killed in among the cavalry horses and returned to the village with some soldiers' horses they had captured. Hawk caught Yellow Nose's war horse and brought it back to camp. Much to the surprise of everyone Yellow Nose turned up two days later, his arm in a sling which he had cut from his shirt, having made the trip on foot. The soldiers did lots of shooting during this night attack, but fired so wildly no one was hit. Mr. J. J. White, who was down here some time ago getting stories from the old people, told me that many years ago he bought the shield and lance, which Yellow Nose lost, from one of the officers of Carr's command present at this night fight.

Parties of Dog Soldiers had fights almost every day with the troops and Pawnee scouts. In one of these fights Howling Magpie was shot through both thighs. He was too weak to ride, so two of his cousins with this war party pushed on to the Indian village, the cousins following with a mule dragging Howling Magpie's travois. When the war party reached the village they were to send out relatives to care for the wounded man. But the soldiers and Pawnee scouts jumped the village before anyone could go out and Howling Magpie and his cousins, Shave Head and Little Man, were never again seen alive. Another war party found their dead bodies some time later. Years afterward, when the Pawnees and Cheyennes made peace, some Pawnees who were scouting with Major Carr at this time told how they came on these three Cheyennes and killed them. The Pawnees say they were scouting in advance of the troops and jumped the little Cheyenne party. Shave Head and Little Man put up a good fight and, refusing to leave their wounded cousin, were soon killed.

Howling Magpie, crippled by his wounds, was killed lying in the drag.[3]

After the little night fight Carr left his wagons under strong guard and pushed on after the Dog Soldiers. William F. Cody (Buffalo Bill) was chief of scouts for Major Carr, and Major Frank North commanded the Pawnee scouts. The reason this command did so much damage, the Indians say, was because of the presence of the Pawnee scouts. They always showed up first and the Cheyennes mistook them for friendly warriors.

The Dog Soldiers and these two Sioux villages, under Whistler and Two Strikes, now decided to go north and join the Northern Cheyennes and Sioux under Red Cloud. They had no trouble in distancing Carr's outfit, but when they reached the South Platte the river was so high that they were compelled to lie in camp waiting for the flood to subside. Tall Bull sent scouts to the south, in which direction the Indians had their last fight with Carr, but no scouts were sent to the east, as they did not expect any troops from that direction. Pawnee scouts came up on two Cheyenne men and one old woman who were following the village and they killed the two men. The Pawnees told the Cheyennes later that the woman refused to be captured and they were compelled to kill her also. These scouts told Carr which way the trail went.

Tall Bull was anxious to cross the Platte rivers [north and south forks] and get up into the Black Hills country. He sent Two Crows and five other Cheyennes on ahead to try the South Platte and find a place where it might be forded. This party crossed the South Platte and found the river so high in some places that the water ran over their horses backs. Then they found a place where it was not so high and marked it with sticks. It was evening when they returned to the village and reported to Tall Bull. There was a great deal of excitement in the camp at this time, as a war party of Sioux had come in and reported troops following the trail. Nevertheless Tall Bull sent

[3] *The Record of Engagements* reports a fight in this vicinity on July 5, 1869, and says three Indians were killed.—G.H.

criers through the camp to announce that they would camp where they were for two days; then they would cross over and camp in the high bluffs near the square butte, known to the whites as Court House Rock, where they could watch for soldiers and could not be surprised. Many of the Sioux, however, insisted on crossing the river that evening. But the Cheyennes went into camp at this place, called by the whites Summit Springs. This is at the base of Freemont Butte or White Butte, and here heads a little stream called White Butte Creek. The Cheyennes say it was poor judgment for Tall Bull to insist on going into camp instead of crossing the South Platte that evening and this error was the cause of the village being surprised next day.[4]

The Cheyennes agree that the Pawnees and soldiers took them completely by surprise next day (July 11, 1869). The day was a misty one, "smoky" the Indians say. They had been burning the grass to destroy their trail; they say everything looked indistinct. Brave Bear and Two Crows say they were eating the mid-day meal when Carr attacked them. Some of the Indians were lounging on a little hill, but most all were eating. Little Hawk, riding some distance from the camp, first discovered the troops. But he had a slow horse and the Pawnee scouts beat him to the camp. The day being so smoky his signals were not seen. He joined some of the fugitives from the village and got away with them. The Pawnee scouts were in the lead in the charge on the camp, shooting and yelling. Most of the horses were herded close to the camp, and many were tied near the lodges. At the first sound of firing all ran to catch horses before they stampeded. Those with horses in camp quickly mounted the women and children, while the men got ready to fight. Brave Bear and Two Crows ran out of their lodge toward the horses just in time to see all of Tall Bull's own herd stampede. As they ran they heard Tall Bull call in a loud voice, "All of you that are on foot and cannot get away follow me." A number of people ran with Tall Bull and his two wives to a little ravine with sharp high banks. By this time the troops were all

[4] Located about six miles south of Atwood, Logan County, Colorado, and east of Colorado State Highway 63.—S.L.

around, except on the south side of the camp, and the excitement was terrifying. Horses were stampeding in all directions, the Pawnees and soldiers yelling and shooting, women and children screaming with fright, Cheyenne and Sioux men shouting orders to the women and fighting off the attackers. Many people, mounted and on foot, streamed out to the south and scattered over the prairie in little groups, the men fighting off the pursuing Pawnees. Tall Bull's party in the ravine helped divert the soldiers and scouts from the fleeing Indians. The Pawnees, the Cheyennes say, did most of the killing and also captured the greater part of the pony herd. Two Crows ran across the prairie with a party of Cheyennes and Sioux, who covered the flight of a number of Cheyenne and Sioux women and children. Some were mounted, many on foot, and they were strung along the open prairie. The Pawnees followed, shooting and killing, but their horses seemed very tired after their long run up the hill to the Indian camp. Fighting in the rear of these women and children were Kills Many Bulls, Two Crows, and Lone Bear, the latter mounted, the other two on foot. Lone Bear was very brave, Two Crows says, charging again and again into the party of Pawnees chasing them, thus covering the flight of Two Crows and Kills Many Bulls as well as the women and children they were protecting. These three kept turning and fighting off the Pawnees; men in other groups did the same. Once Lone Bear charged right in among the Pawnees and went down fighting like a wild animal. Other Cheyennes say Two Crows was very brave, though he speaks sadly of running away and leaving so many Cheyenne and Sioux women and children to be killed by the Pawnees. After killing Lone Bear, Two Crows says, the Pawnees seemed to have stopped chasing the people. Two Crows had been badly kicked in the shins by a Pawnee horse he was trying to catch. In some way this horse got away from its rider and ran past Two Crows.

Tall Bull, the Dog Soldier chief, had three wives. One of those he put on a horse when the shooting started and she got away with a daughter of the first wife. The other two wives, the youngest and the eldest, went with Tall Bull to the ravine. In the fighting here the youngest was killed and other was captured. Powder Face, an old chief, and his Sioux wife went with Tall Bull; also the son of Powder Face, Black Moon, who had been badly wounded some days before and was still very weak. Big Gip and his wife also ran with this party to the ravine. A young Dog Soldier, named Wolf with Plenty of Hair, was very brave and staked himself out with a dog rope at head of the ravine. It was the custom for the Dog Soldier wearing a dog rope to pin himself down in running fights or when a party was taken by surprise as in this case. The fighting was so hot around the ravine that no one had time to pull the picket pin for Wolf with Plenty of Hair, and after the fight was over he was found where he had staked himself out. The Cheyennes in the ravine put up a desperate fight. Bill Cody and Frank North claim they killed Tall Bull, but the Pawnees say no one knows who killed him, as they were all shooting at him. White Buffalo Woman, wife of Tall Bull and sister of Good Bear, was allowed to come out of the ravine and surrender. She is still living at Tongue River Reservation. The rest of the Cheyennes were killed in the ravine.[5]

This was one of the severest blows struck against the Dog Soldiers. The troops captured most of the horses and mules and burned and destroyed the camp. The Cheyennes say the surprise was so complete that they wonder why more people were not killed and give the Pawnees the credit for the damage that was done. The names of the Cheyenne men killed were Tall Bull, Black Moon (named after a total eclipse of the moon), Wolf with Plenty of Hair, Powder Face, White Rock, and Lone Bear. A large number of women and children were killed.[6] Of the Sioux we do not know how many were

[5] Cf. Grinnell, *Fighting Cheyennes*, 316–18; Russell, *Lives and Legends of Buffalo Bill*, 138–48. Bent may have made the most acceptable statement about who killed Tall Bull, inasmuch as self-interest on the part of Luther North imbues the claims for his brother Frank, and W. F. Cody's carelessness about the contents of "autobiographies" put together by others for him clouds his part in the affair.—S.L.

[6] Fifty-two Indians were reported killed, both Cheyenne and Sioux, but Special Order No. 17, issued by Headquarters Republican River Expedition, July 11, 1869, does not account for the killed by sexes. Seventeen women and children were listed as captured. The plunder taken, aside from an estimated ten tons of Indian items destroyed, was very impressive: 690 buffalo robes, 361 saddles, 84 lodges complete,

killed. Brave Bear and Yellow Nose were with a party that remained hiding and a month later crossed the Platte and joined the Indians in the north. Both these men married women up there. Yellow Nose did not come south again until Dull Knife's band came down in 1877. Those that went north spent one winter there and then the majority came south again and joined the Southern Cheyennes. Most of the Dog Soldiers, however, straggled south and joined the Southern Cheyennes on the South Fork of the Canadian, staying with the Southern Cheyennes from that time on. I was living near Camp Supply at this time with the Southern Cheyennes.

At this period the Dog Soldiers were the most famous of the Cheyenne bands and the least understood by the whites. This band was originally one of the six Cheyenne soldier societies. These societies or brotherhoods are very old; each has its own peculiar dances, songs, ceremonies, and regalia. In the old days almost every Cheyenne man belonged to one of these societies. New members were brought in on the invitation of older members.[7] No man who had murdered or even accidentally killed a fellow tribesman could join a soldier society, and if a member was guilty of such a crime he was expelled and outlawed. In 1837 Porcupine Bear, the leader or chief of the Dog Soldiers, killed Little Creek in a drunken fight. For this Porcupine Bear was expelled from the society and outlawed, and compelled by custom to camp apart, with his family and relatives, from the rest of the tribe. Another Cheyenne, still living in the south, although a good man and highly respected as a warrior, was never permitted to join a soldier society because he accidentally killed

9,300 pounds of dried meat, 274 horses, 144 mules, and $1,500 in gold and bank notes, in a listing of 44 items of varying usefulness in Indian camp life. Rister, *Border Command*, 152–53; Grinnell, *Fighting Cheyennes*, 318; Berthrong, *Southern Cheyennes*, 343.—S.L.

[7] Grinnell, *The Cheyenne Indians*, II, 56–79; G. A. Dorsey, *The Cheyenne: Ceremonial Organization*, 16–30; Llewellyn and Hoebel, *The Cheyenne Way*, 99–131, contain detailed accounts of the Dog Soldiers and other Cheyenne soldier societies. Of particular significance in Bent's account, however, is the information on the intermarriage of Dog Soldiers and Sioux, the development of separate and ascendant position in the Cheyenne hierarchy, and the determined wildness of the Dog Soldiers.—S.L.

another Cheyenne in 1873. Ice, or White Bull, the famous Northern Cheyenne medicine man, was expelled from the Foolish Dog Society because his uncle fired at another Cheyenne in a quarrel about a dog. Though this man was not even wounded, nor was White Bull directly concerned in the trouble, he was expelled from the society because of his uncle's act. Ice later became a member of the Crooked Lance or Bone Scraper Society.

These soldier societies policed the camp and took charge of the tribal hunts. The chiefs selected a society for these duties, and after one society had acted as police for a time it went off duty and the chiefs selected another society to serve. When on duty the soldiers were very strict and punished anyone who broke rules or disobeyed orders. At times they acted in a very arbitrary manner. When Crook's soldiers were drawing near to attack Dull Knife's village in November, 1876, the leader of the Fox Soldiers carried things with a high hand and threatened to have his men punish severely anyone who attempted to leave the camp. The result was that people were so cowed that no one dared suggest moving, and so the village was taken at a disadvantage and destroyed and many people killed.[8] I have often seen these men "soldiering" offenders.

About 1838 the Bowstring Society wanted to form a war party, but were afraid to start until the ceremony of exposing the sacred arrows was performed. They asked Gray Thunder, the sacred arrows' keeper, to do this, but he refused, alleging that the time was not ripe. The Bowstrings insisted, and Gray Thunder, persisting in his refusal, was severely quirted by the soldiers and forced to comply with their demand. Strange to say, the war party came to a disastrous end, being annihilated by the Kiowas in a desperate fight. Though Gray Thunder was over seventy years old at this time, not even his age nor his sacred office protected him from the wrath of the soldiers. This

[8] Colonel Ranald S. Mackenzie completely routed the Cheyennes under Dull Knife on the north fork of the Powder River on November 25, 1876. Mackenzie was serving in General George Crook's command. Crook, *General George Crook: His Autobiography* (edited by Martin F. Schmitt), 214.—S.L.

was about the strongest action a soldier society ever took and it brought them bad luck.

Among the Cheyennes there were six warrior societies, as follows:

Woksihitaneo, or Kit-fox Men; the leader carried a club with the skin of a kit-fox hanging therefrom.

Himoiyoqis, the Crooked Lance or Bone Scraper Society. The leaders carried a lance with a crooked one end and during their dances a man made a noise by scraping a piece of elk horn made in the shape of a lizard. This was Roman Nose's society; I was also a member.

Mahohivas, Red Shields or Bull Soldiers. They carried red shields with the tail of a buffalo bull hanging from the shield. In early days the members of this society all resigned. Most of them were getting old, so they held a big ceremony on the Republican River and all the men resigned from the society, each man putting in a young man of promise in the society to fill his place. This is why the Republican River is called Red Shield River by our tribe.

Himatanohis, or Bowstring Men. The name comes from a peculiar lance, shaped like an elongated bow with a lance head at one end; this lance was carried by the leader. This society was also called *Konianutqio*, or Wolf Warriors. The Bowstring Men were good warriors, but were very headstrong. One of their war parties was annihilated by the Crows about 1819 and another party by the Kiowas and Comanches in 1837.

Hotamimasaw, Foolish or Crazy Dogs; an organization of very young warriors, boys just beginning their careers. This is a Northern Cheyenne society, a good deal like our Bowstring Society. We have no Crazy Dog Society down here among the Southern Cheyennes.

Hotamitaneo, or Dog Men; called Dog Soldiers by the whites. This society became the most famous of all the Cheyenne societies. In early days the Dog Men were purely a soldier society, but in later years they came to be looked on as a band or division of the tribe. To understand this change clearly it should be remembered that the soldier society was an organization of warriors, while the band or clan was an organization of families. About 1830 the old Cheyenne

337

clan system began to break up, and about 1837 the Dog Soldier Society, led by the famous outlaw, Porcupine Bear, broke through the old tribal custom and changed itself from a society of warriors to a camp or separate division. One of the old Cheyenne divisions, the *Masikota*, went over in a body and joined the Dog Soldier camp; famous warriors from other divisions also joined the Dog Soldiers, who soon became famous for the bravery and enterprise of their leaders and warriors. In this way a large number of ambitious young men were attracted to the new camp and the Dog Soldier band became stronger as other bands weakened. The Dog Soldier men dropped the old custom by which a man, when he married, went to live in the camp of his wife's band. They brought their wives home to their own camp. For a long time the Dog Soldiers were looked upon almost as outlaws by the rest of the tribe; but when the big wars came with the whites, and the Dog Soldiers took such a leading part in the fighting, the rest of the tribe came to show them the greatest respect.

The Dog Soldiers did not wear the common war bonnet of eagle feathers, but a peculiar round bonnet of crow feathers, without a tail; that is, without the string of feathers hanging down the warrior's back. One of the customs of this band was that, when hard pressed by the enemy, the warriors must give up their horses to the women and remain behind on foot to fight off the foe. The strangest and least understood of their customs was the use of the dog rope. This was a sash of buffalo skin several inches wide and about eight feet long, slit near one end for a few feet to make a loop which was thrown over the right shoulder and under the left arm of the wearer. At the lower or trailing end of the sash or "rope," as it was always called by the Indians, was a wooden picket pin. The rope was ornamented with porcupine quills, dyed in various bright colors; no beadwork was ever used. There were from two to four of these ropes in the society at all times, and the bravest men were selected to wear them. The wearer of the rope fought on horseback like other warriors, but, when caught in a desperate situation, the wearer of the dog rope dismounted and drove the picket pin into the ground. Here he must

338

remain. Should the fight go against his party he would be disgraced if he pulled up the pin and retreated. However, another warrior could release him by pulling the picket pin and driving the wearer of the dog rope off the field by striking him a few times with his quirt. The idea was that the wearer of the sash was so brave that he would not retreat after staking himself to the ground and that the man who released him had to whip him like a dog to compel him to retreat. The fight in which Tall Bull was killed in 1869 was the last occasion in which a dog rope was used. Wolf with Plenty of Hair staked himself out at the head of the ravine and died where he stood. Dog ropes were also used by the Arapahos, Mandans, Kiowas, and Prairie Apaches. The custom of wearing these ropes was very old, dating back to the time when the Indians had no horses and fought on foot. About one hundred years ago the Cheyennes and Mandans had a fight on the Upper Missouri and both sides used dog ropes in their fight. In the fight east of Denver about the year 1837, the Kiowas and Cheyennes both used dog ropes. The Kiowa chief who wore the dog rope in this fight was very brave. He charged the Cheyennes several times all alone. He did not dismount and picket himself out, but was killed on horseback.

After the Dog Soldiers set themselves up as a separate band they occupied in the Cheyenne camp circle the position formerly taken by the *Masikota*. The camp circle invariably opened toward the east like a single tepee.

The Dog Soldiers lived on the Republican and Smoky Hill rivers most of the time and were great friends of the Oglala and Brulé Sioux, who hunted and camped in that region. The Dog Soldiers and Sioux intermarried a great deal. Tall Bull's mother was a Sioux woman, and a great many of the Dog Soldiers were half Sioux. The young men of this band were very wild and reckless, great raiders, and being hard to control were always in mischief. In this way they got the rest of the tribe into trouble. These young men would make a raid and get out of the way and the troops would come and stumble across some other band of Cheyennes and punish them for what the Dog Soldiers had done.

With the destruction of Tall Bull's village, and the consequent breaking up of the Dog Soldiers as a band, some going to the Northern Cheyennes and others to the south, the power of this famous society was broken and never since have they been a factor in the wars of the Cheyenne tribe.

CHAPTER FOURTEEN

THE FETTERMAN FIGHT

A WORD NOW ABOUT affairs in the North from the time I left, in 1865, with Little Wolf's (Honi-i-ha-ket) band to rejoin Black Kettle and the main body of Southern Cheyennes—from a land to which few of us were ever to return, the dearly beloved hunting grounds of the Cheyenne tribe, teeming with game at this time, and whose mountains, valleys and plains, with their abundance of cold water, were to the Cheyennes a land of health and happiness.

Gold had been discovered in western Montana, and to reach this land the settlers and miners attempted to go through the heart of the Indian hunting ground by what became known as the Bozeman Trail, running from Fort Laramie, Wyoming, on the North Platte, along the eastern base of the Big Horn Mountains, due west from Fort C. F. Smith[1] to Bozeman, Montana, a shorter and better route than the famous Bridger Road. The Indians naturally resented this, the young fighting men of the Northern Cheyennes and Arapahos and the Sioux foolishly confident of holding off the white invaders, the wiser chiefs fearful of the future with the annihilation of the game and loss of their country. This was the famous Powder River country, for the preservation of which the allied Cheyennes and Sioux fought bitterly for over ten years, the high-water mark of resistance being the famous battle of the Little Big Horn.

---

[1] Fort C. F. Smith, established August 12, 1866, on the east bank of Big Horn River, eight miles above the mouth of Rotten Grass Creek, at the then eastern edge of the Crow Indian country; originally named Fort Ransom, soon changed to Fort C. F. Smith in honor of Major General Charles Ferguson Smith, d. 1862; abandoned July 29, 1868, after the Fort Laramie Treaty of 1868. Frazer, *Forts of the West*, 84.—S.L.

The government sent out troops in the summer of 1865 to keep open the famous Bozeman Trail in the Powder River country from Fort Fetterman to Fort Reno, to Fort Phil Kearny, to Fort C. F. Smith on the Big Horn River, and thence west. Opposed to the troops were strong war parties of Cheyennes and Sioux, with some Northern Arapahos. The opposition of the Indians was so determined that in the fall of this year commissioners were sent from Washington to secure the consent of the Indians to the opening of the road. The Sioux and Cheyenne chiefs absolutely refused to attend any council for this purpose.[2] In June, 1866, another council was held, this time at Fort Laramie.[3] Spotted Tail and a few other chiefs of the Brulé Sioux signed the treaty, and Big Mouth, a leader of a band of the Oglala Sioux known as the "Laramie Loafers," also signed. A strange thing in this connection is that in 1869, at the old Whetstone Agency, Spotted Tail shot and killed Big Mouth in a quarrel which followed a feud of some months' duration, and Spotted Tail himself met a violent death at the hands of a fellow tribesman, Crow Dog, in 1881. Dull Knife and a few of the headmen of his band also signed this treaty a few days later; but this action was utterly repudiated by Two Moons, Ice or White Bull, and the other ruling spirits of the Northern Cheyennes. In fact, the Indians were so bitter that they threatened to depose Dull Knife, who in defense

[2] Bent is here referring to the proposal of Governor Newton Edmunds of Dakota Territory, and its approval by the Indian Office in Washington, in 1865, to negotiate a peace treaty with the Sioux, following the outbreak of hostilities after the Sun Dance of late June, early July, 1865, on Powder River. Edmunds was able to secure assent only of the peaceful bands along the Missouri, with the Oglalas of Red Cloud and the Brulés of Spotted Tail, as well as the hostile Northern and Southern Cheyennes and Arapahos in the Powder River country unaccounted for in the treaty negotiations. Hyde, *Spotted Tail's Folk*, 107—S.L.

[3] In October, 1865, Big Ribs and a few other friendly Sioux from near Denver were the only Indians who could be prevailed upon to carry a peace message from Fort Laramie to the northern camps, which began to drift in during March and April, 1866, for the Fort Laramie peace talks with Colonel H. E. Maynadier, preparatory to the meeting with the commissioners headed by E. B. Taylor of Washington in June. On June 27, seven chiefs of the Brulés and six of the Oglalas signed the treaty. Hyde, *Spotted Tail's Folk*, 113–15.—S.L.

claimed that he had been deceived by the interpreters of the council as to the terms of the treaty.

The hostile element of the Sioux was led by Red Cloud, whose power had been steadily growing. Efforts were made to have him attend the council, and at first he flatly refused, but later on, in June, he attended and announced his opposition to the plans of the government. While Red Cloud was addressing the council, troops arrived to assist in building forts along the trail, and on being apprised of their purpose he abruptly left the council with his headmen, openly defiant of the commissioners.

The government now proceeded to establish three forts along the trail: Fort Reno (rebuilt) and Fort Phil Kearny, both on Powder River; and Fort C. F. Smith on the Big Horn River.[4] This action infuriated the already excited Indians. Young men from the Sioux bands flocked to Red Cloud's camp, and even Spotted Tail soon found himself with but few followers. All the Northern Cheyennes were hostile, and so were the Northern Arapaho bands of Black Coal and Eagle Head. The Indians made things so hot for the troops that travel over the road was absolutely prevented.

At Fort Phil Kearny it was impossible for the troops to bring in hay or wood except under heavy guard. On December 21, 1866, Lieutenant Fetterman and a party of eighty-one men were cut off from the fort and all killed. Many accounts of this fight have been written, but little from the Indian side. Two Moons, who is still living at Tongue River Agency, told me his story of the fight while on a visit to Colony, Oklahoma, some years ago.

Two Moons' Story[5]

These big Indian camps were made up of the Sioux under Red

---

[4] Fort Reno, Wyoming, was established June 28, 1866, located a mile north of Fort Connor, established 1865, which it replaced; it was on the west bank of the Powder River. Fort Phil Kearny, established July 13, 1866, at the foot of the Big Horn Mountains, Wyoming, between Big and Little Piney creeks just before they unite, fifteen miles north of the present town of Buffalo. Frazer, *Forts of the West,* 183–84.—S.L.

[5] Another informant, White Elk, a Cheyenne, accompanied George Bird Grinnell

Cloud, Pawnee Killer, and Blue Horse; the Cheyennes under Strong Wolf (or Brave Wolf), Little Wolf, and Dull Knife; and the Arapahos under Black Coal and Eagle Head. The Sioux alone had over one thousand fighting men. For some time the Indians had been running off stock, making attacks on small parties near the fort, but always falling back when attacked by the soldiers. This encouraged the soldiers to chase the small raiding parties, which was just what we wanted, as the chiefs always advised us not to fight the soldiers. A small party, of which I was one, was sent out to spy on the fort and see if it could be taken without much loss. We saw it was too strong to take and so reported. Then the leaders decided to follow the usual plan of drawing the soldiers out by a small decoy force and then kill them all when out of reach of the fort. [This was the plan followed at Julesburg in 1865 and at Platte Bridge later on in the same year.] One morning a strong body of soldiers came out with wagons to get timber for the fort. When they were about half-way to the pine woods, a small party of Indians were sent to attack them. The wagons drew up in a circle, and, as planned by our leaders, another force was sent out from the fort to help the soldiers with the wagon train. [This relief expedition was under Lieutenant W. J. Fetterman.] Now a select party of warriors, mounted on the best and swiftest ponies, were sent over to the crossing of Lodgepole Creek. These men, not many in number, were ordered to draw the soldiers into the hills where the big body of Indians were hiding. The Indians attacking the wagon train rode off as the soldiers from the fort drew near, and these now turned to the right, crossing the creek, in pursuit of the Indians at Lodgepole Creek. These Indians did their work well and fell back slowly toward the Lodgepole hills. The soldiers followed fast and were well into the hills before the big body of Indians attacked them. The soldiers now turned back for the fort, but were surrounded and had to dismount. Then they turned loose their horses and fought on foot. The fight was soon over and every

---

over the battle ground and gave him a detailed, graphic account of what took place. White Elk was a young man in his late teens, forty-eight years before the telling, which dates the account in 1914. Grinnell, *Fighting Cheyennes*, 235–44.—S.L.

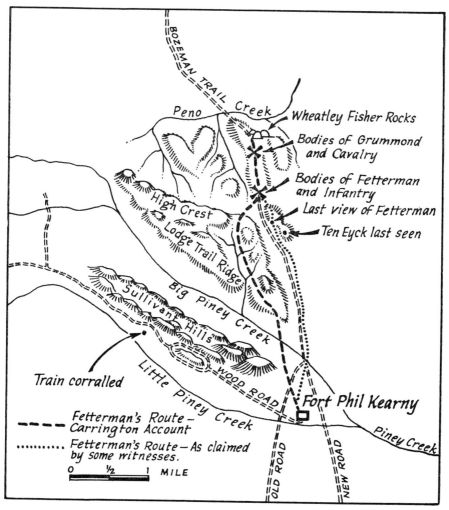

Peno

Creek

Wheatley Fisher Rocks

Bodies of Grummond
and Cavalry

Bodies of Fetterman
and Infantry

Last view of Fetterman

Ten Eyck last seen

High Crest

Lodge Trail Ridge

Big Piney Creek

Sullivant Hills

WOOD ROAD

Little Piney Creek

Train corralled

Fort Phil Kearny

Piney Creek

OLD ROAD

NEW ROAD

Fetterman's Route —
Carrington Account

Fetterman's Route — As claimed
by some witnesses.

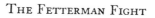

0   ½   1   MILE

From J. W. Vaughn, *Indian Fights*

The Fetterman Fight

345

soldier killed. The Cheyennes had two men killed in this fight, the Arapahos one, and the Sioux eleven.

[End of Two Moons' story.]

Little Wolf's brother was one of the Cheyennes killed in the fight. Little Wolf told me about this when in the South in 1877. When the Fetterman party was trapped, Little Wolf dismounted from the white war horse he had ridden in so many battles. This horse he turned over to his younger brother, a boy of twenty, called Swift Hawk (Inois). He also gave the boy his scalp shirt, and war bonnet, and the lance he had carried in his many famous fights, saying as he did so: "With all these warriors looking on, it is a good time to show how a Cheyenne brave can die." This boy was the first to ride against the dismounted soldiers and he was killed fighting among them. The white war horse was also killed. The main body of Indians charged in after the boy and like a mighty wave flowed over the troops. Little Wolf told me that he buried his brother with all the things he wore in battle.

The success of the Indians in their opposition to the opening of the road through the Powder River country was so pronounced that a new commission was appointed in 1868 to treat with them. The Indians demanded that the forts be abandoned and the building of roads through their hunting grounds stopped. The authorities were anxious to complete the building of the Union Pacific Railroad, which would give an easy route to the Montana gold fields from the south, and hence the Bozeman Trail would lose its importance. Finally the commissioners, Generals Harney and Sanborn, made a new treaty, which was signed April 29, 1868, the government agreeing to withdraw the troops from the forts in question and abandon the Bozeman Trail. Red Cloud was still defiant and refused to sign the treaty until the troops had been actually withdrawn and the forts abandoned. He finally signed in November, 1868.

Agencies were now established for the various bands of Sioux, the Northern Cheyennes and Arapahos. The Spotted Tail Agency was placed on Whetstone Creek, on the Missouri, later to be moved west to the White River. The Red Cloud Agency, famous for many a year thereafter, was located on the North Platte below Fort Laramie, but in 1873, was moved to the White River, in South Dakota. The Northern Cheyennes roamed over the region of the Yellowstone–Big Horn country, at intervals staying with their friends, the Sioux, at the Red Cloud Agency and occasionally with the Gros Ventres at the Milk River Agency, in Montana. They were very wild and impatient of any restraint, and made a great deal of trouble for the agents when they visited the agencies. Raids against the Crows and Shoshones were frequent, both by the Northern Cheyennes and by the Arapahos, as well as the Sioux, and by parties made up from all three tribes.

To the northwest of the agencies were large camps of free and unrestrained Sioux and some Cheyennes, along the Powder, Tongue, and Big Horn rivers. These seldom, if ever, went to the agencies and they absolutely refused to recognize the authority of the government agents. They were known variously to the whites as the "wild," "hostile," and "Northern" Indians, and were the magnet that drew away from the influence of the agents the wild young people of the various tribes. The only white man who ever had nerve enough to visit these wild camps was Father [Pierre Jean] De Smet, the great Jesuit missionary. He visited the camp of the Hunkpapa Sioux, then on the Powder River, and met Sitting Bull, Black Moon, Gall, and a number of other chiefs made famous later by the Custer fight, and he speaks of the great reception given him while in these hostile camps.

The Northern Cheyennes never associated much with Sitting Bull's band and knew very little about him either at this time or later. The Oglalas, and especially those at the Red Cloud Agency, were their great friends among the Sioux. Crazy Horse was leader of a small Oglala band at this time and was very intimate with the Northern Cheyennes, often joining them in raids on the Crows and Shoshones in the early 1870's, when he made his reputation as a fighter. As far as known, he never went to the agencies. The Cheyennes still consider him the bravest man among the Sioux.

347

Early in the 1870's, the government commenced to negotiate with the Indians for the right to run the Northern Pacific Railroad through their territory. It was from the so-called Northern Indians that the greatest opposition was encountered. As usual, commissioners were sent out to talk with the Indians, with the customary distribution of presents to get the chiefs and headmen to sign agreements they never understood. The commissioners were always too hurried to wait for a complete understanding with the real Indian leaders. New commissioners would come again in a few months, more hasty talks and presents followed, but never any definite understanding. No wonder the Indians did not know whom or what to believe. Game was becoming scarcer and the number of buffalo plainly fewer each year. The removal of the Red Cloud Agency was the cause of constant squabbling between the authorities and the Indian leaders; but late in the summer of 1873 this was accomplished, the agency being moved to the White River, near the Black Hills, and Fort Robinson was established near the agency.

In 1873 a delegation of Northern Cheyennes and Arapaho chiefs and headmen were sent to Washington in reference to the project of removing all the Northern Cheyennes to the Southern Cheyenne Reservation in Oklahoma. The Northern Cheyennes were bitterly opposed to the plan but had to send a delegation anyway. At this time there were nineteen hundred Northern Cheyennes credited to the Red Cloud Agency. The delegation arrived in Washington on November 6, 1873. At this time there was also in Washington a delegation of Southern Cheyennes and Arapahos, and a party of Utes under Ouray. With the Southern Arapahos was a Ute boy who had been captured when about seven years old and was thought to be the son of Ouray. The Utes were very anxious to get this boy back; but he was so well satisfied that he refused to leave the Arapahos and had no recollection of Ouray as his father, a bitter disappointment to this famous Ute chief. The Northern delegation was under the direction of General John E. Smith, with Jules Coffee and William Rowland as interpreters. The party was made up of Dull Knife, Strong Wolf,

348

Black Hawk, Little Wolf, Spotted Wolf, Lame White Man, Crazy Head, Crow, Old Wolf, Bear Who Pushes Back His Hair, and White Powder.

On November 3 the Northern Cheyennes and Arapahos had an interview with President Grant, who told them that under the treaty of 1868 they must go south to the Indian Territory. Plenty Bears, a Northern Arapaho, replied that they did not wish to go south, were well satisfied where they were, and as he understood the treaty they were not to go south for thirty-six years. Dull Knife also answered the President and said that when he signed the treaty he understood that the Northern Cheyennes were not to go south at all. President Grant answered "Then the fault must have been with the interpreters, as General Sherman had no intent to deceive you." As a matter of fact the President was wrong and Dull Knife was right.[6]

Dull Knife and Plenty Bears later reiterated to the secretary of the Interior and the commissioner of Indian Affairs that they never understood the treaty of 1868 to oblige them to give up their home in the North. The talk came to nothing, as the Northern Cheyennes

---

[6] According to the treaty with the Northern Cheyennes and Arapahos concluded at Fort Laramie on May 10, 1868 (see *Statutes at Large*, XV, 655), under Article II, the Indians "Agree to accept as a permanent home that portion of the reservation set apart for the Southern Cheyennes and Arapahos by the Treaty of Medicine Lodge of October, 1867, or some portion of the reservation set apart for the Brulés and other bands of Sioux Indians by the Treaty of April 29, 1868. Within one year of the date of the treaty, they will attach themselves permanently either to the agency provided for near the mouth of Medicine Lodge Creek or to the agency about to be established on the Missouri River near Fort Randall, or to the Crow Agency near Otter Creek on the Yellowstone provided by the treaty of May 7, 1868, and it is hereby understood that one portion of said Indians may attach themselves to one of the aforementioned reservations and another portion to another of said reservations as each part or portion of said Indians (Cheyennes or Arapahos) may elect." Any Indian electing to farm could select land within the said reservation. The treaty was signed for the government by Generals Sherman, Harney, Terry, Augur, and Messrs. Sanborn and Tappan; for the Indians by Wah-tah-nah, Black Bear; Bah-ta-che, Medicine Man; Oh-cum-ga-che, Little Wolf; Ichs-tah-en, Short Hair; Non-ne-se-be, Sorrel Horse; Ka-te-u-nan, The Under Man; Ah-che-e-wah, Man in the Sky; We-ah-se-vose, Big Wolf; Ches-ne-on-e-ah, The Beau; Mah-ah-ne-we-tah, The Man Who Falls from His Horse; O-e-na-ku, White Crow; A-che-kan-koo-ani, White Shield; Tah-me-la-pash-me, Dull Knife.—G.H.

and Arapahos were firm in their determination not to go south to live. What a pity the government insisted some years later on sending Dull Knife's band to the South and to the terrible end which followed the decision of the government to keep them there.

Meanwhile the government continued its temporizing policy with the Northern Indians, thinking, perhaps, that with the building of the Northern Pacific Railroad, and the consequent opening of the country to settlement, game would become so scarce that the wilder Indians would be forced onto the reservations. The buffalo were rapidly disappearing under the wanton slaughter of white hide hunters and the horde of Red River half-breeds from Canada. To the Indian, the buffalo was life itself. Without this animal the Plains Indians were helpless.

It is probable that in the natural order of things conditions would so adjust themselves that little trouble would be experienced in the north from the wild bands; but unfortunately gold was discovered in the Black Hills. In defiance of the treaty rights guaranteed them in 1868, the government, in 1874, sent a military expedition into the Hills to investigate the finding of gold. This expedition was under command of General Custer, who wrote a flowery description of the Black Hills country, reporting it rich in gold.[7] A flood of miners followed, and consequent clashes with the infuriated Indians. Detachments of troops made a faint-hearted attempt to drive out the miners. In May, 1875, another government expedition, under a strong military escort, was sent into the Hills to map the entire district, laying lines for roads and military posts. That the Indians had any right to hold this country, with its mineral and other lands guaranteed to them by the treaty of 1868, apparently never entered anybody's head. That the mines could be worked on royalty or on shares for the Indians, or leased, as are the oil fields of Oklahoma at present,

---

[7] Custer was ordered from Fort Abraham Lincoln on the Missouri, in Montana, with ten companies of cavalry and two of infantry on July 1, 1874. On August 3, Custer sent his scout, Charlie Reynolds, to Fort Laramie with reports of the expedition, after which the few flecks of gold found incidentally by the men of the expedition became headline news throughout the country. Parker, *Gold in the Black Hills*, 24–26.—S.L.

the timber lands of the Chippewas, and the grazing lands of the Crow, Cheyennes, and Blackfeet, was evidently never seriously considered. No trouble had been experienced in obtaining the consent of the Indians to the relinquishment of their hunting rights in Nebraska and on the Republican Fork of the Smoky Hill River in June, 1875, for the sum of twenty-five thousand dollars; yet these hunting rights had been guaranteed by the treaty of 1868. That the Indians had any right to the Black Hills country after gold was discovered seemed preposterous to the white people.

However, in June, 1875, a commission was appointed, under the direction of the President, to proceed to the Sioux country and treat with the Indians for the sale of their rights in the Black Hills. The council opened on September 20 with representatives from the various Sioux divisions and the Northern Cheyennes and Arapahos. A powerful element of the Indians opposed giving up the Hills at any price. Others were ready to sell, but their demands were considered so exorbitant that no agreement could be reached. To give up their interest in the Big Horn country was a proposition the Indians absolutely refused even to consider.[8]

Although by the treaty of 1868 all the land east of the Big Horn Mountains (the Powder River country) was considered Indian territory, yet in December, 1875, General Sherman issued an order that all Indians off the reservations at the end of the following month would be treated as hostile and war made against them. The agents were ordered to notify the "wild" Indians of this order. It is extremely doubtful if the Northern Cheyennes absent from the Red Cloud Agency ever heard of such an order. Sitting Bull claimed he never did, and so did Crazy Horse. And it is also doubtful whether they would pay any attention to the order anyway, knowing that they

[8] Various abortive efforts were made by Generals Sherman, Sheridan, and E. O. C. Ord to stem the tide of the gold rush to the Black Hills in 1874 and 1875, and Grant hmself had to admit that stopping mining operations would prove an almost impossible task. The loss of the Black Hills by the Indians entailed also the loss of minerals. Between 1878 and 1962, the Homestake Mine at Lead, South Dakota, accounted for no less than $715,000,000 in bullion. Parker, *op. cit.*, 27–52, 196–97. —S.L.

were within their rights while they stayed within the region assigned them by the treaty of 1868.

To add to the excitement over the Black Hills affair, a large number of Southern Cheyennes, who had broken away from the agency in the south following the war of 1874–75, had come North to their kinsmen on the Powder River, an element dangerous to the peace, of course, with their stories of wrongs endured from the soldiers and settlers and news of the extermination of the buffalo in the south, events which will be treated of in the next chapter.

CHAPTER FIFTEEN

ADOBE WALLS

To the camps of the Cheyenne bands in the South gradually came drifting the broken Dog Soldiers, many on foot, a bit subdued over the loss of their leader and the destruction of their village. The main body of the Southern Cheyennes was then (1869) around Fort Supply, the agency not having yet been established. It was not until the following year, in May of 1870, that the agency was opened at Darlington. This was named after Brinton Darlington, a Quaker and the first agent for the Cheyennes and Arapahos; he retained me as interpreter.[1] From this time until the spring of 1874 the Cheyennes were peaceful, wishing only to be left alone and dealt with according to treaty stipulations. In 1872 the Kiowas urged the Cheyennes to join with them in a war on the whites but the Cheyennes refused.[2] Game was still abundant, though the buffalo were

[1] Brinton Darlington, a Quaker, was chosen agent for the Upper Arkansas Agency, under Enoch Hoag, superintendent of the Central Superintendency, with the election of U. S. Grant as president of the United States. Darlington arrived at his post July 6, 1869, but found that the Cheyennes had not kept their promise to settle on their reservation near Camp Supply. The Indians objected to the location on the Salt Fork of the Arkansas, the water there being bad. Commissioner of Indian Affairs Ely S. Parker ordered Darlington to select a new agency, and on May 3, 1870, Darlington took up the new and permanent site near present El Reno, Canadian County, Oklahoma. Berthrong, *Southern Cheyennes*, 345, 355.—S.L.

[2] The picture was a good deal more complex than Bent here indicates, with the Dog Soldiers under Bull Bear reluctant to come to the reservation and slow in doing so, and the Kiowas and Comanches frequently inducing small numbers of the younger Cheyennes to join them in raids into Texas. The threat of war from the Cheyenne side was not infrequent after 1870, but the Arapahos kept rigidly in the paths of peace. Berthrong, *op cit.*, 346–67.—S.L.

353

becoming scarcer. In fact, the slaughter of buffalo was the main cause of the next war in the South, the unrestrained action of the horde of white hunters who killed for the hides alone, leaving the carcasses to rot on the plains by the thousands, filling the Indians with bitterness and indignation.

Another of the primary causes for the disturbance of the peace in the south was the presence of a number of white horse thieves who made their headquarters at Dodge City, Kansas, and raided the Indian camps at every opportunity. These bands of thieves were made up of the roughest and most lawless men of the border. In 1873 a delegation of Southern Cheyennes and Arapahos visited Washington and protested against the outrages committed by these horse thieves. President Grant promised Little Robe that the Indians would receive protection. But, like so many others, this proved to be an empty promise. To raid the Indian herds and get away was of course attended with some risk; but once in town the thieves were safe from molestation, and the fruits of their raids could be converted into cash without interference from any legal authority. There was not much law on the border at this time for any one, and none at all for the Indian. Had the military authorities, in protection of the Indians on reservations, but expended a fraction of the money later spent in putting down Indian uprisings a different story might be told and many innocent women and children saved from horrible suffering and death. White men lack patience and sympathy in dealing with a weaker people. Only too often has the red man been left a prey to the crafty and unscrupulous, notwithstanding solemn treaty obligations.

The Union Pacific Railroad had practically split the buffalo into two great herds. The southern herd was now subjected to an attack by organized bands of white hunters the like of which was never seen. This slaughter went on even in the hunting grounds reserved for the Indians by the recent treaties, while the military stood in apparent sympathy with the hide hunters. For this wanton destruction of the Indian food supply resentment against the whites was smouldering. The Plains Indians believed that the buffalo was created especially

354

for his use. From the hide he made his tepees, winter robes, parfleche cases, saddle covers, winter moccasins, cradles, and shields; from the horns, his spoons and dishes; from the long hair of the head, ropes and lariats; the sinew gave him his thread and bowstrings and backed his bows; the shoulder blades and other heavy bones were used as instruments in dressing hides and the brain, liver, and fat in tanning; from the tail were made knife scabbards, handles for clubs, and wands used in medicine dances; the hoofs and horns were made into glue; in fact so varied were the uses of the buffalo that its destruction was like taking away the Indians' life. With the acquisition of the horse, the buffalo made the Cheyenne one of the proudest and most independent men that ever lived.

In addition to the hide hunters, the white horse thieves were a source of irritation to the Cheyennes in the spring of 1874. These men made their headquarters at Fort Dodge and at the Big Bend of the Arkansas. My herd was stolen early in the spring and taken to the Big Bend. Soon after this Little Robe's band, then camped at the head of Salt Creek, had its herd stolen one night by white thieves. Next morning a party of Little Robe's men started in pursuit. The trail led toward the Cimarron River. The best horses had been stolen and the Indians soon abandoned the chase, being unable to gain with their poor ponies. However, two Cheyenne men continued the pursuit: Little Robe's son, Sitting Medicine, and Curious Horn, or White Bear, son of Bull Sign. When these two reached the Cimarron they located the camp of the horse thieves, but were discovered by the white men and fired on. The Cheyennes, being greatly outnumbered, made for a rocky bluff and, dismounting, returned the fire. Sitting Medicine was twice wounded, and under the circumstances the Cheyennes retired at dark. Though the Cheyennes were still at peace, and despite the promise of the President, nothing was done to punish these thieves.

The hide hunters grew bolder and established themselves in the heart of the Indian hunting ground at an abandoned trading post, called Adobe Walls, situated in the panhandle of Texas on the South Fork of the Canadian River, about a mile from the mouth of a small stream called Bent's Creek. This post had been built many years before, probably before 1840, by my father and Ceran St. Vrain, and was principally used in trading for horses with the Kiowas, Comanches, and Apaches, who captured many horses on their raids into old Mexico. Bent and Company employed Mexicans to break the horses thus obtained in trade. The fort had been abandoned for many years, being considered by my father to be too far south for his purpose.[3] It was from this fort that the hunters sallied forth and killed thousands of buffalo, the hides being piled near the fort. Wagons from Dodge City hauled supplies for the hunters and returned with buffalo hides. At this time Robert M. Wright and Charles Rath were supplying the outfit at Adobe Walls.[4]

Between the horse thieves and hide hunters, and dissatisfaction at

[3] The time of construction of the Adobe Fort on the Canadian, in Hutchinson County, Texas, is uncertain. Grinnell dated it prior to 1840; Philip St. George Cooke, from information given him in conversation by Charles Bent, put it in the fall of 1842; but Lieutenant James W. Abert (*Western American in 1846-1847: The Original Travel Diary of Lieutenant J. W. Abert, Who Mapped New Mexico for the United States Army*, edited by John Galvin, p. 74) speaks in his entry of December 24, 1846, at Santa Fe, of having seen Mr. St. Vrain. "I asked if he had any trading house on the Canadian. He told me that the Kioways had sent and warned him not to come down this year, as the Comanches had determined to revenge themselves on the whites for the death of their children. This nation have suffered much from the measles . . . As I have not more than 18 men I determine to give up my project of going in by the Canadian, but should take the route by Bent's Fort." He was on his way to Fort Leavenworth the morning of Monday, December 28 after a raging snowstorm had continued from the night into the day. This much we know, then, that the Bents and St. Vrain had the Adobe Fort on the Canadian but operated it irregularly until they (more likely William Bent) attempted to destroy it between 1848 and 1850, according to Grant Foreman (*Marcy and the Gold Seekers*, 226). Cf. Lavender, *Bent's Fort*, 405n., 412-13n.—S.L.

[4] Two years before, Charles Rath had forty thousand buffalo hides stacked in his yard at Dodge City. He was joined in his enterprise in the winter of 1872-73 by Robert M. Wright and reported that the firm shipped two hundred thousand hides that season. Also prominent in the hide trade at this time were the Mooar brothers, J. Wright and John, and their cousin Charles, who were partners. J. Wright Mooar, as hunter, once killed 96 buffalo from a single stand; not to be outdone, Charles Rath killed 107 on the Canadian River in 1873; Frank Collinson (*Life in the Saddle*, 55) says "my best score was 121 buffalo on one stand north of where Childress is now located." Cf. Wayne Gard, *The Great Buffalo Hunt*, 110-13, 128-29.—S.L.

the new agencies over supplies, the Indians were in a state of excitement and unrest. The Comanches, especially, were very bitter, and so were a large portion of the Kiowas, because the whites continually pushed out into the Indian hunting grounds, south of the Arkansas, guaranteed to them by the treaty.[5]

John D. Miles was now agent at Darlington for the Cheyennes and Arapahos and I was his interpreter.[6] A Comanche medicine man, named Isatai,[7] now claimed to be possessed of supernatural powers and was the leader of the discontented element. His harangues worked the Comanches and Kiowas up to the fighting point, and delegations from these tribes came to the Cheyenne camps, asking for help to drive out the white hunters. Agent Miles sent runners to the Cheyennes warning them to keep out of trouble, and I tried to influence them for peace. Whirlwind was against going to war and moved his band in near the agency, and later was followed by Little Robe's people. White Shield, with his small band, moved in soon after. By the hostile Cheyennes these friendly members of the tribe were derisively called "Penataka," from the name of a Comanche band who lived with the Wichitas, Caddos, and Delawares, and who were accused by their fellow tribesmen as acting as government scouts against their own people.[8] But with two exceptions these friendly Cheyennes refused to serve as scouts against their fellow tribesmen. As a matter of fact, many of those later classed as hostile would have

[5] The Comanches were not without blame in the great slaughter of the herds. Frank Collinson wrote, "On one occasion I saw hundreds of Comanche Indians on a buffalo 'surround.' They were escorted by the United States Cavalry and killed around two thousand buffalo with guns, pistols, and arrows." *Op. cit.*, 63.—S.L.

[6] Brinton Darlington had died May 1, 1872; his successor, John D. Miles, arrived at the agency on May 31, 1872. Berthrong, *Southern Cheyennes*, 368.—S.L.

[7] Isatai's name may be rendered into English as Rear-End-of-a-Wolf. Nye, *Carbine and Lance*, 244.—S.L.

[8] The Comanches were divided into twelve bands, of which the Penateka, or Honey Eaters, here referred to by Bent were one of the largest. Others with frequent contacts with the whites, either in peace or in war, were the Quahadi, of which band, the "Antelopes," Quanah became a great leader at the ensuing Battle of Adobe Walls. Muriel Wright, *A Guide to the Indian Tribes of Oklahoma*, 118; Ernest Wallace and E. Adamson Hoebel, *The Comanches: Lords of the South Plains*, 24–31.—S.L.

preferred to have gone into Darlington, but were prevented from doing this by the soldier societies; the Bowstring men, in particular, kept many men in the hostile camps by threats of punishment. After the soldiers took the field against them the Cheyennes, of course, stuck together and gave the troops a run for their money.

The main body of the Cheyennes were camped on the headwaters of the Washita River, holding a sun dance under the direction of Crazy Mule, a medicine man. This dance lasted four days and was participated in by a party of twenty-two Arapahos, led by Yellow Horse, who had come out from Darlington agency in a very hostile mood. The sun dance had just come to an end, at the close of a fine June day, when a long line of warriors were seen riding toward the Cheyenne village. They were Comanches, with a few Kiowas, magnificently arrayed in war rigs and splendidly mounted, the Comanches at this time being very rich in fine horses. In a long line the visiting warriors rode inside and outside the great Cheyenne camp circle, chanting war songs, their war bonnets tossing in the breeze. Isatai rode at the end of the long line, making appeals, in Comanche, for the Cheyennes to join the war party, promising them much plunder when they wiped out the hunters at Adobe Walls, who, as was well known, had loads of supplies. "My medicine is strong," he chanted, "and the hunters' bullets will not harm us." The Cheyennes needed little urging, and next day most of the young men joined the war party, as did also the visiting Arapaho delegation. The Adobe Walls were not many miles away from the Cheyenne camp and so easy a victory was promised by Isatai that a large number of women and children went along to pack the plunder.[9]

[9] Who did the urging for the fight at Adobe Walls remains a question. W. S. Nye's informants among the Comanches included Timbo, son of Parra-ocoom; Yellow Fish, an old Quahadi; and Poafebitty. They related that a great smoker held simultaneously with the sun dance, attended by Kiowas, Comanches, Cheyennes, and Arapahos, the talk was of attacking the Tai-bos (whites), but first the Tonkawas, accused of cannibalism on Comanches killed in a skirmish in Texas, should be taken care of. When the latter idea was abandoned, Quanah of the Comanches urged that all ride against Adobe Walls. Isatai and Quanah then took charge. Nye, *Carbine and Lance*, 245.—S.L.

The advance of the Indians was made skilfully, and at daybreak a few days later the Indians lined up half a mile from the fort in a grove of trees. The medicine man went alone to the top of a nearby bluff to reconnoitre the camp. He wore a headdress of sagebrush and could see the white men's camp clearly from the top of the hill.

I have talked with nearly all of the Cheyennes who took part in this battle and survived the war of 1874; also with many of the Arapahos who were present. I also knew some who were present on the whites' side. Billy Dixon was there and often talked with me about this fight.[10] I have read a few accounts of the battle, which took place on June 27, 1874, and, as usual, they contain many details which are utterly without foundation. One writer says that the field was covered with dead white horses, lately issued to the Cheyennes by the government. As a matter of fact, no horses of any color were issued to these tribes at this time. The list of Indian leaders given by white writers is ridiculous. Red Moon, Eagle Head (called Minimic by the whites), Gray Beard, and many other Cheyenne chiefs were in this fight, but fought simply as warriors. Isatai, the Comanche, was the actual leader. Only a few Kiowas were present at this battle.

Isatai's plans were good: To take by surprise the sleeping hunters and strike quickly in the gray dawn of day. Only an accident prevented the success of the plan. The night was warm, and inside the fort the heat was so oppressive that a number of men slept in the empty wagons outside. They gave the alarm, though themselves cut off, such was the speed with which the Indians made their attack. A cracking overhead had awakened the hunters in the fort, who feared the roof was falling, just as the Indians charged. This probably saved the white men. The Comanches, being the best mounted, led the charge across the plain to the adobe buildings. Round and

---

[10] Dixon was barely twenty-three years of age at the time he participated in the fight at Adobe Walls, but he had come out to Kansas from West Virginia in 1864 at the age of fourteen and was by now a veteran mule-skinner, buffalo hunter, and frontiersman. Bat Masterson, only twenty, was another of a number of young participants. There were twenty-eight white defenders in all. Cf., Olive K. Dixon, *Life of Billy Dixon*; Billy Dixon, *Life and Adventures of Billy Dixon of Adobe Walls.*—S.L.

round the fort they rode, but could make no impression on the thick walls. They backed their horses against the doors to force them open, but the hunters piled goods against them to prevent this. The hunters cut loopholes through the walls and the Indians fell back to the protection of the piles of hides and the empty wagons, where they kept up a hot but useless fire. Daring warriors made futile charges to the walls of the fort. A young Cheyenne named Horse Road, already wounded, rode around the walls taunting the white men, and was killed hammering on the door with his gun. A young Comanche warrior was also shot near the door of the stockade. But they could do nothing against the thick walls of the fort. The women and children yelled encouragement to the warriors from a nearby hill, but Isatai's medicine had failed. The Indians captured or killed most of the hunters' horses. But the adobe walls could not be burned or forced and the Indians gave up the fight. Six Comanches were killed. Five Cheyennes were killed outright, and one, badly wounded, was carried off to die later. The Cheyennes killed were Horse Road, Stone Teeth, Coyote, Spotted Feathers, Walks on the Ground, and Stone Calf's son. Nine of the dead Indians were left on the field lying so close to the fort that it was impossible to carry them off. After the Indians left, the hunters abandoned the fort. Some days later Prairie Chief and a party of Cheyennes went back to look for the dead. The hunters had gone, but had cut off the heads of the nine dead warriors and stuck them on boards nailed to a long pole in the ground.[11]

Most of the Arapahos were so disappointed over the failure of the Comanche medicine man's promises that they returned to the agency. But the majority of the Cheyennes were for war. On July 3 a small party of Cheyennes attacked Patrick Hennessy's wagon train near what is now Hennessy, Oklahoma. I knew Pat Hennessy very well, as he frequently freighted for the trader I sometimes worked for at this time. He was warned not to make this trip, but, being utterly fearless himself, refused to see any danger. Hennessy's train was

---

[11] Grinnell in his account of the fight makes no mention of the Indian heads (*Fighting Cheyennes*, 322–24).—S.L.

loaded with goods for Agent James Haworth, of the Kiowa and Comanche agency. Hennessy was killed, also his three teamsters: George Fand, Thomas Calloway, and Ed. Cook. A large party of Osage buffalo hunters came up just after the fight and threw Hennessy's body in the grain wagon and burned it. They also secured most of the plunder.

The military, in four columns, now took the field against the hostiles and kept them on the jump all summer and up to the middle of the following winter. The troops were never able to inflict much damage on the Cheyennes, but they followed them so closely that the Indians found it impossible to get any supplies during the winter following, which was very severe.

On August 30, 1874, Colonel Nelson A. Miles, with eight troops of cavalry, four companies of infantry, and artillery, had a running fight with the Cheyennes on the headwaters of the Washita River. One Indian was killed. When the troops took the field against the hostiles, the Cheyennes had as guide a Comanche named Mule Smoking, called Black Comanche by the Cheyennes on account of his very dark color. The Comanches told the Cheyennes that Mule Smoking knew all the water holes on the Staked Plains, a region not well known to the Cheyennes. So, as a precaution for the campaign they knew would follow, the Cheyennes were glad to avail themselves of the services of the expert Comanche trailer. Yet he was killed in the first engagement, this one with Miles's outfit. Mule Smoking was struck with a piece of artillery shell. Colonel Miles had a number of Delaware scouts with him, under old Fall Leaf. One of these scouts was riding ahead of the command early in this fight and the Cheyennes suddenly turned and charged, a warrior, with a lance, knocking the Delaware off his horse. The Cheyennes did not harm the Delaware, but took his horse, saddle and bridle, and gun. The pony was very poor, and the saddle and bridle hardly worth taking. The Cheyennes say that the troop commander should have been ashamed to send a man in advance on such a mount.

On September 11, scouts Billy Dixon and Amos Chapman, with four soldiers carrying dispatches from Miles to Major William E.

361

Price's command, had a fight with a small party of Kiowas on the north bank of the Washita River. The whites took refuge in a buffalo wallow and held off the Indians until help came. Amos Chapman, who is a squaw man and lives near Colony, told me that they did not kill any Indians, but Chapman lost a leg. One of the soldiers was killed and all were wounded. Satanta, the Kiowa chief, came into Darlington some time after this fight and told us about it.[12]

Late in September a party of Cheyennes, with some Comanches and Kiowas, were returning from the Staked Plains to the Red River. They met a force under Colonel Ranald S. Mackenzie, and the Cheyennes attacked the troops. They were driven off after a sharp fight, and Mackenzie followed their trail of the main camp in the Palo Duro Canyon, near the Red River of Texas. He took the Indians by surprise and destroyed the camp, capturing a lot of stock, most of which belonged to the Kiowas and Comanches, who were rich in horses at this time, the Cheyennes not being so well off in this particular. One Kiowa was killed just as he was leaving his lodge. The day previous these troops killed a Cheyenne warrior named Chief Hill.[13]

On November 6 Lieutenant H. J. Farnsworth and twenty-eight men of the Eighth Cavalry were attacked as they came in sight of a Cheyenne village on McClellan Creek, Texas. When the hosstiles charged, Farnsworth's troops retreated, and a soldier was dismounted in the flight. Next morning he was found on foot by Many Crows and Spotted Wolf. The soldier had a gun, but was killed by Many Crows. Farnsworth had with him a Cheyenne guide named Brown Blackbird. He jumped off his horse when the Cheyennes

[12] The fight described by Bent seems to be part of a much larger one, described by Nye from information gathered from army records and Kiowa and Comanche informants. It was a phase of the attack on Capatin Wyllys Lyman's wagon train hauling supplies from Camp Supply to Colonel Miles at the edge of the Llano Estacado. Nye, *Carbine and Lance*, 274–82.—S.L.

[13] Mackenzie's forces took 1,400 head of Indian ponies in the surprise attack on the large Indian encampment in Palo Duro Canyon, south of present Amarillo, September 27, 1874. He destroyed the herd, knowing he could not move them. Mumsukawa, a Comanche informant, provided the post-battle narrative from the Indian side. Nye, *Carbine and Lance*, 284–89.—S.L.

charged down on the troops and was made prisoner. He was not killed. This scout was one of the two Cheyennes who served with the troops in this campaign of 1874–75. The other was Little Snake, a brother-in-law of Ben Clark, Miles's chief of scouts in this campaign. Little Snake went out from Camp Supply with the troops and was later sent back with dispatches. He did not go out any more, as he had contracted tuberculosis.

Farther east and north, in the middle of September a war party of Cheyennes, under Medicine Water, operating in western Kansas, on the Smoky Hill River, had captured four girls named Germain, an event which afterwards brought a great deal of trouble on the Cheyennes. Following the capture of these white girls, this Cheyenne party was hotly pressed by the troops. Naturally the lot of the girls was not a pleasant one; but that they suffered any greater hardships than the rest of the party the Cheyennes positively deny. There was little to eat for any one and game was scarce; the country was thick with columns of troops from the forts and stations nearby, and the Indians were kept on the jump. Afraid to come into Darlington, this party made for Gray Beard's camp on the north branch of McClellan Creek, Texas. The morning they arrived, November 8, the camp of one hundred and ten lodges was attacked by troops under Lieutenant F. D. Baldwin. The Indians broke camp hurriedly and left the two younger Germain girls on the ground eating hackberries. The rear guard of the Cheyennes, posted in the hills, waited until they saw the troops pick up the two white girls. The two elder girls were not released until Stone Calf brought in his band in January, 1875, and turned the girls over to Agent John D. Miles at Darlington. When Lieutenant Baldwin sent these two younger girls in to the agency, Agent Miles organized an entertainment for their benefit. It was repeated for two or three nights and was crowded with agency employees and soldiers.

In the latter part of November (the 28th) Captain C. A. Hartwell had a running fight with Cheyennes near Muster Creek, Texas, but never got near enough to hurt any Indians.

Another affair, called by the military authorities an engagement, has a different side to it according to the Indian account. There was but little grass near the agency in the late fall and early winter, and the herds of the friendlies were sent out to graze on the Kingfisher, about eighteen miles from the agency. Agent Miles issued passes to the Indian herders for identification in case of interference by the military, who were very active in pursuit of the hostiles. Whirlwind sent word to Lieutenant Colonel Thomas H. Neill and Agent Miles that a small party of hostiles were in the vicinity, and Captain A. S. B. Keyes, was sent out with a company of Negro troops from the Tenth Cavalry. I knew Captain Keyes very well, as I was stationed at Darlington at this time. He followed the trail of a small party into the herders' camp, and, not being able to distinguish between the friendlies and hostiles, brought in the whole party. The Indians made no resistance. My herder was in the camp with my herd and made himself known to Captain Keyes. The Captain did not bring him in, but brought in all the others. The leader of this small hostile party was Big Moccasin, who had planned to steal fresh horses from the agency and go north.

The winter of 1874–75 was one of great severity. Game being scarce and the troops active, the lot of the Cheyenne hostiles was a hard one. Not being able to stand punishment like the Cheyennes, most of the Comanches and Kiowas had drifted back to Fort Sill and surrendered. In this war the bulk of the fighting was done by the Cheyennes, the main body of which was still out. Their situation being desperate and the outlook hopeless, runners from the friendly bands were sent out by Agent Miles to induce the hostiles to come in and surrender. In January, 1875, White Horse and Stone Calf came in with the Dog Soldiers. In February Stone Calf and Red Moon were sent out and had a talk with the remnant of the hostiles, with the result that early in March Gray Beard and the majority of the Cheyennes came in and were disarmed. The war of 1874–75 was now over.

It was decided by the military authorities that the leaders in the war from each tribe would be arrested and confined in the military prison of Fort Marion, Florida. Nine Comanches, twenty-six Kiowas, two Arapahos, and thirty-three Cheyennes were selected for punishment. Of the Cheyennes one was a woman, Calf Woman, wife of Medicine Water, and was with the war party that killed the Germain family and captured the four girls. Now, the older Indians never understood the white man's system of arrest. Grown men were never made prisoners by the Plains Indians. If captured, they were promptly killed. This was understood and was accepted as a matter of course. To be ironed and confined was past their understanding, and for this reason trouble always followed when an Indian was confined in the old days. Satank, the Kiowa, when arrested in 1871, slipped his manacles and with only a small knife attacked the heavy guard of soldiers and was shot to death. Crazy Horse resented his arrest and was bayoneted by the guard in 1877.[14]

The selection of the Cheyenne prisoners was made with but little tact by Colonel Neill. His interpreter, Romeo, the Mexican, told me he was under the influence of liquor at the time, and this the Cheyennes believe. Be that as it may, his methods aroused the resentment of the Indians. One day, early in April, all the late Cheyenne hostiles were lined up so that the ringleaders might be selected for punishment. After taking the chiefs, Gray Beard, Heap of Birds (Many Magpies), Eagle Head (Minimick), Lean Bear, Medicine Water and his wife, Calf Woman, and others to the number of fifteen, it grew dark, and to complete the list Colonel Neill "cut off eighteen from the right of the line," intending at some future time to eliminate the innocent and substitute others. But this was never done, and a few days later, on April 6, 1875, while the prisoners were being put in leg irons by Wesley, the Negro blacksmith, an outbreak occurred. A lot of women were sitting a short distance from the prisoners singing war songs.[15] Several of the Cheyenne men had been put in irons

[14] Crazy Horse of the Oglala Sioux was killed at Camp Robinson, in northwestern Nebraska, September 5, 1877, Hyde says through a dirk thrust from his own hand, deflected by Little Big Man, who was attempting to restrain him as he was being put in the guardhouse; others say from a bayonet thrust by a soldier. Hyde, *Spotted Tail's Folk*, 253.—S.L.

[15] Seventy-two prisoners in all were to be transported in April, 1875, to Fort Marion, Florida, thirty-one of them Cheyennes, the rest Arapahos, Kiowas, Coman-

when suddenly Black Horse, excited by the songs of the women, kicked the blacksmith under the chin and made a dash for the camp of White Horse, some distance away on the north side of the north fork of the river. The guard opened fire. Bullets raining through the Cheyenne camp in the distance wounded several people, and in a panic men, women, and children ran for the sand hills across the river and a mile south of the Indian village. The women, with axes and short-handled hoes, and the men, with their knives, dug rifle pits and holes for the women and children, while other warriors with bows and rifles returned the fire of the guard. It was now about 2 P.M. and the guard had been reinforced by three troops of cavalry and a Gatling gun and later on by some infantry. Big Shell, while standing at the door of his lodge, was shot in the head by a sergeant riding by when the fight started. I rode up to Big Shell just as he was shot. The cavalry made a charge on the sand hills, but so many were wounded that they quickly fell back. White Horse only had about one hundred warriors in his camp, and these were poorly armed, but they successfully held off the troops from 2 P.M. until nightfall, a few spasmodic attempts being made to storm the Indian position during the afternoon. These attacks always broke down under the Indian fire. Two Cheyennes were killed in the sand hills: Little Bear and Dirty Nose. Black Horse was shot in the side as he made his run for White Horse's camp and though reported dead by Colonel Neill and the Indian agent, lived for many years afterwards. He died a few years ago. To take a position held by entrenched Indians is a hard matter, as the troops found out several times in the Nez Percé and other Indian campaigns, so reinforcements were brought up during the night and thrown around the Indian position, plans being made for an attack next day. During the night the Indians—

---

ches, and Caddos. The "historian" of the Cheyenne sojourn in the Florida prison-fortress was a man named Mohe, who became "Cohoe" through a mistake in white record-keeping. The story of Cohoe and reproductions of his paintings and sketches made at Fort Marion between 1865 and 1868 appear in *A Cheyenne Sketchbook*, by Cohoe, with commentary by E. Adamson Hoebel and Karen Daniels Petersen. —S.L.

men, women and children—slipped quietly through the troops, and when morning came the Indian position in the sand hills was found deserted.

Little Bull's party of hostiles had been out all winter and were coming in to Darlington at this time. Meeting the fleeing Indians from White Horse's camp, the news of the attack threw them into a panic. So, about twenty lodges decided to make a run for the North. The remainder were persuaded by friendly Indians to come back to the agency.

When the main body of Cheyennes, under Stone Calf, Gray Beard, and Bull Bear, decided to go in and surrender, a small part of Gray Beard's band, under Little Bull, a great warrior, refused to go in and planned a dash through the troops to join the Northern Cheyennes. When this deplorable fight occurred following Black Horse's break, Little Bull's party was camped on the North Fork of the Canadian, about twenty-five miles away. The refugees from White Horse's camp reached Little Bull's camp early in the morning and reported that the troops were killing the Cheyennes at the agency. To the number of about twenty lodges, Little Bull decided to take his party to their relatives, the Northern Cheyennes. The military soon received notice of the whereabout of this party and plans were made to head off the Indians, a force leaving Fort Wallace, Kansas, for this purpose under command of Lieutenant Austin Henely. After crossing the Smoky Hill River the Cheyennes discovered that troops were on their trail, and on the hard high ground they split up into smaller bands to shake off their pursuers. Their ponies were in very bad shape after the hard winter campaign, and though they managed to puzzle the troops they could not lose them. Spotted Wolf, still living, had a small party with him, and for a while was followed by the soldiers. He watched the troops closely and discovered that Lieutenant Henely had abruptly swung off his trail and headed for the northeast. When the troops turned off, Spotted Wolf told Chicken Hawk to go ahead and notify Little Bull that the soldiers were coming. Chicken Hawk says his pony was in bad shape and he was unable to gain on the troops. Some of Chicken

Hawk's relatives were with Little Bull, so he was anxious to reach him. Little Bull's party had stopped to rest in a secluded spot on the North Fork of Sappa Creek, in the northwest part of Kansas, a good place in which to hide but a poor one to defend in a fight, as it turned out. Henely, it seems, was floundering around doubtfully when he ran on to some buffalo hunters, who directed him to the Indian camp and went along for the sake of plunder. But for this chance meeting it is probable that the soldiers would never have discovered Little Bull's camp.

The little band was encamped on a low tongue of land where the Sappa made a horseshoe bend, back of them a sharp bluff, and beyond were the plains and their pony herds. The troops attacked at daybreak of April 23, 1875, taking the Cheyennes by surprise, though a number got away over the bluffs to the pony herds. The troops rushed across the creek and took up a position where they could pour a cross fire into the Indians. The long-range guns of the buffalo hunters did much execution, and though the Indians put up a stiff fight they suffered severely. So many of the women and children were killed and wounded that Little Bull and Dirty Water went out to parley with the soldiers. A sergeant came out to meet them. White Bear, from his position near the creek bed, shot and killed the sergeant, and the troopers promptly killed Little Bull and Dirty Water, who was standing close behind. Blind Bull told me that he could not understand why White Bear killed the sergeant. This killing caused Little Bull and Dirty Water, an old man, to be shot down. For some time after the killing of the sergeant the troops kept up a hot fire on the Indians and finally turned off in the direction taken by those who had escaped at the opening of the fight. Blind Bull says that, as the troopers started away, White Bear rose up and fired at them. They turned and shot him and he fell into the creek. His stepfather, Black Hairy Dog, later the keeper of the Medicine Arrows, with his wife, was in the party that got away. Little Bear was also one of those that broke through to the pony herd. After catching his pony, he suddenly announced to his companions that he would ride back to the gully where the Indians were fighting. Little Bear went back and charged into the troops and was killed. His father and mother had also been killed here earlier in the fight. Strangely enough, Little Bear's horse was picked up by some Arapahos six months after the battle on the North Fork of the Canadian River.

White Bear's war bonnet, tipped with two buffalo horns, was taken from the battlefield by Lieutenant Henely. He also took a woman's silver belt from the body of a young woman named Yellow Body Woman, who was killed in the gully. At Fort Lyon, some time afterwards, these articles were shown by Lieutenant Henely to a Cheyenne woman married to a cattleman at Las Animas. She recognized the things and predicted that Lieutenant Henely, who was then on his way to Arizona, would come to a violent end. He was drowned in Arizona a year later.

Seven Cheyenne men and twenty women and children were killed in this fight.[16] The names of the men killed were: Little Bull, Tangle Hair, Dirty Water, The Rat, White Bear, Young Bear, and Stone Teeth. Dull Knife's band avenged their deaths when they swung through this part of Kansas in 1878.

[16] Lieutenant Henely reported after the battle that nineteen Cheyennes and eight women and children had been killed. Berthrong, *Southern Cheyennes*, 404.—S.L.

Abert, Lieutenant James W. *Western America in 1846–1847: The Original Travel Diary of Lieutenant J. W. Abert, Who Mapped New Mexico for the United States.* Edited by John Galvin. San Francisco, 1966.

Athearn, Robert G. *William Tecumseh Sherman and the Settlement of the West.* Norman, 1956.

Beck, Warren A. *New Mexico: A History of Four Centuries.* Norman, 1962.

Bent, George. Letters. William Robertson Coe Collection, Yale University Library, New Haven, Connecticut.

———. Letters. Western History Department, Denver Public Library, Denver, Colorado.

Berthrong, Donald J. *The Southern Cheyennes.* Norman, 1963.

Bougainville, Louis Antoine de. *Adventure in the Wilderness: The American Journals of Louis Antoine de Bougainville, 1756–1760.* Edited by Edward P. Hamilton. Norman, 1964.

Cohoe. *A Cheyenne Sketchbook.* Commentary by E. Adamson Hoebel and Karen Daniels Petersen. Norman, 1964.

Collinson, Frank. *Life in the Saddle.* Edited by Mary Whatley Clarke. Norman, 1963.

Crook, General George. *General George Crook: His Autobiography.* Edited by Martin F. Schmitt. Norman, 1946.

Custer, George Armstrong. *My Life on the Plains.* Edited by Edgar I. Stewart. Norman, 1962.

Dixon, Billy. *Life and Adventures of "Billy" Dixon of Adobe Walls.* Compiled by Frederick S. Barde. Guthrie, Okla., 1914.

Dixon, Olive K. *Life of "Billy" Dixon.* Dallas, 1927.

Dorsey, G. A. *The Cheyenne: Ceremonial Organization.* Field Columbian Museum *Publication No. 99,* Vol. IX, No. 2. Chicago, 1905.

Estergreen, M. Morgan. *Kit Carson: A Portrait in Courage.* Norman, 1962.

Foreman, Grant. *Marcy and the Gold Seekers: The Journal of Captain R. B. Marcy, with an Account of the Gold Rush over the Southern Route.* Norman, 1939.

Frazer, Robert W. *Forts of the West: Military Forts and Presidios and Posts Commonly Called Forts West of the Mississippi River to 1898.* Norman, 1965.

Gard, Wayne. *The Great Buffalo Hunt.* New York, 1959.

Garrard, Lewis H. *Wah-to-yah and the Taos Trail.* Norman, 1955.

Gregg, Josiah. *Commerce of the Prairies.* Edited by Max Moorhead. Norman, 1954.

Grinnell, George Bird. *The Fighting Cheyennes.* Norman, 1956.

———. "Bent's Old Fort and Its Builders," Kansas State Historical *Collections,* XV (1919–22). Topeka, 1923.

Hadley, James A. "The Kansas Nineteenth Cavalry and the Conquest of the Plains Indians," Kansas State Historical Society *Collections,* X. Topeka, 1908.

Hafen, LeRoy R. "When Was Bent's Fort Built?" *Colorado Magazine,* Vol. XXXI, No. 2 (April, 1954).

Henry, Alexander. *The Manuscript Journals of Alexander Henry ... and of David Thompson ... 1799–1814.* Edited by Elliot Coues. New York, 1897.

Hodge, Frederick Webb. *Handbook of American Indians North of Mexico.* Bureau of American Ethnology *Bulletin No. 30.* 2 vols. Washington, 1910.

Hoig, Stan. *The Sand Creek Massacre.* Norman, 1961.

Hyde, George E. *Red Cloud's Folk: A History of the Oglala Sioux Indians.* Norman, 1937.

————. *Spotted Tail's Folk: A History of the Brulé Sioux*. Norman, 1961.

Inman, Henry. *The Old Santa Fe Trail: The Story of a Great Highway*. New York, 1897.

Jones, Douglas. *The Treaty of Medicine Lodge*. Norman, 1966.

Jones, Robert Huhn. *The Civil War in the Northwest*. Norman, 1960.

Kennerly, William Clark. *Persimmon Hill: A Narrative of Old St. Louis and the Far West*. Norman, 1948.

Lavender, David. *Bent's Fort*. Garden City, N.Y., 1954.

Lecompte, Janet. "Gantt's Fort and Bent's Picket Post," *Colorado Magazine*, Vol. XLI, No. 2 (Spring, 1964).

Llewellyn, Karl N., and E. Adamson Hoebel. *The Cheyenne Way: Conflict and Case Law in Primitive Jurisprudence*. Norman, 1941.

Lowe, Percival G. *Five Years a Dragoon*. Edited by Don Russell. Norman, 1965.

Luebers, H. L. "William Bent's Family and the Indians of the Plains," *Colorado Magazine*, Vol. XIII, No. 1 (January, 1936).

Mayhall, Mildred P. *The Kiowas*. Norman, 1962.

McReynolds, Edwin C. *The Seminoles*. Norman, 1957.

Miles, Nelson A. *Personal Recollections*. Chicago and New York, 1897.

Mooney, James. *Calendar History of the Kiowa Indians. Seventeenth Annual Report*, Bureau of American Ethnology. Washington, 1898.

Moorhead, Max. *New Mexico's Royal Road: Trade and Travel on the Chihuahua Trail*. Norman, 1958.

National Archives. Ceran St. Vrain to Lieutenant Colonel Eneas Mackay, July 21, 1847, General Land Office Records. Washington.

————. Document No. 97, Abstract of Licenses, Office of Indian Affairs, St. Louis Superintendency. Washington [1835].

Nye, Wilbur Sturtevant. *Bad Medicine and Good: Tales of the Kiowas*. Norman, 1962.

———. *Carbine and Lance: The Story of Old Fort Sill*. Norman, 1937.

Parker, Watson. *Gold in the Black Hills*. Norman, 1966.

Preble, Rear Admiral George Henry. *The Opening of Japan: A Diary of Discovery in the Far East, 1853–1856*. Edited by Boleslaw Szczesniak. Norman, 1962.

Rister, Carl Coke. *Border Command: General Phil Sheridan in the West*. Norman, 1944.

Roe, Mrs. Francis Marie Antoinette. *Letters of an Army Officer's Wife*. New York, 1909.

Rosa, Joseph G. *They Called Him Wild Bill*. Norman, 1964.

Russell, Don. *The Lives and Legends of Buffalo Bill*. Norman, 1960.

Seger, John Homer. *Early Days Among the Cheyenne and Arapahoe Indians*. Norman, 1934.

Spring, Agnes Wright. *Caspar Collins: The Life and Exploits of an Indian Fighter of the Sixties*. New York, 1927.

Stewart, Edgar I. *Custer's Luck*. Norman, 1955.

U.S. Congress, Senate, "Sand Creek Massacre," *Report of the Secretary of War. Sen. Exec. Doc. 26, 39* Cong., 2 sess. (1867).

U.S. Government, "Journal of a March of a Detachment of Dragoons, under Command of Colonel Dodge, during the Summer of 1835," *American State Papers*, Vol. VI. Washington, 1861.

———. Carr to Sheridan, November 1, 1868, War Department, Office of the Adjutant General, Letters Received, Carr *Report*.

Vaughn, J. W. *The Battle of Platte Bridge*. Norman, 1964.

Wagner, Henry R., and Charles L. Camp. *The Plains and the Rockies: A Bibliography*. San Francisco, 1937.

Walker, Henry Pickering. *The Wagonmasters: High Plains Freighting from the Earliest Days of the Santa Fe Trail to 1880*. Norman, 1966.

Wallace, Ernest, and E. Adamson Hoebel. *The Comanches: Lords of the South Plains*. Norman, 1952.

Ware, Captain Eugene F. *The Indian War of 1864.* Topeka, 1911.
Wright, Muriel H. *A Guide to the Indian Tribes of Oklahoma.* Norman, 1951.
Zornow, Frank William. *Kansas: A History of the Jayhawk State.* Norman, 1957.

Black Moon: 303 ff., 334, 347
Black Shin: 19, 55, 243, 253, 306
Black Stone: 326
Black Whetstone: 240
Black White Man: 64–67, 249
Blair, Francis (Frank) Preston, Jr.: 84–86, 110
Blair, Montgomery: 85n.
Blind Bear: 322
Blind Bull: 368
Block, Phil: 281
Blue Horse: 253, 317 & n., 322, 344
Blunt, Gen. James G.: 143–46
Bobtail Bear: 320
Bobtail Porcupine: 309 ff.
Boggs, Tom: 70, 252, 292 & n.
Boone, Col. Albert D.: 94, 114 & n., 121 n.
Boone, Daniel: 94, 114 n.
Border Ruffians: 102
Bowstring Society (*or* Wolf Warriors): 22–24, 72–75, 78, 201, 271, 336–37, 358
Bozeman Trail: 341 ff.
Brave Bear: 99n., 332, 335
Brave Wolf: 102, 122
Bridger, Jim: 63n., 228
Bridger Road: 341
Broken Arrow: 309 ff.
Broken Hand: 86 & n.
Brown Blackbird: 362
Brulé Sioux: 53, 90–92, 112–13, 137–39, 164 n., 167 ff., 194 ff., 201 n., 208, 252n., 272, 339, 342 & n., 349n.
Buffalo Arrows: 52–53
Buffalo Bull Society: *see* Red Shield Society
Buffalo Cap: 50, 200
Buffalo Goad: 279, 281
Bull (personal name): 50–51
Bull Bear: 126, 143, 256 ff., 268n., 284, 294 ff., 303, 308, 353n., 367
Bull Hump: 42–44, 71–72
Bull Sign: 355
Bull-Telling-Tales: 122 ff.

Bull that Hears: 249
Butterfield, David A.: 268 & n.
Byers, W. N.: 107

Caddo Indians: 269, 357, 366n.
Calf Woman: 365
California Joe: 316n., 318n.
Calloway, Thomas: 361
Camp Cottonwood: 137–38
Camp Dodge: 204 n.
Camp Ellsworth: 188
Camp Fillmore: 148n.
Camp Mitchell: 186, 188, 193, 211
Camp Rankin: 170 ff., 183
Camp Robinson: 365n.
Camp Sanborn: 122
Camp Supply: 292, 313, 315n., 321, 325 ff., 335, 362n., 363
Camp Weld: 124
Carpenter, Capt. Louis H.: 305 ff., 309–11
Carr, Maj. Eugene A.: 291n., 209, 311–13, 328–35
Carson, Kit: 62–68, 72, 83, 87, 245–47, 292 & n.
Cedar Grove (personal name): 21
Chapman, Amos: 293n., 361–62
Cheyenne Indians: family of, 3; name of, 3; origins of, 3–4; as lake dwellers, 4–8; meet Sioux, 6; discover Red Pipestone Quarry, 7; first see white men, 7; attacked by Assiniboins, 11–12; acquire guns, 11–12; raided by Ojibwas, 12n.; leave Minnesota, 12–13; relations with Moiseyu, 12–13; encounter Sutaio Indians, 13; meet Rees and Mandans, 14; at village at Standing Rock, 15–16; relations with Mandans and Rees, 16; move into Black Hills, 16–17; acquire horses, 17; meet Arapahos, Kiowas, and Crows, 17; become plains tribe, 17–21; form alliance with Arapahos, 21; secure guns, 21; form alliance with Sioux, 22; conflict with Crows,

Plumb, Col. Preston B.: 204–205
Poafebitty: 358n.
Pockmark, Jim: 269
Pointed Lance Men: 22–23n.
Poisal, John: 285n.
Poor Bear: 117, 250 ff., 283 ff.
Pope, Gen. John: 224 n., 287n.
Porcupine Bear: 21, 60, 74–75, 78 ff., 82, 335, 338
Porcupine Bull: 45, 60n.
Potawatomi Indians: 3
Powder Face: 290 n., 334
Powhatan Indians: 3
Prairie Apache Indians: 21, 135, 251, 339, 356; live with Kiowas, 22, 249; known for horses, 37–42; trade at Adobe Fort, 68; at battle of Wolf Creek, 79–82; join Cheyennes and Arapahos, 249; move south to avoid Hancock, 268; at council of Medicine Lodge, 283–85
Prairie Bear: 302, 305
Prairie Chief: 19, 360
Pratte, Cabanné, and Company: 59n.
Price, Col. Sterling: 88 & n.
Price, Maj. William E.: 361–62
Prophet, the: 72
Pushing Ahead: 77–78

Quahadi Comanches: *see* Northern Comanche Indians
Quanah: 357n., 358n.

Rat, The (personal name): 369
Rath, Charles: 267, 356 & n.
Red Arm (*or* Red Sleeve): 265
Red Bead (*or* Red Drop): 275
Red Bird: 322
Red Bull: 257
Red Cloud: 99n., 139, 195 ff., 200, 201 n., 209, 215, 216 & n., 231 n., 244, 324, 331, 342n., 343 ff.
Red Cloud Agency: 347, 351
Red Hair: 324
Red Leaf: 99n.

Red Moon: 244, 294, 359, 364
Red Shield Society (*or* Buffalo Bull Soldiers): 7, 23n., 74, 78, 201, 337
Red Shin: 317
Red Sleeves: 71
Red Teeth: 322
Ree Indians: 14, 16 & n., 21
Remick, Dr.: 322
Reynolds, Charlie: 350n.
Ridge Men (*Hisiometanio*) Clan: 159
Riding on the Cloud: 269
Ripley, W. D.: 122 & n.
Robinson, A. M.: 113n.
Rock Forehead: 41–42, 102, 251, 253, 325
Roman Nose: 201n., 216 & n., 221, 239–40, 242ff., 253 & n., 257ff., 275, 294, 300 ff., 306–307, 324, 337
Roman Nose Thunder: 320, 321 n.
Romeo (Mexican interpreter): 365
Rowland, Capt. E. S.: 235n.
Rowland, William: 208, 348

Sac and Fox Indians: 3, 280 ff.
St. Vrain, Ceran: 43n., 59–62, 88 & n., 89n., 93n., 292 & n., 356 & n.
Sanborn, Gen. John B.: 247ff., 280n., 283, 345, 349n.
Sand Creek Massacre: 60, 97, 151–63, 180, 223, 244, 247ff., 253n., 256
Sand Hill: 121n., 159, 251, 325
Sans Arc Sioux: 201n., 235
Satank (Sitting Bear): 285, 365
Satanta (White Bear): 135n., 250, 267, 284ff., 362
Sawyers, James A.: 231–33
Second Missouri Light Artillery: 235n., 236
Sedgwick, Maj. John: 95n., 105
Setangya (Sitting Bear): 134
Seven Bulls: 249
Seventh Cavalry: 264n., 275, 293n., 313ff.
Seventh Iowa Cavalry: 138, 170, 209
Shave Head: 330

Touching the Sky: 304, 320, 321 n.
Trade: intertribal, 31–32; at Bent's
  Fort, 68, 83–84
Treaties: see Fort Laramie Treaty of
  1868; Fort Wise Treaty of 1861;
  Little Arkansas, treaty of; Medicine
  Lodge, treaty of
Trudeau, Pierre: 305
Turkey Leg: 272, 276ff., 295
Turkey Without Feathers: 303
Twins: 221
Twin Woman: 15
Two Crows: 273ff., 298, 303ff., 311,
  328, 331ff.
Two Face: 208
Two Moons: 342ff.
Two Strikes: 298, 331
Two Thighs: 181

U. S. Volunteers: 232
Union Pacific Railroad: 276–78, 345,
  354
Upper Arkansas Agency: 113n., 114n.,
  353n.
Under Man, The (personal name):
  349n.
Ute Indians: 42, 45, 121, 315, 323, 348;
  as scouts for Custer, 245

Valverde, battle of: 68
Van Dorn, Gen. Earl: 111
Virgil: 87

Walker, Col. Samuel: 226, 231 & n.,
  233–42
Walking Coyote: 43
Walking Whirlwind: 42
Walks on the Ground: 360
Wallen, Maj. Henry D.: 136
War Bonnet: 143, 159
Ward, Lt. E. W.: 328n.
War Department: 97ff., 108, 162, 225,
  231, 291
Ware, Lt. E. F.: 171, 174 & n., 177

Weasel Bear (also called Ermine Bear
  or White Bear): 302ff.
Wesley (Negro blacksmith): 365
Whetstone Agency: 342
Whirlwind: 102, 284, 357, 364
Whistler: 137, 331
White, J. J.: 330
White Antelope: 41, 102, 143, 154–55,
  159 & n., 289
White Bear: 283, 322, 368ff.
White Buffalo Bull (or Ice Bear): 307
White Buffalo Woman: 319ff., 334
White Bull: 102, 201n.
White Crow: 349n.
White Elk: 343–344n.
White Face Bull: 19
White Frog: 6, 8n.
White Horse: 126, 144ff., 256, 258,
  263, 268n., 284, 298, 302ff., 308,
  328ff., 364, 367
White Leaf: 143–44, 181
White Man's Ladder: 309ff.
White Powder: 349
White Rock: 334
White Shield: 349n., 357
Whiteshirt, Tom (also called Tom
  Wilson or Graham Wilson): 257
White Thunder: 42n., 48, 51–53, 68,
  72, 80, 97n., 302ff.
Wichita Indians: 247, 278ff., 357
Williford, Capt.: 232
Wilson (soldier): 257
Wilson and Graham Circus: 257
Wind Woman: 323
Wise, Gov. Henry A.: 108, 110
Wolf (personal name): 322
Wolf Belly (or Bad Heart): 301, 306
Wolf Chief: 42, 60, 98n., 131–32, 205,
  326
Wolf-Coming-Out: 122ff.
Wolf Creek, battle of: 79–82, 91,
  228–31
Wolf Man (or Bullet-Proof): 309ff.
Wolf Robe: 143, 145n.

Life of George Bent has been set on the Linotype in 11½-point Caslon Old Face with 1½-point spacing between the lines. Handset Caslon has been selected for display to preserve the continuity of typographic design.

The paper on which the book is printed bears the watermark of the University of Oklahoma Press and is designed for an effective life of at least three hundred years.